AFRICAN HISTORICAL DICTIONARIES
Edited by Jon Woronoff

1. *Cameroon,* by Victor T. LeVine and Roger P. Nye. 1974. Out of print. See No. 48.
2. *The Congo,* 2nd ed., by Virginia Thompson and Richard Adloff. 1984
3. *Swaziland,* by John J. Grotpeter. 1975
4. *The Gambia,* 2nd ed., by Harry A. Gailey. 1987
5. *Botswana,* by Richard P. Stevens. 1975. Out of print. See No. 44.
6. *Somalia,* by Margaret F. Castagno. 1975
7. *Benin [Dahomey],* 2nd ed., by Samuel Decalo. 1987. Out of print. See No. 61.
8. *Burundi,* by Warren Weinstein. 1976
9. *Togo,* 2nd ed., by Samuel Decalo. 1987
10. *Lesotho,* by Gordon Haliburton. 1977
11. *Mali,* 2nd ed., by Pascal James Imperato. 1986
12. *Sierra Leone,* by Cyril Patrick Foray. 1977
13. *Chad,* 2nd ed., by Samuel Decalo. 1987
14. *Upper Volta,* by Daniel Miles McFarland. 1978
15. *Tanzania,* by Laura S. Kurtz. 1978
16. *Guinea,* 2nd ed., by Thomas O'Toole. 1987
17. *Sudan,* by John Voll. 1978. Out of print. See No. 53.
18. *Rhodesia / Zimbabwe,* by R. Kent Rasmussen. 1979. Out of print. See No. 46.
19. *Zambia,* by John J. Grotpeter. 1979
20. *Niger,* 2nd ed., by Samuel Decalo. 1989
21. *Equatorial Guinea,* 2nd ed., by Max Liniger-Goumaz. 1988
22. *Guinea-Bissau,* 2nd ed., by Richard Lobban and Joshua Forrest. 1988
23. *Senegal,* by Lucie G. Colvin. 1981. Out of print. See No. 65.
24. *Morocco,* by William Spencer. 1980
25. *Malawi,* by Cynthia A. Crosby. 1980. Out of print. See No. 54.
26. *Angola,* by Phyllis Martin. 1980. Out of print. See No. 52.
27. *The Central African Republic,* by Pierre Kalck. 1980. Out of print. See No. 51.
28. *Algeria,* by Alf Andrew Heggoy. 1981. Out of print. See No. 66.
29. *Kenya,* by Bethwell A. Ogot. 1981
30. *Gabon,* by David E. Gardinier. 1981. Out of print. See No. 58.
31. *Mauritania,* by Alfred G. Gerteiny. 1981
32. *Ethiopia,* by Chris Prouty and Eugene Rosenfeld. 1981. Out of print. See No. 56.
33. *Libya,* 2nd ed., by Ronald Bruce St John. 1991
34. *Mauritius,* by Lindsay Rivière. 1982. Out of print. See No. 49.
35. *Western Sahara,* by Tony Hodges. 1982. Out of print. See No. 55.

36. *Egypt*, by Joan Wucher King. 1984. Out of print. See No. 67.
37. *South Africa*, by Christopher Saunders. 1983
38. *Liberia*, by D. Elwood Dunn and Svend E. Holsoe. 1985
39. *Ghana*, by Daniel Miles McFarland. 1985. Out of print. See No. 63.
40. *Nigeria*, by Anthony Oyewole. 1987
41. *Ivory Coast*, by Robert J. Mundt. 1987
42. *Cape Verde*, 2nd ed., by Richard Lobban and Marilyn Halter. 1988. Out of print. See No. 62.
43. *Zaire*, by F. Scott Bobb. 1988
44. *Botswana*, by Fred Morton, Andrew Murray, and Jeff Ramsay. 1989
45. *Tunisia*, by Kenneth J. Perkins. 1989
46. *Zimbabwe*, 2nd ed., by R. Kent Rasmussen and Steven L. Rubert. 1990
47. *Mozambique*, by Mario Azevedo. 1991
48. *Cameroon*, 2nd ed., by Mark W. DeLancey and H. Mbella Mokeba. 1990
49. *Mauritius*, 2nd ed., by Sydney Selvon. 1991
50. *Madagascar*, by Maureen Covell. 1995
51. *The Central African Republic*, 2nd ed., by Pierre Kalck; translated by Thomas O'Toole. 1992
52. *Angola*, 2nd ed., by Susan H. Broadhead. 1992
53. *Sudan*, 2nd ed., by Carolyn Fluehr-Lobban, Richard A. Lobban, Jr., and John Obert Voll. 1992
54. *Malawi*, 2nd ed., by Cynthia A. Crosby. 1993
55. *Western Sahara*, 2nd ed., by Anthony Pazzanita and Tony Hodges. 1994
56. *Ethiopia and Eritrea*, 2nd ed., by Chris Prouty and Eugene Rosenfeld. 1994
57. *Namibia*, by John J. Grotpeter. 1994
58. *Gabon*, 2nd ed., by David Gardinier. 1994
59. *Comoro Islands*, by Martin Ottenheimer and Harriet Ottenheimer. 1994
60. *Rwanda*, by Learthen Dorsey. 1994
61. *Benin*, 3rd ed., by Samuel Decalo. 1994
62. *Republic of Cape Verde*, 3rd ed., by Richard Lobban and Marlene Lopes. 1994
63. *Ghana*, 2nd ed., by David Owusu-Ansah and Daniel Miles McFarland. 1995
64. *Uganda*, by M. Louise Pirouet. 1994
65. *Senegal*, 2nd ed., by Andrew F. Clark and Lucie Colvin Phillips. 1994
66. *Algeria*, 2nd ed., by Phillip Chiviges Naylor and Alf Andrew Heggoy. 1994
67. *Egypt*, by Arthur Goldschmidt, Jr. 1994

Historical Dictionary of GHANA
Second Edition

by
DAVID OWUSU-ANSAH
and
DANIEL MILES McFARLAND

African Historical Dictionaries, No. 63

The Scarecrow Press, Inc.
Metuchen, N.J., & London
1995

DT
510.5
.M38
1995

British Library Cataloguing-in-Publication data available

Library of Congress Cataloging-in-Publication Data

Owusu-Ansah, David.
 Historical dictionary of Ghana / David Owusu-Ansah and Daniel
Miles McFarland. -- 2nd. ed.
   p. cm. -- (African historical dictionaries ; no. 63)
   Rev. ed. of: Historical dictionary of Ghana / Daniel Miles
McFarland. 1985.
   Includes bibliographical references.
   ISBN 0-8108-2919-3 (alk. paper)
   1. Ghana--History--Dictionaries. I. McFarland, Daniel Miles.
II. McFarland, Daniel Miles. Historical dictionary of Ghana.
III. Title. IV. Series.
DT510.5.M38 1995
966.7'003--dc20   94-18978

To Jo

CONTENTS

Acknowledgements v

Editor's Foreword vii

Abbreviations and Acronyms ix

Chronology xix

INTRODUCTION 1

 Map of Administrative Regions
 and National Boundaries 2

 Map of Physical Regions of
 Ghana 4

 Map of Major Ethnic and Linguistic
 Distributions of Ghana 6

THE DICTIONARY 9

BIBLIOGRAPHY 257

Appendix A
(British Administrators of the
Gold Coast) 379

Appendix B
(Ghanaian Leaders from 1951) 381

About the Authors 383

ACKNOWLEDGEMENTS

One cannot engage in a project of this nature without extensive solicitation of previous works. I am, therefore, indebted to many and I thank them all. I am particularly thankful to my co-author, Dr. Daniel M. McFarland, whose first edition of the *Historical Dictionary of Ghana* served as the base for the present work. During the two and one half years of researching and writing this project, I came to depend on the services of a number of students. Kim Cornell Belcher and Geoffrey Coats helped with the library research. Nicole O'Neill, Vickie Fowler, and Angela Chapson typed sections of this work, while Keith Pultz, Stephanie Callahan, and Meg Gardner contributed the maps. I acknowledge Dr. Stephen Wright of the Department of Geography for allowing his students to produce the maps as part of their class project. Dr. Michael Galgano, Head of the Department of History at James Madison University, arranged my teaching schedules in a manner that allowed me time to research. Drs. Lee Congdon, Jacqueline B. Walker, Christopher Arndt, and Raymond Hyser were supportive. Gordon Miller and the Inter-Library Loan Department of James Madison University Library were of great help. I am also thankful to Paula See, whose managerial skills made my other responsibilities at the Department of History easier to combine with work on this project. This work is dedicated to my wife, Jo Eye Ansah, whose love and support have made teaching and research possible. Again, I am grateful to Dr. Daniel Miles McFarland, my co-author, for allowing me to dedicate this work to Jo.

David Owusu-Ansah
Harrisonburg, VA
May 1993

EDITOR'S FOREWORD

It has taken a long time, but things are coming full circle in Ghana. When it achieved independence under a charismatic leader, most observers predicted the best: economic prosperity, grass-roots democracy, a world role.... That, alas, is not what happened. There was little democracy, the economy was ruined, and few cared what went on in Ghana. Indeed, from a position of leadership in many fields, it fell behind less promising African states. Now, finally, there is some positive news. The economy shows signs of improvement, the multiparty elections were tolerable, and an opposition emerged. Ghana is even praised in certain circles as an example to be followed rather than one to be shunned.

So, this book appears at a very opportune moment. For it covers not only the pre-colonial period, colonization, and the struggle for independence but more of the post-independence woes and the still tentative upturn. It includes numerous entries on the major players and others on crucial events and essential institutions. There is information on the economy, society and culture, key geographical features, and prominent ethnic groups. Ghana's long history is documented further in an extensive chronology stretching from the first inhabitants to the latest political events. And, to learn more, there is a list of acronyms and abbreviations, a vital guide for a country where they abound.

This second edition of the *Historical Dictionary of Ghana* was written by David Owusu-Ansah. Born and educated in Ghana, and then the United States, Dr. Owusu-Ansah initially taught in Ghana, and then the United States. He is presently associate professor of history at James Madison University. He has thus had more opportunities than most to study the country, to observe its successes and failures and also to explain them to others as a teacher, lecturer, panelist and author. He could thus build on the first edition by co-author Professor Daniel M. McFarland, an American Africanist.

Jon Woronoff
Series Editor

ABBREVIATIONS AND ACRONYMS

ACDC	Army Central Defence Committee
ACI	African Cultural Institute
ACP	Action Congress Party
ADC	Agricultural Development Corporation
AFDC	Armed Forces Defence Committee
AFRC	Armed Forces Revolutionary Council
AGC	Ashanti (Asante) Goldfield Corporation
AGCC	African Gold Coast Corporation
AGI	Association of Ghana Industries
APP	All-People's Party
APRP	All-People's Republican Party
ARPS	Aborigines' Rights Protection Society
AWAM	Association of West African Merchants
AYB	African Youth Brigade
BARADEP	Brong-Ahafo Regional Agricultural Development Program
BARDEC	Brong-Ahafo Regional Development Corporation
BHC	Bank for Housing Construction
BIAS	Bulletin of Institute of African Studies (Legon)
BNI	Bureau of National Investigation
BSL	Black Star Line
CA	Constitutional Assembly
CA	Consultative Assembly
CAST	Consolidated African Selection Trust
CCDEF	Coordinating Committee of Democratic Forces
CCE	Center for Civic Education
CCG	Christian Council of Ghana
CDR	Committee for the Defence of the Revolution
CEDEP	Center for the Development of People

CGMC	Chamber of Ghanaian Mining Concessionaires
CID	Criminal Investigation Department
CIP	Community Initiated Project
CMB	Cocoa Marketing Board
CME	Council of Muslim Elders
CMS	Church Missionary Society
CO	Colonial Öffice
COCOBOD	Cocoa Board (Ghana)
COV	Companion of the Order of the Volta
COYA	Committee on Youth Associations
CPA	Cocoa Producers Alliance
CPC	Cocoa Purchasing Company
CPP	Convention People's Party
CRIG	Cocoa Research Institute of Ghana
CSIR	Center for Scientific and Industrial Research
CUT	Committee for Togolese Unity
CVC	Citizens' Vetting Committee
CYO	Catholic Youth Organization
CYO	Committee on Youth Organization
DA	District Assembly
DAO	District Administrative Officer
DAPIT	Development and Application of Intermediate Technology Program
DC	District Commissioner
DEC	District Executive Committee
DIC	Divestiture Implementation Committee
DMC	Diamond Marketing Corporation
DPO	District Political Officer
DS	District Secretary
DYLG	Democratic Youth League of Ghana
ECOMOG	ECOWAS Monitoring Group
ECOWAS	Economic Community of West African States
ECRAG	Entertainment Critics and Reviewers Association of Ghana
EDP	Entrepreneurship Development Program
EEC	European Economic Community
EFF	Extended Fund Facility
EREDEC	Eastern Regional Development Corporation

ERP	Economic Recovery Program
FAO	Food and Agricultural Organization
FDC	Food Distribution Corporation
FEAC	Foreign Exchange Auction Committee
FOREX	Foreign Exchange Bureaux
FPD	Front for the Prevention of Dictatorship
FPIB	Forest Production Inspection Bureau
FYO	Federated Youth Organization
GAAS	Ghana Academy of Arts and Sciences
GAS	Ghana Academy of Sciences
GAW	Ghana Association of Writers
GAWU	Ghana Agricultural Workers' Union
GAWW	Ghanaian Association for Women's Welfare
GBA	Ghana Bar Association
GBC	Ghana Bauxite Company
GBC	Ghana Broadcasting Corporation
GC	Gold Coast
GCARPS	Gold Coast Aborigines' Rights Protection Society
GCD	Ghana Consolidated Diamonds, Ltd.
GCEU	Gold Coast Ex-Servicemen's Union
GCFA	Gold Coast Farmers' Association
GCHC	Ghana Cargo Handling Company
GCMA	Ghana Co-operative Marketing Association
GCP	Ghana Congress Party
GCSA	Ghana Civil Servants Association
GCTUC	Gold Coast Trade Union Congress
GDM	Ghana Democratic Movement
GDP	Gross Domestic Product
GEC	Ghana Enterprises Commission
GEPC	Ghana Export Promotion Council
GES	Ghana Education Service
GET	Ghana Educational Trust
GFDC	Ghana Food Distribution Corporation
GFIC	Ghana Film Industry Corporation
GHA	Ghana Highway Authority
GHAPSO	Ghana People's Solidarity Organization
GIHOC	Ghana Industrial Holding Corporation

GIMPA	Ghana Institute of Management and Public Administration
GJA	Ghana Journalists Association
GMA	Ghana Manufacturing Association
GMA	Ghana Medical Association
GMFJ	Ghana Movement for Freedom and Justice
GNA	Ghana National Archives
GNA	Ghana News Agency
GNAT	Ghana National Association of Teachers
GNCC	Ghana National Chamber of Commerce
GNCC	Ghana National Commission on Children
GNCC	Ghana National Construction Corporation
GNFC	Ghana National Farmers' Council
GNMC	Ghana National Manganese Corporation
GNPC	Ghana National Petroleum Corporation
GNTC	Ghana National Trading Corporation
GNYC	Ghana National Youth Council
GOIL	Ghana Oil Company
GOPDC	Ghana Oil Palm Development Corporation
GPHA	Ghana Ports and Harbors Authority
GPM	Ghana Patriotic Movement
GPP	Ghana Peoples' Party
GPPF	Ghana Progressive Popular Front
GPSC	Ghana Peace and Solidarity Council
GPTU	Ghana Private Transport Union
GRC	Ghana Railways Corporation
GSB	Ghana Standards Board
GSC	Ghana Shippers Council
GSD	Geological Survey Department
GSMC	Ghana State Mining Corporation
GTMB	Ghana Timber Marketing Board
GTMO	Ghana Timber Millers Organization
GTP	Ghana Textile Printing
GTPCWU	General Transport, Petroleum and Chemical Workers' Union
GUNSA	Ghana United Nations Students' Association
GUP	Ghana Universities Press
HSWU	Health Service Workers' Union

IAS	Institute of African Studies (Legon)
IASB	International African Service Bureau
IBRD	International Bank for Reconstruction and Development (World Bank)
ICC	Industrial Co-operative Corporation
ICCO	International Cocoa Organization
ICO	International Coffee Organization
ICWU	Industrial and Commercial Workers' Union
IDA	Irrigation Development Authority
IDC	Industrial Development Corporation
IMC	Interim Management Committee
IMF	International Monetary Fund
INCC	Interim National Coordinating Committee
INEC	Interim National Electoral Commission
IRI	Industrial Research Institute
ITTU	Intermediate Technology Transfer Unit
JAMB	Joint Admissions and Matriculation Board
JCC	Joint Consultative Committee
JFM	June Fourth Movement
JP	Justice Party
JPC	Joint Provincial Council of Chiefs
JSS	Junior Secondary School
JWAC	Joint West Africa Committee
KMAC	King's Medal for African Chiefs
KNRG	Kwame Nkrumah Revolutionary Guards
LRP	Labor Re-deployment Program
LSNA	Legon Society on National Affairs
LVB	Land Value Board
MAC	Military Advisory Council
MAP	Muslim Association Party
MATS	Military Academy and Training School
MBE	Member Order of the British Empire
MFJ	Movement for Freedom and Justice
MI	Military Intelligence
MOV	Member of the Order of Volta
MYC	Muslim Youth Congress

NA	Native Authority
NADECO	National Development Company
NAFTI	National Film and Television Institute
NAG	National Archives of Ghana
NAL	National Alliance of Liberals
NALCO	National Association of Local Councils
NAO	Native Administration Ordinance
NARAC	National Agricultural Resources Allocation Committee
NASSO	National Association of Socialist Students Organizations
NBSSI	National Board for Small-Scale Industries
NBTPE	National Board of Technical and Professional Examinations
NCBWA	National Congress of British West Africa
NCC	National Commission for Culture
NCD	National Commission for Democracy
NCGW	National Council of Ghana Women
NCP	National Convention Party
NCWD	National Council for Women and Development
NDC	National Defence Committee
NDC	National Democratic Congress
NDF	National Democratic Front
NDM	National Democratic Movement
NDPC	National Development Planning Commission
NEB	National Energy Board
NEC	National Economic Commission
NERC	National Economic Review Committee
NES	National Employment Service
NGA	New Generation Alliance
NGP	New Ghana Party
NHC	National House of Chiefs
NIB	National Investment Bank
NIP	New Independence Party
NJO	Native Jurisdiction Ordinance
NLC	National Liberation Council
NLCD	National Liberation Council Decree
NLM	National Liberation Movement
NMP	National Mobilization Program
NORDEC	Northern Regional Development Corporation

NPP	New Patriotic Party
NPP	Northern People's Party
NRC	National Redemption Council
NSC	National Security Council
NSC	National Service Corps
NSS	National Service Scheme
NT	Northern Territories
NTC	Northern Territories Council
NTTC	National Teacher Training Council
NUGS	National Union of Ghana(ian) Students
NUS	National Union of Seamen
NVTI	National Vocational Training Institute
NYA	Northern Youth Association
NYC	National Youth Council
NYOC	National Youth Organizing Committee
OAC	Organization for African Community
OATUU	Organization of African Trade Unions Unity
OAU	Organization of African Unity
OCDR	Organizing Committee for the Defence of the Revolution
OFY	Operation Feed Yourself
OOV	Officer of the Order of Volta
OPRI	Oil Palm Research Institute
ORC	Office of Revenue Commissioners
OTDC	Overseas Trade Development Council
PAC	Pan-African Club
PAMSCAD	Program of Action for the Mitigation of the Social Consequences of Adjustment for Development
PAP	People's Action Party
PBD	Produce Buying Division (of Cocoa Marketing Board)
PC	Provincial Commissioner
PDA	Preventive Detention Act
PDC	People's Defence Committee
PEA	People's Educational Association
PFP	Popular Front Party
PHP	People's Heritage Party
PIB	Price and Incomes Board
PIP	People's Independent Party

PMFJ	People's Movement for Freedom and Justice
PMMC	Precious Minerals Marketing Corporation
PNC	People's National Convention
PNDC	Provisional National Defence Council
PNDCL	Provisional National Defence Council Law
PNP	People's National Party
POGR	President's Own Guard Regiment
POYA	Popular Youth Association
PP	Progress Party
PPC	Petroleum Promotion Council
PPDD	Popular Party for Democracy and Development
PPF	People's Popular Front
PPP	People's Popular Party
PRELOG	People's Revolutionary League of Ghana
PRP	People's Revolutionary Party
PSC	Police Service Commission
PSWU	Public Services Workers' Union
PTWU	Post and Telecommunications Workers' Union
RAC	Royal African Company
RC	Regional Commissioner
RDC	Regional Development Corporation
RWAFF	Royal West African Frontier Force (WAFF)
SAG	Senior Advocate of Ghana
SAL	Structural Adjustment Loan
SAP	Structural Adjustment Program
SCMB	State Cocoa Marketing Board
SCOA	Société Commerciale de l'Ouest Africain
SDF	Social Democratic Front
SEC	State Enterprises Commission
SGMC	State Gold Mining Corporation
SMC	State Mining Companies
SMC	Supreme Military Council
SMCD	Supreme Military Council Decree
SOERP	Stated-Owned Enterprise Reform Program
SPG	Society for the Propagation of the Gospel
SPP	Special Public Prosecutor
SRC	Students' Representative Council
SSNIT	Social Security and National Insurance Trust

STAFAMS	State Farms Corporation
TC	Togoland Congress
TCC	Technology Consultancy Center
TCOR	Trusteeship Council Official Records
TCP	Togoland Congress Party
TDC	Tema Development Corporation
TEDB	Timber Export Development Board
TF	Third Force
TGCTHS	Transactions of the Gold Coast and Togoland Historical Society (Achimota and Legon)
THSG	Transactions of the Historical Society of Ghana (Legon)
TMB	Timber Marketing Board
TUC	Trades Union Congress
TVT	Trans-Volta Togoland
UAC	United Africa Company
UAF	United Action Front
UAT	United African Trust
UCC	University of Cape Coast
UG	University of Ghana
UGCC	United Gold Coast Convention
UGFC	United Ghana Farmers' Council
UGFCC	United Ghana Farmers' Council of Cooperatives
UN	United Nations
UNC	United National Convention
UNIFIL	United Nations Interim Force in Lebanon
UNP	United Nationalist Party
UNTSO	United Nations Truce Supervision Organization
UP	United Party
UST	University of Science and Technology
VAG	Veterans Association of Ghana
VALCO	Volta Aluminum Company
VBRP	Volta Basin Research Project
VLRDP	Volta Lake Research and Development Project
VORADEC	Volta Regional Agricultural Development Corporation
VORADEP	Volta Regional Agricultural Development Project
VRA	Volta River Authority

VRF	Volta River Federation
VRP	Volta River Project
WAAC	West African Airways Corporation
WANS	West African National Secretariat
WASU	West African Students' Union
WAYL	West African Youth League
WDC	Workers' Defence Committees
WREDEC	Western Regional Development Corporation
YPM	Young Pioneer Movement
YSG	Youth Study Group

CHRONOLOGY

c. 10,000 B.C.   Probable human habitation at Jiman on the Oti River (8°37'N, O°06'E) is earliest recorded site located within modern Ghana.

c. 8000 B.C.   Probable human habitation around Lake Bosumtwi in modern Asante.

c. 4000 B.C.   Oldest date for pottery found at the Stone Age site on Gao Lagoon near Accra.

c. 3300 B.C.   Late Stone Age site at Bosumpra Rockshelter, Abetifi, Kwahu.

c. 1500 B.C.   The beginnings of Kintampo Culture.

c. 100 B.C.   Early Iron Age at Tema.

c. 150 A.D.   Early Iron Age at Kpone.

c. 700 A.D.   Iron technology had developed around New Buipe.

c. 1000   Iron technology existed at Bonoso in the nuclear area of the Brong.

1076-1077   The Almoravids conquered ancient Ghana on the edge of the Sahara.

c. 1200   The Guan began to move down the Volta from the Gonja area toward the Gulf of Guinea.

c. 1298   Asaman founded the Bono (Brong) kingdom.

xix

c. 1400   Increased Dyula commercial activities at Begho.

c. 1450   The Guan had reached the coast west of modern Accra and had settled the Akuapem area.

1472   The Portuguese had reached the Gold Coast and were trading for gold at Shama near the Pra.

1479   Castilian, English and Italian ships had joined the Flemish and Portuguese on the Gold Coast.

c. 1480   Dagomba, Mamprusi and Nanumba were in the process of state formation.

19 Jan. 1482   A Portuguese squadron under Diogo de Azambuja reached the Benya and soon began construction of the Fort of San Jorge, Elmina.

15 Mar. 1486   John II of Portugal gave Elmina the status of a Municipality and took the title "Lord of Guinea."

7 June 1494   The Treaty of Tordesillas recognized Portuguese claims to the coast of West Africa.

c. 1500   Adanse and Akwamu, early Akan states, had emerged. The Ga, under Ayi Kushi, had settled in the Accra Plains by this time.

25 July 1503   The paramount chief of Efutu and a thousand others were baptized on Santiago Hill outside Elmina.

c. 1550   The Mande began the conquest of Gonja.

1553   Englishmen were contesting the Portuguese monopoly of trade on the Gold Coast.

1580   The French set up a factory at Accra, taken by the Portuguese in 1583.

1595   Dutch vessels were trading on the Gold Coast.

1598	The Dutch established posts at Mouri and Butri.
c. 1620	The Gonja attacked Dagomba at Daboya and the Dagomba were forced to move their capital to Yendi.
1624	The Fante and the Dutch formed an alliance against the Portuguese.
c. 1630	Oti Akenten began his leadership of the Asante.
1631	The English built a lodge at Kormantin.
16 June 1633	The Dutch estimated five tons of gold being brought from the Gold Coast annually.
26 Aug. 1637	A Dutch force landed at Cabo Corso (Cape Coast) and began a final push against the Portuguese.
29 Aug. 1637	San Jorge Castle was surrendered to the Dutch and the Dutch moved their headquarters there from Mouri.
c. 1640	Tobacco was introduced from America.
8 Feb. 1642	The Dutch took Fort Saint Anthony at Axim, the last Portuguese post on the Gold Coast.
20 Aug. 1642	The Accra gave the Dutch permission to build a post near Osu.
1645	Swedes captured an old Portuguese base at Osu.
c. 1646	By this date the Akwamu had conquered the Gua in the Akuapem area.
1650	The Swedes established themselves at Cabo Corso (Cape Coast) and Takoradi.
1652	The Swedes began Fort Carlsborg at Cabo Corso, and established themselves also at Osu. The Dutch base at Accra was named Fort Crevecoeur.

1657-1658   Denkyira defeated Adansi and emerged the major
              Akan power in the west. Danes arrived on the Gold
              Coast and began to take Swedish posts.

1661   The Ga ceded the beach at Osu to the Danes, who
              began Christiansborg Castle.

1663   The British established a base at Komenda.

1664-1665   The Anglo-Dutch War resulted in conflicts between
              those two nations on the Gold Coast. In May 1664
              the English took Cabo Corso from the Dutch, who
              had taken it from the Swedes the year before. The
              English called the place Cape Coast. It would be
              their headquarters for two hundred years.

1665   The Dutch took Kormantin from the English and
              named it Fort Amsterdam.

1672   The Royal African Company replaced the Company
              of Royal Adventurers as the English agents of the
              Gold Coast trade. The English began James Fort at
              Little Accra.

1677   The Akwamu under Ansa Sasraku sacked and burned
              the Ga capital at Great Accra (Ayawaso).

1679   The Akwamu moved east from Great Accra into
              Ladoku. The English began a fort at Anomabo. The
              Portuguese took Christiansborg Castle, but returned it
              to the Danes in 1683.

c. 1680   Kumasi emerged as capital of Asante during the early
              reign of Asantehene Osei Tutu.

1681   Akwamu burned Little Accra and Osu.

1682   Brandenburgers began to build a series of posts at
              Princestown, Takrama, and Akwida, but these
              Germans did not stay long.

1688	The Akwamu conquered Ladoku. The French established themselves at Komenda, but soon left. The Dutch began Fort Vredenburg at Komenda. The Dutch began to sign alliances with peoples along the west coast.
c. 1691	The Adom-Ahanta war, which was to last many years, began about this time.
1691	The English established Fort Metal Cross at Dixcove.
1694	A war of the Komenda against the Dutch began. The English built a fort at Winneba.
1698	Denkyira defeated Assin.
c. 1700	The Mamprusi court moved from Gambaga to Nalerigu.
1701	The Akwamu crossed the Volta and advanced eastward into modern Benin (Dahomey). Osei Tutu and the Asante defeated Ntim Gyakari and the Denkyira in the Battle of Fayiase.
1702	The Asante defeated the Akyem Kotoku, allies of Denkyira. The Akwamu army pulled out of the area between the Volta and Whydah.
1707	The Akwamu army conquered the Ewe of Krepi, but failed in an invasion of Kwahu. The advance carried the Akwamu to Ho and Kpandu.
1708-1710	Akwamu campaigned against Kwahu and was finally successful.
c. 1713	Yendi Dabari, seat of the Dagomba, fell to the Gonja under Kumpatia.

11 Apr. 1713   The Treaty of Utrecht granted the English a contract to supply slaves to Spanish America, initiating the most active period of slave trade on the Gold Coast.

1717   Akyem inflicted a costly defeat on the Asante army on the Pra River; Asantehene Osei Tutu was killed.

13 Aug. 1720   The Dutch West India Company acquired claim to all Brandenburg (Prussian) properties on the Gold Coast.

1724   The Akwamu and Fante campaigned against Agona. The Dutch took Gross Friedrichsburg, at Princestown, from John Konny, an Ahanta merchant.

1730   The Akyem and their allies defeated Akwamu and forced the Akwamu across the Volta.

1731   The Concord of Abotakyi created the state of Akuapem (Akwapim).

1734   The Danes began Fort Fredensborg at Ningo.

1737   Troops from Dahomey (modern Benin) raided the area about Keta.

1742   Opoku Ware of Asante defeated the Akyem forces, making Asante the major power on the Gold Coast.

1744   Gonja became a tributary state to Asante.

1745   Dagomba became a tributary to Asante.

1750   Opoku Ware died and civil war broke out on the succession of Kusi Obodum as Asantehene. A war, between Anlo on one side and Ada, Akuapem and Akyem Abuakwa on the other began.

Apr. 1752   The Royal African Company was replaced by the Company of Merchants Trading to Africa.

May 1752   The Rev. Thomas Thompson arrived at Cape Coast as a missionary for the SPG.

1757   The French failed in an attempt to take Cape Coast.

1764   The Asante army crossed the Volta and was almost wiped out in an ambush by Oyo and Dahomey troops. Kusi Obodum was destooled, several tributary states rebelled against Asante, and Osei Kwadwo became the new Asantehene.

1765   Asante forces came within a few miles of Anomabo and Cape Coast, establishing a camp at Abora in Fante territory, but a shortage of food forced an Asante retreat. Coastal states formed an alliance against Asante.

1766   Philip Quaque began his missionary career for the SPG at Cape Coast.

1768   The English began Fort Apollonia at Beyin.

1777   Osei Kwadwo died and was replaced by a minor, Osei Kwame, as Asantehene.

Jan. 1782   Accra, Osu, Labadi, Krobo, Tema, Ningo, Ada and others along the eastern coast recognized Danish authority.

18 Apr. 1782   The English captured Fort Crevecoeur from the Dutch and demolished it.

25 Mar. 1784   The Danes and their allies began a campaign against the Anlo.

18 June 1784   The Danes signed a peace treaty with the Anlo.

1786   Paul Erdmann Isert explored Akuapem.

1787   The Danes built a fort at Teshi, completing their control of trade along the eastern coast between Accra and the Volta.

21 Dec. 1788   Paul Erdmann Isert for Denmark signed a treaty with Akuapem by which the Danes gained use of all unused land in Akuapem, but the plantation did not last long after Isert's death.

16 Mar. 1792   The Danish King ordered an end to the slave trade by his subjects after 1 January 1803.

31 Mar. 1792   Archibald Dalzel arrived as Governor at Cape Coast Castle, a position he was to hold until 1802.

1800   Osei Tutu Kwame (Osei Bonsu) replaced Opoku Fofie as Asantehene.

1802   Denmark became the first nation to outlaw the Atlantic slave trade.

1805   The Asante defeated Assin at Kyikyiwere in the Moinsi Hills. The Assin chiefs fled to the Fante.

7 Feb. 1805   George Torrane arrived at Cape Coast Castle as Governor for the Company of Merchants.

1806-1807   The Asante army occupied much of the territory between Accra and the Volta. They also invaded Fante territory in pursuit of two fugitive Assin chiefs. The Dutch surrendered Fort Amsterdam at Kormantin to the Asante. Mankesim was destroyed and the British base at Anomabo was attacked.

1807   After doing great damage along the coast, the Asante army, under Osei Bonsu, was forced to retreat due to smallpox and dysentery.

Mar. 1807   The British and the United States outlawed all dealing and trading in slaves in Africa and their transport elsewhere was declared unlawful after 1 January 1808.

19 May 1817	An English expedition under Frederick James and Thomas Bowdich, nephew of the Governor of Cape Coast Castle, reached Kumasi to negotiate trade relations with Osei Bonsu.
7 Sept. 1817	An agreement was reached between the English and Asante to maintain peace between the two nations. A British officer would reside at Kumasi and some children of the Asantehene would be educated at Cape Coast.
1819	Joseph Dupuis went to Kumasi as the first Crown envoy to negotiate an agreement between the English and the Asante.
23 Mar. 1820	An agreement reached by Joseph Dupuis with the Asantehene provided that the Asante and English would share jurisdiction on the coast. The English officials at Cape Coast repudiated the agreement.
7 May 1821	An Act of the English Parliament abolished the Company of Merchants Trading to Africa and transferred all its property to the Crown.
3 July 1821	British posts on the Gold Coast were placed under the Governor of Sierra Leone.
Apr. 1822	Sir Charles MacCarthy arrived at Cape Coast and began to prepare for war with Asante.
4 June 1823	The Asante army crossed the Pra to begin a campaign against Denkyira, Wassa, Fante and the British.
Oct. 1823	Osei Bonsu died and the Golden Stool was seized by Osei Yaw Akoto.

21 Jan. 1824	Between Bonsaso and Nsamankow in Wassa the Asante and a British force under Sir Charles MacCarthy accidentally met. MacCarthy and eight other officers were killed. The head of MacCarthy was believed to have been taken to Kumasi as a trophy.
7 Aug. 1826	The Asante army under Osei Yaw Akoto suffered a serious defeat at Katamanso, near Accra. The battle is sometimes called the Battle of Dodowa. The victorious forces were made up of Ga, Fante, Denkyira, Akyem, Akwamu, and British forces.
1828	The British government transferred control of Gold Coast British interests to a committee of London merchants. At Cape Coast and Accra the merchants were to elect a council, which in turn would choose a president.
18 Dec. 1828	The first Basel Missionaries arrived at Osu.
15 Feb. 1830	George Maclean assumed duties as President of the Council of Merchants at Cape Coast.
1831	Conflict between Asantehene Osei Yaw Akoto and Dwaben climaxed in the occupation of the town by Asante forces. This caused many from Dwaben to flee, seeking protection in Akyem.
27 Apr. 1831	Asante agreed to peace terms with the English and English allies on the coast. Peace between Asante and Denmark and Danish allies was reached during the summer.
1833	The first Methodist missionaries arrived in the Gold Coast.
1 Aug. 1834	Slavery was abolished in the British Empire. The Act passed Parliament in August 1833.

1843   The Basel Mission established schools at Osu and Akuropon. The British government resumed control of English posts on the Gold Coast from the Company of Merchants.

6 Mar. 1844   The Bond of 1844 signed this date marked the climax of Anglo-Fante friendship.

1847   The Bremen Mission (German) began work on the Gold Coast.

1850   During the year Denmark turned over all its interests on the Gold Coast to the British.

24 Jan. 1850   Queen Victoria issued a charter to the forts and settlements on the Gold Coast which provided for a Governor and Legislative Council to govern the area between 10°0'W and 10°0'E longitude, subject to the Queen and her Council.

1852   Coastal areas under British jurisdiction were subjected to taxation under what was known as the Poll Tax Ordinance of 1852. Opposition to the tax developed quickly and no real effort was made to collect the tax after 1862.

26 Apr. 1853   The British established a system of courts to deal with civil and criminal cases in areas under their control.

1856   The British expanded their protectorate to include Akuapem, Krobo and Krepi.

1857   Charles Bannerman established the *Accra Herald* (later the *West African Herald*) at James Town, Accra. This was the first newspaper run by Africans on the Gold Coast.

10 May 1858   The Municipal Corporations Ordinance provided for municipal government with power to assess house

taxes in British areas. The Poll Tax Ordinance was amended in a vain attempt to make it more acceptable to Africans. The District Assemblies Ordinance established District Councils in the British Protectorate. The Ordinance was disallowed the next year.

Mar. 1863   The Asante invaded the British Protectorate in a dispute over extradition of two fugitives from Asante territory. Economic activities along the coast were severely dislocated.

25 Oct. 1864   People in the Cape Coast area protested to the British Governor that they were not British subjects and should not be subject to British tax without their consent.

1865   John Zimmerman finished a translation of the Bible into Ga. Ada and Anlo began a war which lasted for several years, with the British eventually siding with Ada and the Asante supporting Anlo.

24 Aug. 1865   A British Parliamentary Report recommended a gradual British withdrawal from the Gold Coast.

19 Feb. 1866   British Gold Coast interests were returned to the jurisdiction of authorities in Sierra Leone. This was the situation until 1874 when a separate administration for the Gold Coast and Lagos was created.

5 Mar. 1867   The British and Dutch agreed to exchange their posts on the Gold Coast to separate their jurisdictions at the Sweet River, just east of Elmina. They also agreed to establish common tariffs.

21 Mar. 1867   The British deposed King John Aggery of Cape Coast, abolished his position, and announced that in the future the people of Cape Coast would elect a

headman, who would have to swear allegiance to England.

27 Apr. 1867   Asantehene Kwaku Dua I died. His successor was 35-year-old Kofi Kakari.

28 Aug. 1867   Akwamu and England reached an agreement of amity and commerce.

1868   Attempts to transfer English posts at Komenda to Dutch control raised a storm of protest. A meeting at Mankesim forced an alliance of Africans to resist transfer of Komenda, Dixcove, Sekondi, and Beyin to the Dutch. The alliance became the Fante Confederacy.

1 Feb. 1868   The Dutch bombarded Komenda.

Fall 1868   The Asante army crossed Akyem and invaded Krepi.

1869   The Asante armies threatened the whole coastal area.

June 1869   Asante forces took Anum and Ho during an expedition in the Volta area. F. A. Ramseyer and J. Kuhne, of the Basel Mission, and a French businessman, J. Bonnat, were captured and taken to Kumasi as prisoners.

25 Aug. 1869   The Fante Confederacy held a meeting in Mankesim, to discuss the Asante threats.

Nov. 1869   The Dutch proposed to turn over all their Gold Coast interests to the British.

19 Dec. 1870   African leaders in Elmina protested the proposed transfer of Elmina from Dutch to English control.

18 Nov. 1871   Fante leaders adopted a constitution for a Fante Confederacy at Mankesim.

30 Nov. 1871	British authorities at Cape Coast arrested a number of Fante leaders who had played roles in the creation of the Fante Confederacy.
12 Feb. 1872	British authorities at Cape Coast issued a proclamation warning against anyone taking office under the Fante Confederacy and condemned the Confederacy constitution.
17 Feb. 1872	The Dutch agreed to turn over their Gold Coast possessions to the British.
6 Apr. 1872	Elmina Castle was transferred to the British by the Dutch. Within a short time Axim, Dixcove and Sekondi were also transferred to English control.
30 July 1872	Fante leaders, meeting at Mankesim, selected their leaders.
9 Dec. 1872	The Asante Army left Kumasi in a move to protect their interests on the coast.
6 June 1873	Fante leaders appealed for British protection.
2 Oct. 1873	Major General Sir Garnet Wolseley ("Sagrenti" in Akan traditions) arrived at Cape Coast to organize forces against the Asante.
22 Dec. 1873	The Asante army began a retreat to Kumasi.
Jan. 1874	Forces under Wolseley began the advance toward Kumasi. They entered Kumasi by 4 February 1874 and sacked the town. That was the first time in Asante history that enemy forces entered the capital.
13 Feb. 1874	A treaty of peace was signed at Fomena between the Asante and British.
22 June 1874	By the treaty of Dzelukofe, Anlo recognized British control east of the Volta.

24 July 1874   The British established the Gold Coast Colony (including Lagos) under a governor, executive council and legislative council. The seat of government was established at Accra.

6 Aug. 1874   An Order in Council empowered the Gold Coast Legislative Council to legislate for all areas on the Gold Coast under British protection.

21 Oct. 1874   Kofi Kakari was deposed as Asantehene. Mensa Bonsu, a younger brother of Kofi Kakari, was elected Asantehene.

17 Dec. 1874   The British Gold Coast government emancipated all pawns and slaves in areas under their jurisdiction.

12 Sept. 1875   The Asante army attacked Dwaben. The result was further migration of people from Dwaben to Akyem Abuakwa, where they settled about Koforidua.

7 Dec. 1875   Marie-Joseph Bonnat set out up the Volta with five canoes and 27 men on a journey to Salaga. Bonnat, a former prisoner in Kumasi, became an Asante agent.

1876   The Wesleyans opened a secondary school at Cape Coast. In time this school would unite with other schools to become Mfantsipim.

30 Jan. 1876   Marie-Joseph Bonnat and British Special Commissioner Dr. V. S. Gouldsbury reached Salaga. Each man hoped to control trade through Salaga.

8 Mar. 1876   Dr. Gouldsbury signed a commercial treaty for the British with Kete Krakye.

1877   Marie-Joseph Bonnat joined a company to prospect for gold along the Ankobra river. Geraldo de Lema and the Anlo were active in resistance to British control of trade in the Ada-Keta areas.

19 Mar. 1877   The British formally moved their seat of government from Cape Coast to Christiansborg.

1878   Tetteh Quashie introduced cocoa seedlings from Fernando Po to Akuapem. His first harvest was in 1883.

Dec. 1879   The British extended their jurisdiction around the Keta Lagoon as far as Aflao.

2 Sept. 1880   The British created the Volta River District with jurisdiction over Krobo, Akuapem, Shai and Krepi.

May 1881   A Roman Catholic Mission was established at Elmina.

15 Oct. 1881   Captain R. La Touche Lonsdale began his trip to Kumasi, Salaga and Yendi. He reached Salaga on Christmas Day and continued on to Yendi.

May 1882   The British provided for general and local boards of education, and for inspectors of schools for the Gold Coast.

1883   The Public Labor Ordinance provided powers for the British to recruit paid African labor.

15 Jan. 1883   A reenactment of the Native Jurisdiction Ordinance of 1878 based the powers of African chiefs and tribunals on English authority.

8 Mar. 1883   Mensa Bonsu was destooled as Asantehene and banished from Kumasi. This touched off a long period of anarchy in Asante.

27 Apr. 1884   Kwaku Dua II was enstooled as Asantehene, but he died of smallpox 71 days later.

5 July 1884   The Germans announced a protectorate over Togoland.

1885	The first cocoa was exported from the Gold Coast. By 1911 the Gold Coast was the world's largest producer of cocoa.
7 Jan. 1885	The British arrested Geraldo de Lema. He was rescued by Anlo friends but soon recaptured. The British held him at Elmina from May 1885 to the end of 1893.
13 Jan. 1886	Lagos was separated from the Gold Coast. Organization of the Legislative Council of the Gold Coast was also changed to allow for four nominated unofficial members, two Europeans and two Africans.
14 July 1886	The British and Germans reached an agreement on the border between the Gold Coast and Togoland.
24 July 1886	Edmund Bannerman and others began a campaign in Accra to raise funds to send a deputation to London to protest actions of the colonial officials in the Gold Coast.
27 July 1886	Akwamu became part of the Protectorate as part of the Gold Coast.
7 Oct. 1886	Krepi formally submitted to Gold Coast rule.
18 Feb. 1887	Swefi signed a treaty for protection with the British at Wiawso.
1888	John M. Sarbah became the first African member of the Gold Coast Legislative Council.
14 Mar. 1888	The English and Germans agreed upon a neutral zone north of the Daka River.
26 Mar. 1888	Agyeman Prempe was elected Asantehene, ending a four-year interregnum. He could not be formally installed as Kwaku Dua III (Prempe I) until 1894.

5 May 1888	Kwahu submitted to British protection by a treaty signed at Abetifi.
8 Oct. 1888	Louis Binger, a French explorer, reached Salaga from the north.
1889	The Fante National Political Society was formed at Cape Coast. This was one of the earliest nationalist movements on the Gold Coast.
10 Aug. 1889	The French and British reached their first agreement defining the boundary between the Gold Coast and the Ivory Coast.
1890	A Department of Roads and a Department for Education were created by the Gold Coast Colony.
1 July 1890	The Heligoland Agreement between Germany and England further demarcated the boundaries between Togo and the Gold Coast, leaving Ho, Kpandu and part of Peki in German hands.
25 Nov. 1890	Atebubu recognized British protection.
1891	The first Gold Coast census showed a population of 764,185 for the colony. A Department of Telegraph and a Department of Prisons were established.
25 Apr. 1892	George Ekem Ferguson began his trip into the territory north of Salaga to secure British interests in that area.
26 Aug. 1892	Nanumba signed a treaty of friendship and trade at Bimbila with the British.
12 July 1893	England and France divided Gyaman, with the chief city of Gyaman, Bonduku, going to the Ivory Coast.

Nov. 1893   The Asante invaded Atebubu in an attempt to destroy the Brong Confederation and open the route to Salaga for Asante traders again.

15 Nov. 1893   The British extended an offer of aid to the Brong Confederation in case of Asante threats.

1894   During the year many groups in the north signed agreements with the British. The Trade Roads Ordinance authorized chiefs to require up to six days of labor per quarter on the public roads of all their people. Coastal towns from Axim to Lome were connected by a telegraph line. The Town Council Ordinance provided for municipal governments for Accra, Cape Coast and Sekondi, to be financed by a house tax. A bill to vest all "waste lands" in the Crown was introduced into the Legislative Council, but was withdrawn due to the great protest.

12 Apr. 1894   Bona signed a trade friendship treaty with the British.

4 May 1894   The Dagaba (Dagarti) signed a treaty with the British at Wa.

28 May 1894   The Mamprusi signed a treaty with the British at Gambaga.

4 June 1894   Kwaku Dua III (Prempe I) was enstooled Ashantehene.

2 July 1894   The Mossi signed a treaty with the British at Ouagadouga (Burkina Faso).

28 Mar. 1895   A delegation from Asante left the Gold Coast for England to protest British policy against Asante. The Asante delegation was not received in London.

8 Apr. 1895   William Edward Maxwell replaced Brandford Griffith as Governor of the Gold Coast.

23 Sept. 1895 Governor Maxwell sent an ultimatum to the Asantehene demanding that the Asante consent to a British resident in Kumasi.

18 Oct. 1895 The Adansi signed a treaty for protection with the British.

17 Jan. 1896 British forces occupied Kumasi. The Asantehene and many of his chiefs were arrested and exiled to the Seychelles Islands in the Indian Ocean.

14 Aug. 1896 The British established a garrison of African soldiers at Kintampo.

16 Aug. 1896 The British proclaimed a protectorate over Asanteland.

4 Dec. 1896 The Germans defeated a Dagomba army at Adibo, and the following day the Germans destroyed Yendi.

24 Dec. 1896 British troops under Donald Stewart occupied Gambaga.

1897 The Obuasi gold mines were opened. The Bank of British West Africa opened a branch in Accra and a branch was opened in Kumasi in 1908. The British tried again to get a bill to vest unused lands in the Crown through the Legislative Council, but opposition again forced the measure to be withdrawn. The debate gave rise to the Aborigines' Rights Protection Society (ARPS).

14 Mar. 1897 The French and their allies defeated Babatu and his Zabrama forces at Gandiago.

29 Mar. 1897 British forces under Francis B. Henderson clashed with the forces of Samori Toure. Troops of Samori had been along the Black Volta over a year.

7 Apr. 1897   George E. Ferguson was killed near Wa during a battle between the British and Samori's forces.

20 Apr. 1897   The French and British at Yariba reached a temporary agreement on boundaries for their spheres of control in what would become the Upper Volta (Burkina Faso) and the Northern Territories of the Gold Coast.

May 1897   The ARPS was organized at Cape Coast.

23 June 1897   French forces defeated Babatu at Doucie.

Oct. 1897   The British began a campaign to end the influence of the Zabrama. By June of the following year Zabrama power had been broken.

1898   The African Methodist Episcopal Zion Church was founded in Cape Coast. It was the first independent Christian denomination on the Gold Coast run solely by Africans.

1 Jan. 1898   The ARPS began to publish *The Gold Coast Aborigines* at Cape Coast.

24 May 1898   The ARPS sent a delegation to London to protest land policy of the government of the Gold Coast.

14 June 1898   The French and British reached an agreement on the northern limits of British control behind the Gold Coast. Formal ratification of the agreement took place in 1899.

13 July 1898   Africans on the western Gold Coast petitioned for representation in the Legislative Council.

Aug. 1898   Construction of a railroad from Sekondi to the hinterlands began. It reached Tarkwa in 1901, Obuasi in December 1902, and Kumasi in October 1903.

5 Aug. 1898   The Colonial Office in London received the ARPS delegation protesting the land policy.

14 Nov. 1898   Germany and England agreed on their borders in the north. A previously existing neutral zone was abolished, thus allowing Mamprusi to go to the British. Dagomba was split, and Chakosi went to Germany.

5 Feb. 1900   Cecil Hamilton Armitage arrived in Asante with Hausa troops for an abortive search for the Golden Stool.

25 Mar. 1900   Governor F. Mitchell Hodgson arrived in Kumasi. He announced, during his visit, that the Asantehene would never be allowed to return to Kumasi; that the Asante were responsible for public work. He also demanded the Golden Stool.

31 Mar. 1900   The Asante went to war with the British in what is called the Yaa Asantewa War, after the queen mother of Ejusu who was one of the leaders against Hodgson and the British occupation of Asante.

15 Apr. 1900   The chiefs of Kumasi demanded a return of Prempe, restoration of the slave trade, an end to conscript labor and the expulsion of all foreigners from Kumasi.

25 Apr. 1900   The siege of the British fort in Kumasi began.

23 June 1900   Governor Hodgson and others escaped from Kumasi.

15 July 1900   The siege of the fort at Kumasi was broken and most of the rebellion collapsed but some resistance continued until the end of the year.

26 Sept. 1900   Asante and the Northern Territories were annexed to the British crown under the Governor of the Gold Coast effective as of 1 January 1902.

1902	A Department of Native Affairs was created in the Gold Coast Colony administrative organization.
1 Jan. 1902	The Gold Coast officially became the Colony, Asante and the Northern Territories.
May 1906	The White Fathers began their mission at Navorongo. They opened a school the following year.
1907	Tamale and Wa were connected to the coast by telegraph. British headquarters in the Northern Territories was moved from Gambaga to Tamale and changed from a military to civil status.
1909	A government college for the training of teachers and a Technical School opened in Accra. Also in Kumasi and Tamale, government schools were opened.
13 Sept. 1911	A bill for the establishment of forest reserves was enacted by the Legislative Council, but dropped because of opposition.
14 Aug. 1914	As a result of the outbreak of World War I, Yendi, capital of Dagomba (and under German control), was occupied by the Northern Territories Constabulary.
26 Aug. 1914	German forces in Togoland surrendered to an Anglo-French force. The area was divided between the two allied powers.
Sept. 1916	Governor Hugh Clifford announced the "Clifford Constitution." The Legislative Council was enlarged to 21 members: 12 official and nine unofficial. Three of the unofficial members would be paramount chiefs, and three would be other Africans.
2 Feb. 1918	*The Gold Coast Leader* issued the call which was to bring about the organization of the National Congress of British West Africa (NCBWA).

6 May 1919   The Supreme Council of the League of Nations assigned Togoland as a mandate to the British and French. This action was confirmed by the whole League on 20 July 1922.

28 June 1919   Germany renounced its claims to Togoland when it signed the Treaty of Peace at Versailles.

10 July 1919   The Milner-Simon Declaration fixed the boundary between British and French Togoland. The English-mandated section covered 13,000 square miles.

9 Oct. 1919   Frederick Gordon Guggisberg arrived in Accra as the new Governor of the Gold Coast.

30 Oct. 1919   Governor Guggisberg met in Kumasi with the Kumasi Council of Chiefs and sympathetically listened to their requests that Prempe be returned from exile.

17 Nov. 1919   Governor Guggisberg presented his Ten Year Development Program to the Legislative Council. He also called for improved transportation, education, health care, utilities, port facilities, prisons, and more Africans in government service.

5 Mar. 1920   The Governor's Committee on Educational Matters recommended that education at the local level on the Gold Coast be in the local vernacular.

15-28 Mar. 1920 The NCBWA held its first conference in Accra.

1921   An Anthropological Department was organized for Asante under Robert S. Rattray.

23 June 1921   Governor Guggisberg announced a plan to speed replacement of Europeans by Africans in government service.

1923   The railroad from Accra to Kumasi was completed. Construction had started in 1905.

11 Oct. 1923   The northern part of the Togo mandate was placed under the Northern Territories for administration and the southern part of the mandate was to be administered as part of the Colony.

8 Apr. 1924   The Constitution of 1925 provided for 15 official and 14 unofficial members for the Legislative Council.

11 Nov. 1924   Prempe returned to Kumasi from exile.

17 May 1926   The Provincial Councils of Chiefs met for the first time in face of considerable opposition from educated Africans.

11 Nov. 1926   Prempe was installed as Kumasihene.

Jan. 1927   Prince of Wales (Achimota) College was opened, offering courses from kindergarten through college.

19 Apr. 1927   Nana Ofori Atta introduced the Native Administration Ordinance in the Legislative Council. This was the first time that a bill had been offered by an unofficial member.

1929   The British government established a Colonial Development Fund. The United Africa Company was created as a subsidiary of Lever Brothers.

17 Apr. 1930   The Youth Conference held its first meeting at Achimota.

Fall 1930   Cocoa farmers organized a boycott of the cocoa market to try to keep up prices.

12 May 1931   Prempe I (Kwaku Dua III) died. On June 22 that year, Kwame Kyeretwie was elected as Kumasihene.

24 Apr. 1933   The Kumasihene was installed as Asantehene Osei Agyeman Otumfo, Prempe II.

1934   The Chief Commissioner of the Northern Territories became a member of the Gold Coast Executive Council. The Waterworks Ordinance and the Sedition Ordinance both passed in the Legislative Council with a clear division of African and European members on the votes.

1935   The Executive Council of Gold Coast Colony was empowered to act for Asante and the Northern Territories. The Asante Confederacy was restored.

Oct. 1937   Cocoa farmers began a boycott of European firms buying cocoa. The hold-up lasted until the next April in Akuapem and Akyem Abuakwa.

21 June 1940   France fell to Germany in World War II. The Ivory Coast, Upper Volta (Burkina Faso), and Togoland declared their loyalty to the Vichy government in France, and all the land borders of the Gold Coast were closed.

1942   Ofori Atta I of Akyem and Kobina Arku Korsah of Saltpond were appointed the first Africans on the Governor's Executive Council.

1942   Alan Burns became Governor of the Cold Coast.

20 Aug. 1943   An Income Tax Ordinance finally was enacted by the Legislative Council.

1944   The Youth Conference launched a major campaign for changes in the Gold Coast Constitution.

29 Mar. 1946   The Burns Constitution was announced. The Gold Coast became the first British African colony with a majority of Africans in the Legislative Council.

Dec. 1946   A council of chiefs was established in the Northern Territories for the first time.

13 Dec. 1946   Following the defeat of Germany in World War II, the British Togoland Trusteeship was approved by the United Nations.

4 Aug. 1947   The United Gold Coast Convention (UGCC) was inaugurated at Saltpond.

16 Dec. 1947   Kwame Nkrumah returned to the Gold Coast after many years' absence in the US and England to become General-Secretary of the UGCC.

1948   The University College of the Gold Coast was established, with classes to be held at Achimota until a campus was built at Legon.

26 Jan. 1948   A boycott of imported goods from Europe was initiated under the leadership of Nii Bonne. The boycott climaxed at the end of February with riots and the looting of stores.

20 Feb. 1948   J. B. Danquah and Kwame Nkrumah spoke to a mass rally at the Palladium Cinema in Accra.

28 Feb. 1948   Rioting began along Christiansborg Road in Accra and spread throughout the Gold Coast. It did not subside until the middle of March.

12 Mar. 1948   Six leaders of the UGCC (the Big Six) were arrested and sent to the Northern Territories. Nkrumah and Danquah were among those arrested.

15 Apr. 1948   J. B. Danquah proposed that the name of the country be changed from the Gold Coast to Ghana.

June 1948   A British commission under the direction of Andrew Aiken Watson issued a report on the causes of the February riots. It recommended that the people of the Gold Coast be allowed to write their own constitution and that educational development be greatly accelerated.

3 Sept. 1948 Kwame Nkrumah established the *Accra Evening News*.

Jan. 1949 An all-African committee under Sir Henley Coussey was established to prepare new constitutional recommendations. The Coussey Committee began its meetings on March 14, 1949.

12 June 1949 After a conflict with the leadership of UGCC, Nkrumah announced the formation of the Convention People's Party (CPP). Nkrumah called for "Self-Government Now" from British rule.

29 June 1949 Charles Arden-Clarke was appointed Governor of the Gold Coast.

23 Oct. 1949 Nkrumah addressed a crowd at the West End Arena in Accra on "What I Mean by Positive Action."

26 Oct. 1949 The Coussey Committee plan for a new constitution was made public.

20 Nov. 1949 Nkrumah convened a massive assembly at the West End Arena. He called the group the Ghana People's Representative Assembly. The group rejected the Coussey recommendations, called for the election of a constituent assembly to write a constitution, and demanded immediate self-government as a British Dominion.

7 Jan. 1950 The Trades Union Congress (TUC) began a strike.

8 Jan. 1950 Nkrumah announced the beginning of his Positive Action campaign, calling for a general strike, a boycott of foreign business, and non-cooperation with the government. Within a short time public services began to be disrupted in the larger towns of the Gold Coast.

11 Jan. 1950   Governor Arden-Clarke proclaimed an emergency.

12-13 Jan. 1950 Many demonstrators were arrested in Accra and Sekondi-Takoradi.

19 Jan. 1950   The leaders of the TUC called off the general strike.

21 Jan. 1950   Police took over CPP headquarters and arrested a number of CPP leaders. Nkrumah was arrested on the 22nd. The CPP press had been banned by this time.

14-22 Feb. 1950 Nkrumah was tried and sentenced to three one-year terms in prison.

Apr. 1950   The CPP won all seven seats in the Accra Municipal Council elections.

Nov. 1950   The CPP won all the seats in the Kumasi Town Council elections.

30 Dec. 1950   The new Gold Coast Constitution was published by the government.

5-10 Feb. 1951 Elections were held for the Legislative Assembly. The CPP won 34 of the 38 popularly contested seats.

13 Feb. 1951   At Christiansborg Castle, Governor Arden-Clarke met with Nkrumah and asked him to form a government.

20 Feb. 1951   The new Legislative Assembly met with Nkrumah as Leader of Government Business. E. C. Quist was selected as President of the Assembly. On February 26, six seats were allotted to CPP members in the new government.

Nov. 1951   The Local Government Ordinance ended most of the powers of chiefs over local affairs.

1952   The College of Arts, Science and Technology was established at Kumasi.

10 Mar. 1952   The Constitution was amended to provide for a prime minister, to be nominated by the Governor and confirmed by the Assembly. The Executive Council would become a Cabinet with the Governor to serve as President of the Cabinet.

21 Mar. 1952   In a secret ballot Nkrumah was elected Prime Minister by the Assembly.

10 July 1953   Nkrumah made his "Motion of Destiny" to the Assembly. The Assembly approved the motion requesting independence within the Commonwealth "as soon as the necessary constitutional arrangements are made."

7-8 Dec. 1953 The Sixth Pan-African Conference met in Kumasi to consider speeding the liberation of Africa and the creation of a West African Federation. Nkrumah and Nnamdi Azikiwe of Nigeria attended the conference.

10-11 Apr. 1954 The Northern People's Party was created.

28 Apr. 1954   Constitutional changes were announced. Indirect elections were ended and seats in the Legislative Assembly were increased to 104. There would be an all-African Cabinet.

15 June 1954   The first elections under the 1954 Constitution were held. In an election contested by seven parties, the CPP won 72 out of the 104 seats.

12 Aug. 1954   The Legislative Assembly called on the government to ban all political parties based on racial or religious principles.

14 Aug. 1954   An Act fixing the price of cocoa passed the Assembly, causing great discontent in Asante.

19 Sept. 1954   The National Liberation Movement (NLM) began in Asante.

21 Oct. 1954   The Asantehene and his Council adopted a resolution in support of the idea that a federal form of government be adopted for the Gold Coast.

Jan. 1955   Several people were killed and many arrested in acts of violence in Kumasi.

7 Jan. 1955   The Governor banned carrying arms in Asante.

9 Mar. 1955   The Northern People's Party endorsed the concept of federalism.

27 July 1955   A select committee appointed by the government in April to study the form of government the Gold Coast should have after independence rejected federalism in favor of a centralized form of government.

12 Aug. 1955   Asante and the Northern Territories submitted proposals for a federal constitution to the Governor.

26 Sept. 1955   Sir Frederick Bourne arrived in Accra to advise the government on organization of constitutional matters.

16 Nov. 1955   The Legislative Assembly gave lesser chiefs in Asante the right to appeal from the Asante Council direct to the Governor in constitutional disputes.

23 Dec. 1955   Sir Frederick Bourne recommended that the independence constitution should provide a "substantial transfer of power from the center to the regions."

17 Feb. 1956   The Achimota Conference, proposed on 1 January by Nkrumah to study Bourne's constitution began. It lasted until 16 March. The Asante Council and the NLM refused to take part in the meeting.

18 Apr. 1956   Sir Kobina Arku Korsah became the first African Chief Justice of the Gold Coast.

19 Apr. 1956   Nkrumah published his blueprint for an independence constitution. He suggested that the new nation should be called "Ghana," that there should be a centralized form of government, and that Brong, which had hitherto been part of Asante, would be given a separate regional status.

9 May 1956   A plebiscite on union with the Gold Coast was held in the British-mandated section of Togo. The voters approved unification by overwhelming margins everywhere except in the southern Ewe section.

11 May 1956   The British Secretary for Colonies called for a general election to resolve the constitutional impasse in the Gold Coast. After the election the question of the form of government would be left to the new Assembly.

17 July 1956   In general elections the CPP won 71 of 104 seats in the new Assembly.

3 Aug. 1956   The Legislative Assembly voted for independence within the Commonwealth under the name of Ghana by a vote of 72 out of 104.

18 Sept. 1956   The British Colonial Secretary announced that independence would be granted on 6 March 1957.

16 Oct. 1956   A conference in Accra on the form of government for independent Ghana could reach no agreement. Asante and the Northern Territories now demanded a federal form that would recognize their separate identities.

15 Nov. 1956   The Assembly endorsed Nkrumah's unitary form of constitution by 70 to 25 votes.

20 Nov. 1956   The NLM and NPP sent a resolution to the Secretary for Colonies demanding separate independence for Asante and the Northern Territories.

10 Dec. 1956   The British Colonial Office issued a statement in opposition to the division of the Gold Coast.

18 Dec. 1956   The Ghana Independence Bill passed in the British House of Commons. It became law on 7 February 1957.

26 Jan. 1957   The Secretary for Colonies came to the Gold Coast in an attempt to resolve the constitutional predicament.

8 Feb. 1957   The Colonial Office published the draft of a compromise constitution.

12 Feb. 1957   Both Nkrumah and Busia endorsed the draft as proposed by the British government.

13 Feb. 1957   It was announced that the Queen would appoint Governor Charles Arden-Clarke as first Governor-General after independence.

21 Feb. 1957   Prime Minister Harold Macmillan announced that all Commonwealth prime ministers had approved Ghana's independence and membership in the Commonwealth.

22 Feb. 1957   The Queen approved the new Constitution, to become effective 6 March.

6 Mar. 1957   Independence Day. The British colony of the Gold Coast became the independent nation of Ghana within the Commonwealth.

8 Mar. 1957   Ghana became the 81st member of the United Nations.

11 June 1957   Kojo Botsio announced the formation of a national merchant marine line, the Black Star Line.

22 July 1957   The Deportation Act gave the government power to deport any foreigner whose presence in Ghana was not conducive to the public good.

7 Sept. 1957   Geoffrey Bing, former Labor Member of the British Parliament, was appointed Attorney-General of Ghana.

13 Oct. 1957   Three opposition parties and several regional groups joined to form the United Party (UP) under the leadership of Kofi Busia, Simon Dombo, Joe Appiah and Joseph Boakye Danquah.

Nov. 1957   All local and ethnic organizations were made illegal and tribalism was declared a criminal offense.

13 Nov. 1957   William Francis Hare was sworn in as Ghana's second and last Governor-General.

Dec. 1957   The Avoidance of Discrimination Act outlawed all parties based on religious considerations.

15-22 Apr. 1958   The first Conference of Independent States of Africa met in Accra.

16 July 1958   Ghana Airways began international flights to London.

18 July 1958   The Preventive Detention Act gave the government power to detain persons up to five years without trial or appeal for conduct prejudicial to the security of the state or its foreign relations.

3 Sept. 1958   The government announced the Asante Stool Lands Act, which gave the central authorities in Accra control over all Asante lands.

24 Sept. 1958   Ofori Atta II of Akyem Abuakwa was arrested and was forced to live in Accra until 1966.

10 Nov. 1958   Arrests of many members of the opposition UP under the Preventive Detention Act began. They were accused of a plot to overthrow the government.

21 Feb. 1959   The government introduced an amendment to the Constitution dissolving regional assemblies.

Apr. 1959   The Brong-Ahafo Region was created from Asante.

6 Apr. 1959   A law expelled any member of the National Assembly who was detained under the Preventive Detention Act.

May 1959   Nkrumah and Sekou Toure announced the Ghana-Guinea Union. Mali would join later.

29 June 1959   A Stool Lands Act took over all stool lands in Akyem Abuakwa. Kofi A. Busia reached exile in England. He later was expelled from the Assembly and S. D. Dombo became leader of the opposition.

19 July 1959   Ghana, Guinea and Liberia signed an agreement to create the Community of Independent African States.

10 Nov. 1959   A number of the leaders of the UP in Asante, including Baffour Akoto, the senior linguist to the Asantehene, were detained under the Preventive Detention Act.

6 Mar. 1960   Nkrumah announced plans for a new constitution which would turn Ghana into a republic. The draft provided for eventual surrender of Ghanaian sovereignty to a Union of African States.

15 Mar. 1960   The draft republican constitution was approved by the National Assembly, 75 votes to 10.

19, 23, 27 Apr. 1960	Dr. J. B. Danquah, UP candidate for Head of State, was defeated 1,016,076 to 124,623 by Nkrumah, CPP candidate, in a presidential election. The republican constitution, which was also voted upon, was ratified overwhelmingly in a plebiscite.
29 June 1960	The Regions of Ghana Act adjusted the boundaries of all the regions and created the Central Region from the Western Region and the Upper Region from the Northern Region.
1 July 1960	The Ghanaian Republic was inaugurated with Kwame Nkrumah as first President.
16 July 1960	Ghanaian troops joined other UN troops in the Congo.
25 Aug. 1960	Accra attempted to establish a policy for succession to the skin (throne) of Dagomba.
1 Oct. 1960	The President's Own Guard Regiment was established.
24 Dec. 1960	Mali announced that it had joined the Ghana-Guinea union.
Jan. 1961	The Third Battalion of the Ghanaian Army in the Congo mutinied and its Commander, Col. David Hansen, was severely beaten.
7 Mar. 1961	Nkrumah addressed the General Assembly of the UN in New York on the Congo situation.
8 Apr. 1961	Nkrumah, in a famous Dawn Broadcast, promised to clean the CPP of corruption. This marked the beginning of a campaign against the old guard of the CPP. On 22 April, Nkrumah addressed a CPP Study Group on Building a Socialist State.

27-29 Apr. 1961   The presidents of Ghana, Guinea and Mali met in Accra and agreed to create a union to be known as the Union of African States.

28 Apr. 1961   Ghanaian troops at Port Francqui in the Congo were attacked by Congo troops of Joseph Mobutu. Forty Ghanaian soldiers were killed.

1 May 1961   Nkrumah took full control of the CPP, assuming the office of General-Secretary, Life Chairman, and Chairman of the Central Committee.

29 Aug. 1961   A law made it an offense to insult President Nkrumah in writing, print or speech subject to imprisonment for up to three years.

4 Sept. 1961   Attempts of the government to deduct five percent compulsory saving from workers' wages led to a general strike. The strike, which began among the railway and dock workers in Sekondi-Takoradi, was joined by municipal bus workers in Accra on 6th and 7th September; petrol and motor workers in Accra joined on 18th September. The government ordered all striking workers back to work on 17th September. The strike was not called off until 22 September 1961.

22 Sept. 1961   Nkrumah became Supreme Commander of the Ghanaian armed forces, and all non-Ghanaian officers attached to the Ghanaian forces were relieved of their commands.

28 Sept. 1961   Nkrumah dismissed Komla Gbedemah, Kojo Botsio and other old comrades from his government and replaced them with people from the left wing of the CPP.

3 Oct. 1961   J. B. Danquah, Joe Appiah and other UP leaders plus many of the recent strike leaders were detained under the Preventive Detention Act.

16 Oct. 1961   Komla Gbedemah denounced Nkrumah in the National Assembly. A few days later he and his family went into exile.

30 Oct. 1961   A special criminal division of the High Court was created to try offenses against the safety of the state at the discretion of the President. Verdicts of this division were not subject to appeal.

4 Nov. 1961   Two bombs exploded in Accra, one damaging the statue of Nkrumah in front of Parliament House.

7 Nov. 1961   Hundreds of opponents of the CPP were arrested all over Ghana.

9-20 Nov. 1961   Queen Elizabeth began a tour of Ghana.

20 June 1962   A group of political detainees, including J. B. Danquah and Victor Owusu, were released from prison.

July 1962   The CPP's eleventh congress met in Kumasi and adopted Nkrumah's "Plan for Work and Happiness."

1 Aug. 1962   At Kulungugu a grenade was thrown at Nkrumah. The explosion killed several and injured many others, but the President was not seriously hurt.

29 Aug. 1962   Foreign Minister Ako Adjei, Information Minister Tawia Adamafio, and the Executive Secretary of the CPP, Cofie-Crabbe, were all arrested under the Preventive Detention Act and dismissed from their posts, charged with the Kulungugu incident.

7 Sept. 1962   The National Assembly proclaimed Nkrumah to be President for life.

9 Sept. 1962   A bomb exploded near Flagstaff House, where the President lived, killing one person and injuring others.

Shortly afterwards Nkrumah surrounded himself with security guards from Communist bloc nations.

11 Sept. 1962   The National Assembly adopted a resolution calling for a one-party system in Ghana.

22 Sept. 1962   Bombs exploded in Accra. A state of emergency with dusk to dawn curfew was imposed in Accra and Tema.

28 Sept. 1962   All news leaving Ghana was subjected to censorship.

11 Jan. 1963   A Special Court was established to hear cases involving crimes against the security of the state. There would be no appeal from verdicts.

Mar. 1963   The National Assembly adopted a Seven-Year Development Plan for 1963-1970. This was to be the first stage of a program that would establish a full socialist state in two decades.

17 Mar. 1963   Kojo Botsio was appointed Foreign Minister. In September 1961 Botsio had been dismissed as Minister of Agriculture, and had been obliged to resign from the National Assembly in February 1962.

25 May 1963   Ghana became one of the charter members of the Organization of African Unity in Addis Ababa.

9 Aug. 1963   The treason trial of Ako Adjei, Tawia Adamafio, H. H. Cofie-Crabbe, and two others began before the Special Court on treason cases.

Sept. 1963   The last Ghanaian troops were removed from the Congo.

4 Nov. 1963   The Preventive Detention Act of 1958 was extended for five more years, after heated debate, in the National Assembly.

9 Dec. 1963   Sir Arku Korsah, Chief Justice of the Special Court, acquitted Ako Adjei, Tawia Adamafio and H. H. Cofie-Crabbe of charges that they were involved in the attempt to kill Nkrumah in August 1962. On 11 December 1963, Nkrumah dismissed Chief Justice Arku Korsah from office. The National Assembly, on December 23rd, gave the President authority to override decisions of the Special Court. New trials for the acquitted individuals were ordered the next day.

31 Dec. 1963   Nkrumah announced that a referendum would be held to make Ghana a one-party state, adopt the CPP party flag as the national flag, and give the President power to dismiss judges.

2 Jan. 1964   Police Constable Seth Ametewee fired five shots at President Nkrumah in Flagstaff House. Nkrumah was not hurt, but a security guard was killed.

8 Jan. 1964   J. B. Danquah was arrested under the Preventive Detention Act.

24-31 Jan. 1964   A national referendum overwhelmingly approved a new flag, made Ghana a one-party state, and gave the President power to dismiss judges.

21 Feb. 1964   Ghana became the Convention People's Republic, a one-party state. The CPP party flag, overprinted with a black star on the center stripe, replaced the old national banner.

1 Oct. 1964   The Special Branch of the Ghana police was dissolved and its security functions were placed under the President's Security Services.

4 Feb. 1965   Dr. J. B. Danquah, 69, former leader of the UP and opponent of Nkrumah in the presidential election of 1960, died in prison, where he had been for more than a year.

9 June 1965   CPP candidates for membership in the National Assembly were returned without contest. The membership in the Assembly was increased from 104 to 198.

10 June 1965   The new National Assembly unanimously elected Nkrumah for a second five-year term as President. Construction was begun on the 2,162-foot-long bridge on the lower Volta at Sogakofe.

19 July 1965   Ghana adopted a decimal currency based on the cedi, which replaced the Ghanaian pound.

31 Aug. 1965   President Nkrumah took over direct command of the armed forces and all senior officers were required to take an oath of allegiance to the President.

10 Sept. 1965   The National Assembly passed a provision which provided that any member of the Assembly that lost the support of Nkrumah could be recalled.

22 Nov. 1965   The Ghana Trading Corporation was created.

22 Jan. 1966   Nkrumah inaugurated the Volta River Project at Akosombo, 65 miles (104 km) northeast of Accra.

21 Feb. 1966   Nkrumah left Accra for a trip to Peking and Hanoi, hoping to bring peace to Vietnam.

24 Feb. 1966   The Convention People's Republic of Ghana was overthrown by a military coup. The National Liberation Council (NLC) was established with Rtd. Major-General Joseph A. Ankrah as Chairman, and Commissioner of Police John W. K. Harley as Deputy Chairman. The CPP and the National Assembly were dissolved. Colonel Emmanuel K. Kotoka was promoted Major-General and became Commander of the Ghanaian Army. Nkrumah learned of his removal from office in China.

1 Mar. 1966	Political parties were banned by the NLC. The NLC began to expel all Soviet and Chinese personnel from Ghana.
2 Mar. 1966	Nkrumah was welcomed to Guinea by President Sekou Toure, who proclaimed Nkrumah to be co-President of Guinea.
19 Mar. 1966	Kofi Busia returned to Accra after seven years of exile.
24 Mar. 1966	The NLC placed local government in the hands of management committees which began a purge of CPP sympathizers.
5 Apr. 1966	The Preventive Detention Act was revoked.
16 June 1966	K. A. Gbedemah returned to Ghana after more than four years of exile.
30 June 1966	The NLC established an advisory Political Committee with Edward Akuffo-Addo as Chairman and Kofi Busia as Vice Chairman. Joe Appiah, Simon Dombo, William Ofori Atta, Joseph A. Braimah and other anti-Nkrumah figures were appointed to the Committee.
1 Sept. 1966	The NLC established a Constitutional Commission to submit proposals for a new constitution.
28 Sept. 1966	The Jiagge Commission was established to investigate assets of former members and officials of the CPP. Mrs. Annie Jiagge, Chairperson, was a High Court Justice.
1 Dec. 1966	The NLC removed all chiefs enstooled during the Nkrumah period by the CPP.
17 Apr. 1967	An attempted coup took place. A reconnaissance regiment from Ho came to Accra with plans to take

over the government. Lt. General E. K. Kotoka and several other soldiers were killed before order was restored.

9 May 1967   Lt. Samuel Arthur and Moses Yeboah were executed at Teshie for their roles in the attempted coup of 17 April.

30 June 1967   The NLC established a 21-member Executive Committee responsible for the general direction of the government.   Two-thirds of the Committee were civilians.

11 July 1967   The NLC established a National Advisory Committee to replace the earlier Political Committee.   Dr. K. A. Busia was Chairman of the new Committee.

26 Jan. 1968   The Constitutional Commission, chaired by Justice Edward Akuffo-Addo, presented its draft constitution.

29 Jan. 1968   The NLC announced that a 140-seat Constituent Assembly would be established to debate the constitutional proposals of the Akuffo-Addo Commission.   The Elections and Public Disqualification Decree banned many former CPP members from public office for ten years. Komla A. Gbedemah, former minister in the Nkrumah administration, was exempted from the disqualification decree on 7 November 1968.

28 Oct. 1968   Gen. Ankrah announced that each of the country's 49 administrative districts would elect a member of a constituent assembly through local councils, 91 members would be elected by occupational and civic groups, and 10 members would be appointed by the NLC.

7 Nov. 1968   The funeral of Abdullai III, Ya Na of Yendi, touched off a struggle for the skin (throne) of Dagbon (Dagomba).

6 Jan. 1969   The Constituent Assembly, elected in December 1968, began work on a new constitution. The Assembly rejected a motion to have their work approved by a national referendum and adopted a motion that their approved draft would become the constitution of the second Ghana republic.

2 Apr. 1969   Lt. General Joseph A. Ankrah was forced to resign as Head of State after admitting that he had received money for political purposes. Brig. Akwasi Amankwaa Afrifa became the new chairman of the NLC and Head of State.

28 Apr. 1969   A decree prohibited political parties based on tribal or religious grounds.

1 May 1969   The NLC lifted the ban on political activity.

12 May 1969   The Jiagge Commission recommended that one and a half million cedis be recovered from 21 top former members of the CPP.

6 June 1969   A decree prohibited the reorganization of the CPP as the People's Popular Party.

16 Aug. 1969   The Constituent Assembly approved a new Constitution for the Second Republic.

22 Aug. 1969   Togo, Dahomey (Benin), and Ghana signed an agreement with the Volta River Authority for the purchase of power produced at Akosombo. A Presidential Commission was established to oversee the transition to civilian government.

29 Aug. 1969   A national election was held for a new National Assembly. Dr. K. A. Busia's Progress Party (PP) defeated K. A. Gbedemah's National Alliance of Liberals (NAL), winning 59 percent of the popular votes. The PP won 105 and the NAL 29 seats in the Assembly.

3 Sept. 1969   Akwasi Afrifa, J. W. K. Harley and A. K. Ocran of
the NLC took oaths as the Presidential Commission.
K. A. Busia was sworn in as Prime Minister.

30 Sept. 1969   Ghana officially returned to civilian rule.

16 Oct. 1969   Prime Minister Busia departed on a trip to the US and
Europe to try to find help with the nation's debts.
While in New York he addressed the UN.

18 Nov. 1969   The government ordered the expulsion of all aliens in
Ghana without residence permits.

Feb. 1970   The government began a purge of the civil service.
Renewal of appointments was denied to 568 (the
"Apollo 568") persons who had served during the
Nkrumah period. E. K. Sallah appealed to the courts
against dismissal and won his case. Busia refused to
reemploy him.

May 1970   Asantehene Osei Agyeman Prempe II died and J.
Matthew Poku became Asantehene Opoku Ware II.

7-11 July 1970 At a London meeting with 15 creditor nations, Ghana
was able to refinance most of the debt from the
Nkrumah period with a two-year moratorium on 50
percent of the amount due.

30 July 1970   The National Assembly voted to abolish the
Presidential Commission created the year before.

28 Aug. 1970   Edward Akuffo-Addo was elected President of the
Second Republic by an Electoral College, made up of
members of the National Assembly plus 21 chiefs.

20 Oct. 1970   Three opposition parties combined as the Justice Party
(JP).

Dec. 1970   General Albert K. Ocran demanded that all members
of the Assembly declare their assets as required by the

Constitution. Many members refused to make the declarations.

Apr. 1971   The National Union of Ghanaian Students (NUGS) demanded free education, wholesale nationalization of business and amnesty for political exiles.

27 July 1971   The government published its austerity budget. Public services and benefits for public employees were to be cut and taxes were to be raised.

Aug. 1971   All "direct or indirect" mention of Nkrumah or the CPP was outlawed.

3 Sept. 1971   The Labor Ministry announced firm action to prevent the Trades Union Congress (TUC) from initiating strike action in opposition to the new taxes.

10 Sept. 1971   The National Assembly dissolved the TUC.

8 Jan. 1972   Prime Minister Busia traveled to London for treatment of an eye condition.

13 Jan. 1972   A military coup ended the Second Republic and established a government of the National Redemption Council (NRC) under Lt. Colonel Ignatius Kutu Acheampong as Chairman.

5 Feb. 1972   The NRC repudiated part of Ghana's foreign debt.

27 Apr. 1972   Kwame Nkrumah died in Bucharest, Romania, where he was undergoing treatment for cancer.

31 Apr. 1972   The body of Nkrumah was flown from Romania to Conakry, Guinea.

7 July 1972   The body of Nkrumah was flown to Accra, and the next day it lay in state in the Conference Hall of the State House.

9 July 1972   Nkrumah was buried at Nkroful (the body was removed in 1992 and reburied at the Kwame Nkrumah Memorial Park in Accra).

18 July 1972   The NRC issued a decree making it a capital offense to attempt to overthrow the NRC.

14 Aug. 1972   The Aidoo Asset Commission began to investigate the assets of K. A. Busia and the ministers in his administration.

12 Sept. 1972   The NRC abolished the Supreme Court.

3 July 1973   The last detainees of the Busia government were freed.

31 Aug. 1973   Kojo Botsio, one of Nkrumah's lieutenants, was arrested and charged with plotting to overthrow the NRC.

Dec. 1973   A plot by former Nkrumah supporters to replace the NRC was uncovered. Death sentences were imposed and later commuted to life.

1974   The world oil price crisis and inflation began to seriously erode standards of living in Ghana.

13 Jan. 1974   Acheampong announced a National Economic Planning Council to create a national self-reliance program.

11 Feb. 1974   The nation's universities were closed for more than a month because of what the government described as subversive activities on the campuses.

13 Mar. 1974   A Debt Settlement Agreement was reached with Western creditors by which many debts were rescheduled at lower rates of interest with longer periods for repayments.

9 Oct. 1975   A seven-member Supreme Military Council (SMC) was established as the highest legislative and administrative organ of the state. A reorganized NRC continued as an executive council.

7 Mar. 1976   Ignatius Kutu Acheampong was promoted to the rank of General.

30 June 1976   An SMC decree became effective which limited foreign control of many business activities and required foreign companies to sell part (30 to 50 percent) of their stocks to Ghanaians.

1977   Economic conditions deteriorated rapidly. Near-famine conditions existed in the Upper Region, and food shortages were common all over Ghana.

10 Jan. 1977   The SMC announced creation of the Koranteng-Addow Committee to prepare proposals for a union form of government.

June 1977   The Ghana Bar and Medical Associations threatened to strike if the SMC did not hand power over to civilians. Pharmacists, engineers, accountants and teachers joined in protests in July.

1 July 1977   General Acheampong, in a dawn broadcast, announced that power would be transferred to an elected government as soon as practicable.

4 Oct. 1977   The Koranteng-Addow Committee made its report, proposing a constitution with a president and a legislature selected "on merit" without resort to political parties. The proposed constitution became known as the "Union Government" plan.

13 Jan. 1978   Police broke up mass meetings of university students and arrested many. The students' demonstration was in opposition to the Union Government idea.

27 Jan. 1978   The People's Movement for Freedom and Justice (PMFJ) was organized to oppose Union Government. Komla Gbedemah, Akwasi Afrifa and William Ofori-Atta were among the leaders of the movement.

30 Mar. 1978   The Union Government Referendum was held with low voter turnouts. Brong-Ahafo, Asante and the Eastern regions all opposed Union Government, yet the SMC reported 60 percent for Union Government to only 40 against.

3 Apr. 1978   All organized groups which had opposed the Union Government plan in the referendum were banned.

5 Apr. 1978   Many of the leaders in opposition to Union Government were placed in detention. Among them were Gbedemah, Ofori-Atta, Victor Owusu, John Bilson and Adu A. Boahen. Many others went into exile or hiding.

30 Apr. 1978   A Constitutional Drafting Commission was named by the SMC. The Commission was headed by Thomas A. Mensah. It began work on 31 May and was scheduled to finish its work by October.

5 July 1978   General Acheampong was forced to resign and he was replaced by Lt. General Frederick W. K. Akuffo, who had been Acheampong's deputy since 1977.

Aug.-Nov. 1978 Widespread labor unrest and strikes disrupted the Ghanaian economy.

28 Aug. 1978   Kofi Busia died in exile in England.

6 Nov. 1978   The SMC imposed a state of emergency as strikes and unrest spread.

7 Dec. 1978   A Constituent Assembly was announced. New district councils elected 64 delegates, the SMC appointed 29

members, and 27 persons were nominated by various interest groups.

21 Dec. 1978   The Constituent Assembly convened to approve a draft constitution.

30 Dec. 1978   The SMC published a list of 105 persons it disqualified from holding public office.

1 Jan. 1979   The ban on political activities was lifted. Within a month almost twenty parties were organized, but by April only six of these groups were really viable.

15 May 1979   The Constituent Assembly presented its approved draft for a constitution and adjourned. An attempted coup by junior officers was suppressed and several were arrested, including an Air Force officer named Jerry John Rawlings.

4 June 1979   A group of junior officers seized control of the government, released Flight Lieutenant Jerry John Rawlings, arrested General Frederick Akuffo, and replaced the SMC with the Armed Forces Revolutionary Council (AFRC) under Rawlings.

12 June 1979   The AFRC began trials of former government officials and others for corruption and crimes against the state.

16 June 1979   General Ignatius Kutu Acheampong and General E. K. Utuka, former Commander of the Border Guard, were executed by the AFRC for squandering government funds.

18 June 1979   Elections for President and the new National Assembly were held. The People's National Party (PNP) gained 71 seats to 42 seats for the Popular Front Party (PFP), 13 for the United National Congress (UNC), and 10 for the Action Congress Party (ACP). Dr. Hilla Limann of PNP and Victor

Owusu of PFP were ahead of several other candidates in the presidential race, and they had to face each other in a runoff.

26 June 1979   Former heads of state Generals Frederick W. K. Akuffo and Akwasi A. Afrifa were executed by the AFRC. Former Foreign Minister Roger Felli, former Chief of Defense Staff Major General Robert Kotei, Air Marshal George Yaw Boakye, and Admiral Joy Amedume were also executed.

9 July 1979   Hilla Limann of PNP was elected President in a runoff election against Victor Owusu of PFP.

24 Sept. 1979   Hilla Limann and Joseph William Swain de Graft-Johnson were inaugurated as President and Vice-president of the Third Republic for four-year terms. A Special Tribunal took over all cases of corruption still pending before People's Revolutionary Courts set up by the AFRC. Transitional provisions placed this Special Tribunal above control of the National Assembly.

27 Nov. 1979   Rawlings was retired from the army on the grounds that his position was not compatible with his status as former Head of State.

29 Mar. 1980   A number of soldiers were arrested and charged with an attempt to start a mutiny. AFRC supporters claimed the arrests were an attempt to discredit its former members.

11 June 1980   Military Intelligence began surveillance of Rtd. Captain Kojo Tsikata, who was one of the founders of the June 4th Movement and an associate of Rawlings.

Summer 1980   The economy declined steadily and popular discontent mounted during the summer.

Aug. 1980 Parliament rejected two judges nominated by President Limann to the Supreme Court. This touched off a constitutional crisis which eroded the strength of the PNP.

Sept. 1980 The government warned that all public employees who resorted to strikes would be summarily dismissed.

15 Oct. 1980 Security forces raided the home of Rawlings and arrested a foreigner accused of being a left-wing radical in the country to train members of the June 4th Movement in political subversion. Rawlings was briefly detained on suspicion of subversive activities.

Nov. 1980 President Limann revamped the economic machinery of his government in an attempt to deal with the growing economic stagnation and inflation.

31 May 1981 All military personnel associated with the AFRC were retired from the Ghana Armed Forces.

23 June 1981 Five opposition parties announced plans for a merger as the All People's Party (APP). The union did not hold together and during the year several small political groups tried to organize as parties.

30 June 1981 The Budget for 1981-82 was announced, calling for cuts in expenditures, higher taxes and a large deficit. The inflation rate ran as high as 107 percent.

31 Dec. 1981 A coup ended the Third Republic, and Flight Lieutenant Jerry John Rawlings again became Head of State as Chairman of the Provisional National Defense Council (PNDC). By the time of the coup, Ghana's foreign debts equaled twice the total value of 1981 exports. Annual inflation was running above 140 percent.

2 Jan. 1982   Rawlings announced suspension of the Constitution and dismissal of all the officers of the Third Republic, and he proscribed all political parties.

21 Jan. 1982   The PNDC announced appointment of !7 secretaries as heads of ministries.

15 Mar. 1982   The PNDC ordered all labor unions to withdraw demands for wage increases.

4 Apr. 1982   The PNDC organized the 31st December Youth Brigade to create a program of national service for all Ghanaian youth.

4 July 1982   The bodies of three High Court judges and a retired army officer, abducted four days before, were discovered near Akuse.

21 Sept. 1982   All the borders of Ghana were closed indefinitely in a campaign to halt smuggling.

16 Dec. 1982   The PNDC announced the decision to split the Upper Region into Upper West and Upper East Regions.

30 Dec. 1982   The PNDC announced its four-year economic program of austerity and sacrifice.

17 Jan. 1983   Nigeria ordered all aliens out of that country. This order affected over one million Ghanaians.

29 Jan. 1983   The border at Aflao, closed in September, was opened to admit Ghanaians expelled from Nigeria. The Nigerian expulsion order touched off a national emergency in Ghana.

Apr. 1983   A drastic food crisis reached the point of desperation during April. Many commodities disappeared from markets. Prices for the few items that were available quadrupled from the start of the year.

23 Apr. 1983   Kwesi Botchwey, Secretary for Finance and Economic Planning, presented the 1983 budget. It called for tight controls on spending and imports.

6 May 1983   University students marched from Legon into Accra in a demonstration against the PNDC. Workers began a counter-demonstration and fighting ensued.

14 June 1983   Several people were arrested for plotting to overthrow the government.

19 June 1983   Many persons died in an attempted coup. Prisons were opened and many opponents of the PNDC escaped.

21 June 1983   Members of the Workers' Defense Committees of Accra and Tema took over the Supreme Court, the Cadbury Factory, and two presses in Accra.

1-27 July 1983   The National Defense Committee held a cadre training school for more than a thousand supporters of the PNDC on the campus of the University of Ghana at Legon.

13 Aug. 1983   Four soldiers were executed for their part in coup attempt in June.

17 Aug. 1983   Those convicted of the murders of the High Court judges and retired army officer the previous year were executed.

1 Oct. 1983   An Exploration and Production Law of 1983 was passed. The law, which placed all petroleum deposits in the country within the jurisdiction of the state, empowered the Secretary for Fuel and Power to represent the country in negotiations for and entry into petroleum agreements.

11 Oct. 1983   The PNDC announced the most drastic devaluation of the cedi in the history of Ghana.

4-8 Nov. 1983   Joint military exercises of the forces of the Upper Volta (Burkina Faso) and Ghana were observed by the heads of state of both countries in a demonstration of solidarity between the revolutionary governments of the two countries.

31 Dec. 1983-
Mar. 1984   Grace period set by the former Citizens Vetting Committee, later on to be called the Office of Revenue Commissioners, for payment of all outstanding taxes to the state.

3 Jan. 1984   An action program for the redeployment of all redundant workers in the public sector was announced.

12-13 Jan. 1984 At an annual meeting of the Ghana Bar Association, the organization called on the PNDC to release all political detainees and those against whom no legitimate charges had been brought.

5 Mar. 1984   The Ghana Democratic Movement (GDM), a new opposition movement to the PNDC, was launched in London.

6 Mar. 1984   The PNDC hinted at the possibility of beginning discussions that might lead to political reforms aimed at creating "better and well-represented governmental institutions not based on wealth and influential people."

16 Mar. 1984   The University of Cape Coast became the first of the nation's three universities to reopen for completion of the 1982-83 academic year. The universities were closed in May 1983 following mass demonstrations by students.

24 Mar. 1984   Three soldiers were arrested and executed for participating in an attempted military overthrow of the PNDC.

5 June 1984   A Commission on Education recommended to the PNDC that a loan scheme under which university students would borrow money to cover their maintenance and personal expenses be established. The Commission also recommended that students be made to pay for their boarding, lodging, and textbooks while the government continues to pay for the full cost of tuition.

Aug. 1984   Preliminary results of the 1984 census were unveiled. Population figures of 12,205,574 were reported. This indicated that the country's population grew at a rate of 2.6 percent annually since 1970.

27 Aug. 1984   A law providing for the establishment of a National Public Tribunal to hear and determine appeals from and decisions or orders of regional public tribunals was published in Accra.

Sept. 1984   An amendment to the Special Military Tribunal Law of 1982 (PNDCL 9) was passed. According to the amendment, any member of the Ghana Armed Forces, including deserters and those retired, who incited, assisted or procured any person to invade Ghana or unlawfully subverted any part of Ghana or assisted in the preparation of any such invasion or attack was guilty of an offense.

18 Oct. 1984   University of Ghana, Legon, reopened to begin its normal 1984-85 academic year.

1 Dec. 1984   The PNDC announced the dissolution of the National Defense Committee (NDC) and Workers' Defense Committees (WDCs). Both political organizations were replaced with Committees for the Defense of the Revolution (CDRs).

3 Dec. 1984   The PNDC directed that Interim Management Committees (IMCs) of public boards and statutory corporations, excluding banks and financial

institutions, be abolished with immediate effect and be replaced by Joint Consultative Committees (JCCs). The JCCs would act as advisory bodies to the managing directors.

11-12 Dec. 1984   At a donors' meeting held in Paris, industrialized countries agreed to increase their loan commitment to Ghana by 9 percent for the 1985 fiscal year.

31 Jan. 1985   An abortive plan to assassinate Rawlings in Kumasi was uncovered.

26 June 1985   Great Britain canceled Ghana's aid debts worth £51 million.

14 July 1985   Four laws on the rights of inheritance to property were passed.

15 July 1985   The government signed an investment code that provided a legal framework for the utilization of the nation's natural resources.

10 Sept. 1985   The *Eagle*, a new bi-weekly newspaper to serve as the mouthpiece of the Committee for the Defense of the Revolution, was launched.

6 Nov. 1985   Certain soldiers from the Ghana Armed Forces were arrested for plotting to overthrow the government of the PNDC. This was the thirteenth reported attempt against the PNDC since coming to power in 1981.

28 Nov. 1985   Four United States diplomats were expelled from Ghana. They were accused of engaging in "activities not conducive to good relations." The United States government retaliated by expelling four Ghanaian diplomats.

8 Dec. 1985   J. H. Mensah, former finance minister in the Busia administration, was arrested with two other people in

the United States on charges of illegally attempting to export firearms.

Jan. 1986   The Ministry of Local Government and the Ministry of Rural Development and Cooperatives were merged. The new administrative unit was designated as Ministry of Local Government and Rural Development.

13 Jan. 1986   The second phase of the Economic Recovery Program (ERP) was announced to run from 1986 through 1988.

19 Jan. 1986   The PNDC confirmed the appointment of Mr. Justice E. N. P. Sowah as Chief Justice.

5 Mar. 1986   The trial by public tribunal of two groups accused of subversion began in Accra.

8 Mar. 1986   The New Democratic Movement held a symposium at the Accra Community Center on the topic "Ghana Since Nkrumah." Many of the speakers criticized the PNDC administration for "compromising the revolution" by adopting conservative policies.

3 Apr. 1986   Seventeen judges were dismissed by the government on charges of corruption.

15 Apr. 1986   Eight persons whose trial began on 5 March 1986 on charges of attempting to subvert the PNDC government were sentenced to death by firing squad.

16 Apr. 1986   Four persons belonging to the Kwame Nkrumah Revolutionary Guard, New Democratic Movement, African Youth Command, and African Youth Brigade were arrested on charges of inciting workers against the government.

May 1986 A new compensation law replacing the Workmen's Compensation Act, 1963, was signed by Chairman Rawlings.

5 May 1986 At a press conference in Accra, a spokesperson for the National Union of Ghana Students (NUGS) expressed concern about what the organization described as the "arbitrary and unwarranted arrests" by the government. The spokesperson was referring to the arrests of four persons on 16 April 1986.

27 May 1986 Two Ghanaians, arrested on 8 December 1985 with J. H. Mensah and charged with illegal purchase of missiles and heavy arms, were sentenced to three years' probation and two hundred hours of community service by a United States Federal Judge in New Jersey. The jury could not arrive at a decision in the case of J. H. Mensah.

22 June 1986 Sixteen people were executed by firing squad. Seven of them were among the eight previously charged with conspiring to subvert the government of the PNDC. The rest had previously been found guilty of murder and armed robbery.

23 July 1986 The Land Title Registration Law of 1986 was passed to replace the Land Registration Act of 1962. The new law called for compulsory land registration throughout the country.

Aug. 1986 The PNDC abolished the Ministry of Culture and Tourism. Responsibilities for culture were transferred to the Ministry of Education while tourism became the responsibility of the Ministry of Trade.

1 Aug. 1986 Four members of the New Democratic Movement and the Kwame Nkrumah Revolutionary Guard detained in mid-April were released.

20 Aug. 1986 Public sector hiring was frozen.

24 Aug. 1986 A Ghanaian delegation headed by the Secretary for Finance and Economic Planning, Dr. Kwesi Botchwey, conducted negotiations in Washington, D.C., with the International Monetary Fund (IMF).

26-29 Aug. 1986 The occasion for the special Pan-African tomb dedication for Dr. W. E. B. Du Bois coincided with the 23rd anniversary activities of his death.

9 Sept. 1986 Ivorian officials confirmed the arrest of the ship *Hercules One* on information that it was carrying illegal arms for a Ghanaian opposition group.

23 Sept. 1986 Radio Togo announced an attempted military overthrow of the government of President Eyadema. The report also identified the coup plotters as a "terrorist commando unit" which had crossed into Togo from Ghana. Togo immediately closed its border with Ghana.

18 Nov. 1986 A legislative instrument that gave effect to the implementation of an extradition treaty between Ghana, Togo, Benin, and Nigeria was published in Accra. The agreement was first signed by the participating countries in December 1984. The treaty was subsequently ratified by Ghana on 15 January 1985.

19 Nov. 1986 The government enacted a new law on the retirement of judges in the country.

26 Nov. 1986 A five-member OAU delegation led by the Secretary-General, Mr. Ode Oumarou, met Flt. Lt. Rawlings to discuss the ongoing conflict between Ghana and Togo.

7 Feb. 1987 In what the government described as "the spirit of reconciliation," subversion charges against 12 individuals were dropped. Victor Owusu, former

presidential candidate in the Third Republic, was one of those to benefit from the amnesty.

20 Feb. 1987   The Secretary of Finance and Economic Planning announced major highlights of the 1987 budget in Accra. A 25 percent increase in the minimum wages for civil servants was to take effect from 1 January 1987.

Mar. 1987   Two new departments, Policy, Planning and Monitoring, and Animal Health and Production, were established under the Ministry of Agriculture to help maximize the use of limited resources in the agricultural sector of the economy.

6 Apr. 1987   Chairman Rawlings expressed concern about what he described as the "culture of silence" in the country. His statement generated intense debate in the national newspapers throughout the month on the role of the press in developing democracies.

12 Apr. 1987   The PNDC approved the establishment of an Islamic education unit within the Ministry of Education and Culture. Among other things, the unit would make sure that Islamic schools strictly adhered to policies of the education ministry.

6-7 May 1987   Donor countries at their consultative group meeting in Paris pledged some $300 million more than Ghana had requested.

8 May 1987   The government ordered the closure of the University of Ghana, Legon, after students refused to attend classes to protest the arrest of Kakraba Cromwell, former secretary of the National Union of Ghana Students (NUGS).

17 May 1987   Akoto Ampaw, Kwesi Pratt and Kwesi Adu-Amankwah were arrested and charged with involvement in activities intended to undermine the

authority of the government. Kwesi Adu-Amankwah was a member of the National Democratic Movement and head of the TUC's political department.

23 May 1987   The Ghana-Togo border, closed since 24 September 1986, was reopened.

26 May 1987   The Chieftaincy (Amendment) Law of 1987 (PNDCL 180), giving legal effect to the preservation of stool property, was passed.

3 June 1987   A commission to advise the PNDC on the defense needs of the nation was set up under the chairmanship of Lt. Gen. Emmanuel A. Erskine, former head of the United Nations Peacekeeping Force in Lebanon. The commission was officially inaugurated on 26 August 1987.

12-14 June 1987 All three universities in Ghana (Kumasi, Cape Coast, and Legon) were closed following demonstrations by students. According to the *Mirror* report, students were protesting fee payments proposed by the commission on educational reforms.

1 July 1987   The National Commission for Democracy (NCD) announced district assembly elections to be held in the last quarter of 1988. The Commission also announced the creation of 110 districts to replace the previous 65.

21 Aug. 1987 As part of its privatization program, the government approved the decision of the Ghana Cocoa Board to sell 52 of its 92 cocoa and coffee plantations to individual Ghanaians, organizations, and foreign companies.

28 Aug. 1987 The University of Ghana, Legon, was the first of the nation's three universities to reopen for the completion of the 1986-87 academic year.

Sept. 1987   The Legal Aid Scheme of 1987 (PNDCL 184) under which low-income people would be represented in both civil and criminal matters was established.

1 Sept. 1987   The Junior Secondary School (JSS) system commenced.

20 Sept. 1987   The nation's newest region, the Upper West Region, was officially inaugurated. The region had been in existence as an administrative unit since December 1982.

1 Oct. 1987   The National Commission for Democracy launched a national exercise to register voters for district assembly elections.

30 Dec. 1987   Kwesi Pratt and Yao Graham, detained on 17 May 1987 and 15 July 1987, respectively, were released.

20 Jan. 1988   Six foreign nationals were sentenced to death by firing squad for crimes "intended to sabotage the economy." The alleged crimes included illegal transfers of more than $4 million to other West African banks.

20 Jan. 1988   PNDC Chairman Rawlings and Capt. Blaise Compare (Head of Burkina Faso) met at Tamale in northern Ghana. This was the first meeting between the two leaders since the 15 October 1987 military coup in which Capt. Thomas Sankara died.

2 Feb. 1988   The Ministry of Foreign Affairs warned Ghanaians to obtain genuine travel documents before departing the country. The ministry expressed concern about the "rampant violation of immigration laws by Ghanaians abroad."

22 Feb. 1988   A two-day conference held by Ghana to discuss a proposed Program of Action to Mitigate the Social Cost of Adjustment (PAMSCAD) ended in Geneva

(Switzerland). The conference, which was chaired by Dr. Kwesi Botchwey (Secretary for Finance and Economic Planning), was attended by 14 bilateral government representatives, 12 multilateral agencies, and 16 non-governmental organizations. The purpose of the conference was to inform donor institutions of the social cost of Ghana's economic recovery program.

2 Mar. 1988   A compulsory land title registration exercise, aimed at reducing the incidence of land litigation often associated with agricultural tenancies, was launched.

12 May 1988   The W. E. B. Du Bois Memorial Center for Pan-African Culture in Accra was adopted as a subsidiary research and documentation center of the African Cultural Institute (ACI).

30 June 1988   All three universities were closed following student demonstrations.

13 Sept. 1988   The National Commission for Democracy announced the appointment of 550 individuals to serve on the proposed district assembly committees.

8 Oct. 1988   The government announced the establishment of a Judicial Council in the wake of criticisms from the Bar Association that the absence of such a council undermined the judiciary and encouraged corruption.

12 Oct. 1988   The National Commission for Democracy announced the division of the country into three zones for district election purposes.

14-17 Oct. 1988   All three universities were reopened for students to complete their final examinations. According to university officials, students were required to leave campus immediately after the examination.

1 Nov. 1988	Union workers at the Ghana Broadcasting Corporation (GBC) went on a four-hour demonstration. Transmissions on all main channels were delayed during the demonstration. The government responded with an immediate dismissal of union leaders of the GBC.
9 Nov. 1988- Feb. 1989	Campaigning for and district assembly elections in 28 all zones took place.
16 Dec. 1988	The PNDC Secretary for Education, K. B. Asante, announced at a press conference that the government would no longer "be responsible for the maintenance of students at the secondary and university levels."
23 Dec. 1988	The National Union of Ghana Students released a statement critical of the educational reform package made public on 16 December 1988.
28 Dec. 1988	Kwame Karikari, lecturer at the University of Ghana and former chairperson of the National Democratic Movement (NDM), was released from detention. He was first detained in July 1987.
7 Feb. 1989	A series of legislative instruments that gave legal backing to the establishment of the 110 district assemblies was published. The documents also contained a detailed description of the 87 functions of the district assemblies.
10 Feb. 1989	The nation's three universities were reopened for the 1989-90 academic year.
24 Feb. 1989	Ghana and Nigeria signed a trade cooperation agreement that facilitated the free movement of people and goods between the two countries.
27 Mar. 1989	The Ministry of Information revoked the registrations of all newspapers and magazines published in the nation. Forty out of the nation's 49 newspapers and

magazines were approved for republication under the Newspaper Licensing Law, 1989 (PNDCL 211), and Law 11417. According to the ministry, the exercise was an attempt to introduce "order and decency into the nation's journalism."

14 June 1989   The PNDC government passed the Religious Bodies (Registration) Law of 1989. The law, (PNDCL 221), was made retroactively effective from 1 June 1989.

22 Sept. 1989   Chairman Rawlings took direct command of the Ghana Armed Forces. Lt. Gen. Arnold Quainoo, former Commander of the Armed Forces, was redeployed and charged with the responsibility of establishing the National Planning and Development Commission. Gen. Quainoo remained a PNDC member.

6 Oct. 1989   The Ministry of Defense issued a statement announcing the arrest of Major Courage K. Quashigha and four others. Maj. Quashigha was former Chief of Operations at PNDC headquarters and former Commander of Military Police.

29 Dec. 1989   The PNDC government announced a major Cabinet reshuffle.

5 Mar. 1990   The Tripartite Committee set a new national daily minimum wage of 218 cedis. The new rate, which affected only those who made less than 218 cedis a day, was a 28 percent raise over the previous daily minimum wage of 170 cedis.

1 June 1990   A demonstration demanding respect for human rights and multiparty constitutional rule in Ghana was held outside the Ghana High Commission in London. The protest was organized by the London-based Democratic Alliance of Ghana, an opposition to the PNDC administration.

6 July 1990   At the four-day conference that ended this date at Cape Coast, the Ghana Bishops Conference called on the PNDC government to open a national debate on the nation's political future.

1 Aug. 1990   A new organization, the Movement for Freedom and Justice (MFJ), was launched in Accra. The stated goal of the movement was to "campaign for the restoration of democratic rule in Ghana."

24 Aug. 1990   About 110,300 pupils from the nation's middle schools took the Middle School Leaving Certificate examination (MSLC). The class of 1990 was the last to take the examination, which would be replaced by the Basic Certificate of Education, to be taken by students from the new Junior Secondary Schools.

4 Sept. 1990   A nine-member coordinating committee of the London branch of the Movement for Freedom and Justice was launched.

9 Jan. 1991   Structural Adjustment Program III (1991-92) was inaugurated.

25 Mar. 1991   A Committee of Experts was created by the government to draft a constitutional proposal for the country.

26 Mar. 1991   The National Commission for Democracy presented its report on "District Assemblies and the Democratic Process" to the government. Receiving the document, Chairman Rawlings hinted that a National Consultative Body to draft a new constitution would start work in July and the modalities for its composition would be announced not later than May.

10 May 1991   The PNDC announced its acceptance of multipartyism in Ghana.

14-15 May 1991   A Consultative Group on Ghana, comprising nine countries and 11 international organizations, met in Paris and pledged $950 million in support of Ghana's 1991 economic development plans. The amount pledged was $100 million in excess of what was recommended by the World Bank.

19 June 1991   The government of the PNDC announced an amnesty for all political exiles who had not been found guilty of offenses against the state.

21 June 1991   Deadline set by the National Commission for Democracy for the election of a Consultative Constitutional Assembly. The assembly was to discuss proposals submitted earlier by the Committee of Experts.

2-5 July 1991   The Ghana Catholic Bishops Conference called on the government of the PNDC to return the nation to constitutional multiparty rule.

31 July 1991   The Committee of Experts submitted its 252-page report on constitutional proposals to the government.

6 Aug. 1991   Eleven opposition groups joined together to form the Coordinating Committee of Democratic Forces (CCDEF) of Ghana.

14 Aug. 1991   A new minimum wage of 460 cedis was announced to take retroactive effect from 1 July 1991.

26 Aug. 1991   The Consultative Assembly, which was elected to discuss proposals submitted by the Constitutional Committee of Experts, was inaugurated. The first day of official business of the assembly was 30 September 1991.

1 Sept. 1991   Free Medicare and limited insurance for civil servants and retired officers of the Ghana Armed Forces became effective.

28 Feb. 1992   Mr. Justice D. Annan was replaced as Chairman of the National Commission for Democracy by Nana Agyeman Badu, Omanhene of the Dormaa Traditional Area.

6 Mar. 1992   Chairman Rawlings presented the following timetable for the return to constitutional rule: referendum on the new Constitution to be conducted on 28 April 1992; ban on party politics to be lifted on 18 May 1992; Presidential elections to be held on 3 November 1992; Parliamentary elections to be held on 8 December 1992; and Fourth Republic to be inaugurated on 7 January 1993.

20 Mar. 1992   Major Courage Quashigha and others, arrested in October 1989 on charges of plotting to overthrow the PNDC government, were granted amnesty. They were, however, discharged from the Ghana Armed Forces.

27 Mar. 1992   Final sitting of the Consultative Assembly on the Draft Constitution. At this 99th sitting, the Assembly adopted the 26-chapter and 299-section draft constitution. The document was presented to the PNDC on 31 March 1992.

28 Apr. 1992   In a referendum, over 80 percent of registered voters in Ghana approved the Draft Constitution submitted by the Consultative Assembly.

18 May 1992   Registration and formation of political parties became legal. This marked the official lifting of the ban on political party activities since 1981.

14 Sept. 1992   Rawlings officially retired from the Ghana Armed Forces.

3 Nov. 1992   Presidential elections were held in Ghana under the supervision of the Interim National Electoral Commission (INEC) and Commonwealth Observers.

Five parties presented candidates and they were as follows: Mr. Kwabena Darko for the New Independence Party (NIP); Dr. Hilla Limann for the People's National Convention (PNC); Flt. Lt. Rawlings for the National Democratic Congress (NDC); Gen. (Rtd.) Emmanuel Erskine for the People's Heritage Party (PHP); and Professor Adu Boahen for the New Patriotic Party (NPP). The results of the elections from the nation's 200 constituencies were reported as follows: Rawlings (58.3%); Adu Boahen (30.4%); Limann (6.7%); Darko (2.8%); and Erskine (1.7%).

4-5 Nov. 1992   A dusk-to-dawn curfew was imposed in Kumasi and Accra. Following the declaration of the National Democratic Party's candidate, Flt. Lt. Jerry Rawlings, as winner of the presidential elections, the opposition called the election results into question and accused the PNDC and National Democratic Party of election irregularities.   According to a report from the Commonwealth Observers, however, the elections were considered fair. To stabilize the situation in the country, the INEC postponed the Parliamentary elections to 29 December 1992.

29 Dec. 1992   NPP and some opposition parties boycotted the Parliamentary elections.

7 Jan. 1993   The Fourth Republic was inaugurated.

INTRODUCTION

Ghana, the former British Gold Coast, shares borders with three French-speaking nations: the Ivory Coast to the west, Togo to the east, and Burkina Faso (former Upper Volta) to the north. The Gulf of Guinea of the Atlantic Ocean forms the southern border of Ghana (see Map 1). Created at independence in 1957 from the British Gold Coast Colony, Asante, the Northern Territories, and the United Nations Trust Territory of British Togo, Ghana covers a total land area of about 92,000 square miles (239,000 sq km). The country lies entirely in the tropical zone with its southernmost coast extending to Cape Three Points--4°30' above the equator. The Greenwich Meridian (longitude 0°) runs through Tema, an industrial town 17 miles (27 km) to the east of Accra.

The physical relief of the country is generally low as the Precambrian rock system that composed most of the territory has been worn down by erosion to almost a plain. However, five geographical regions can be distinguished (see Map 2). The coastal plains that stretch across the southern part of Ghana comprise the coastal savanna, the Volta Delta, and the Akan Lowlands. The grassy and scrubby lowland is an undulating country. To the north of this lie the Asante Uplands. Within the Asante Uplands are the Southern Uplands and the Kwahu Plateau. Of these two features, the Kwahu Plateau is important as it serves as one of the significant physical divides in Ghana. The Afram and Pru rivers flow into the Volta River on its eastern sector while, on the other side, the Pra, Birim, Ofin, Tano and others meander southward into the sea. To the eastern boundaries of Ghana are the Akuapem-Togo Ranges. Beginning from the west of Accra and continuing in a northeasterly direction through the Volta Region into Togo, many prominent heights in this area are composed of volcanic rocks. Ghana's highest point at Mount Afadjato (2905 ft.) is located in

1

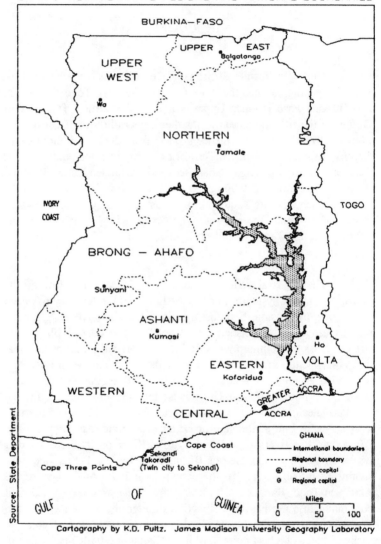

GHANA: ADMINISTRATIVE REGIONS AND NATIONAL BOUNDARIES

Cartography by K.D. Pultz. James Madison University Geography Laboratory

the Akuapem-Togo Ranges. To the west of the ranges lies the Volta Basin, which covers about 45 percent of the nation's total land surface. Apart from the Gambaga Scarp in the north and the Konkori Scarp to the far west, the basin of the Volta River is relatively low.

The combination of Ghana's geographical location and its physical relief determine its climatic conditions. The southwest monsoon, with its cool, moist breezes coming in across the Gulf of Guinea, brings rain to the southwestern part, while the northeast Harmattan, with its desiccating gales from the desert, brings periods of drought to the Upper and Northern regions. Consequently, the major forested areas of the country lie to the south of the Kwahu Plateau. To the south of the plateau are also the nation's major population centers such as Ghana's capital of Accra on the eastern coast, Kumasi in the interior, and Cape Coast and Sekondi-Takoradi on the western coast. Within this triangle are the gold, diamond, bauxite, and manganese deposits of the country. It was the area south of the Kwahu Plateau, therefore, that came into greater contact with European traders and missionaries in the pre-colonial period.

While the ethnic groups constituting the population of Ghana had already settled in their present locations prior to the end of the sixteenth century (see Map 3), the centuries preceding British control of the Gold Coast in the late nineteenth century were marked by the formation and expansion of states and, therefore, the subjugation of others by more powerful local entities. The argument has been made that the processes of state formation and development in the Gold Coast were influenced by attempts by various local groups to participate in, or control, trade with the Europeans who began arriving at the coast as early as the fifteenth century. To a considerable extent, however, the growth and/or decline of these states and the relations among them were responses to patterns of trade, particularly between north and south, that preceded European incursions and to internal dynamics peculiar to the states themselves.

Like most African countries south of the Sahara, the rise of a national consciousness in Ghana developed only in the twentieth century in response to colonial policies. Even though the call to freedom came from a militant few, in the post-World War II environment of disintegrating colonial empires, the concept of independence captured

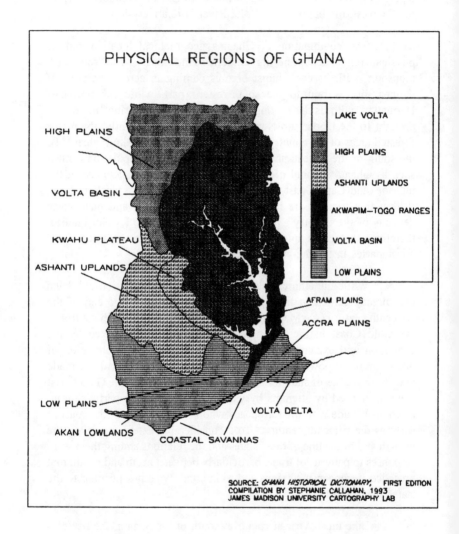

PHYSICAL REGIONS OF GHANA

HIGH PLAINS

VOLTA BASIN

KWAHU PLATEAU

ASHANTI UPLANDS

LOW PLAINS

AKAN LOWLANDS

COASTAL SAVANNAS

VOLTA DELTA

ACCRA PLAINS

AFRAM PLAINS

LAKE VOLTA

HIGH PLAINS

ASHANTI UPLANDS

AKWAPIM—TOGO RANGES

VOLTA BASIN

LOW PLAINS

SOURCE: *GHANA HISTORICAL DICTIONARY*, FIRST EDITION
COMPILATION BY STEPHANIE CALLAHAN, 1993
JAMES MADISON UNIVERSITY CARTOGRAPHY LAB

the imagination of many and gained popular support. The nature of the timetable for freedom and the structure that the modern political society in Ghana was to adopt were, however, not perceived equally by all. While members of the United Gold Coast Convention (UGCC) (q.v.) advocated a federal system of government, the opposing Convention People's Party (CPP) led by Kwame Nkrumah (qq.v.) called for immediate independence under a centralized political structure of the state. The fundamental differences among the nationalist parties have left an indelible mark on Ghana's politics since independence in 1957.

The government of the First Republic was a visible supporter of liberation movements. Ghana's anti-colonial stand was best articulated in Nkrumah's independence speech when he proclaimed that the nation's freedom would be "meaningless unless it was linked to the total liberation of Africa." To achieve this goal, much of Ghana's resources were committed to aid anti-colonial movements. Ghana was a founding state of the Organization of African Unity (OAU) which Nkrumah perceived would mature into a United States of Africa. For the nation to lead the liberation cause, there was the need to train domestic manpower. It was also essential to create an industrial base. For the government of the CPP, the national agenda could only be realized if it was not distracted by the politics of the opposition (q.v.). Hence, as early as 1958, a Protective Detention Act (q.v.) was passed by the CPP-dominated parliament. The law allowed the head of state power to detain without trial those who were considered a threat to the nation. The government of the First Republic used the detention laws to intimidate leading members of the opposition. Some of them were co-opted, others were either driven into exile or jailed. By 24 February 1966, when Nkrumah's administration was overthrown by the National Liberation Council (q.v.), Ghana was a one-party state.

Since the fall of the First Republic, the "Black Star of Africa" came to resemble many ordinary African countries. The Second Republic, inaugurated in 1969, lasted less than three years in office before it was overthrown by the military. The administration of the Supreme Military Council (SMC) (q.v.) lasted until 1979 when it, too, was overthrown in the bloodiest coup in the history of Chana. The decade of the 1970s was characterized by hyperinflation, students' unrest, and strikes by workers' unions. The national economy hardly grew. While the SMC preferred to blame previous administrations,

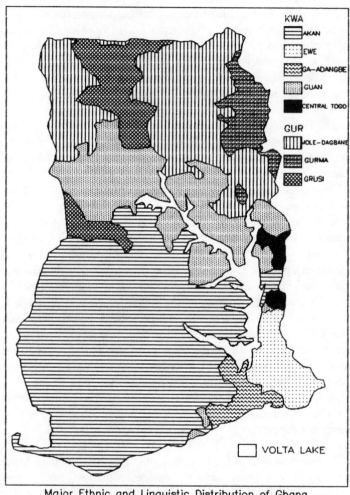

Major Ethnic and Linguistic Distribution of Ghana
Source: Irving Kaplan et al., *Area Handbook for Ghana* (Washington, D.C.: GPO for The American University, 1971).
Produced by Meg Gardner in the JMU Geography Lab, 1993.

natural disasters, and the Arab oil embargo for the nation's predicaments, the Armed Forces Revolutionary Council (AFRC) (q.v.) which came to power put the blame squarely on the leadership of the Ghana Armed Forces. Thus, prior to the inauguration of the Third Republic later that year, Flt. Lt. J. J. Rawlings and the AFRC purged the military.

The Limann (q.v.) administration of the Third Republic lasted only until 31 December 1981 before it was also overthrown, ushering in an eleven-year reign by the government of the Provisional National Defense Council (PNDC)--also led by Rawlings (qq.v.). Emerging from a radical left-wing position, the PNDC vowed to purge the civilian sector as the AFRC had done in 1979 to the military. The ultimate goal of the government was to start a grass-roots political revolution. If successful, the people whose political consciousness was to be raised would call on politicians to be accountable. It was in the pursuit of these goals that the government justified the creation of Workers' and People's Defense Committees and Public Tribunal (qq.v.).

While the PNDC administration was accused by its opponents of being a dictatorship, political observers found the government to be pragmatic. The government was praised by the World Bank and the International Monetary Fund for its Economic Recovery and Structural Adjustment programs (qq.v.) which were introduced in phases throughout the 1980s. The effectiveness of the PNDC economic recovery policies was shown by a significant fall in the rate of inflation, increased domestic production, and an overall confidence that Ghana was on the verge of a political recovery. This was further demonstrated by the 1992 presidential and parliamentary elections which signified the reintroduction of constitutional rule. With Rawlings elected President of the Fourth Republic, the question is raised whether he could oversee via parliamentary means the political and economic recovery he achieved as head of a military government.

THE DICTIONARY

- A -

ABANKESIESO. Original capital of the Denkyira (q.v.) state. It was located not far from modern Adansi Obuasi in the Asante Region (qq.v.).

ABETIFI. 6°40'N, 0°45'W. Kwahu town in the Eastern Region. Archaeologists unearthed Neolithic remains at Bosumpra Cave near here. Abetifi was an important mission center in the colonial period.

ABONSE (Abonce). The old market town of Great Accra, located inland from modern Accra. This market was frequented by merchants from the interior, who brought gold, ivory, and slaves to trade for salt and European goods. It appears on a 1629 Dutch map as "A.B.C."

ABORIGINES' RIGHTS PROTECTION SOCIETY (ARPS). A group organized at Cape Coast in 1897 to conduct a campaign of opposition to the Lands Bill (q.v.) of that year. The Lands Bill threatened traditional land tenure by proposing that all land not in actual use be in the control of the British government. Jacob Wilson Sey of Cape Coast and Anomabo (qq.v.) was first head of the ARPS.

ABOSOM (singular. obosom or bosom). Akan (q.v.) gods and goddesses, considered to be children of the supreme deity. These divinities have personalities and may take residence in inanimate objects such as rocks, caves, and special places, where their shrines are attended by priests and priestesses.

ABOTAKYI, CONCORD OF. An alliance of Guan, Akyem and others to unite against Akwamu and create Akuapem (Akwapim) (qq.v.). The agreement was reached about 1731.

ABRADE. The people who founded the Akwamu (q.v.) state with a center at Nyannaoase about 1600.

ABRAHAM, WILLIAM E. Born 1934. Onetime head of the philosophy department at the University of Ghana (q.v.). He was also a confidant and speech-writer of President Nkrumah (q.v.) and author of *The Mind of Africa*. In November of 1964 he was appointed by President Nkrumah to chair a committee of nine to purge the country of literature critical of socialism. The next year he became a member of the State Publishing Corporation board, a group established to control all publishing and distribution of printed materials in Ghana. He became Pro-Vice Chancellor of the University of Ghana (q.v.) at Legon in 1965. After spending nine months in prison following the 1966 military takeover of the Nkrumah administration, Abraham left politics to become a priest.

ABRAMBO (Abramboe, Abrem, Abrembo). An Etsi (q.v.) state north of Komenda (q.v.) which appears on a 1629 Dutch map. It was east of the Pra (q.v.).

ABREMPON (singular. birempon). Hereditary titles held by the Akan territorial chiefdoms, especially of the Asante Confederacy (qq.v.). The title was also attainable by achievement by the very wealthy.

ABRON see BRONG

ABRUQUAH, JOSEPH WILFRED. Born 1921. Native of Saltpond. He was educated at Mfantsipim and in England and once served as Headmaster of Mfantsipim (q.v.). He was a schoolteacher in Cape Coast and at Keta (qq.v.) between 1949 and 1963. His writings included *The Catechist* (1965) and *The Torrent* published in 1968.

ABUAKWA AKYEM (Abuakwa Akim). The eastern and largest branch of the Akyem. Their origins are traced to the Adansi (q.v.), one of the earliest Akan (q.v.) groups. During their earliest history they were settled about a place called Kokobiante. Under Ofori Panin (q.v.) they migrated from Adansi to the Atewa Hills (qq.v.). Kibi (q.v.) is their chief city today. It was founded around 1700.

ABURI. 5°51'N, 0°11'W. Located in the Eastern Region at the edge of the Akuapem (q.v.) Ridge. The town is some 20 miles (32 km) north of Accra (q.v.). It appeared on a 1729 map as Abura and was known to the Dutch as Aboera. The Basel missionaries (q.v.) began a school for girls here in 1847, and it has been an educational center since then. A nursery for cocoa (q.v.) was started in 1886, and this developed into the present Botanical Gardens. The town has long been a resort for bureaucrats escaping the heat and bustle of Accra.

ABUSA. The farm contract system by which farm laborers served as tenants in exchange for one-third the produce of the land.

ABUSUA. Akan (q.v.) matrilineal clans in which members trace their lineage from a common ancestress and blood. There are seven (or eight) Akan clans. The Aduana and Oyoko (qq.v.) trace their origin to Asantemanso (q.v.), the nuclear point from which one tradition traces Akan beginnings.

ACCANY see AKANNY

ACCRA. 5°33' N, 0°13'W. One of the original Ga (q.v.) coastal settlements, first known as Small Accra. It became the Ga capital in 1677 after Akwamu (q.v.) destroyed Great Accra; located some 10 miles (16 km) inland, Accra became an important trade center during the Atlantic slave trade era, especially after several European posts were built. In 1876 it replaced Cape Coast (q.v.) as the British administration center, and in 1957 it became capital of Ghana. From a population figure of about 16,000 in 1891, the city has expanded to incorporate surrounding towns as neighborhoods extending to the coast. It is by far the largest urban area in Ghana and it was estimated in 1988 to have a population of about 949,113.

ACCRA PLAINS. The flat, dry triangle between Accra, Ada, and Akosombo (qq.v.). Kpesi (q.v.) people lived in the area from early times. Ga, Adangbe, and Ewe (qq.v.) moved in at later dates. The Plains experience very low rainfall, but the region is fairly free of tsetse (q.v.), and therefore it is suitable for livestock.

ACCRA PLAINS AGRICULTURAL DEVELOPMENT. Primary studies for the creation of an Accra Plains Agricultural Development began in April 1984. The program was part of a government decision to launch pilot schemes aimed at utilizing available resources in abandoned agricultural estates and potential areas in the Accra plains (q.v.) for intensive food production. According to a government statement, the Accra Plains Agricultural Development project was to be the first of many such schemes to be established across the country. The construction of irrigation schemes was to be part of the government effort to increase agricultural (q.v.) productivity in the area.

ACHEAMPONG, IGNATIUS KUTU. Born on 23 September 1931; died on 16 June 1979. Head of State. Educated at Catholic schools in Kumasi and Ejura, and Central College of Commerce, Agona-Swedru. Teacher and principal, 1949-1952. Commissioned in the army in 1959. Attended military training programs in England and Kansas. Leader of the military coup in 1972. Head of State and Chairman of the National Redemption Council (q.v.), 1972-1978. Removed from his offices by his colleagues in the Supreme Military Council (q.v.) on 5 July 1978. After being held in custody for a time, he was released, dismissed from the army without benefits, and disqualified from holding office again. In June 1979 he was arrested by the Armed Forces Revolutionary Council (q.v.) and executed by firing squad.

ACHIMOTA. 5°37'N, 0°14'W. A town in the Accra capital district six miles (10 km) north of Accra (q.v.). Location of Achimota

School (q.v.), the first government-sponsored higher education institution in the country.

ACHIMOTA SCHOOL. The foundation stone for Achimota was placed in 1925 and unveiled by the Prince of Wales, for whom the school was at first named. Prince of Wales College was formally opened in January 1927. The school was conceived by Governor Frederick G. Guggisberg (q.v.), and it became one of the finest schools in Africa under the administration of A. G. Fraser (q.v.). For many years, it took male and female students from kindergarten through college. The college campus built near Achimota at Legon in 1948 is now the University of Ghana (q.v.).

ACRON see AKRON

ACTION CONGRESS PARTY (ACP). A political party organized to contest the 1979 elections. Retired Colonel Frank Bernasko (q.v.), once agricultural minister under Acheampong (q.v.), was leader and presidential candidate of the party, and Kofi Awoonor (q.v.) (famous author and university lecturer), was general secretary. Most of the support for the party came from the Fante (q.v.) area of the Central and Western regions. The party won ten seats in the assembly in the June 1979 elections. The ACP was known as the party of "progressive intelligentsia."

ACULO. Grusi-speaking (q.v.) group in the Upper Region who are closely related to the Sisala (q.v.) and Kasena.

ADA (Addah). 5°47'N, 0°38'E. Coastal town on the right bank of the Volta (q.v.). The twin town of Ada Foah (Ada proper) and Big Ada is about 71 miles (114 km) east of Accra (qq.v.). The Volta is wide at this point. Constantly shifting sand impedes navigation, but access in small launches is possible from here up the river 50 miles (80 km) to Akuse (q.v.) most of the year, and to the Senchi Rapids (q.v.) in the rainy seasons. The town was an important trade Center for slaves from up the Volta River in the eighteenth century. A ferry crosses the river from Ada to Anyanui, on the left bank of the Volta.

The Danes built Fort Kongensten (q.v.) at Ada in 1784. Eight years later they outlawed the slave trade in thearea, a dictate often ignored by many of the traders on the lower Volta. Palm oil, hides, and salt were the main commodities traded here during the nineteenth century. In 1850 the Danes sold out to the English, who finally crossed the dreaded Ada bar in the steam launch *Eyo* in 1868. During the British-Asante War of 1873, Captain John Glover established his headquarters there. G. A. Henty and Henry Stanley visited Glover there that year. Robert Bannerman, M. J. Bonnat (qq.v.), Alexandre Duman, Geraldo de Lima (q.v.), and other famous traders operated in the region during the last four decades before 1900. Commander Paget Jones set out from Ada in 1899 to explore the Volta.

ADAE. Akan (q.v.) sacred day which occurs twice in every forty-three days on Sundays (Great Adae) and Wednesdays (Little Adae). These are days of rest when the ancestors are remembered, their spirits are propitiated, and the royal ancestors are honored and solicited.

ADALI-MORTTY, GEORMBEEYI. Poet and educator. He was born in the early twentieth century at Gbogame, Northern Eweland, and was educated at Achimota and Cornell University. After spending many years as a government official, and slowly building a reputation as a poet, he was asked to join the faculty of the University of Ghana (q.v.), Legon. He was a respected member of the School of Administration and Public Relations Management. He joined the private sector upon retirement from the university and died in 1986 at an advanced age.

ADAMAFIO, TAWIA. Ga (q.v.) political leader. Christened Joseph Tawia Adams at birth, he changed his name in 1946 while a clerk for the Supreme Court in Accra. Though at first in opposition to Nkrumah and the Convention People's Party CPP) (qq.v.), he was won over. He wrote for the *Evening*

News (q.v.). In 1956 he went to England to study law, and while there he organized the National Association of Socialist Students Organizations (NASSO) (q.v.) to support the CPP in London. Upon returning to Accra, he became General-Secretary of the CPP for seventeen months. By mid-1961 Adamafio was Minister of Presidential Affairs with an office in Flagstaff House. He was an ally of John Tettegah of the Trades Union Congress (qq.v.), one of the leaders of the left wing of the CPP, and he was often spoken of as Nkrumah's heir. During this period he became Minister of Information and Broadcasting, and in this role he is credited with beginning the campaign to exalt Nkrumah. He also was active in a Study Group which attempted to work out a new socialism as the program for the CPP. After an attempt on Nkrumah's life in August 1962, Adamafio was one of those charged with the assassination attempt. He was arrested on 29 August 1962, tried by a special court, found not guilty, but held in preventive detention (q.v.) by Nkrumah until the coup in 1966. Adamafio returned to favor in 1972 when the military ended the Second Republic. In 1977 he headed the Continental African Youth Command, and in 1978 he was active in the Supreme Military Council campaign of Union Government (qq.v.). Adamafio's memoirs were entitled *By Nkrumah's Side: The Labour and the Wounds.*

ADAMANSO. 5°16'N, 1°52'W. Place in the Western Region in Wassa (qq.v.) country near which the British Governor, Sir Charles MacCarthy (q.v.), was killed in a skirmish with the Asante (q.v.), on 21 January 1824. The skirmish is also called Bonsaso (q.v.) or Nsamakow by different authorities.

ADANGBE (Adampa, Adangme, Dangme). People associated with the Ga (q.v.) in southeastern Ghana. Many of these people live along the coast and on inselbergs in the Accra Plains (q.v.). Ada, Kpong (qq.v.), Kronbo, Ningo, Shai (q.v.), Prampram (q.v.), and Osudoku are identified as Adangbe. They are closely related to the Ewe (q.v.). See the writings of Kropp-Dakubu for literature on these peoples.

ADANSI. One of the earliest Akan (q.v.) states, probably founded in the first half of the sixteenth century. It was located between the Oda and Fum tributaries of the Pra (q.v.) in the Kwisa and Moinsi Hills, also known as the Adansi Hills. It was astride the major north-south trade route. The traditional founder was Opon Enim (q.v.). The first capital was at Adansimanso which was later replaced by Fomena (qq.v.) as Adansi capital.

ADANSI HILLS (also Moinsi). A ridge running from Lake Bosumtwi (q.v.) across a strip of the Central Region to the Huni Valley and Tarkwa.

ADANSIMANSO. 6°18'N, 1°33'W. The earliest capital, located southwest of Lake Bosumtwi (q.v.) about 15 miles (24 km). This is the heartland of the Akan (q.v.) people.

ADDO, EDWARD AKUFO. Born 1906. Attorney, Chief Justice, and President of the Second Republic. He was born in Akropong-Akuapem and educated in Presbyterian schools, Achimota, and Oxford. He was a brother-in-law to William Ofori Atta and son-in-law of Sir Ofori Atta I (qq.v.). In 1940 he received his law degree, and soon after his return to Ghana, he became active in politics. He was a founding member of the United Gold Coast Convention (UGCC) (q.v.) in 1947, and the following year he was one of the "Big Six" arrested by the British authorities in connection with the riots. In the elections of 1951, 1954, and 1956, he was an anti-Nkrumah candidate. In spite of his opposition to Nkrumah (q.v.), he was appointed to the Supreme Court and was one of the judges in the treason trial of Adamafio and Ako Adjei (qq.v.) in 1963. After the court found the defendants in the treason trial innocent, Nkrumah dismissed Addo from the Supreme Court. After the coup of 1966 which toppled Nkrumah, Akufo-Addo became an important figure in the National Liberation Council (q.v.) government as Chairman of the Political Committee. He also chaired the committee that drafted the constitution for the Second Republic. In the elections for the chief executive of the Second Republic, he was elected as President by the electoral commission as the candidate of the Progress Party.

Soon thereafter he suffered a stroke and retired from politics after the 1972 military coup.

ADDO-DANKWA I. Died 1838. Ruler of Akuapem, 1816-1836. He was a member of the alliance that defeated Asante at Katamanso (Dodowa) (qq.v.) in 1826. Near the end of his reign the Basel Mission began its work in Akuapem (qq.v.). In 1836 he was deposed by a pro-Danish faction, and he died two years later.

ADIBO. 9°18'N, 0°01'E. A village in the Northern Region in Dagomba just south of Yendi (qq.v.). Here in 1896 the Germans defeated the Dagomba before moving on to sack Yendi.

ADINKRA CLOTH. Cotton cloth stamped with various traditional designs. The stamps were once made from pieces of calabash. Originally, the dye came from the bark of the badie tree. Each design has a special meaning to the Akan (q.v.).

ADISADEL COLLEGE. A school started in 1910 as the Church of England Grammar School in Cape Coast (q.v.). It is currently one of Ghana's most prestigious secondary schools.

ADJEI, AKO. Born 1915. A Ga attorney who was a student with Nkrumah (qq.v.) in the United States and London. In 1947 he was offered the secretaryship of the United Gold Coast Convention (q.v.), but suggested Nkrumah instead of himself. He was arrested during the 1948 riots, and became one of the famous "Big Six" imprisoned with Nkrumah, Danquah (q.v.), and others. Adjei joined the Convention People's Party (q.v.) in 1952, and became a member of Nkrumah's government in 1954. He was the Foreign Minister from 1959 to 1962. In 1962 he was arrested and charged with complicity in the attempt to murder Nkrumah. Acquitted by the court, he still was held in prison by Nkrumah under preventive detention (q.v.) until released after the 1966 coup.

ADJETEY, CORNELIUS FREDERICK. 1893-1948. Veteran soldier and Ghanaian martyr. A native of Labadi, near Accra, who was educated at Osu Presbyterian Primary School and served in the Gold Coast forces from World War I through World War II (qq.v.), with service in East Africa in the First World War and in Burma during the Second World War. On 28 February 1948 he was killed while leading a group of ex-servicemen towards the Castle at Osu (q.v.) in protest against conditions in the Gold Coast. His death touched off the chain of events that led to the British decision to withdraw from the Gold Coast.

ADOMI (Adome). 6°14'N, 0°06'E. Place on the Volta just north of Senchi and south of Akosombo where a single-span steel arch bridge, built between 1955 and 1957, takes the Accra-Ho highway across the Volta River (q.v.). The bridge replaced the ferry at Senchi and was the first bridge built across the Volta proper.

ADONTEN. The main body of an Akan (q.v.) army, it is under the command of an Adontenhene.

ADUANA (Abrade). One of the principal Akan clans.

ADU BOFFO (Adu Bofo). Died 1883. Son of Gyasewahene Opoku Frefre of Asante (q.v.). Adu Bofo himself became Gyasewahene (q.v.) by the second half of the nineteenth century and distinguished himself as an able military commander. His most important mission was his command of the Asante army of the eastern Volta expedition of 1867 which occupied the trans-Volta area and took the Basel missionaries Ramseyer and J. Kuhne and the French trader Marie Joseph Bonnat (qq.v.) prisoners. In the Asantehene's (q.v.) council, he was a leading opponent of any détente with the Europeans. In 1873 he commanded the west wing of the Asante forces attacking the coast toward Elmina (q.v.).

ADUMFO. An Akan state executioner.

AFADJOTO, MOUNT. 7°02'N, 0°34'E. At 2,905 feet (885 m), this peak in the Volta (q.v.) Region on the Togo border is the highest elevation in Ghana.

AFLAO. 6°07'N, 1°11'E. The most eastern town in Ghana. This coastal border town is the last stop before entering Togo and is only a few miles from the Togo capital city of Lome.

AFRAM. A western tributary of the Volta River which rises northwest of Mampong in the northern part of the Asante Region and flows into Lake Volta (qq.v.).

AFRAM PLAINS. Large area of underdeveloped land between the Afram and Sene arms of Lake Volta (q.v.). The plains are sparsely settled by Guan-speaking (q.v.) people who mainly support themselves by fishing. Soils are frequently flooded in the wet season and parched the rest of the year. The savanna woodlands are spotted with red ironwood and shea trees. Here and there baobabs grow. Tall elephant grass grows near the water. It was once an important hunting area, but much of the game, especially the elephants, is gone. Part of the area is set aside as a game reserve. Tsetse (q.v.) flies are a major problem. Attempts began in the 1980s to improve infrastructure that would facilitate the agricultural development of the area.

AFRICAN COMPANY OF MERCHANTS. A British company organized to replace the Royal African Company (q.v.) for trade on the coast of Africa in 1750. Membership in the new company was open to all British merchants who paid a forty-shilling fee. Parliament made an annual grant to help maintain trade posts for the company on the coast of Africa.

AFRICAN MORNING POST. An Accra newspaper which Nnamdi Azikiwe edited in the early 1930s. The journal was the mouthpiece of the West African Youth League (q.v.), an early nationalist organization.

AFRICAN STEAMSHIP COMPANY. A merchant marine company chartered in 1852 for the purpose of trading with West African ports. It carried the mail to the Gold Coast (q.v.) for many years. In 1891 it became part of the Elder-Dempster Lines. The British and African Steam Navigation Company, organized in 1869, also became part of Elder-Dempster by 1894.

AFRIFA, AKWASI AMANKWAA. 1936-1979. This soldier and politician was born in Asante Mampong (q.v.). He attended Adisadel College in Cape Coast before joining the army in 1956. Part of his military training occurred in England, where he went to Officer Cadet School at Aldershot and the Royal Military Academy at Sandhurst. After returning to Ghana in 1961 he served in the Congo as a member of the UN peacekeeping force.

    Afrifa was one of the officers of the Ghana Armed Forces who directed the coup which ended the reign of Kwame Nkrumah and established the National Liberation Council (NLC) (qq.v.) of 24 February 1966. Afrifa's accounts of the military coup was published in his book *The Ghana Coup: 24th February 1966.* He was a member of the NLC's Executive Council. He served also as Minister of Finance, Economic Affairs, and Trade. In 1969 he became NLC Chairman and Head of State following the resignation of General Ankrah (q.v.), a position he held till the establishment of the Second Republic under Dr. K. A. Busia (q.v.).

    Though disappointed with progress under Busia, Afrifa defended the Second Republic against another military coup, and when the army again returned to power, as the National Redemption Council (q.v.), at the beginning of 1972, Afrifa was arrested, and spent more than a year in detention. After his release, he lived in retirement for some time, returning to active participation in public life as a member of the People's Movement for Freedom and Justice (q.v.). In 1979 he helped organize the United National Convention Party (q.v.), and was elected to Parliament on that ticket in the election held on 18 June that year. Just a week later, he was executed on an order of the Armed Forces Revolutionary Council (q.v.).

AFUTU see EFUTU

AGGREY, JAMES EMMAN KWEGYIR. 1875-1927. Educator.
Born in Anomabo, Aggrey was educated in the Methodist school at Cape Coast. He was one of the early members of the Aborigines' Rights Protection Society (q.v.). In 1898 he went to Salisbury, North Carolina, where he attended Livingstone College for four years. After his graduation he married a lady from Virginia, received a doctorate in divinity, and remained a member of the faculty of Livingstone until 1924. In October 1924 he returned to the Gold Coast to become vice-principal of Achimota (qq.v.). In 1927 he returned to the United States to study at Columbia in New York, but died suddenly on 30 July 1927.

AGGREY, JOHN. 1809-1869. Fante ruler of Cape Coast (qq.v.), 1865-1866. As ruler of Cape Coast, Aggrey claimed sovereignty to the walls of the English Castle. He petitioned the British to respect his authority in Cape Coast, a request the English took to be a challenge to their prerogatives. The British arrested Aggrey in December 1866 and sent him into exile in Sierra Leone. In 1869 he was allowed to return to Cape Coast, but he died shortly after his homecoming. He is honored in Ghana as the first traditional ruler on the Gold Coast (q.v.) to resist colonial rule.

AGOGO. 6°48'N, 1°05'W. Town in the Asante Region, about 40 miles (64 km) east of Kumasi (q.v.). It was an early mission center and continues to be known for its schools for girls.

AGONA. One of the Akan Abusua (qq.v.) clans.

AGONA ASANTE. 6°56'N, 1°29'W. Town in the Asante Region on the Great Northern Road between Kumasi and Mampong (qq.v.). It was one of the principal divisions of the Asante (q.v.) nation. Its paramount chiefs are the descendants of Okomfo Anokye, the chief priest of Asantehene Osei Tutu (qq.v.).

AGONA STATE (Agua, Aguna, Agwano, Agonna, Janconcomo). One of the larger states shown on a 1629 Dutch map, located between Fante and Accra (qq.v.). On the 1729 Anville map it is shown between Akron (q.v.) and Akra, with a note that it was "very powerful." It was conquered by Akwamu (q.v.) in 1689. Nsaba (5°39'N, 0°45'W) in the Central Region was the seat of the Omanhene, or paramount chief, of Agona from 1693 to 1931. Senya Beraku and Winneba (qq.v.) are the important ports of the area, and Swedru (q.v.) is its most important inland city.

AGRICULTURE. Among the common crops grown in Ghana for home consumption are cassava, cocoyam, yam, maize, rice, plantain, and millet. Even though a large number of small-scale farmers have been engaged in the production of these crops, food prices continued to be high in the 1980s due to the rapidly increasing population and the high cost of collecting, assembling, transporting, storing, and distributing these agricultural commodities.

Ever since cocoa (q.v.) beans were exported from the country in 1891, the crop has received more government attention than any other crop in the nation. The continued attention paid to the industry is evident by the fact that, even though it provided only 15 percent of the gross agricultural production in 1988, it was allocated about 29 percent of the capital spent in agriculture and about 67 percent of the recurrent expenditure in the agricultural sector, hence the higher food prices during that decade.

It became increasingly obvious in the 1980s that agricultural production had to be boosted as part of the national recovery plan (see ECONOMIC RECOVERY PROGRAM; EXPORT PROMOTION; INVESTMENT CODE). To accomplish that objective, the Ministry of Agriculture established various linkages that were to make the results of research, modern agricultural techniques, and technologies available to farmers. Policies were also put in place to rationalize efficiency and to improve the delivery of public sector services in the field of research, extension, input supplies, and credit facilities to farmers (see GLOBAL 2000 FOUNDATION). Furthermore, through government efforts, the Ghana-Italian-FAO projects in the Afram Plains (q.v.) opened that area to mechanized agriculture. Thus, by 1986, it was reported that the amount of arable land in Ghana under cultivation for food and cash crops had increased from 11 percent in 1981 to 13.6 percent. Palm oil production, for example, increased dramatically.

While higher agricultural production in the decade of the 1980s could be attributed partly to better natural circumstances such as good rains, it can also be argued that the relatively stable political environment and some government policies of the period helped. The acquisition of World Bank funding for the Ghana Oil Palm Development Corporation (GOPDC) and certain local mills, for example, could only have happened with government support. As part of the privatization program, the Ministry of Agriculture also announced its intention to abolish its policy of fixing minimum guaranteed prices for agricultural produce. This, it was reasoned, would ensure that producers received market prices for their goods (see COCOA MARKETING BOARD). Notwithstanding these improvements in the production of exportable agricultural produce, Ghana's annual population growth of 2.5 percent makes continued success in the production of traditional foodstuffs crucial to the nation's general stability.

AGUNA see AGONA STATE

AHAFO. Sefwi (q.v.) territory between the Bia and Tano (q.v.) rivers which was conquered by Opoku Ware of Asante (qq.v.) in about 1721. The name means "hunting ground of the Asantehene." Today the area is part of the Brong-Ahafo Region (q.v.).

AHANTA (Anda, Anta, Hanta). Coastal area of the Western Region between the Ankobra and Pra rivers (qq.v.). Busua (4°48'N, 1°56'W) is the center. Ahanta was shown on the 1629 Dutch map as Anta and on the Anville map of 1729 as Hante. The state runs inland from the coast for a short distance. Sekondi, Takoradi, Dixcove, Cape Three Points, Prince's Town, and Axim (qq.v.) were some of the important outlets to the area. The Prussians, Portuguese, Dutch, and English all vied for trade here.

AHASIA see GREAT INKASSA

AHEMA (Ahemaa, Hemaa). Plural of Ohemaa. Akan (q.v.) for queen mothers. The Queen Mother of Asante is the Asantehemaa (qq.v.). The Queen Mother in Asante and Akan society is the second most important person after the king or chief. She nominates the candidate for chief, and if the council of king-makers (elders) does not select her choice she can veto anyone of whom she disapproves. She can give advice to the chief, she sits next to the ruler in court, and she alone can rebuke the chief. She can also hold her own court.

AHENE (Ahenfo). The plural of ohene. Chief or king among the Akan (q.v.). Usually perceived to be the custodian of ancestral land.

AHENEMMA. Princes of the Golden Stool (q.v.). Even though Asante (q.v.) is a matrilineal society and sons (princes) by tradition have not inherited the throne, many occupants of the Golden Stool employed their sons in administrative positions.

AHMADIYYAH. A Muslim (q.v.) brotherhood founded in India in the late nineteenth century. It appeared in the Gold Coast during World War I (qq.v.). These Muslims do not consider Muhammad (the orthodox prophet of Islam) to be the last of the prophets. Their initial history in Ghana is characterized by conflict with orthodox Muslims, especially at Wa (q.v.) in the Upper West Region. They have conducted an aggressive educational program and published thousands of religious tracts. Today, the movement in Ghana runs a number of schools including secondary and vocational training centers.

AHUBAW. A popular Akan (q.v.) festival to celebrate the yam harvest. During the colonial period, celebrations would frequently get out of hand due to public drunkenness and disorder. The 1892 Native Customs Ordinance tried, unsuccessfully, to limit excesses in the celebrations in the major coastal cities.

AHWENE KOKO (Affindio Coco, Old Wankyi). The traditional first capital of Wenchi (q.v.). It was destroyed by the Asante (q.v.) around 1712.

AIDOO, CHRISTINA AMA ATA. Born 1940. Author, university lecturer, and once Secretary of Education. Aidoo was born at Abeadzi Kyakyiakor (near Saltpond) in the Central Region. She was educated in Methodist schools, and graduated from the University of Ghana (q.v.), Legon. She studied also in England and the United States. She is author of many poems and short stories. Her collection of short stories, *No Sweetness Here*, published in 1970 received worldwide acclaim, and her first play, *Dilemma of a Ghost*, has been performed in many theaters. She was with the Department of English at the University of Cape Coast (q.v.) before 1982 when she was appointed Secretary of Education in the Provisional National Defense Council (q.v.) government, a position she held until June 1983. Now residing in Harare, Zimbabwe, she chaired the 1990 Commonwealth Writer Prize regional panel. Her recent publication, *Changes* (1991), received great reviews. She has been described by reviewers as a "feminist writer."

AJENA GORGE. 6°16'N, 0°03'E. Place where the Volta once broke through the Akuapem-Togo (qq.v.) (Akwapim-Togo) range of mountains. The narrow gorge was only 30 yards (28 m) wide. The gorge is now the location of the Akosombo Dam (q.v.), completed in 1965. Akosombo village is just south of the dam.

AKAN (Akanny, Akani, Acanjj, Hecanny, etc.). One of the major ethnic groups of West Africa, the majority living in Ghana. They are grouped around a number of clans, most of them having traditions of origins in the Adanse region around Lake Bosumtwi (qq.v.). They have matrilineal systems of descent.

AKAN CLANS. The Abusua (blood) clan is matrilineal. The Fante have seven female clans and the Asante (qq.v.) have eight. The Asante clans are: Aduana (Aduena), Agona (qq.v.), Asinie (Asena), Asokore, Asona, Oyoko (qq.v.), and, depending on sources, Abrade, Beretuo, and Ekuana (qq.v.). These are totemic clans. All Akan (q.v.) belong to one of them. The totem of the Oyoko is a parrot, of the Aduana a frog, of the Asona a crow, etc. Every Akan also belongs to his father's family, called the ntoro or spirit family, but inherits from the mother's line.

AKAN DIVISIONS. The Akan divisions in Ghana include the Akuapem, Akyem (Akim), Kwahu, Ahafo, Asante, Brong, Denkyira, Assin, Nzema, and Fante (qq.v.).

AKAN LANGUAGE. The language is today known as Akan. It was once known as Twi (q.v.). The Akan of the Asante (q.v.) is the most widely used. The Akuapem dialect was the first to be written. The Fante (q.v.) version of Akan is spoken along the coast. The Brong (Abron) and Bawle (Baule) (qq.v.) of the Ivory Coast also speak Akan. Akan is a tonal language.

AKANNY (Akanni, Acanny, Hacany, etc.). The old Akan state around Lake Bosumtwi and southward to the Pra (qq.v.). Adansi and other Akan (qq.v.) now occupy the area.

AKANTAMANSU (Akantamanso, Katamanso). 5°44'N, 0°05'W. A place in the Accra Plains (q.v.) where the great battle took place in August 1826 between the British and their local allies and the Asante under Asantehene Osei Yaw Akoto (qq.v.). The British referred to the conflict as the battle of Dodowa (q.v.), but Dodowa and Akantamansu at the Accra Plains are 8 miles (13 km) apart. Arabic manuscripts believed to have been carried by Asante to this battle and lost at Akantamansu were located at the Royal Library in Copenhagen by Ray Kea in 1963.

AKIM see AKYEM

AKOSOMBO. 6°18'N, 0°03'E. Village in the Eastern Region near the Ajena Gorge (q.v.) and the Akosombo Dam. It is now a port from which boats go northward to Kete-Krakye, Kpandu, Yeji, and Yapei (Tamale Port) (qq.v.). The town is 65 miles (104 km) northeast of Accra (q.v.).

   The Akosombo power project was started in 1961 and was operational by the end of 1965. The dam was an earth-and-rock-fill type structure 370 feet (113 m) high and 2,100 feet (640 m) long at its crest. When the reservoir behind the dam was completely filled, Lake Volta (q.v.) extended 250 miles (402 km) into the north, forming one of the largest man-made lakes in the world. The dam experienced its first major drought in 1983, affecting the supply of electricity. Power supplied from the dam is exported to both Togo and Benin.

AKRAMAN see GOMOA

AKRON (Acron, Akrong). A polity on the coast between Fante and Agona (qq.v.) in what is now the Central Region of Ghana. On the 1729 Anville map it is shown as Great Akron to the interior, and was referred to as Akron on the coast. Apam (q.v.) was the chief town.

AKROPONG see AKUROPON

AKUA BA (pl. Akuamma). An Akan (q.v.) doll carved of wood with flat oval head, long neck and small round body. It is often called a "fertility doll," and is sometimes carried by pregnant women as a protection for the unborn child. It has come to be one of the symbols of Asante (q.v.) art.

AKUAPEM (Akawapim, Aquapim). An Akan polity in the Eastern Region northeast of Accra on the Akuapem Ridge (qq.v.). It covers about 330 square miles (885 sq km). The area was once part of Akwamu (q.v.) empire from around 1680 to 1730, before it gained its independence. The seat of the paramount chief was first at Asamankese, then Nyanawase, and today at Akuropon (Akropong) (qq.v.). There are some nineteen major towns in the polity. Aburi, Dawu, Mampong-Akuapem, and Akuropon (qq.v.) are among the more important. Its healthy climate, good land, industrious people, heavy missionary influence, and proximity to Accra (q.v.) make Akuapem one of the most progressive areas of Ghana.

AKUAPEM-TOGO RANGE (Akwapim-Togo). Folded hills that run from the mouth of the Densu river (q.v.) in a northeasterly direction to the Togo frontier. They are cut by the Volta at the Ajena Gorge (qq.v.). In Togo they continue as the Togo-Atakora Mountains. In Ghana their average height is 1,500 feet (457 m).

AKUFFO, FREDERICK W. K. 1937-1979. Soldier, Head of State. Native of Akuropon in Akuapem (qq.v.). He joined the army in 1957, was trained at Sandhurst in England, was commissioned in 1960, and served in the UN peacekeeping force in the Congo. At the time of the coup against Busia (q.v.) and the Second Republic, Akuffo was a colonel. By 1976 he was a member of the Supreme Military Council (SMC) (q.v.) and Chief of the Defense Staff. On 5 July 1978 he seized power from Acheampong (q.v.), becoming Chairman of the Supreme Military Council (q.v.). Less than a year later, on 4 June 1979, Akuffo was overthrown by the Armed Forces Revolutionary Council (q.v.). He was executed on 26 June 1979.

AKUMADAN (Akomada, Akomadan). 7°24'N, 1°57'W. Town on the western road from Kumasi to Wenchi near the northern border of the Asante Region (qq.v.). It is 56 miles (90 km) northwest of Kumasi. The town is known for its local markets.

AKUROPON (Akropon, Akropong). 5°5'8N, 0°05'W. Seat of the Okuapemhene of Akuapem (qq.v.). Town in the Eastern Region, on the Akuapem Ridge, about 32 miles (51 km) northeast of Accra. Akuropon was an early site of educational and agricultural activities of the Basel missionaries (q.v.), and later of similar activities of the Presbyterians. One of the earliest training colleges for teachers was founded here.

AKUSE. 6°06'N, 0°08'E. River port on the west side of the Volta some 55 miles (88 km) above Ada (qq.v.). It is on the tidal limit of the river, and navigation generally ends here except in the rainy season from August to December. It was one of the earliest inland trading centers depending on river transport from Ada, and a ferry still plies the Volta from here. The Basel Mission (q.v.) once had a station at Akuse. The British had a District Commissioner resident in the town as early as 1895, one of two on the Gold Coast (q.v.). The town is in the Eastern Region and is part of Manya (Eastern) Krobo (q.v.).

AKWAMU (Aquamboe, Oquie). One of the early Akan (q.v.) kingdoms. Traditions link Akwamu origins to the north, but by the early sixteenth century the kingdom was in the Atewa Hills with a capital at a place called Asamankese (qq.v.). Later the capital was moved to Nyanawase, near modern Nsawam, not far above Accra by 1681, and Agona (qq.v.) by 1689. By 1702 the armies of Akwamu held power all the way to Ouidah (Benin) in the east. Kwahu (q.v.) fell to Akwamu in 1710. That was to be the point of greatest expansion. From 1729 a series of reverses contracted the limits of Akwamu power to a small area north of Krobo (q.v.). They submitted to the British on 27 July 1886.

AKWAMUFIE. 6°17'N, 0°05'E. The Akwamu (q.v.) capital. A town in the Eastern Region near the Volta and the Akosombo (qq.v.) Dam. The Akwamu moved here after a defeat by the Akyem and Akuapem (qq.v.) in 1730.

AKWAPIM see AKUAPEM

AKWATIA. 6°03'N, 0°25'W. Town in the Eastern Region that is the center of diamond mining.

AKWIDA (Akoda). 4°45'N, 2°01'W. Coastal village on Cape Three Points between Prince's Town and Dixcove in the Western Region (qq.v.). The Bradenburgers built Fort Dorothea (qq.v.) here in 1685. This post was later taken over by the Dutch. Only the ruins of Fort Dorothea remain today.

AKYEASE (Achiasi). 5°50'N, 1°00'W. Town on the railroad below Oda (q.v.) in the southwestern corner of the Eastern Region. The railway line through the town made it possible for rail travel from Accra to Sekondi-Takoradi possible without having to go through Kumasi (qq.v.).

AKYEM (Akim, Achim). One of the major Akan (q.v.) groups of Ghana. Akyem tradition traces their origin as a state to the modern Adansi (q.v.) area in the sixteenth century. Pressure from the Denkyira (q.v.) in the seventeenth century forced Akyem movement eastward into the area of the Atewa Hills and the Birim River between the modern towns of Kibi and Oda (qq.v.). Reindorf (q.v.) says Akyem means "salt trader." At one time they were also active in the gold and slave trades. The Akyem are divided into three major divisions: the Akyem Abuakwa, the Akyem Bosume, and the Akyem Kotoku (qq.v.).

AKYEM ABUAKWA. The senior and largest Akyem (q.v.) division. These Akyem migrated into the Atewa Hills around Kibi in the late seventeenth century from the Adansi (qq.v.) area. They established their capital at Banso, near their modern center at Kibi.

AKYEM BOSUME. The southernmost and smallest Akyem (q.v.) division. These Akan moved from Adansi (qq.v.) into their present position as a result of pressure from the Asante (q.v.) early in the eighteenth century. Their chief town today is Akyem Swedru (5°51'N, 1°01'W).

AKYEM KOTOKU. The middle Akyem (q.v.) division. When they first moved into the Atewa Hills (q.v.) they established a capital at Jedem (Jyadem, Gyadam), only a short distance from their present capital at Oda (q.v.) (Nsuaem).

ALEXANDER, HENRY TEMPLER. 1911-1977. British officer, Scottish Rifles. He served as Nkrumah's (q.v.) Chief of Defense Staff from January 1960 to September 1961 during the early stages of the UN Congo operations. He wrote of his experiences in Ghana and the Congo in *Africa Tightrope*, published in 1965.

AMANFU (Amanfro, Amanfur, Amanful, Mount Manfro). The location just a few hundred yards east of the Castle at Cape Coast (q.v.). The Danes built Fort Frederiksborg (q.v.) here around 1660, but sold their claims to the British in 1685. About 1699 the English rebuilt the fort and named it Fort Royal. Almost no traces of the fort are there today.

AMANHENE (singular. Omanhene). Akan (q.v.) paramount chiefs.

AMANKWATIA (Amankwa Tia, Aman Quatia, Amanquattiah). Ca. 1833-1874. Bantamahene and Commander of the Asante (qq.v.) army against the British, 1872-1873. Amankwatia owed his position to Asantehene Kofi Kakari (q.v.), and he became one of his master's closest advisers. He belonged to the group that counseled a hard-line policy against British pretensions on the Gold Coast (q.v.). During 1872 he persuaded the Asantehene to allow him to occupy the trade routes as far as the Fante (q.v.) borders. Permission was granted, and on 9 December 1872 Amankwatia left Kumasi (q.v.) at the head of an Asante army. By the middle of 1873 the army was within a few miles of Cape Coast (q.v.). But anti-war sentiment in Kumasi in the second half of 1873 undermined Kofi Kakari's resolution, and in November Amankwatia was ordered to retreat to Asanteland. A British and Fante force followed under Sir Major-General Garnet Wolseley (q.v.). Amankwatia died in defense of Kumasi.

AMANSIE (Amanse, Amansi). The area around Lake Bosumtwi, between the upper Oda and Anum rivers, which is the Asante (qq.v.) heartland. The territory was settled by members of the Oyoko clan from Adansi (qq.v.) around 1600. According to Asante tradition, the first Asante people originated from Asantemanso (q.v.) in the Amansie area.

AMANTOO STATES. The chief states forming the Asante (q.v.) Confederacy (q.v.). They are Kumasi, Dwaben, Mampong, Nsuta, Kokofu, and Bekwai (qq.v.). Kumawu (q.v.) is at times mentioned in relation to the early Asante states.

AMARIA (Hamaria, Amariya). Zambrama-Grusi (qq.v.) leader who was born in Santijan, located at 10°32'N, 1°32'W in the Sisala-Builsa area 50 miles (80 km) southwest of Bolgatanga (qq.v.). When Amaria was about seven he was captured by Alfa Hano (q.v.), first of the Zabrama leaders. In the following years he distinguished himself as a leader under Alfa Gazare and Babatu (q.v). In 1894 he broke from his allegiance to the Zabrama, allied himself with the Europeans, and helped break the power of the Zabrama in the northern basin of the Volta (q.v.).

AMEDUME, J. K. Naval officer who was a close associate of Acheampong (q.v.), 1975 to 1978. During this time he was Minister of Labour, Social Welfare, and Cooperatives. In the last year of Supreme Military Council (SMC) (q.v.) rule he was promoted to Rear Admiral and naval chief. He was executed by the Armed Forces Revolutionary Council (AFRC) (q.v.) in June 1979.

AMEDZOFE (Amedzope). 6°51'N, 0°26'E. Old German mission station in the Volta Region Avatime section, midway between Ho (qq.v.) and Hohoe. It is a beautiful mountain town in the Togo Hills in the shadow of Mt. Gami and in sight of the Biakpa, Kabakaba, and Peki Hills. There are several interesting waterfalls near Amedzofe.

AMETEWEE, SETH. A police constable who was assigned to guard duty at Flagstaff House. On New Year's Day 1964 he shot at Kwame Nkrumah (q.v.) in an abortive attempt to kill the President.

AMSTERDAM, FORT. 5°12'N, 1°05'W. A fort near Kormantin (Kromanti, Kormantine) on the coast in the Central Region near Saltpond (qq.v.). It was started by the English in 1638. The Dutch took it over in 1665, and gave it the name by which it is still known. It changed hands between the English and Dutch several times. The Asante (q.v.) took it in 1807, and in 1811 Anomabo (q.v.) held it a short time. The British held it after 1868. In 1951 a restoration project was undertaken, but this was not completed. Most of the slaves sent to the British Caribbean journeyed through this post.

ANKOBEA. (Amkobia) The Asantehene's (q.v.) personal security force and bodyguard. These persons were appointed by and responsible only to the Asantehene.

ANKOBRA RIVER. River which rises near Bibiani and flows through the Western Region (qq.v.) to reach the Gulf of Guinea just west of Axim (q.v.). It flows through Ghana's gold-producing region. In October 1983 a modern bridge near Axim replaced the old one-vehicle ferry to facilitate the construction of the Pan-African highway. The Ankobra is navigable in small boats for about 50 miles (80 km). The Mansi and the Bonsa are the major tributaries.

ANKRAH, JOSEPH ARTHUR. Died in 1992. Soldier and Head State. Born in Accra, Ankrah was educated in the schools of the city. He later joined the army, and by the start of World War II he was a warrant officer. During the war he took officer training in England and became a commissioned officer. He served in the UN peacekeeping forces in the Congo. He was Deputy Chief of the Defense staff when, in July 1965, Nkrumah (q.v.) retired him from the armed forces. In 1966, after the 24 February coup, he was reinstated in the army with the rank of Lieutenant-General, appointed Commander of the Armed Forces, and named Chairman of the National Liberation Council (q.v.). As Head of State, Ankrah was largely a figurehead, but he apparently had ambitions to keep his job. He accepted money from foreigners to conduct a poll to determine his chances if he were to become a candidate when popular elections were allowed again. This touched off a scandal which resulted in his resignation from public offices in 1969. Ankrah remained in quiet retirement till his death in late 1992.

ANLO (Awuna). An Ewe (q.v.) group who live along the coast to the east of the Volta River (q.v.). Other peoples in the area called them the Awuna. The legendary seventeenth century founders of Anlo (Sri and Wenya) are said to have come from Notsie in the area of modern Togo. From the settlement of the Anlo around the Keta Lagoon, there were wars between Anlo and Ada and Accra (qq.v.) over fishing rights and the salt and slave traffic. More than half the population of Anloland are said to have been killed in fighting in 1776. Later the Danes joined Ada and the allies of Ada in a war with Anlo, and on 18 June 1784 the Anlo had to submit to Danish rule. The Danes surrendered their prerogatives over Anlo to the English in 1850. The fierce competition with Ada continued, and England frequently resorted to military force to subdue the Anlo. In June 1874, with the Treaty of Dzelukofe, Anlo surrendered.

ANLOGA (Awunaga). 5°48'N, 0°54'E. Capital of the Anlo, located 11 miles (18 km) southwest of Keta on the spit of land between the Keta Lagoon (qq.v.) and the Gulf of Guinea. Zion College of West Africa, the oldest in the Volta Region, was opened here in October 1937.

ANOKYE, OKOMFO (Anonkye, Anotche, Anotchi). Kwame Frimpong Anokye, known in Asante traditions as Okomfo Anokye, was an Akwamu priest who helped Osei Tutu (qq.v.) establish the traditions of the Asante Union, including the Golden Stool (q.v.), soul of the Asante nation. He helped work out the Asante Constitution and the tradition of the Odwira Festival. Francis Fuller referred to Anokye as the "Cardinal Wolsey" of Asante, and in a 1986 *Journal of African History* article, Thomas McCaskie, a British historian of Asante, questioned whether Okomfo Anokye ever existed. Asante tradition, however, describes Okomfo Anokye as a powerful seventeenth-century priest whose magical abilities contributed immensely to the rise of Asante as a hegemonic Akan (q.v.) power. His descendants sit on the stool of Agona (q.v.), Asante.

ANOMABO (Anomobo, Anomabu). 5°10'N, 1°07'W. Fante (q.v.) town in the Central Region 10 miles (16 km) east of Cape Coast (q.v.). It was founded in the sixteenth century as a fishing village. The name means "Bird Rock." The Dutch built a lodge to trade here about 1640, and the town was in turn captured by Danes, Swedes, and English. It was bombarded by the French in 1794, and attacked by the Asante (q.v.) in 1807. The English built Fort Charles at Anomabo in 1679, and in the 1750s built another fort called Anomabo Fort. This was restored in the 1950s. Anomabo was a major British commercial depot for many years.

ANOUFOU or ANUFO see CHOKOSI

ANSA SASRAKU. Ruler of Akwamu (q.v.) in the latter part of the seventeenth century. He defeated the Ga (q.v.) in 1677, and by the time of his death in 1689 he ruled the coast from the Volta to Agona (qq.v.).

ANTOR, SENYO GATROR. Born 1913. Ewe political leader in the Volta Region (qq.v.). Educated in Bremen Mission at Amedzofe, the Presbyterian Training College, Akuropon, and the Theological College at Ho. Editor, *UN Newsletter*, 1949-1953. One of the leaders in the formation of the Togoland Congress Party (q.v.) in 1951. He wanted an Ewe homeland under Ewe control and was opposed to the integration of British Togo into the Gold Coast (q.v.). He was a member of the Legislative Assembly, 1954-1957. After independence he was arrested in connection with unrest in the Volta Region. He was sentenced to six years, but released after appeal. He served in the National Assembly, 1958-1961. In 1961 he was detained by Nkrumah (q.v.) and was left in prison without trial until the coup in 1966. Under the National Liberation Council (q.v.) he served as a member of the Political Committee, and he was a member of the Constituent Assembly, 1968-1969. In the Second Republic he was ambassador to Togo, 1970-1972.

ANUM. A tributary of the Pra which rises northeast of Kumasi, near Effiduasi, in the old Dwaben area of the Asante Region (qq.v.), and flows southward until it joins the Pra at 6°12'N, 1°12'W.

ANUM-BOSO. A Guan (q.v.) group that lives mostly in the Eastern Region.

ANYIDOHO, KOFI. Born 1947. Poet and university professor. Born at Wheta in the Volta Region, Anyidoho was trained at the Advanced Teacher Training College (Winneba) and at the Institute of African Studies (q.v.) (Legon). Now described by critics as one of Ghana's best poets, Kofi Anyidoho was the product and one of the founding members of the Creative Writers Association at the University of Ghana (q.v.), where he is now an Associate Professor of Literature. His works include *Elegy for the Revolution* (1978), *Cross Rhythms* (1983), *A Harvest of Our Dreams* (1984), and *Earth Child* and *Brain Surgery* (1985). Anyidoho has been described as a writer of "mood poetry." "Feelings of disillusionment, cynicism, and optimism" are all reflected in his poetry. Some commentators have associated these moods with the author's personal and deep identification with his subject--the nation of Ghana.

AOWIN (Awowin). An Anyi-Bawle group of Akan (qq.v.) who live along the Ivory Coast border in the Western Region between the Nzema and Sefwi (qq.v.).

APAM (Appam). 5°17'N, 0°44'W. Coastal city just to the west of Winneba and 43 miles (69 km) west of Accra (qq.v.). The Dutch began Fort Leydsaamheid here in 1697. It was taken briefly by the Akyems (q.v.) in 1811 and by the British in 1868. In the present century the fort became a police station.

APO CEREMONY. An eight-day holiday when all Akan (q.v.) are supposed to cleanse their souls (sunsum) of evil by saying and doing what is on their minds.

"APOLLO 568." In 1970 Prime Minister Kofi Busia dismissed 568 civil servants who had served while Nkrumah (qq.v.) was president, and who still seemed to be loyal to the former president. This caused a clash with the judiciary, which ruled that one of the dismissed, E. K. Sallah, could not be removed from his position. Busia refused to obey a court order which obliged him to reemploy Sallah. The case was cited by the opposition as a sign that Busia disregarded the supreme court of the state.

APOLLONIA (Appolonia, Amanahia, Apolonia). The early Christian missionaries referred to Nzema (q.v.) country as Apollonia. The British built a fort at Beyin (q.v.) in 1768-1770 which they called Fort Apollonia. The fort was transferred to the Dutch in 1868. It is in ruins today.

APPIAH, JOSEPH MANUEL. 1918-1990. An Asante (q.v.) and Ghanaian politician. Educated at Wesleyan Primary School in Kumasi, and Mfantsipim at Cape Coast, he worked for the United Africa Company (q.v.) in Accra, Takoradi, and Freetown (Sierra Leone). Appiah went to England to study law in 1943, and passed the bar in 1954. While in England, Joseph Appiah became friends with Kwame Nkrumah (q.v.), and they both attended the Pan-African Conference in Manchester in 1945. It was also in England that Appiah met and married Peggy Cripps, daughter of Sir Stafford Cripps (Labor Chancellor of Exchequer). While still in England, he was one of the founders of the West African National Secretariat.

Upon returning to the Gold Coast, Appiah joined the Convention People's Party (CPP) (q.v.), but in early 1955 he quit that party and joined the opposition National Liberation Movement (NLM) (q.v.). Elected to the Legislative Assembly in 1946, he became head of the opposition in 1957. His bitter opposition to Nkrumah's "cult of personality" landed him in prison in October 1961. He was not released from Ussher Fort (q.v.) Prison until December 1962.

Following the coup of 1966, Appiah was made a Roving Ambassador for the National Liberation Council (q.v.), and was later placed on the Political Committee. In the 1969 elections he organized the United Nationalist Party, but was defeated in an attempt to get a seat in the National Assembly.

During the Second Republic he joined the Justice Party, and was active in opposition to Busia (qq.v.). With the National Redemption Council (q.v.) coup in 1972 he returned to favor once again. He became a close adviser to Acheampong (q.v.). He was given the job of Roving Ambassador again, and represented Ghana at the United Nations for a time. He was active in the campaign for Union Government in 1978. Then, when the Supreme Military Council (q.v.) was replaced by the Armed Forces Revolutionary Council (q.v.), he found himself, briefly, in prison once more. In his later years, he was a member of the Synod of the Methodist church. His memoirs were entitled *Joe Appiah: The Autobiography of an African Patriot.*

AQUAMBOE see AKWAMU

AQUAPIM see AKUAPEM

AQUOWOA see KWAHU

ARCANIA or ARCANES see AKANNY

ARDEN-CLARKE, CHARLES NOBLE. 1898-1962. British colonial officer. After service in the army, 1917-1920, Arden-Clarke joined the Colonial Service and worked in Nigeria, 1920-1936; Bechuanaland, 1936-1942; Basutoland, 1942-1946. He was then elevated to Governor of Sarawak, 1946-1949; Governor of the Gold Coast (q.v.), 1949-1957; and first Governor-General of Ghana, March-May 1957, when he was replaced by a Labour peer, the Earl of Listowel. As the last British Governor of the Gold Coast, Arden-Clarke worked unusually well with Kwame Nkrumah (q.v.) toward the smooth transfer of power from Great Britain to Ghana.

ARMAH, AYI KWEI. Born 1939. Author. Armah is from Takoradi in the Western Region (qq.v.). He was educated at Achimota, Groton (Massachusetts), and Harvard University. His BA degree was in sociology. After graduation he worked briefly as a translator in Algiers. Then he taught English at

Navrongo and got a job writing scripts for Ghana Television. In 1967 he studied briefly at Columbia and wrote for a few months for *Jeune Afrique*. Later he lectured on African Literature at the University of Massachusetts and since 1972 he has been teaching at the University of Tanzania, Dar es Salaam. He is Ghana's most prolific novelist. His first novel was *The Beautiful Ones Are Not Yet Born*, published in 1968. This was followed by *Fragments*, 1970; *Why Are We So Blest?* 1972; *Two Thousand Seasons*, 1973; and *The Healers*, 1978. Armah has also published short stories and poems. He is the subject of several interesting monographs.

ARMED FORCES OF GHANA. Composed of the army, navy, and air force. The army was divided into two brigades of eleven battalions. The navy bases were at Sekondi and Tema (qq.v.). The air force had airmen divided into five squadrons. There were paramilitary forces, including the border guards who were incorporated into the army in the mid-1980s. The Military Academy has been located at Teshi, near Accra (qq.v.).

Since February of 1966, members of the Armed Forces of Ghana have organized at least four successful military coups. There have been countless unsuccessful attempts to overthrow governments. For some commentators, the frequent involvement of the Armed Forces in politics was indicative of problems in institutional discipline among the forces. In that situation, the officer corps became decimated in the political turmoil, especially that which took place in 1979. The result was that the officers still in service were afraid of the men under them. Esprit de corps was almost nonexistent. The military was also reported to have terrorized the civilians they were supposed to protect.

By the end of 1983 Flt. Lt. J. J. Rawlings, Chairman of the Provisional National Defence Council (PNDC) (qq.v.), was in the process of organizing a Peoples' Militia to advance the cause of his revolution. In 1984 the PNDC amendment to the Special Tribunal Law of 1982 (PNDCL 9) was passed with the intent of instilling some discipline in the armed forces while creating conditions by which the army could be depended upon to protect the civilian population. The

constitutional proposals of 1992 also barred members of the
public service, including the 11,900-strong armed forces, from
politics.

ARMED FORCES REVOLUTIONARY COUNCIL (AFRC).   A
group of junior officers and enlisted soldiers, led by Jerry John
Rawlings (q.v.), which overthrew the Supreme Military
Council on 4 June 1979 with the avowed purpose of
conducting a "house-cleaning" exercise within the army. Eight
high-ranking officers, including three former heads of state--
Afrifa, Acheampong, and Akuffo (qq.v.), were found guilty of
corruption and executed. Many other persons were sentenced
to long terms at hard labor and had their properties confiscated
by the state. After four months in power, during which
elections were held, the AFRC surrendered power to a civilian
government under Hilla Limann (q.v.), on 24 September 1979.

ARMITAGE, CECIL HAMILTON.   1869-1933.   Colonial officer.
Armitage entered Gold Coast (q.v.) service in 1894 and was
part of the British expedition against Asante (q.v.) in 1895-
1896. He was secretary to Governor Frederic Hodgson (q.v.)
for a time, and in 1900 he was sent to Kumasi to find the
Golden Stool (qq.v.), a mission in which he failed. He was
acting Resident of Kumasi during the siege of the Fort in
Kumasi in 1900.
　　　　Armitage was Chief Commissioner, Northern
Territories, 1910-1920, during which time he was criticized by
Governor Hugh Clifford (qq.v.) for his failure to prevent
excesses in the way his subordinates sometimes dealt with
people under their control. While in the North, Armitage
wrote *The Ashanti Campaign of 1900* and made several
valuable reports on conditions in the Northern Territories.
　　　　Cecil Armitage became Governor of The Gambia in
1920 and held the position until 1927, when he retired.

ART. Ghana is famous for its wood carvings, especially stools, *oware*
boards, and *Akua ba* dolls. Masks and human or animal
figures in wood are not traditional in most Akan (q.v.)

societies. Drums, combs, and other objects made of wood are often decorated with designs.

Brass ceremonial vessels (*kuduo*) and brass boxes and containers are sometimes interesting. Metal-casting by the lost-wax method is developed to a fine art, especially among the Asante (q.v.), who are known for their gold weights, ornaments, and jewelry.

Ghanaian pottery is generally undistinguished. Most pots are blackened after firing by placing the hot pot in leaves. Smoke then turns the pot black. Some pots, especially from the northern regions, are decorated with interesting designs. Terra-cotta heads were once used in funerals.

Contemporary Ghanaian artists compare favorably with any in Africa. Saka Acquaye excels in music, writing, and art. He is a sculptor of note, and his wood panel inlay murals grace a number of public buildings in Accra. Oku Ampofo, Kofi Antubam, and Vincent Kofi are other important sculptors. Among Ghana's notable painters are Kobina Bucknor, A. O. Bartimeus, Alex Amofa, and Sylvanue Amenuke. W. C. Owusu, J. O. T. Ansah, and Daniel Cobblah are ceramists. S. K. Prah, S. H. Kyei, S. K. Nkansah, and J. C. Okyere are among the better-known wood-carvers. The Gold Coast Society of Artists was formed in 1946, and Ghana today continues to have an active community of talented and skilled artists. A Ghana Art Council also exists.

ASAFO. Communal or militia groups organized for defense or group enterprises. Asafo companies often ruled sections of villages or towns, and they often fought pitched battles against each other, as in Cape Coast in 1859. The companies were sometimes seen as organizations of young men that checked the power of traditional leadership.

ASAFOHENE. Captain of an Asafo (q.v.) Company, or a ceremonial head of a group of kinsmen.

ASAFU-ADJAYE, EDWARD OKYERE. 1903-1976. Lawyer and political leader. Educated in Kumasi, at Adisadel, and the University College of London. Passed his bar examination in

1936. He and F. V. Nanka-Bruce (q.v.) represented the Gold Coast at the coronation of George VI in 1937. Member of the Legislative Assembly from 1946 to 1956 and member of the National Assembly in 1956. Minister of Local Government in 1951 and of Trade and Labor in 1955. One of the Gold Coast representatives at the coronation of Elizabeth II in 1953, and Ghana's first High Commissioner to the Court of St. James, 1957-1961. He resumed his law practice in 1961.

ASAMAN. The traditional founder of Bono-Manso. The date of the foundation of Bono-Manso is disputed. Some authorities give a date of about 1297 and others give a date as late as 1400. The settlement was near Techiman (q.v.).

ASAMANKESE. 5°52'N, 0°40'W. An old capital of Akwamu (q.v.), it is a large town in the Eastern Region about 50 miles (80 km) northwest of Accra.

ASAMENI (Asomani, Asemmani). An Akwamu merchant who learned several European languages so as to deal with the Europeans at Accra (qq.v.). In June of 1693 he overpowered the Danish garrison of Christiansborg (q.v.), and he ruled that post as governor for about a year, trading with the English, French, and Dutch. After Christiansborg was restored to the Danes, Asameni continued to play an important role in Akwamu affairs.

ASANTE (Ashanti). A region, a people and an Akan (q.v.) nation. Asante is the proper Akan spelling, although other English spelling as Ashanti and Ashantee can be found in print. The divisions of Asante are Kumasi (Kumase in Akan), Mampong, Bekwai, Kokofu, Nsuta, Dwaben (Juaben) (qq.v.), Effiduase, Asokore, Ejisu (Edweso), Bonwire, Asumegya (qq.v.), and Senfi.

According to a tradition, the Asante-speaking Akans migrated from the Adansi area around Lake Bosumtwi (q.v.) to the neighborhood of the trading town of Tafo (qq.v.). This migration took place in the early seventeenth century under Obiri Yeboa, a member of the Oyoko (qq.v.) lineage. The ruling clans of Asante were described as having originated from Asantemanso (q.v.), also near Lake Bosomtwi. By 1690, Osei Tutu (q.v.) was the Asante leader. He formed the alliance with Mampong, Bekwai, Kokofu, Dwaben, Nsuta, and others, which became the Asante Union. According to tradition, Osei Tutu was aided by Okomfo Anokye to establish the traditions of the Golden Stool (q.v.), the Odwira, and the Asante Constitution.

The eighteenth century saw the steady expansion of Asante influence. Denkyira, a former overlord of the Asante states, fell in 1701; Assin, Aowin (qq.v.), Amanahia, Wassa, Twifo, and Wenchi (qq.v.) by 1720; Techiman, Banda, Gyaman, and Western Gonja (qq.v.) by 1740; Kete Krakye, Central and Eastern Gonja, Dagomba, Akyem, and Akwamu (qq.v.) by 1755. By 1760 all Asante's neighbors save the Fante (q.v.) were under the spell of the Golden Stool (q.v.). The Fante were vulnerable too, but they were in the British sphere.

As the Asante attempted to open routes to the coast, it was perhaps inevitable that they would come into conflict with the Europeans and the European allies on the coast. From 1807, when Asante pushed hard toward the coast, clashes began to occur. In 1826 the Asante army was defeated at Katamanso (Dodowa) (qq.v.). That battle proved to be an important test of Asante hegemony. In 1874 the British marched into Kumasi, leaving it a city of ashes. In 1896 the British returned again, and this time they sent the Asantehene and many important individuals into exile. He was allowed to return again only in 1924. By then the power of Asante was no more. But they were still a proud people. In 1935 the British allowed the Asante Union to be re-created, but it would never again be a sovereign power. Asante is now one of the ten regions of modern Ghana.

ASANTE, DAVID. 1834-1892. A Basel (q.v.) missionary. He was educated in the Basel school in Akuropon, and in Basel, Switzerland. After he returned to Akuapem (q.v.), he gained some note as a writer on African religion and as a translator. He helped J. G. Christaller (q.v.) with a translation of the

Bible into Twi or Akan (qq.v.), and he translated John Bunyan's *Pilgrim's Progress* into Twi.

ASANTEHEMAA.   Queen-mother of Kumase and an important adviser to the Asantehene (qq.v.).   Her position is a personification of the Asante matrilineal system.   See AHEMA.

ASANTEHENE.   The Omanhene of Kumasi and head of the Asante (qq.v.) Union.   He is the keeper of the Golden Stool and therefore the king of Asante (qq.v.).

ASANTE-KOTOKO-UNION SOCIETY.   A society founded in Kumasi in 1916 as a patriotic Asante (qq.v.) association of Asante merchants, clerks, and teachers. J. E. Bandoh was the first president of the society, and J. W. K. Appiah was the first secretary. E. P. Owusu, who later became Prempe II (q.v.) in 1931, was a charter member.

ASANTEMANHYIAMU.   The High Council or Assembly of the Asante (q.v.) Union.   It served as the highest tribunal of the nation.   All the provincial rulers, the senior Kumasi (q.v.) officials, and the queen-mother were members.   Its regular annual sessions took place during the annual Odwira (q.v.) Festival.   Extraordinary sessions of the council were held in times of emergency.

ASANTEMANSO   (Santemanso).   Place where Asante (q.v.) traditions say the first of their ruling clans originated. R. S. Rattray (q.v.) referred to Asantemanso as the "most hallowed spot in all their territory." The grove where Asante history is supposed to have begun is not far from Lake Bosumtwi (q.v.).

ASASE YAA (Asase Ya, Asase Efua). The earth goddess. Thursday is the day set aside by the Akan (q.v.) to honor the earth goddess. The soil is not tilled on Thursday; it is a day of rest from farmwork. Asase Yaa is not regarded as a divinity. There are no priests, shrines, or temples, but Asase Yaa is recognized as the source of truth. Offerings are sometimes placed upon the ground for the earth spirit.

ASEBU (Saboe, Sabu, Sabou, Sabue). 5°13'N, 1°12'W. Village in the Central Region. A 1629 Dutch map shows Saboe (Asebu) as a coastal state with Futu to the west and Fante (q.v.) to the east. The locality was known for its salt. Mouri (q.v.) is an Asebu village. The Dutch dominated the trade of this place from the late sixteenth century. It was also subject to Fante domination by 1725.

ASENE. 5°55'N, 0°56'W. The Battle of Asene took place here in 1824. Asene Krofoso is on the north bank of the Pra (q.v.) near Obogu and Dampong (q.v.). Here, a two-day battle was fought in 1824 between the Akyem-Akuapem allies on one side and an Asante (qq.v.) army on the other side. As a result, Akyem Kotoku regained sovereignty from Asante rule.

ASENIE (Asinie). One of the principal Akan (q.v.) clans.

ASESEWA. 6°23'N, 0°08'W. Famous Manya Krobo (q.v.) market in the Eastern Region some 30 miles (48 km) northeast of Koforidua and near Lake Volta (qq.v.).

ASHANTI see ASANTE

ASHANTI CONFEDERACY COUNCIL. Group created by the British at Kumasi in January 1935 to represent the Asante (qq.v.) people in the revived Asante Union. It was assigned only limited powers, in keeping with the policies of Indirect Rule (q.v.) proclaimed by the British at the time. By the end of the Second World War in 1945 it had been called together 11 times.

ASHANTI GOLDFIELD CORPORATION (AGC). A corporation organized in 1897 with E. A. Cade as the chief figure. The corporation gained a 100-square-mile (259-sq-km) concession for mining, trading, rubber and timber extraction, and road building. It opened its first mine at Obuasi (q.v.) in 1898. In 1975 the National Redemption Council (q.v.) took over 55 percent ownership of Ashanti Goldfield Corporation. Major rehabilitation of AGC infrastructure in the mid-1980s resulted in an increase in its production of gold. Also in the mid-1980s, AGC announced its intent to engage in agricultural ventures.

ASOKORE. One of the Akan (q.v.) clans.

ASONA. One of the Akan (q.v.) clans, called the "fox" clan.

ASSIN (Asen, Asin). Akan (q.v.) group that today is found in the Central Region east of the Pra with the Denkyira and Twifo to the west, the Adansi to the north, the Akyem to the east, and the Fante (qq.v.) to the south. They have been intermediaries in the trade between the hinterland and the coast, and have often been subject to pressures from their more powerful neighbors. Both Denkyira and Asante (q.v.) have ruled them at different times. The Assin have frequently allied themselves to Wassa, Twifo, and Fante (q.v.), and their lands were frequently devastated in wars between these people and the Asante.

The Assin are divided into two groups. The Assin Apemanim (Apimenem) are mostly on the east side of the Cape Coast-Kumasi highway, with a capital at the old slave depot of Manso (q.v.). The Assin Attendansu (Atandanso) are mainly to the west of the road, with a capital at Nyankumasi.

ASSOCIATION OF WEST AFRICAN MERCHANTS (AWAM). A group of European businesses which united during the depression of the 1930s to fix prices and divide markets in West Africa. Their agreement about the Gold Coast (q.v.) markets was reached in July 1934.

ASUMAN see SUMAN

ASUMEGYA. One of the original metropolitan states of Asante (q.v.). The Asumegyahene (ruler of Asumegya) by tradition was the commander of the left wing of the Asante forces.

ATABIA. Died ca. 1742. Mamprusi (q.v.) ruler. His reign of half a century, from about 1688, saw a great expansion of Mamprusi in what is now the Northern and Upper regions. At first his capital was located at Gambaga, but about 1700 he moved to Nalerigu (qq.v.), 7 miles (11 km) to the east of Gambaga.

ATEBUBU (Tebu). 7°45'N, 0°59'W. An old capital of the Brong (q.v.), the town is on the Great Northern Road 85 miles (136 km) northeast of Kumasi (q.v.). It is the western end of an old road that used to go off to the ferry at Kete-Krakye, but now goes to Lake Volta (qq.v.). It was a stopover place for the cattle drivers from the north.

ATEWA HILLS. 5°59'N, 0°40'W. Hills in the center of the Eastern Region. The Birim River rises in this area, and the Akyem capital of Kibi (qq.v.) is located in these hills. Diamonds were discovered in the hills in about 1919, and there are also deposits of bauxite in the area. Altitudes rise to 2,400 feet (732 m) on these densely forested slopes.

ATTOH-AHUMA, SAMUEL RICHARD BREW. 1863-1921. Methodist minister, nationalist, author. He was an officer in the Aborigines' Rights Protection Society (q.v.).

ATWIA. Early inhabitants of what became the Akyem area between the Pra and the Densu (qq.v.).

AUGUSTABORG, FORT. A Danish fortification built on the location of an earlier Dutch post in 1787. It was bought by the British in 1850. The ruined fort would have been located at modern Teshi (q.v.) had it remained.

AVATIME (Afatime). Central Togo people who form an enclave in Ewe territory in the Volta Region (qq.v.). The paramount chief lives at Vane. Amedzofe is the more important town. The area is in one of Ghana's most beautiful mountain districts.

AVOLIENU see NEWTOWN

AWASO (Awaaso). 6°14'N, 2°16'W. Town in the Western Region. It is the terminal of a rail line from Dunkwa (q.v.), built at the end of World War II to bring out bauxite. The area is also an important source for timber.

AWHAITEY, BENJAMIN. Adangbe (q.v.) military officer who in December 1958 was Commander of Giffard Camp at Accra. He was arrested for being involved with others in a plot to overthrow or assassinate Nkrumah (q.v.). From this point, the government began to use the Preventive Detention Act (q.v.) of 18 July 1958 against its opposition. Awhaitey was convicted and dismissed from the army.

AWONA (Anwona). Akan name for Ewe (qq.v.).

AWOONOR, KOFI (George Awoonor-Williams). Born 1935 at Wheta, Anlo South, Volta Region near Keta (qq.v.). One of Ghana's best-known writers. He was educated at Achimota, Legon, London, and Stony Brook, New York. He was managing director of Ghana Film Industries, 1965-1967, and has had several academic appointments in the United States and Ghana. Awoonor is best known as a poet, but he is author of a novel, *This Earth, My Brother* (1971), and a survey of the history, culture, and literature of Africa south of the Sahara, *The Breast of the Earth* (1975). In 1975, while on the faculty of the University of Cape Coast (q.v.), he was arrested by the military government of the National Redemption Council (q.v.) for helping Brigadier Alphonse Kattah, accused head of an Ewe (q.v.) plot to overthrow the government, escape into Togo. He was held for eleven months before being convicted and sent to prison. In 1983 Awoonor was appointed Ambassador to Brazil by the Provisional National Defense Council (PNDC) (q.v.) and later transferred to New York as Ghana's United Nations Permanent Representative. He continues to write despite a busy diplomatic schedule. His book *The Ghana Revolution: Background Account from a Personal Perspective* generated varied responses.

AWOONOR-RENNER, KWEKU BANKOLE (Kweku Awuno-Bankole). 1898-1970. Journalist and politician. Born at Elmina and educated in Catholic school at Cape Coast, in the 1920s he went to the United States and attended Tuskegee Institute (Alabama) and Carnegie Institute (Pennsylvania). While in the US he was once secretary of the African Students' Association, and he wrote *The Crisis* for the NAACP. From the US he went on to Russia, where he attended the University of Toilers of the East in Moscow. In 1928 he published a book of poems, *This Africa*, in Moscow. An English version of this book was published in 1943.

Back in the Gold Coast (q.v.) by 1931, Awoonor-Renner edited the *Gold Coast Leader* (Sekondi) for awhile, and then moved to Accra, where he became active in the Gold Coast Youth Conference (q.v.). He helped organize the Asante Freedom Society, an attempt to block re-creation of the Asante Union. He also became a vocal Communist in the Gold Coast, and joined the Accra Muslim Party. In 1942 he was elected to the Accra Town Council. By the last year of World War II he went to London to study law. There he was quickly involved in the West African National Secretariat (q.v.), where he got to know George Padmore and Kwame Nkrumah (qq.v.). He attended the Pan-African Congress at Manchester in 1945. The following year he published a pamphlet, "The West African Soviet Republic."

Awoonor-Renner was back in the Gold Coast during the heyday of the organization of the Convention People's Party (CPP) (q.v.). He was an active supporter of Nkrumah, and he was sent to James Fort Prison with Nkrumah, Kojo Botsio (q.v.), and other CPP leaders in 1950. Once the CPP achieved power, Awoonor-Renner separated himself from his CPP comrades. For a time he devoted his energies to the Muslim Association Party (q.v.), and in 1957 he joined other opposition leaders in the United Party (q.v.). But poor health curtailed his political activities after 1957.

AWOWA (Ahoba ni). Pawns. Persons (or property) held as collateral for debts or obligations.

AWOWIN see AOWIN

AWUTU (Obutu). A Guan group, most of whom live in the Gomoa (qq.v.) area.

AXIM (Axem). 4°52'N, 2°14'W. Coastal town in the Nzema (q.v.) area of the Western Region just to the east of the Ankobra River, and 40 miles (64 km) west of Takoradi (qq.v.). It is on a beautiful, small bay, and just offshore is Bobaysi Island with its lighthouse. The Portuguese first reached Axim in the early 1470s and had a small base there by 1503. They began Santo Antonio de Axem (St. Anthony) in 1515. The fortress was erected on a bluff above the small harbor. The fortress was the last Portuguese stronghold and was evacuated on 8 February 1642 when it was attacked by the Dutch. The property was ceded to the British in 1872. The fort was restored in the 1950s, and it is now used for government offices.

AYAWASO (Ayaso). 5°40'N, 0°17'W. A small village just outside of Accra (q.v.) on the Nsachi River where King Ayite of the Ga Asere dynasty established the Ga (q.v.) capital about the middle of the sixteenth century. The place was sacked and burned by the Akwamu (q.v.) in 1677.

AYENSU RIVER. 5°22'N, 0°35'W. A river which rises in the Atewa-Atwiredu hills south of Kibi (q.v.) and flows into the Gulf of Guinea just east of Winneba (q.v.). It is the major source of the water supply of Winneba.

- B -

BAAH, KWAME R. M. Born 1938. Soldier. Native of Dormaa Ahenkro in the Brong Ahafo (q.v.) Region. He attendedsecondary school in Kumasi, joined the army in 1959, and was commissioned in 1962, after cadet training at Teshi and in India. He served in the Congo under the command of Acheampong (q.v.). Kwame Baah was assigned to the Ghanaian embassies in London and Washington. In 1972 he joined Acheampong and the National Liberation Council (q.v.) in the coup that ended the Second Republic. He was Commissioner of Lands and Mineral Resources in 1972 and Commissioner of Foreign Affairs from 1973 to 1975. After the creation of the Supreme Military Council (q.v.), Baah was dropped from the Cabinet and retired from the army. He was, however, sentenced to fifty years in prison by the Armed Forces Revolutionary Council (q.v.) in 1979.

BAAKO, KOFI. 1926-1984. Politician and nationalist from Saltpond (q.v.). A founding member of the Committee on Youth Organization and the League of Ghana Patriots (qq.v.). He was a key member of the Convention People's Party (CPP) (q.v.) from its beginning and one of Nkrumah's (q.v.) closest confidants. In 1949 Baako became editor of the CPP *Cape Coast Daily Mail*, and he soon joined other nationalists in prison for his opposition to colonial rule. He was elected to the Legislative Assembly in 1954 from Saltpond and represented his hometown until the coup of 1966 ended the rule of Nkrumah and the CPP.

Kofi Baako held a number of positions in the CPP administration. He was Minister of Information and Broadcasting in 1958 and leader of the National Assembly in July 1961; later he was Minister of Parliamentary Affairs, and finally Minister of Defense. He also acted as General-Secretary of the party and was a member of the party's Central Committee. Kofi Baako was identified with the socialist wing of the party advocating a one-party state.

BABATU (Babato, Baba, Mahama dan Issa). Zabrama (Zabarima or Zerma) leader who followed his father, Alfa Gazari (qq.v.), as leader of a band which dominated a large area of what is now northern Ghana and central Burkina Faso. He succeeded his father in 1883. The Grusi (q.v.) people under Amaria (Hamaria) (q.v.) rebelled against Babatu and joined the French in destroying Zabrama suzerainty. Babatu was defeated at Gandiaga in March 1897 and at Doucie (Ducie) in June. With his forces decimated, Babatu retreated into Dagomba (q.v.), where he joined the Dagomba in resistance to British incursions. Babatu died about 1900.

BADU, KOFI. Born 1935. Journalist and politician. A native of the Asante Region, Badu was an active member of the Convention People's Party (CPP) (q.v.). He was editor and reporter for several Accra papers during the Nkrumah (q.v.) period. He also served in the National Assembly during the First Republic. After the 1966 coup he continued his newspaper career and wrote several critical editorials in *The Spokesman* against the Busia (qq.v.) administration of the Second Republic. Kofi Badu enthusiastically supported the National Redemption Council (NRC) (q.v.) after the 1972 coup. A close adviser to Acheampong after the Supreme Military Council (SMC) (q.v.) was established in 1975, Kofi Badu was appointed Commissioner for Consumer Affairs in 1978.

BAGALE (Bagele). 10°12'N, 0°22'W. A village in the Northern Region where the mausoleum of Dagomba (q.v.) rulers is located.

BALME, DAVID MOWBRAY. 1912-1989. Classical scholar. Graduate of Cambridge and Halle (Germany), who after service in World War II became a lecturer in classics at Jesus College, Cambridge. From 1948 to 1957 he was Principal of the University College of the Gold Coast, Legon. In that position he did much to determine the basic direction of the University along Cambridge lines with residence halls, faculty rule, and intellectual elitism. The library at the University of Ghana (q.v.) is named for Balme. After leaving Legon, Balme taught classics at Queen Mary College, London, from 1957 until he retired in 1978. On 23 February 1989, David Balme died at Leicestershire in the United Kingdom. He was 76.

BALMER, WILLIAM TURNBULL. An English minister who taught at Mfantsipim, Cape Coast, from 1907 to 1911. In 1925 he published *A History of the Akan Peoples*, in which he advanced the idea that the Akan (q.v.) peoples had moved south from ancient Ghana after that old Sahel kingdom came to an end. J. B. Danquah (q.v.) further discussed the idea of dispersion from ancient Ghana in his *Akim Abuakwa Handbook* (1928). This was the reason for Danquah's later proposal that the name of the Gold Coast (q.v.) at independence be changed to New Ghana.

BANKESIESO. An old Denkyira (q.v.) capital. The location is near Obuasi on the route from Kumasi to Elmina in the modern Asante Region (qq.v.).

BANNERMAN, CHARLES EDWARD WOOLHOUSE. 1884-1943. First African to become a judge of the Supreme Court of the Gold Coast (q.v.). He was one of the founders of the National Congress of British West Africa (q.v.).

BANNERMAN, EDMUND. 1832-1903. Grandson of an Asantehene and son of Lieutenant-Governor James Bannerman (qq.v.). He was educated in England as a lawyer. He held a number of positions in the Gold Coast (q.v.) government during his lifetime and was one of the leaders in the movement to have Africans serve on the Legislative Council. In 1886 he was a leader in a movement to send a delegation to England to protest British policy on the Gold Coast.

BANNERMAN, JAMES. 1790-1858. Son of a Scottish commandant at Cape Coast Castle and of an Akan (qq.v.) mother. He married a daughter of the Asantehene (q.v.). By 1850 he was one of the leading merchants in Accra, and in that year he was appointed a member of the first Gold Coast Legislative Council and became civil commandant of Christiansborg Castle (q.v.). At the end of the year he became Lieutenant-Governor of the Gold Coast (q.v.), a position he held until October 1851. James Bannerman established a family which has long been one of the most prominent in the country.

BANTAMA. An important section of Kumasi (q.v.), it is in the northwestern section of the town, between Suntreso and the Mampong Road. The Asante Cultural Center, the Royal Mausoleum, the Okomfo Anokye Teaching Hospital, the Public

Library, the Zoo, and the city's old Race Course are all in the vicinity. In pre-colonial times, rulers of Bantama (the kronti or konti division of Asante forces) commanded many Asante expeditions. Bantama rulers also had, and continue to have, great influence in Asante and Kumasi politics.

BAOULE see BAWLE

BARROS, JOAO DE. 1496-1570. Portuguese factor at Elmina (q.v.) in 1532, Treasurer from 1522 to 1525, commander at Elmina from 1525 to 1528. He wrote one of the earliest accounts of the Gold Coast (q.v.).

BASEL MISSION SOCIETY. A missionary society founded in 1815 in Basel, Switzerland. It began its work on the Gold Coast (q.v.) in 1827. Many of the early missionaries who came to Africa died in their first year in the tropics, but the society persisted in its evangelical, educational, medical, agricultural, and vocational endeavors in spite of all odds. Of nine missionaries sent to Christiansborg between 1828 and 1840, not one made a convert. After 1835 the Akuapem (Akwapim) (q.v.) area became the center of their enterprises. A boys' school was founded there in 1843, followed by a girls' school four years later. By 1881 they had almost fifty schools, mostly in the Eastern Province, and in 1890 there were almost 2,000 students enrolled in their care. By 1900 they operated two Teacher Training schools in the Gold Coast. Since the Basel missionaries used German, they were deported by the British colonial administration during World War I and were not allowed to return until 1926. After that the Basel Mission Church became known as Presbyterian.

BATENSTEYN, FORT. 4°49'N, 1°55'W. A European fort which once stood at Butri, in the Western Region. The Swedes established a trade post there about 1650, but the Dutch built the fort in 1656. The British gained the area in 1872. Today the fortifications are in ruins.

BAWA. The progenitor of the Mole-Dagbani (q.v.) peoples. Tradition says that he came from Gurma and settled at Pusiga (q.v.), in the Upper East Region, near the borders of Burkina Faso and Togo. In Mossi (q.v.) traditions, Bawa is referred to as Nedega, while the Dagomba call him Gbewa (qq.v.).

BAWKU. 11°03'N, 0°15'W. An important town in the Upper East Region near the border with Burkina Faso. It is the principal town of the Kusasi (q.v.) people. The market at Bawku has long been famous, and it is an important contact with the Muslim Sahel to the north.

BAWLE (Baoule, Baule, Bahure). The Anyi-Bawle are the most western Akan (q.v.) group. Most of them live on the border of the Ivory Coast or in the Ivory Coast. They are most closely related to the Sahwi and Aowin (q.v.).

BEGHO (Bahaa, Bighu, Bitu, Insokka, Insoko, Nsoko, Socco). Begho was a fifteenth-century trading center, located in the present Brong Ahafo (q.v.) Region of Ghana. The exact date of its foundation is speculative. It is clear, however, that Begho antedates the rise of both Asante and Gonja (qq.v.). Begho was possibly a Mande colony where Muslim traders from Jenne and the Niger came to trade for gold. By the late sixteenth century, traders from the area began to divert some of their commerce southward to the coast to meet the Europeans. Ivor Wilks (q.v.) is of the opinion that the Asante drive into the northwest, during the period of expansion, was aimed at controlling this trade.

BEGORO. 6°23'N, 0°23'W. Town in the Eastern Region 20 miles (32 km) northeast of Kibi and on the edge of the Kwahu Scarp (qq.v.). It was once an important Presbyterian missionary center.

BEKWAI (Bekwae). 6°27'N, 1°35'W. An Amansie town about 20 miles (32 km) south of Kumasi (qq.v.). Bekwai was one of the original members of the Asante union. The town is not far from Asantemanso, a location claimed to be the origin of the ruling Asante (qq.v.) clans. Bekwai is, therefore, not far from Lake Bosumtwi (q.v.) to the west.

BENKUM. The Left Wing of an Akan army.

BERETUO. One of the Asante (q.v.) abusua, or clans. The rulers of Mampong (q.v.) are identified with the Beretuo (Bretuo). The stool of Mampong is called the Silver Stool, and it is the second most important stool in the Asante Union. In Fante (q.v.) this clan is called Twidan.

BERNASKO, FRANK G. Born 1931. Military officer, lawyer, politician. Born at Cape Coast, Bernasko was educated in Presbyterian schools, at Adisadel College, and at the University of Ghana (Legon), where he graduated in 1960. He later was awarded a law degree from the University. Joining the army, he served a term as Commandant of the Military Academy at Teshi, and after the 1966 coup he became Director of Education in the Ministry of Defense. Following the 1972 coup he was first appointed Commissioner of the Central Region, and in January 1973 he became Commissioner of Agriculture. In this position he gained national attention as the dynamic director of the Operation Feed Yourself (q.v.) campaign of the government. In February 1975 he also took charge of the newly created Ministry of Cocoa Affairs. Bernasko resigned from the National Redemption Council (q.v.) government and from the Ghana armed forces in August 1975. He was a founding member of the Action Congress Party (q.v.) in 1979 and an unsuccessful presidential candidate of that party.

BEYIN (Benyin, Apollonia). 4°59'N, 2°35'W. Coastal town in the Nzema country of the Western Region about 50 miles (80 km) to the west of Dixcove (qq.v.). The Europeans called the area Apollonia (q.v.). The Dutch built a lodge here in about 1660. A British fort here was completed by 1772. The British fortress is still standing The fort was transferred to the Dutch in 1868, but the English purchased it back in 1872.

BIBIANI. 6°28'N, 2°20'W. Town in the Sefwi area of the Western Region (qq.v.). The area around Bibiani is known for its gold-mining industry.

BIGHU see BEGHO

BIMBILA (Bimbia). 8°51'N, 0°04'E. The capital of Nanumba located in the Northern Region about 40 miles (64 km) to the south of Yendi and 75 miles (120 km) north of Kete Krakye (qq.v.).

BIMOBA (Bimawba, B'Moba, Moba). Gurma (q.v.) group who live along the Ghana-Togo border to the west of Sansanne-Mango. Many live in Togo.

BING, GEOFFREY HENRY CECIL. 1909-1977. Once legal adviser to Kwame Nkrumah (q.v.). Bing was a left-wing Ulsterman, educated at Oxford and Princeton, and was a signal officer in World War II. He was a Labour member of the British Parliament from 1945 to 1955, and he helped finalize the terms for Gold Coast (q.v.) independence. After the creation of Ghana he went to Accra as Nkrumah's adviser on legal and constitutional affairs and as liaison with the left wing of the British Labour Party. He was Attorney General of Ghana from 1957 to 1961. After the 1966 coup he spent a few days in prison, but was expelled from Ghana on 24 March 1966. Some months later he published *Reap the Whirlwind; An Account of Kwame Nkrumah's Ghana from 1950 to 1966.* It is a valuable inside story of the Nkrumah years. In 1977, just a few weeks before he died, he returned to Ghana for the first time in over ten years. He praised the Supreme Military Council (q.v.) for pursuing a policy of national reconciliation.

BINGER, LOUIS GUSTAVE. 1856-1936. French colonial officer. In 1887 he began a famous trip through Mali, Burkina Faso, Ghana, and the Ivory Coast. He crossed the Upper and Northern regions to Salaga (qq.v.) in 1888, and from there went to Kong. In 1893 he became the French Administrator of the Ivory Coast. His account of his trip across West Africa was published. See his *Du Niger au Golfe de Guinée par le Pays de Kong et le Mossi.*

BIRIM RIVER. A stream which rises in the Atewa Hills near Kibi and runs in an arch northeast to the foot of the Kwahu Scarp and then bends sharply southwest, flowing across the Akyem country, past Oda, to join the Pra (qq.v.) at 5°58'N, 1°13'W. The Birim area, around Kade and Oda (qq.v.), is known for its diamond mines.

BITU see BEGHO

BLACK STAR LINE. The State Shipping Corporation was established 10 September 1957 with the aid of Israel. The ships were named for the rivers, lakes, and lagoons of Ghana. The *Volta River*, built in 1940, was the first ship purchased for the line. The name "Black Star" came from the US shipping line formed in the 1920s by Marcus Garvey, one of the early African-American nationalists.

BLACK VOLTA (Coumbo). Western tributary of the Volta (q.v.) system. It begins in Burkina Faso near Bobo Dioulasso.

BLANKSON, GEORGE KUNTU. 1809-1898. Merchant, soldier, and member of the Legislative Council, 1861-1873. He was a native of Anomabo. Blankson played an important role in the wars against Asante (q.v.), and negotiated with the Asante and the Dutch on behalf of the British. He was a loyal member of the Methodist Church, often serving as a minister.

B'MOBA see BIMOBA

BOAHEN, A. ADU. Born 1932. Professor of history and politician. Albert Adu Boahen attended Mfantsipim and the University of Ghana (Legon). He received his doctorate in African history from the School of Oriental and African Studies (London) in 1959. His academic career has been at Legon also since 1959. He has been a prolific writer on West African history. His *Topics in West African History, Ghana: Evolution and Change in the Nineteenth and Twentieth Centuries,* and *African Perspective on Colonialism* are three of his publications. Boahen has been a consultant on African history to UNESCO since 1971. Recognition of his scholarship has earned him many visiting professorships to such prestigious institutions as Australian National University (Canberra), Columbia University (New York), Birmingham University (United Kingdom), Johns Hopkins University (Baltimore), and the State University of New York at Binghamton.

Boahen has also been active in his opposition to military rule in Ghana. As a founding member of the People's Movement for Freedom and Justice (PMFJ) (q.v.), he spent several weeks in prison for speaking out against the Supreme Military Council's Union Government (qq.v.) plan in 1978. His continued opposition to military administrations was reflected in his public lecture in Accra in 1989 on the well-publicized topic: "The Ghanaian Sphinx--Reflections on the Contemporary History of Ghana, 1972-1987." What he considered to be the moral dimension or the lack of it in contemporary African politics was the subject of his 1990 lecture at the African Studies Association Conference in Baltimore. He ran for the presidency of Ghana in November 1992 on the ticket of the New Patriotic Party (NPP) (q.v.) but lost to Jerry Rawlings, PNDC chairman and the National Democratic Congress candidate (qq.v). At parliament in the Fourth Republic, Adu Boahen was leader of the Opposition.

BOAKYE, GEORGE YAW. Air Force officer under the National Redemption Council (q.v.) who became the Acting Army Commander after the Supreme Military Council (q.v.) was established in 1975. He was executed by the Armed Forces Revolutionary Council (q.v.) in June 1979.

BOATEN, DAVID SAPONG. Member of parliament and educator. Born in 1943. Royal of the Dwaben stool of Asante and New Dwaben (qq.v.), Sapong Boaten was educated in his hometown of Koforidua. He also attended teacher training institutions at Somanya, Winneba, and the University of Cape Coast (UCC) (qq.v.). Sapong Boaten was president of the students' government at UCC during the 1976 academic year. He ran unsuccessfully for parliamentary position in the Third Republic. From 1981 to 1985, Boaten served first as administrative secretary to the Trades Union Congress (q.v.)

and later as principal of the Ghana Labour College in Accra. He was appointed Under-Secretary for Mobilization and Social Welfare (1986-89) in the government of the Provisional National Defense Council (PNDC) (q.v.), and in January of 1990, he assumed the position of PNDC Secretary of Mobilization and Social Welfare. That was his status when he successfully ran as National Democratic Congress (q.v.) candidate from Koforidua in the elections of 1992.

As PNDC secretary responsible for mobilization and social welfare, Sapong Boaten was actively involved in the government's program to train and redeploy workers. This was part of the Structural Adjustment Program. He was also known to have represented labor and the government at meetings of the International Labor Organization (ILO).

BOLE. 9°02'N, 2°29'W. A town on the Western road in the Northern Region some 77 miles (124 km) south of Wa and about 12 miles (19 km) east of the Black Volta (qq.v.). It was once a Dyula (q.v.) trade depot.

BOLGATANGA. 10°47'N, 0°51'W. Important crossroads, administrative center in the Upper East Region, and marketplace some 100 miles (160 km) north of Tamale (q.v.) and 26 miles (42 km) from the border of Burkina Faso just beyond Paga. The market is famous for its basket ware and straw hats. The town has also been known for its meat-packing industry since independence.

BOND OF 1844. An agreement signed by eight African leaders and the British Lieutenant Governor on 6 March 1844. It defined British legal jurisdiction in the area which came to be known as the Protectorate (q.v.). The general spirit of the "Bond" was that it defined a special relationship between the British and the local chiefs who were parties in the treaty. The British were allowed by this agreement to intervene in the administration of justice in the states when capital punishment was involved. As one writer concluded, the "Bond" allowed the British, in collaboration with local chiefs, "to mould the customs of the land to the general principles of English Law."

BONGO.   10°55'N, 0°48'W.   Town in the Upper East Region near Burkina Faso just northeast of Bolgatanga (q.v.). From April to June in 1916 there was much opposition to British-supported chiefs in the area. The disturbances were ruthlessly crushed by the English. C. H. Armitage (q.v.) was the English officer in charge of the area during the riots.

BONNAT, MARIE JOSEPH.   1844-1881.   French adventurer and trader. Bonnat was an agent for a French firm in the Volta area when captured by the Asante (q.v.) in 1869. He was held prisoner in Kumasi (q.v.) for four years. Finally released in 1874, he was back in Kumasi the following year. On 31 July 1875 Asantehene Mensa Bonsu appointed Bonnat as Asante agent to the area south of Salaga (q.v.), giving him a monopoly of the commerce in that area for six years. He organized an expedition, which traveled most of the way in canoes up the Volta. He reached Salaga (q.v.) on 30 January 1876, becoming the first European to visit that town. In 1877 he led an expedition up the Ankobra River (q.v.) to prospect for gold. This resulted in the formation of a company to exploit the gold deposits at Awudua (5°26'N, 2°05'W) and later at Tarkwa (q.v.). Bonnat died in this region on 8 July 1881.

BONO.   The Bono or Brong state. Purported to be the oldest of the Akan (q.v.) states, the Bono state was believed to have been founded in either 1297 or 1400 A.D. The state was located at the end of the Dyula (q.v.) trade route from the north, and it was also situated near the source of the Tano River. The first capital was at Tutena or Bono-Manso, in the area of modern Techiman (q.v.).   After Bono-Manso was captured and destroyed by the Asante (q.v.) in 1723, Techiman became the most important Bono town. In 1897 Bono came under the protection of the British, and in 1935 it became part of Asante until after independence when the Nkrumah administration created a separate region for Brong and Ahafo (qq.v.).

BONO-MANSO.   Traditional capital of Bono.

BONSASO. 5°17'N, 1°50'W. Located to the southwest of modern Tarkwa (q.v.) in the Western Region. On 21 January 1824, a small British force under Charles MacCarthy (Governor of Sierra Leone and the Gold Coast) clashed with Asante (qq.v.) forces. Charles MacCarthy was killed in the skirmish and his head taken to Kumasi (q.v.) as a trophy. Some sources refer to the 1824 engagement as the Battle of Nsamankow.

BONWIRE (Bonweri). 6°47'N, 1°28'W. A village in the Asante Region near Kumasi (qq.v.). The village of Bonwire is known for its Kente (q.v.) weaving industry.

BORON see BRONG

BOSMAN, WILLIAM. A Dutch factor on the Gold Coast (q.v.) from about 1689 to 1702. His *New and Accurate Description of the Coast of Guinea* is viewed by historians of the Gold Coast as one of the earliest accounts of the Guinea coast.

BOSOME AKYEM see AKYEM

BOSUMTWI, LAKE. 6°30'N, 1°25'W. A natural lake in the Asante Region some 21 miles (34 km) southeast of Kumasi and at the northeastern end of the Moinsi Hills (qq.v.). There is a dispute about whether the lake filled a volcanic crater or resulted from the impact of an ancient meteorite. The caldron covers 19 square miles (49 sq km), reaches a depth of about 230 feet (70 m), and has no outlet. It is regarded as a sacred place by the Asante.

BOTCHWEY, KWESI. Lecturer in economics at the University of Ghana (q.v.) who became Secretary of Finance and Economic Planning for the Provisional National Defense Council (PNDC) (q.v.) from 1982 through 1992. Though considered a Marxist economist, he presided over an Economic Recovery Program (ERP) (q.v.) and Structural Adjustment Programs (SAPs) which were perceived as conservative by the ultraleft (see OPPOSITION POLITICS). According to Dr. Botchwey, however, Ghana's relations with the World Bank and the IMF were determined by pragmatic considerations. Under Dr. Botchwey's stewardship as Secretary for Finance and Economic Planning, Ghana was able to sustain an economic growth averaging about 6 percent through the decade of the 1980s. This was impressive compared to the negative growth inherited by the PNDC in 1981.

BOTSIO, KOJO. Born 1916. Former college teacher and politician. Educated at Adisadel, Fourah Bay (Sierra Leone), and Oxford. Botsio was one of the founders of the Convention People's Party (CPP) (q.v.), and was its first General-Secretary. In 1950 he was held in James Fort Prison with Nkrumah (q.v.). Elected to Parliament in 1951, he became the first Minister of Education and Social Welfare in the new Cabinet. He was Foreign Minister from November 1958 to April 1959 and from March 1963 to June 1965; in 1965 he became Chairman of the State Planning Commission.

After the 1966 coup, Botsio spent some time in custody. When finally released, he joined Nkrumah in exile and was with his former leader when Nkrumah died in Romania in April 1972. It was Kojo Botsio who negotiated the arrangements with the National Redemption Council (NRC) (q.v.) to have the body of the former President returned to Ghana for burial. Botsio was once again imprisoned (1973 through January 1977) on charges of plotting the overthrow of the NRC. By 1979 he was back in politics, becoming Director of Operations and Chairman of the Campaign Committee of the People's National Party (q.v.). Kojo Botsio was a founding member of the Kwame Nkrumah Foundation, a private organization dedicated to sponsoring research activities in the name of the late President Kwame Nkrumah. He supported the National Convention Party (q.v.) in the 1992 presidential elections.

BOWDICH, THOMAS EDWARD. 1790-1824. English writer in the service of the African Company of Merchants (q.v.). He was a member of the first British group to reach Kumasi, on 19 May 1817. Bowdich spent four months in Kumasi (q.v.) negotiating a treaty (signed 7 September 1817). Bowdich's account of Kumasi was published as *Mission from Cape Coast to Ashantee* (1819). After spending some time in Paris and Lisbon, Bowdich returned to Africa in 1823 and died at Bathurst, Gambia, the following year.

BOWLI. A Volta-Central Togo group who live east of Lake Volta in the Volta Region (qq.v.). Their language is called Bowiri.

BRAIMAH, J. A. Civil servant, scholar, politician, and traditional ruler. A member of the Gonja (q.v.) ruling dynasty, he was appointed Kabachewura in 1942 and Yagbouwura (Paramount Chief of the Gonja traditional area) between 1982 and January 1987. J. A. Braimah was Vice-Chairman of the Ghana National House of Chiefs when he died at the age of 71 in January 1987.

Between 1934 and 1950, he served as clerk of the Gonja Native Authority. Among his various responsibilities, J. A. Braimah was appointed to the Gold Coast Legislative Council in 1950. He also served as Minister of Communications and Works between 1951 and 1953, but later broke with the CPP to become a founding member of the Northern People's Party (qq.v.) in 1954. As a member of Parliament, Braimah was a vocal opposition until the 1966 coup. Under the NLC he was a member of the Political Committee and the Constitutional Commission.

Joseph Adam Braimah was also a known historian of Gonja. *The Two Isanwurfos* (1967) and *The Ashanti and the Gonja at War* (1970) were both written by him.

BRANDENBURG. The Brandenburg-Prussian Company that used German soldiers but depended in most cases on the Dutch to run their posts on the coast of the Gold Coast (q.v.). By the end of the seventeenth century, they held posts at Pokoso, Takrama, and Akwida (qq.v.). Gross Friedrichsburg (Princestown) (qq.v.), their largest post, was started in about 1683. These posts were at the southern end of the western trade route to the Asante and Aowin (qq.v.) goldfields. Arrangements which began in 1716 on the transfer of the Brandenburg Company to the Dutch were concluded in 1720.

BREMEN MISSIONARY SOCIETY. A North German missionary society which began educational work on the Gold Coast (q.v.) in 1847. In 1881 it had four schools in the Volta (q.v.) area where most of its activities were concentrated. In June 1916 the Bremen missionaries were deported, and their schools were taken over by the British.

BRETUO see BERETUO

BREW, JAMES HUTTON (Prince Brew of Dunkwa). 1844-1915. Attorney, journalist, businessman, nationalist. He was the son of Samuel Collins Brew (ca. 1810-1881), who was a member of the Legislative Council, 1864-1866. In 1871 James Hutton Brew was active in the Fante (q.v.) Confederacy movement and is said to have been the author of the constitution of the confederation. He founded the *Gold Coast Times* at Cape Coast (q.v.) in 1874. He was known to have conducted a campaign to get elected representation for Africans in the Legislative Council. In November 1885 he organized another paper, the *Western Echo*. He suggested mass meetings of Africans and deputations to England as methods by which Africans could make their opinions known to the authorities in the metropolis. In 1889 he went to London as a self-appointed embassy for African interests, and in 1895 he tried to get English authorities to recognize him as an agent for the Asante (q.v.).

BREW, OSBORNE HENRY KWESI. Born 1928. Poet and writer of note. Born at Cape Coast and educated at schools in Cape Coast, Kumasi, Tamale, and Accra (qq.v.), he became one of the early graduates of the new college at Legon. He entered the Administrative Service of the Gold Coast in 1953 and held posts as Assistant District Commissioner and District Commissioner under the British. After independence he joined the Diplomatic Service of Ghana.

BREW, RICHARD. Died 1776. An Irishman who spent thirty years on the Gold Coast in the service of the Company of Merchants Trading to Africa (qq.v.). He was also a private trader at

Anomabo (q.v.). His wife was a Fante (q.v.), and the famous Brew family of the Gold Coast descended from this couple.

BRISCOE AFFAIR. A 1975 corruption affair which resulted in the dismissal of Generals Lawrence Okai (Chief of Defense Staff) and Charles Beausoleil (Air Force Commander). R. T. Briscoe was a subsidiary of a Danish East Asiatic Company with a long period of operations in Ghana. The case involving Briscoe also led to the loss of company assets in Ghana.

BRONG (Abron, Boron, Borong, Bron, Bono). See BONO.

BRONG-AHAFO REGION. The area west of Asante and south of the Northern Region (qq.v.). It was created in 1958.

BRONG CONFEDERATION. A defensive alliance formed by the Dente Bosomfo of Krakye against the Asante (qq.v.) in the late nineteenth century. The alliance lasted from about 1875 to 1895, by which time the British had established their control over much of the area and had limited the power of the Asante to be a threat to the Brong.

BROWN, EMMANUEL JOSEPH PETER. 1875-1929. Lawyer and author. After teaching for some years in Methodist schools, he worked in the offices of John Mensah Sarbah, and then went to England to study law. In the years just before World War I he was a leader of the Aborigines' Rights Protection Society (q.v.). He was a member of the Legislative Council from 1916 to 1927. His two-volume *Gold Coast and Ashanti Reader* (1929) was a popular collection of folklore and local history.

BROWN, JOSEPH PETER. 1843-1932. Fante (q.v.) teacher and political leader. He was one of the founders of the Aborigines' Rights Protection Society (q.v.), and he served on the Legislative Council from 1904 to 1909. In the 1920s he was active in the National Congress of British West Africa (q.v.).

BUEM. One of the Volta-Central Togo groups of the Volta Region (q.v.).

BUI. 8°16'N, 2°16'W. A small village on the Black Volta (q.v.) near rapids which offered possibilities for hydroelectric development. The project was discussed prior to independence. In 1982 the Provisional National Defense Council (q.v.) announced that Russia would help with the project.

BUILSA (Bulse, Builse, Kangyaga, Kanjaga). One of the Mole-Dagbani groups in the Upper West Region between the Sisala (q.v.) River and the Great Northern Highway. Their language is called Buli (Bulea).

BUIPE (Gbuipe, Ghofe, Ghofon, Goaffi). 8°47'N, 1°32'W. A village in the Northern Region some 60 miles (96 km) southwest of Tamale and just 8 miles (13 km) northwest of a bridge across the Black Volta (qq.v.). This is one of the most important prehistoric sites in Ghana. There is evidence of iron technology in the area by the eighth century of our era. The town was a commercial center from very early times. The tomb of Sumaila Ndewura Jakpa, great ruler of Gonja, is located in Buipe (qq.v.), and the ruler, the Buipewura, is the traditional guardian of the tomb of Jakpa. Buipe lost importance after the chief trade center of Gonja moved to Salaga (qq.v.).

BUKARI-ATIM, CHRIS. Militant student leader who was one of the founders of the June 4th Movement and one of the most aggressive left-wing supporters of Jerry John Rawlings (qq.v.). He was one of the seven members of the initial Provisional National Defense Council (PNDC) (q.v.) in 1982 but was later dropped from the PNDC.

BURNS, ALAN CUTHBERT MAXWELL. 1887-1980. Governor of the Gold Coast, 1941-1947. Alan Burns's father was a colonial civil servant in the West Indies, and the son followed in his father's footsteps, assigned to the West Indies from 1905 to 1912. He then went to Nigeria (1912-1924), returned to the West Indies (1924-1928), was back in Nigeria (1928-1934), and was Governor of British Honduras from 1935 to 1940. He served as Governor of the Gold Coast during the difficult years of World War II (qq.v.). During this time, in 1942, he also filled in as Acting Governor of Nigeria. From 1947 to 1956 he was British Representative on the UN Trusteeship Council. He retired in 1956. He published an autobiography, *Colonial Civil Servant*, in 1950. The most memorable accomplishment of his term as Governor of the Gold Coast was the Burns Constitution of 1946. This provided for an African majority of 18 out of 31 on the Legislative Council and united the Colony and Asante (qq.v.).

BUSIA, KOFI ABREFA. 1913-1978. Teacher, author, politician, Prime Minister. Busia was a member of the royal family of Wenchi, in the Brong-Ahafo Region (qq.v.). He was educated at the Methodist schools in Kumasi, Mfantsipim, and Wesley College, Kumasi. In 1936 he was an instructor at Achimota (q.v.). From there he went to London and Oxford, where he got a doctorate in social anthropology. He then became an officer in the Gold Coast administration. In 1949 he joined the faculty of the new University College at Legon, where he remained until 1956. He authored *The Position of the Chief in the Modern Political System of Ashanti* and *Report on a Social Survey of Sekondi-Takoradi.*

Elected to the Legislative Assembly in 1951, Busia assumed his parliamentary duties while still teaching sociology at Legon. By 1957 he was the leader in organizing the United Party in opposition to Nkrumah's Convention People's Party (CPP) (q.v.). In June 1959 Busia was forced into exile. For the next several years he lived and worked in Holland, Mexico, the United States, and England. During this exile he produced several more books. At the time of the 1966 coup he was at Oxford.

Busia made a triumphant return to Accra shortly after the fall of Nkrumah. He held several important posts under the National Liberation Council (q.v.) government. He was the most influential member of the Constituent Assembly which drew up the constitution for the Second Republic. And while he was working on the new constitution, he founded with others the Progress Party, which won the elections of August 1969, gaining 105 seats to 35 for the National Alliance of

Liberals (qq.v.) and other parties. Busia became the Prime Minister of the Second Republic on 3 September 1969. Busia's administration faced intractable problems unleashed after the many years of one-party politics under the CPP. His suggestions of austerity won him no friends. Early in 1972, while Busia was in England for medical treatment, the army staged another coup. The ousted Prime Minister again found himself in exile. He settled down once more to an academic life at Oxford. He died on 28 August 1978 in exile. His body was returned to Ghana for a state funeral.

BUTRI (Butre). 4°49'N, 1°55'W. A small coastal village in the Ahanta country of the Western Region just east of Dixcove (qq.v.) and at the mouth of Butri Creek. The Swedes had a post here in the middle of the seventeenth century, but the Dutch forced them out and in 1656 began a fort on top of the high hill overlooking the small bay. The fort was called Batensteyn or Batenstein. Over the years the Dutch tried to develop the economy of the area by experimenting with cotton and sugarcane. They set up a rum factory there at the start of the eighteenth century. The fort was ceded to the British in 1872. Today the fortifications are in ruins.

- C -

CABOCEER (Cabocier, Cabeceiro, Cabaça). Of Portuguese origin, meaning "head." The term was adopted by Europeans on the Gold Coast (q.v.) during the eighteenth and nineteenth centuries to address traditional African chiefs and ranked local headmen.

CADBURY BROTHERS. Famous British chocolate business which was founded by George Cadbury (1839-1922). In 1918 it joined with J. S. Fry and Son to become the largest British chocolate company. By 1914 it had purchased most of the cocoa (q.v.) production of the Gold Coast (q.v.).

CAPE COAST (Cabo Corso, Cap Corso, Oguaa, Ogua). 5°06'N, 1°15'W. Fante fishing center which was subject to the Efutu (qq.v.) before the eighteenth century. The Portuguese first traded here in the late fifteenth century. The Portuguese name of the town, Cabo Corso ("Short Coast") was later corrupted by the English as Cape Coast. The Portuguese, English, and Swedes all vied for the trade of the town during the first half of the seventeenth century. Here in 1655, the Swedes constructed a castle which they called Carlsborg (Carolusburg). This structure later changed hands several times. The British took possession of the fortress in about 1664 and it remained their headquarters on the Gold Coast until 1877 when Christiansborg (q.v.) became preferred.

Today Cape Coast is an important commercial, educational, and government center. Some of the best-known secondary schools of Ghana and the University of Cape Coast (q.v.) are located here. Situated just about 8 miles (13 km) east of Elmina (q.v.) (a Portuguese, Dutch, and later a British castle), the area holds great attraction for tourists.

CAPE SAINT PAUL. 5°49'N, 0°57'E. Promontory between Keta and Anloga (qq.v.), on the spit that separates the Keta Lagoon from the Gulf of Guinea.

CAPE THREE POINTS. 4°45'N, 2°06'W. The southernmost point in Ghana, it is located on the coast of the Western Region between Axim and Dixcove (qq.v.). Cape Three Points is 327 miles (526 km) north of the equator.

CARDINALL, ALLAN. 1887-1956. British colonial officer. Cardinall joined the Gold Coast Service in 1914 and spent most of his tour in the Gold Coast in the north, especially at Yendi (qq.v.). He wrote many articles and several books about the Gold Coast. *Natives of the Northern Territories of the Gold Coast* (1920), *A Gold Coast Library* (1924), *In Ashanti and Beyond* (1927), *Tales Told in Togoland* (1931), and *A Bibliography of the Gold Coast* (1932) are his major Contributions. Allan Wolsey Cardinall was Commissioner to the Cayman Islands from 1934 and Governor of the Falkland Islands, 1941-1946.

CASELY-HAYFORD, ARCHIE. Fante from a Cape Coast family, but born at Axim, in the Western Region (qq.v.). He was educated at Mfantsipim, London, and Cambridge, receiving his law degree in London. He was a member of the Legislative Assembly, 1954-1956, and the National Assembly, 1956-1966. During the early days of the Convention People's Party (CPP) (q.v.) he gained the title "Defender of the Verandah Boys" for his defense of Nkrumah (qq.v.) and other CPP members before the Gold Coast courts. Under Nkrumah he served as Minister of Agriculture and Natural Resources, Minister of Communications, and Minister of Interior.

CASELY-HAYFORD, JOSEPH EPHRAIM (Ekra Agyiman). 1866-1930. Author, lawyer, and politician. A Fante, born at Cape Coast (qq.v.) and educated at Fourah Bay College in Sierra Leone and Cambridge. He became a lawyer in 1896. He was a member of the Legislative Council from 1916 to 1926 and a municipal member of the Council from Sekondi from 1927 to 1930. He was a member of the Aborigines' Rights Protection Society and one of the founders of the National Congress of British West Africa (qq.v.). He was the author of *Ethiopia Unbound* (1911) and *Gold Coast Native Institutions* (1903).

CEDI. The official currency of Ghana. A cedi is divided into one hundred pesewas. On 1 January 1980 the official exchange rate was 2.75 cedi for $1 US. The unofficial rate at that time was 14 cedi to the dollar on the black market. The value of the cedi has over the years fluctuated, and has often been determined by what critics saw as external pressures from such institutions as the World Bank and the International Monetary Fund. To stabilize the cedi and also to better regulate supply and demand of the cedi in relation to other currencies, a currency auction market was organized by the Bank of Ghana on 19 September 1986. In 1991 the average rate at which the cedi exchanged to the US dollar was about 350 cedis to $1 US and rising.

CENTRAL TOGO TRIBES. Ethnic groups of the Volta Region between Lake Volta (qq.v.) and the Togo border. The Avatime (q.v.), Nyangbo, Tafi (q.v.), Logba, Likpe, Lolobi, Santrokofi, Akpafu, Bowli (q.v.), Buem, Akposo, Ntrubu, and Adele are the people so classified. They are remnants of the original inhabitants of the area and were there long before the Ewe (q.v.) moved into the region.

CHAKOSSI see CHOKOSI

CHEREPONG see KYEREPON

CHOKOSI (Chakossi, Kyokosi, Tschokossi). An Akan (q.v.) group. These people live in the north, along the Togo border. They are partly Islamized. The French call them Tyokossi. They call themselves the Anufo. Their chief town is Sansanne-Mango in Togo. Many of them were under German rule from 1899 to 1914.

CHRISTALLER, JOHANN GOTTLIEB. 1827-1895. Basel (q.v.) missionary. He came to the Gold Coast in 1853 and was first stationed at Akuropon (qq.v.) for five years. From 1862 to 1865 he was at Aburi, and from 1865 to 1867 he lived at Kibi (qq.v.). From 1867 to 1868 he was back at his first mission at Akuropon. He is best known for his translations of biblical and devotional materials into Akuapem Akan (Twi) (qq.v.) and for an Akan grammar and dictionary.

CHRISTIANSBORG CASTLE (Osu). One of the most famous European structures on the Gold Coast (q.v.). The Swedes first built a lodge at Osu, next to Accra (qq.v.), in 1652. The Danes then took the site. There were brief Dutch, Portuguese (San Francisco Xavier), and Akwamu interludes, with the Danes starting the present structure about 1661. Over the years it has been changed and enlarged many times. The British purchased it in 1850, and it served as the residence of

British governors from 1877 to 1957. Since independence it has been generally known as Government House.

CHU MIENTWI (Twum Antwi). Died ca. 1599. Ruler of Kwaman in Asante and an earlier Oyoko (qq.v.) chief whose dynasty ruled Asante.

CITIZENS' VETTING COMMITTEE (CVC)   A committee established by the Provisional National Defence Council (PNDC) (q.v.) government in 1982 to scrutinize large bank accounts in order to spot illegal incomes. By PNDC Law 80 enacted in December of 1983, the CVC was restructured into the Office of Revenue Commissioners (ORC). The new office was charged with the responsibility of monitoring the operations of all government revenue agencies. The ORC was also to investigate and try persons whose lifestyles and expenditures substantially exceeded their known or declared incomes.

CLARIDGE, WILLIAM WALTON. 1874-1923. Author of one of the better known histories of the Gold Coast (q.v.), *A History of the Gold Coast and Ashanti from Ancient Times to the Commencement of the Twentieth Century* (2 vols., 1915). Claridge was appointed a medical officer to the Gold Coast in 1903. He was senior medical officer in the invasion of Togoland in 1914. He retired in 1919 and died in 1923.

CLIFFORD, HUGH CHARLES. 1866-1941. Colonial officer. Son of a major-general, Clifford began his colonial service in the Malay States. By 1900 he reached appointment as Governor of North Borneo and Labuan. From there he went to the West Indies, 1903-1906, and Ceylon, 1907-1912. He became Governor of the Gold Coast in 1912 and held that position until after the end of World War I (qq.v.). In 1920 he published a history, *The Gold Coast Regiment in the East African Campaign*. While he was Governor, the Legislative Council was enlarged to 21 members, six of whom would be Africans.

From the Gold Coast Clifford went to Nigeria as Governor (1919-1925) and Ceylon as Governor (1925-1927); his last appointment was as Governor of the Straits Settlements and High Commissioner of the Malay States (1927-1929).

COBRE RIVER see ANKOBRA

COCOA. Ghana's most famous export crop. Until recent years, Ghana was the world's major producer of cocoa. Cocoa is native to Central America, and it was introduced to Africa in the 1820s. It was first exported from the Gold Coast (q.v.) in the 1890s. Cocoa was first introduced into the country by the Basel (q.v.) missionaries. However, it was Tetteh Quashie (q.v.) of Accra who has been accredited with the introduction of the crop to Ghana. Returning with a few cocoa plants and pods from Fernanda Po in 1878, Tetteh Quashie was said to have made a small but successful experimental farm from which he sold the yield to Akuapim (q.v.) farmers from 1883 onwards. According to one scholar, it was Sir William Branford Griffith (q.v.), Governor of the Gold Coast (1880-1896), whose efforts caused the rapid development of the cocoa-growing industry in the country. The Governor was said to have imported additional cocoa pods from Sao Tome in 1886 and established a nursery in Aburi (q.v.) from which seedlings were supplied to farmers. Cocoa continues to be a leading cash crop in Ghana. A major crop is harvested between October and March, and a minor crop is produced between May and August. Pods are formed on the tree. They contain beans, which are harvested, fermented and dried. The trees are subject to a number of diseases, especially swollen shoot (a virus carried by mealy bugs), a fungus called black pod, and capsid insects. See also AGRICULTURE.

COCOA MARKETING BOARD (CMB). A board established in 1947 to buy and export all Gold Coast cocoa (qq.v.). Its chief objective was to protect African producers from unfair competition and fluctuating international prices. Before the establishment of the Cocoa Marketing Board, foreign merchants such as Messrs F. & A. Swanzy Ltd. (q.v.), Miller Brothers & Co., and the African Association had monopolized the marketing of cocoa and therefore the profit. By creating the marketing board, the government had hoped to maintain a fund for research on cocoa, but also to use the profit, which had hitherto gone to private merchants, for national development. After 1951, therefore, the government absorbed more and more of the earnings of the CMB for general development plans. This created resentment against the government among the cocoa growers, and smuggling of cocoa into Togo and the Ivory Coast, where prices were higher, became a problem. See also COCOA.

COCONUT. The coconut is common along the coast of the Central and Volta regions. Compared to the cocoa (q.v.) industry, copra production in Ghana is in its developmental stage.

COLONY. In 1874 the British organized the coastal areas under their protection into the "Gold Coast Colony." Ashanti (Asante) and the Northern Territories (qq.v.) were seen as separate administrative units. After these two provinces were brought under British rule in about 1900, the "Colony of the Gold Coast" developed. British rule over the colony lasted until 1957.

COMMITTEE FOR THE DEFENSE OF THE REVOLUTION (CDR) see NATIONAL DEFENSE COMMITTEE

COMMITTEE ON YOUTH ORGANIZATION (CYO). Group organized in Accra in August 1948 which favored a break from the United Gold Coast Convention (q.v.). It advocated "Self-Government Now." K. A. Gbedemah, Kojo Botsio, and Krobo Edusei (qq.v.) were the leaders of this movement. It was the progenitor of the Convention People's Party (q.v.).

COMPANY OF LONDON MERCHANTS. Company organized during the Commonwealth period to trade with the Gold Coast (q.v.), 1651-1658.

COMPANY OF MERCHANTS TRADING TO AFRICA. The successor to the Royal Africa Company (q.v.). This company was a device for maintaining the British posts on the West

African coast from 1751 to 1821. Any English merchant could belong for a small fee.

COMPANY OF MERCHANTS TRADING TO GUINEA. A chartered company operating on the coasts of West Africa, 1632-1651.

COMPANY OF ROYAL ADVENTURERS. A British company chartered by Charles II which managed trade on the Gold Coast (q.v.) from 1663 to 1672.

COMPULSORY LABOUR ORDINANCE OF 1895. An ordinance which required chiefs to provide workers for the government under certain circumstances. It was initially designed to obtain carriers for the Asante (q.v.) campaign, but maintenance of roads and telegraph lines soon became the chief form of public labor demanded by the British.

CONNY, JOHN see KONNY, JOHN

CONSTITUTION OF 1850. In 1850 the Gold Coast Colony (qq.v.) was administered by a Governor who was assisted by an Executive and a Legislative Council. The Executive Council was made up of senior European officials. The Legislative Council was composed of the Executive Council plus unofficial members. The members of both councils were nominated by the Governor.

CONSTITUTION OF 1916. The Clifford Constitution. Hugh Clifford (q.v.) was British Governor from 1912 to 1919. Under Clifford the government of the Gold Coast (q.v.) was reorganized. The Executive Council was made up of the Governor, the Colonial Secretary, the Attorney-General, the Treasurer, the principal medical officer, and the Secretary of Native Affairs. The Legislative Council was composed of the Executive Council plus the Controller of Customs, Director of Public Works, General Manager of Railroads, Commissioners of the Eastern and Western Provinces, and nine unofficial members appointed by the Crown on nomination by the Governor. Of these nine, three were Europeans, three paramount chiefs, and three other Africans.

CONSTITUTION OF 1925. This is sometimes called the Guggisberg Constitution, after Frederick Gordon Guggisberg (q.v.), Governor from 1919 to 1927. The Legislative Council was increased to 15 official and 14 unofficial members. Provincial Councils (q.v.) of paramount chiefs were established for the Western, Central, and Eastern provinces. These councils elected six unofficial members to the Legislative Council. The new Legislative Council touched off the first real political activity in the Gold Coast, because Accra, Cape Coast, and Sekondi (qq.v.) could each elect one unofficial member to the Council. The new enlarged Council met for the first time in August 1926.

CONSTITUTION OF 1946. This is sometimes called the Burns Constitution for Alan Burns (q.v.), Governor, 1941-1947. This charter abolished the Central Province and provided for representation of Asante (q.v.) in the Legislative Council for the first time. The Legislative Council now had six ex-officio, six nominated, and 18 elected members. For the first time there was provision for a clear African majority.

CONSTITUTION OF 1951. This charter is sometimes called the Arden-Clarke Constitution for Governor Charles Arden-Clarke (q.v.), 1949-1957. The Constitution was based on recommendations of a committee headed by J. H. Coussey. There was a Legislative Assembly of 84 members. Thirty-three members were elected in rural districts of the Colony and Asante (qq.v.) by electoral colleges, 37 were elected by Territorial Councils of chiefs, five were elected from the towns of Accra, Cape Coast, Sekondi-Takoradi, and Kumasi (qq.v.), three represented the Chamber of Commerce, three the Chamber of Mines, and three were nominated by the Governor. The Executive Council had a majority of African ministers, responsible to the Governor and to the Assembly. The Northern Territories (q.v.) were now included in the Assembly. In the election, the Convention People's Party (q.v.), in spite of being opposed to the Constitution, won a two-thirds majority. Nkrumah (q.v.) became leader of government business and immediately set out to change the Constitution of 1951.

CONSTITUTION OF 1954. This is the first Nkrumah (q.v.) Constitution. This Constitution ended the complicated electoral procedures of the 1951 charter. All 104 members of the Legislative Assembly were popularly elected. The new Executive Council or Cabinet would be made up of eight members of the Assembly, appointed by the Governor on the advice of the Prime Minister. The Governor retained control of defense and external affairs and retained reserve powers.

CONSTITUTION OF 1957. The second Nkrumah (q.v.) Constitution. This was the independence Constitution of Ghana. The Queen would be Head of State, represented by a Governor-General. The Cabinet of Ministers would be members of the National Assembly, responsible to the National Assembly. A Prime Minister was selected by the National Assembly, and he was Head of the government. A vote of no confidence in the Prime Minister would force a new general election. The National Assembly was made up of 104 members, elected for five-year terms. The country was divided into five regions: Eastern, Western, Trans-Volta-Togoland, Ashanti, and Northern. Each region elected its own Regional Assembly for a term of three years.

CONSTITUTION OF 1960. The third Nkrumah (q.v.) Constitution. It established the First Republic. This Constitution was approved by a plebiscite on 19, 23, and 27 April 1960. The post of Governor-General was abolished, and the Prime Minister became the President. Article 55 gave the President power to rule by decree, and Article 44 allowed the President to appoint and dismiss the Chief Justice.

CONSTITUTION OF 1969. The Constitution of the Second Republic. This Constitution provided for a liberal parliamentary democracy. A President would be ceremonial Head of State. He was selected by an electoral college of members of Parliament plus members of regional assemblies. A Council of State would assist the President in his duties. A Prime Minister was Head of Government and appointed his own Cabinet. The Cabinet was required to resign if Parliament passed a vote of no confidence. The Constitution set up a

National House of Chiefs, to meet in Kumasi (q.v.), and a House of Chiefs for each region of the country. This Constitution was promulgated on 22 August 1969, and the Second Republic took office on 1 October 1969.

CONSTITUTION OF 1979. The Constitution of the Third Republic. This charter provided for a President and Vice-President. They could serve not more than two four-year terms. They could be removed from office by a two-thirds vote of Parliament. Cabinet ministers were appointed by the President, but had to be confirmed by Parliament. Ministers could not sit in Parliament. Legislative power was vested in a unicameral Parliament of no fewer than 140 members elected for a normal term of five years. Parliament selected its own Speaker. A one-party state was unconstitutional. This charter went into force 24 September 1979.

CONSTITUTION OF 1992 see CONSULTATIVE ASSEMBLY

CONSTITUTION OF THE FANTE CONFEDERATION, 1871. An agreement reached by 31 leaders of the Fante at Mankesim (qq.v.), signed on 18 November 1871. It provided for an Executive Council of five elected officials, a Representative Assembly of Kings and principal Chiefs, and a King-President, elected by the kings in the National Assembly each year. The Confederation was a military alliance, but would also concern itself with internal improvements. A poll tax and import and export duties would be levied to pay expenses. The British refused to recognize the Fante Confederation and had many of its leaders arrested.

CONSULTATIVE ASSEMBLY. A Committee of Experts created by the Provisional National Defense Council (PNDC) (q.v.) on 25 March 1991 to write a draft constitution for Ghana's Fourth Republic presented its 252-page report to the government on 31 July 1991. The PNDC submitted the draft constitution to a 260-member Consultative Assembly for discussions. The Assembly, which was inaugurated on 26 August 1991 and included representatives from district, municipal and metropolitan assemblies and about 62 identifiable groups in the nation, submitted its final version of the 1992 Constitution to the PNDC on 31 March 1992.

The Consultative Assembly, in its deliberations, rejected the concept of premiership as defined by the Committee of Experts. Instead, it favored the position of Vice-President similar to the one in the 1979 Constitution. Also dismissed was the proposal that the President of the Fourth Republic be allowed to serve only one five-year term. Instead, the Consultative Assembly proposed two four-year terms. It also proposed the creation of a Judicial Committee of the Council of State. The most controversial issues of the document were Sections 33, 34, and 36 of the Transitional Provisions of the draft constitution which granted indemnity to members of the PNDC administration. The controversy notwithstanding, the draft document was approved as the Constitution of the Fourth Republic on 28 April 1992 in a national referendum.

CONVENTION PEOPLE'S PARTY (CPP). This was the political party of Kwame Nkrumah (q.v.). It was created in June 1949 in a break from the United Gold Coast Convention (q.v.). It demanded "Self-Government Now." It won the elections of February 1951 and remained in power until 1966, when it was disbanded after Nkrumah was deposed. See also NKRUMAH, KWAME.

COUSSEY COMMITTEE, 1949. An all-African committee, chaired by Sir Henley Coussey, (q.v.) which was appointed to make recommendations for a new Constitution. The committee made its report in October 1949, and the report was the basis for the 1951 Constitution (q.v.).

COUSSEY, J. HENLEY. 1895-1958. Lawyer. Educated in England, he became one of the foremost solicitors on the Gold Coast (q.v.). During the 1920s, he was active in the National Congress of British West Africa (q.v.). He became a judge on the High Court in 1943. He was appointed Chairman of a committee to make recommendations on a new form of government for the British Gold Coast in 1949. The report of the Coussey Committee was approved by the Legislative

Council in December 1949, touching off Nkrumah's Positive Action (qq.v.) Campaign for immediate self-government.

CRABBE, HUGH HORATIO COFIE. A Ga leader who joined the CPP as a lieutenant of Tawia Adamafio (qq.v.). Crabbe served as Executive Secretary of the CPP in 1961-1962, but was arrested on 29 August 1962 and charged with complicity in the Kulungugu bombing. He was tried in 1963 and was acquitted, but he was held in prison until after the 1966 coup.

CRACKEY see KRAKYE

CREASY, GERALD HALLEN. Born 1897. Governor. Educated at Rugby and King's College, Cambridge, he served in World War I, and joined the colonial service in 1920. By 1945 he was Chief Secretary of the West African Council, a post he held until he became Governor of the Gold Coast (q.v.). He was Governor of the Gold Coast, 1948-1949, and of Malta, 1949-1954, when he retired. It was Creasy who sent the "Big Six" leaders of the UGCC--J. B. Danquah, Kwame Nkrumah, William Ofori Atta, Akufo Addo, Ako Adjei, and E. Obetsebi Lamptey (qq.v.)--into detention in the Northern Territories after the 1948 riots.

CREPPEE see KREPI

CREVECOEUR, FORT. Fort built at Little Accra by the Dutch between 1642 and 1652. It was almost destroyed by an earthquake in 1862. The British gained the place in 1868, rebuilt it, and named it Fort Ussher (q.v.). It is today a prison.

CROWN LAND BILL OF 1894. A proposal to vest all waste and forest lands and minerals in the Queen. All concessions were to be made by the Crown alone. The British meant the legislation to protect Africans against European exploitation, but Africans thought it was an attempt to take their land. The bill was withdrawn by Governor William Maxwell, and a new lands bill was introduced on 10 March 1897, which was designed to give the Crown control but not ownership. This did not calm African fears, and the outcome was the organization of the Gold Coast Aborigines' Rights Protection Society (q.v.). The British retreated again, substituting the Concessions Ordinance of 1900. This provided that all concessions would be reviewed by the Supreme Court of the Colony (q.v.), which could modify concessions it found to be unreasonable. It also limited the size of concessions, and protected existing rights of Africans.

CRUICKSHANK, BRODIE. Died 1854. Scottish merchant and magistrate. He came to the Gold Coast in 1834 and in a short time rose to a position of great prominence. He was a member of the Legislative Council and Collector-General of the poll tax in 1853, and served briefly as acting Lieutenant-Governor, 1853-1854. He was the author of *Eighteen Years on the Gold Coast*, published in 1853.

- D -

DABOYA (Wasape, Wasipe). 9°32'N, 1°23'W. Village on the White Volta in the Northern Region some 40 miles (64 km) northwest of Tamale (qq.v.). It is the chief town of the Wasipe Division of Gonja (qq.v.). The ruler is called the Wasipewura. Daboya is 70 miles (112 km) northeast of Nyanga, the former capital of Gonja. From ancient times the area about Daboya has been known as a source of rock salt, obtained by boiling soil and extracting salt crystals. The village is the limit of normal canoe traffic on the White Volta and was the terminal port for trade on that river until 1908, when Tamale Port at Yapei (qq.v.) was built.

There is archaeological evidence of human habitation around Daboya since the first century of our era. The people belong to the Tampolensi-Grusi (q.v.) group. They were once under the Dagomba (q.v.), but about 1620 they were conquered by Gonja. During this period the people came under Islamic influences, and a famous old Sudanic mosque is the most interesting edifice in the village today. Most of the village was destroyed by Babatu (q.v.) in 1890, but it was soon rebuilt.

Ferguson persuaded the Wasipewura to sign a treaty of friendship with the British on 8 July 1892.

DaCOSTA, KANKAM. Student leader and politician. Kankam DaCosta was President of the University of Cape Coast (q.v.) students' government (1974-75). Shortly after his graduation in 1976, DaCosta became active in his support of the Union Government concept propagated by the Supreme Military Council (qq.v.). In 1977, DaCosta was appointed Central Regional Coordinator for Union Government activities. During the Third Republic, the government of the People's National Party (q.v.) appointed DaCosta Deputy Minister for Defense, a position he held till the overthrow of that government in 1981. Other than being arrested and kept in detention for a long period following the coup of 1981, very little was heard of DaCosta until 1992 when his name was floated as one of the many possible Vice-Presidential candidates in Dr. Limann's People's National Convention (qq.v.).

DAGBANE. Language of the Dagomba (q.v.).

DAGOMBA (Dagbon). A Mole-Dagbani kingdom in the Northern Region (qq.v.). The Mamprusi are to the north, and the Nanumba (qq.v.) to the south. They call themselves the Dagbamba, their language Dagbane, and their country Dagbong. Tumu is western Dagomba, and Naja is eastern Dagomba. Tradition connects the royal family with the rulers of the Mossi (q.v.), Mamprusi, and Nanumba. Yendi Dabari, on the White Volta, was the original town of the Ya Na (qq.v.), the ruler of Dagomba, but it was destroyed by the Gonja (q.v.) about 1713. Yendi is now the home of the Ya Na, but the largest and most important city in Dagomba today is Tamale (q.v.).

Sitobu, son of Gbewa of Pusiga (qq.v.), is the traditional founder of the Dagomba dynasty. His son, Nyagse (q.v.), founded Yendi Dabari. These two conquered the lands from the White Volta to the Oti from people ruled by earth priests (sing. tindana, pl. tindamba) during the latter part of the fifteenth and early part of the sixteenth centuries. In the early seventeenth century the Gonja took part of Dagomba's western lands, and they administered a severe defeat to Na Dariziegu at Yapei (qq.v.) on the White Volta. Yendi Dabari fell to Gonja in these campaigns, and the Dagomba capital had to be moved eastward to Yendi, a former Konkomba town. The wars with Gonja lasted a century, and hardly had these conflicts subsided before Asante (q.v.) raids bagan. From the 1740s to 1874 the Asante dominated Dagomba, and collected tribute there. By 1874 Dagomba was exhausted, split by factional disputes. The Ya Na Abudulai called in the mercenaries, the Zabrama (q.v.), to try to restore order. And at this point incursions by the British, Germans, and French began. On 4 December 1899 the Germans defeated a Dagomba army at Adibo (q.v.). The following day they destroyed Yendi. By an Anglo-German treaty 14 November 1899 Dagomba was partitioned with Yendi, with most of the eastern part of Dagomba going to the Germans and the western part becoming part of the British Northern Territories (q.v.). Then, in 1914, at the start of World War I, England gathered all Dagomba under its rule.

Dagomba is a patrilineal society. The sub-chiefs are appointed by the Ya Na. The Ya Na in turn is selected from one of the chiefs of either Karaga, Savelugu (q.v.), or Mion. These three towns are called the "gate skins."

DAILY GRAPHIC. Accra newspaper started in 1950 as a subsidiary of the London *Daily Mirror* group of papers. It was eventually taken over by the government of Ghana. The *Sunday Mirror* was the Sunday edition.

DAILY MAIL. The Convention People's Party newspaper at Cape Coast (qq.v.). It was founded by Kwame Nkrumah in December 1949, and its first editor was Kofi Baako (qq.v.).

DAKA RIVER. A stream which rises southeast of Karaga and flows down across Dagomba, passing just west of Yendi (qq.v.), and then being joined by its major tributaries, the Jeba, Kumou (Kumbo), Kbongo, Lumpe. It flows into Lake Volta (q.v.). By an Anglo-German agreement in November 1899, the point at which the Daka flowed into the Volta was the start of a line drawn north and dividing Dagomba into the British and German sections of Dagomba.

DAMBA FESTIVAL. A festival at Wa (q.v.) which commemorates the birth of the Prophet Muhammad.

DAMONGO. 9°05'N, 1°49'W. Town in the Northern Region some 70 miles (112 km) southwest of Tamale (q.v.). The Gonja (q.v.) capital was moved here from Nyanga in 1942. The paramount chief of Gonja is the Yagbumwura.

DAMPONG (Dampon). 6°33'N, 1°03'W. Town in the Asante Region near the upper course of the Pra which was once the chief village of the Akyem Kotoku (qq.v.). About 1824, they moved to Gyadam (Jedem), near Oda (qq.v.).

DANQUAH, JOSEPH KWAME KYERETWI BOAKYE. 1895-1965. Lawyer and nationalist. Danquah was born in Bepong, Kwahu. He was half-brother of Nana Ofori-Atta, Paramount Chief of Akyem Abuakwa (qq.v.). He was educated in Basel Mission (q.v.) schools and at the University of London, and read law at the Inner Temple. While in London, he published *The Akim Abuakwa Handbook, Akan Laws and Customs and the Akim Abuakwa Constitution*, and *Cases in Akan Law* (all in 1928).

Returning home to the Gold Coast, in 1931 he founded the *West African Times* (later the *Times of West Africa*). He also became active in politics, and in 1947 he was one of the founders of the United Gold Coast Convention (q.v.). In March 1948 he was arrested with Nkrumah (q.v.) and others, but in the following year he became a member of the Coussey Committee (q.v.) on Constitutional Reform. By this time he and Nkrumah had come to a parting of the ways. In 1951 Danquah was elected to the Legislative Assembly, and he became one of the leaders of the opposition to Nkrumah.

Danquah lost in the elections of 1954 and 1956. During this period he belonged first to the National Liberation Movement and then the United Party (qq.v.). In 1960 he was the candidate of the United Party for President against

Nkrumah. He received just 10 percent of the vote, winning only the Volta region. In 1961, he was arrested and detained by Nkrumah under the Preventive Detention Act (q.v.) . Released in June 1962, Danquah was rearrested in January 1964. He died in Nsawam Prison on 4 February 1965.

DANQUAH, MABEL DOVE. Died 1984. Writer and editor. Wife of Joseph Boakye Danquah (q.v.). She was the first woman elected to an African legislature.

DARIZIEGU. Died 1620. The Eleventh Ya Na of Dagomba (q.v.), who ruled from 1590 to 1620. Important events that took place in his reign included the loss of large are:.s in the west to Gonja (q.v.) and the move of the Dagomba capital to Yendi (q.v.). Dariziegu was defeated and killed in a battle with Gonja at Yapei (q.v.).

DAWU. 5°59'N, 0°05'W. Site of famous archaeological excavations of Thurstan Shaw. The culture located here was probably at its peak from about 1550 to 1700. The Guan (q.v.) society manufactured iron, bronze, textiles, pottery, ivory, and jewelry.

DE GRAFT, JOE COLEMAN. Born 1932. Novelist, short story writer, poet, and dramatist. He studied English at the University College of the Gold Coast, and for a time was a research fellow at the Institute of African Studies (q.v.) at Legon. *The Secret of Opokuwa* (1967), *Visitor from the Past* (1968), *Through a Film Darkly* (1970), and *Beneath the Jazz and Brass* (1975) are some of his works.

DE GRAFT-JOHNSON, JOHN COLEMAN, JR. Born 1919. Author, economist, historian, diplomat. Educated at Mfantsipim and at Edinburgh University. He received his doctorate in economics at Edinburgh in 1946 with a dissertation on "Cooperation in Agriculture and Banking in British West Africa." This was published in 1958. While still a student he helped organize the Pan-African Congress at Manchester (q.v.) in September 1945. After gaining his doctorate, he was employed at the Colonial Office in London,

1946-1948. He then returned to the Gold Coast to work for the Cocoa Marketing Company, 1948-1949. He was a tutor at the University College from 1950 to 1956. From Legon he went to India and was connected with the University of Dehli, 1956-1961. Back in Legon, he worked at the University for several years until he joined the Ministry of External Affairs and was made Ambassador to Holland and Belgium, 1967-1970. From 1961 to 1967 he was President of the Historical Book Society of Ghana. He is author of many articles and several books. Among his books, *An Introduction to the African Economy* (1959) is perhaps the best known. *African Glory: The Story of Vanished Negro Civilizations*, which was first published in 1954, has gone through several editions.

DE GRAFT-JOHNSON, JOSEPH WILLIAM, SR. 1860-1928. Cape Coast (q.v.) merchant and early nationalist. He was also known as Kwesi Johnson. He was a longtime leader in Cape Coast civic affairs, was a political associate of J. E. Casely Hayford and J. P. Brown (qq.v.), and was one of the co-founders of the Aborigines' Rights Protection Society (q.v.). Joseph William was the son of Joseph Benjamin Johnson, who was a native of Sierra Leone, and of Betsey de Graft, daughter of Joseph de Graft (1756-1843). Joseph William was educated in Cape Coast by a maternal uncle, John Coleman de Graft. At the start of his career, Joseph William worked for F. and A. Swanzy at Elmina (qq.v.), but he established his own business at Cape Coast in the 1890s.

DE GRAFT-JOHNSON, JOSEPH WILLIAM, JR. Son of Joseph William (q.v.) and brother of John Coleman, Sr. He was headmaster of the Wesleyan School at Cape Coast (q.v.) and author of *Towards Nationhood in Africa* (1928) and *Historical Geography of the Gold Coast* (1929).

DE GRAFT-JOHNSON, JOSEPH WILLIAM SWAIN. Born 1933. Members of the famous Cape Coast (q.v.) family, engineer, and Vice-President during the Third Republic. He was educated at Mfantsipim, Leeds and Birmingham universities, and the University of California, where he received his doctorate. He became a member of the engineering faculty at the University of Kumasi (q.v.) in 1968. While on the faculty in Kumasi, he served on many important commissions and committees, including the one which drew up the Constitution for the Third Republic. He was active in the creation of the People's National Party (q.v.) and was nominated as the party's candidate for Vice-President at the party congress in Kumasi, on 20 April 1979. He was elected on the ticket with Hilla Limann (q.v.) two months later. Deposed at the end of 1981, he was arrested a few days later and released from custody in September 1983. He moved to London from where he became an active critic of the Provisional National Defense Council administration with other opposition (q.v.) groups.

DEI-ANANG, MICHAEL FRANCIS. Born 1909. Writer from Mampong, Akuapem. He was educated at Achimota and at the University of London. He was employed in the British Civil Service in the Gold Coast (q.v.) before independence. During the Nkrumah (q.v.) period he was an adviser to Nkrumah on African and foreign affairs and was one of Nkrumah's ghostwriters. He is the author of *Ghana Resurgent* (1964), *Okomfo Anokye's Golden Stool* (a play published in 1960), *The Administration of Ghana's Foreign Relations, 1957-1965: A Personal Memoir* (1975), and several books of poetry. During the final year of Nkrumah's rule, Dei-Anang was Chairman of the State Publishing Corporation.

DE LIMA, GERALDO (de Lema). Died 1912. Trader. Born Aszoviehlo Atiogbe in Dahomey (Benin) about 1835 he, at a very early age, was in the service of a slave trader by the name of Casar Cenquira Geraldo de Lima. When the master died in 1862, the employee took over the boss's business, wife, and name. In 1865 he was expelled from Ada (q.v.) for mistreatment of one of Ada's chiefs. He persuaded the Anlo to take up his quarrel, and the dispute kept the Volta (qq.v.) region in turmoil for over 20 years. He opposed British expansion into the area of the Keta Lagoon (q.v.) because they were a threat to his business dominance of the hinterlands of the lagoon area. As the British moved in and suppressed the slave trade, de Lima was forced to turn to the palm oil trade. Constantly at odds with the British, he tried to organize resistance to British expansion. In 1871 the English bombarded de Lima's home in Anlo and offered a reward for his capture. For some time he evaded arrest, and he smuggled his goods past British officials. When the Germans arrived in 1884, de Lima supported them. He was finally captured by the British, who held him prisoner at Elmina (q.v.) from May 1885 until the end of 1893. He died in 1912 at Keta.

DENKYIRA (Dankyira, Denkera, Denkira, Denkyera). Akan (q.v.) state which before 1701 was the most powerful state in the Gold Coast (q.v.) hinterland. It controlled most of the gold traded to the Europeans from the area between the Tano and Pra (qq.v.) rivers. The old capital was at Abankesieso (q.v.) or Bankesieso, on the Ofin, not far from the modern Obuasi (q.v.). In the summer of 1701 Osei Tutu of Asante (qq.v.) conquered Denkyira under Ntim Gyakari at Feyiase. Denkyira was again crushed by Asante in 1711. Many Denkyira people fled eastward into the lands of the Akyem (q.v.). Today, the area that formed the core of the old Denkyira state is located in the Western Region.

DENSU RIVER. A river which rises in the Atewa-Atewiredu hills west of Koforidua (qq.v.) and flows through the Sakumo Lagoon to reach the sea just west of Accra (q.v.). It is a major source of water for Accra.

DEPORTATION ACT OF 1957. An act passed in July 1957 which allowed the government to void the citizenship of any person who was not born in Ghana of Ghanaian parents. Such persons could be deported if they were perceived a threat to the Convention People's Party (q.v.) government.

DEVELOPMENT AND APPLICATION OF INTERMEDIATE TECHNOLOGY (DAPIT). This program, aimed at establishing and developing a national mechanism to identify, develop, test, produce, and demonstrate to the rural sector appropriate technologies that would contribute to increased production and incomes, was started in 1979. Projects of

DAPIT were implemented through four organs: the Food Research Institute, Industrial Research Institute, Council for Scientific and Industrial Research, and Technology Consultancy Center. In July of 1984, a 12-member sub-committee to select viable projects under phase two of a joint Ghana government/United States Development and Application of Intermediate Technology program was inaugurated. Since then, DAPIT has identified small-scale enterprises as the areas for technology and financial assistance.

DIPALI (Dipalli, Dapali, Yendi Dabari). 9°48'N, O°57'W. A village in the Dagomba part of the Northern Region some 30 miles (48 km) north of Tamale (qq.v.) and near Diari. It is also called Yendi Dabari and was once the capital of Dagomba before the Gonja (qq.v.) invasion forced the Dagomba to establish a new capital at Yendi (q.v.).

DIRECTOR. The title of director applied to all persons formerly referred to as principal secretaries in the public service and managing directors of public corporations. As part of the Provisional National Defense Council (PNDC) (q.v.) government Civil Service Reform Act of 1984, all holders of the highest public service positions in the ministries were also to be referred to as directors and chief directors. Apart from the technical competence required in such positions, the government also demanded that directors and chief directors who worked directly under the PNDC be politically committed.

DISTRICT ASSEMBLIES. Two years after the Provisional National Defense Council (q.v.) created a National Commission for Democracy (NCD) and charged it with the task of coming out with a viable democratic system that will withstand time, the NCD proposed the formation of District Assemblies as local administrations which will offer opportunities to ordinary people to become involved in the political process. On 1 July 1987, the NCD announced District Assembly elections to be held in the last quarter of 1988. The commission also announced the creation of 110 districts to replace the 65 that had existed under previous administrations. The 110 assemblies proposed by the NCD were determined based on minimum population figures of 100,000 for urban areas and 75,000 for rural districts.

DIXCOVE. 4°48'N, 1°57'W. A coastal village in the Western Region just west of Achowa point and east of Butri (q.v.). It is only about 15 miles (24 km) west of Takoradi (q.v.) port. The history of the town suggests that its settlers were independent of the Ahanta (q.v.), and the town itself was ruled by two separate rulers reflecting the different migrations. The English and Dutch built bases here in the seventeenth century. The Portuguese arrived as early as 1503. The Dutch began construction of the fort in about 1642. It was turned over to the British in 1872. The fort was restored in the 1850s, and today is used as offices for the local authorities.

DJERMA see ZABRAMA

DODOWA. 5°53'N, 0°07'W. Town in the Eastern Region about 25 miles (40 km) northeast of Accra (q.v.) and just a short distance from Larteh. It was once the seat of the Joint Provincial Council of Chiefs, and it is the commercial center for the port of Prampram (q.v.).

DODOWA, BATTLE OF   (Dodowa, Akantamasu, Katamanso). Battle fought about 8 miles (13 km) south of Dodowa on 7 August 1826. In this battle, the Ga, Fante, Denkyira, Akyem, Akwamu (qq.v.), and the British united to stop Asante advances into the southeast. The Asante (q.v.) under King Osei Yaw Akoto (q.v.) were badly defeated. This defeat caused a crisis in the Kumasi government in the years that followed.

DOMBO, SIMON DIEDONG.   Born 1923.   Politician, traditional chief (Duori Na since 1949), and businessman. He is a native of Duori in the Upper West Region, near Lawra and Burkina Faso. In 1951 he represented the north in the Legislative Council. In April 1954 he founded the Northern People's Liberation Movement to demand a federal system of government. After Busia's (q.v.) exile in 1959, Dombo became leader of the opposition to the Convention People's

Party (q.v.). He served in the legislative branch of government until the coup of 1966 and was elected again during the Second Republic, serving as Minister of Health and as Minister of the Interior. Following the 1972 military coup, he returned to duties as traditional chief.

DOMPOASE (Dompoasi). 6°18'N, 1°32W. The second Adansi capital, established early in the seventeenth century on the Cape Coast-Kumasi road about 12 miles (19 km) south of Bekwai and just above Fomena (qq.v.). Fomena became the third Adansi capital.

DORMAA AHENKRO (Domaa). 7°17'N, 2°53'W. A border town west of Sunyani in the Brong-Ahafo (qq.v.) Region. At one time these people lived close to Kumasi, but they moved to their present location in an attempt to avoid Asante (qq.v.) rule. Their original home was one of the first places captured by Osei Tutu (q.v.).

DOROTHEA, FORT. 4°45'N, 2°01'W. A small fort located at Akwida in the Western Region near Cape Three Points (qq.v.). The structure was first built by the Brandenburgers (q.v.) in 1685, but it was soon taken over by the Dutch. It is in ruins today.

DU BOIS, WILLIAM EDWARD BURGHARDT. 1868-1963. An African-American leader and intellectual who was one of the founders of the National Association for the Advancement of Colored People (NAACP) and the Pan-African movement. He was the author of several books. In 1961 he joined the Communist Party, and at the invitation of Nkrumah (q.v.), he moved to Ghana and became a Ghanaian citizen. He became the first director of the *Encyclopedia Africana* and was awarded a doctorate by the University of Ghana (q.v.) just a short time before he died on 27 August 1963. He was buried beside the western wall of Christiansborg Castle at Osu, Accra (qq.v.). In 1985, Dr. Du Bois's body and the ashes of his wife, Shirley, were reinterred at the former Du Bois residence at Cantonments. The residence is now the W. E. B. Du Bois

Memorial Center for Pan-African Culture. Since 1988 an annual memorial lecture has been held at the Center. In May 1988 the Du Bois Center became a member of the African Cultural Institute (ACI).

DUNKWA-ON-THE-OFIN. 5°58'N, 1°47'W. Mining center on the railroad between Kumasi and Sekondi-Takoradi (qq.v.). It is 23 miles (37 km) south of Obuasi (q.v.) and 75 miles (120 km) north of Takoradi.

DUPUIS, JOSEPH. A British official sent to Cape Coast (q.v.) in 1819. Crown agent to Kumasi (q.v.) in 1820. While in Kumasi, Dupuis worked out a treaty with the Asantehene Osei Tutu Kwame (q.v.) (Osei Bonsu). It was signed on 23 March 1820. In the treaty, the Asantehene (q.v.) and his chiefs acknowledged themselves as British subjects, but claimed that all the Fante country was part of the Asante (qq.v.) empire. The treaty was never ratified by the British. Dupuis returned to England and in 1824 published the *Journal of a Residence in Ashantee*, an account of his mission on the Gold Coast.

DWABEN (Juaben). 6°49'N, 1°26'W. Located 15 miles (24 km) to the northeast of Kumasi, Dwaben was one of the important early confederate states of Asante (qq.v.). It was once known as Apeayinase before its absorption into Asante. The Dwabenhene was one of the most powerful of Asante chiefs. He once had influence over the Dente Shrine, and there were times when Asante rulers considered Dwaben a threat to the unity of the Confederacy. In 1831 Asantehene Yaw Akoto ordered a military occupation of Dwaben. Many inhabitants of the town sought refuge in Akyem Abuakwa (q.v.) and under British protection. Peace was restored between Kumasi and Dwaben in 1841. The town was occupied again in October 1875 following Dwaben's 1874 declaration of independence from Kumasi. Unsuccessful in attracting British support, on 3 November the Dwaben ran out of ammunition. Hundreds of inhabitants were captured by the union forces and sold into slavery. Again, many others fled to Akyem Abuakwa for British protection. These founded New Dwaben, with its capital at Koforidua (q.v.). Old Dwaben exists as the smaller of the two towns but remains an important member of the Asanteman Council.

DYULA (Dioula, Juula, Wangara). Mande traders originating from old Mali. They were an important factor in the spread of Islam in the Western Sudan and in the Volta (q.v.) basin.

- E -

EAST INDIA COMPANY. Rival East India Companies were created by the French and British to compete against the Portuguese monopoly of trade with the Far East. The British East India Company was formed in London shortly after the Anglo-Spanish war of the late sixteenth century (about 1600) for trade with the East Indies. It controlled English trade with the Gold Coast (q.v.) from 1658 to 1663.

ECONOMIC RECOVERY PROGRAM (ERP). At the start of the 1980s when the Provisional National Defense Council (PNDC) (q.v.) ended the Third Republic, the national economy was in crisis. The conventional market economy which characterized the decade of the 1970s had yielded no visible rewards as the legacy of official corruption, non-accountability, and widespread mismanagement had not been controlled. The national economy which was inherited by the PNDC was characterized by high inflation (about 125 percent), stagnant industrial and agricultural productions, declining per capita income, shortages of imported and local goods, and a gross domestic product (GDP) that had declined between 2 to 5 percent from 1979 to 1980. For the country to pull itself out of the crisis situation, the PNDC government was faced with the task of creating a more stable political environment within which workable economic policies could be implemented. In other words, there was an immediate need to restore the legitimacy of the state and the efficiency of its institutions.

In its attempt to address the nation's economic woes, the PNDC, in coordination with the International Monetary Fund (IMF), launched an Economic Recovery Program (ERP) described by observers as the most stringent and consistent in Africa to date. The first phase of the Structural Adjustment Program (SAP) was evaluated in 1987 to have been very successful--bringing down the inflation rate to 20 percent, and over $500 million in arrears dating back to 1966 was paid to creditors. With confidence enhanced in Ghana's ability and the resolve of the government to pursue policies of recovery, international agencies (including the Paris Club, the World Bank, and the IMF) pledged more than $575 million to the nation's future programs. The pledge was more than 42 percent of the original amount estimated by the government to be needed for Phase Two of the ERP. Targeting the problems of the rural poor, the PNDC engaged in road-building projects, rural electrification programs, and restructuring of the national education (q.v.) system to bring them in line with developmental goals. In all these, the government benefited from World Bank and IMF advice. The success of these policies has been reflected in consistent average GDP growth of between 3 and 5 percent since 1984.

The economic achievements of the 1980s were not without pains. Citizens' vetting committees and public tribunals (qq.v.) were established to ensure public accountability. For some, the tribunals were viewed as agencies for harassment of the well-to-do. Public sector employment was frozen, early retirement of certain public officials was made effective, and others were retrained and redeployed. The resulting unemployment and increased cost of living experienced by many citizens generated negative reactions towards the government, especially from the Trades Union Congress and the National Union of Ghana University Students (qq.v.). Giving credence to these criticisms were the problems of debt servicing, repayment of earlier loans, and other fiscal matters.

Responding to these problems, the PNDC government, with the support of the IMF/World Bank, introduced programs aimed at addressing the social cost of adjustment, including a Program of Action for the Mitigation of the Social Consequences of Adjustment for Development (PAMSCAD) (q.v.). With regard to medium-term programs (including debt servicing and, particularly, repayment of loans to international institutions), extended fund facilities (EFFs) and structural adjustment loans (SALs) were made available to Ghana. In the EFF/SAL package from the IMF, arrangements were made for Ghana to make lower payments on debts, and the pace for eliminating external arrears was regulated with IMF guarantees. Ghana's close relations with the international financial institutions and the successes that resulted from the nation's recovery programs have been described as the fruits of continued lending and policy dialogue with the IMF and the World Bank.

ECOWAS MONITORING GROUP (ECOMOG). The Economic Community of West African States (ECOWAS) created this monitoring group in August 1990. The monitoring group was charged to restore law and order in Liberia, which had been torn by civil war. The member states of ECOWAS that contributed troops to ECOMOG included Ghana, Nigeria, Togo, Gambia, and Mali. The Ghanaian contingent of about 112 men and 5 officers was led by Lt. Gen. Arnold Quainoo, then Provisional National Defense Council (q.v.) member and Chairman of the Ghana National Development Commission. In February of 1991, the Ghanaian contingent was replaced by 856 officers and men. This was indicative of the worsening conditions in Liberia. The conflict in Liberia led to the migration of some Liberian refugees to Ghana. The office of David Sapong Boaten (q.v.), then Secretary of Mobilization and Social Welfare, was actively involved in providing for these refugees.

EDUCATION. Ghana has a well-developed formal educational system. Education along Western lines was first introduced into the country by missionaries as early as 1765. In 1882 the colonial government became active in the supervision of education when it established boards to inspect and standardize the management of schools. Popular demand for education began to increase in the 1930s. Between 1952 and 1961, policies were put in place for the organization of institutions compatible with the developmental needs of independent Ghana. Kindergartens, six-year primary schools, and four-year middle schools constituted the elementary structure of the educational system. Also, there were secondary schools, technical institutions, and teacher training colleges. The Institute for Adult Education at the University of Ghana (q.v.), Legon, began organizing night classes for working adults in 1962. In addition to the University of Ghana at Legon, the University of Cape Coast (q.v.), and the University of Science and Technology (q.v.) at Kumasi, other specialized institutions for advanced studies exist in Ghana.

Reforms in Ghana's educational system, especially at the middle and secondary levels, were extensively discussed in the 1970s. The result was the Dzobo Committee Report of 1974, calling for a more practical or skill-oriented type of education for students at the middle school level, which was to be reorganized into a Junior Secondary School (JSS) system. It was not until 1987 that the Provisional National Defense Council (q.v.) government ended the former middle school system, to be replaced by the Junior and Senior Secondary systems. According to the new structure, instead of a four-year middle school and a five- to seven-year secondary schooling, students graduating from the primary school would immediately enter the compulsory three-year junior secondary school, where they would have combined technical, vocational, and academic studies before proceeding to more specialized studies at the senior secondary level. The diversified character of the new system was also intended to curb the dropout rate at the elementary school level by catering to students with little interest in traditional academic studies and to prepare more students in skills relevant to the modern needs of the country. See also UNIVERSITY OF CAPE COAST; UNIVERSITY OF GHANA; UNIVERSITY OF SCIENCE AND TECHNOLOGY.

EDUSEI, KROBO. 1915-1984. Asante (q.v.) politician. He was educated at the government boys' school in Kumasi. For a time he was reporter and debt collector for the *Ashanti Pioneer*. In 1947 Edusei was one of the founders of the Ashanti Youth Association, and he joined the Convention People's Party (CPP) (q.v.) in 1949. He was imprisoned in the Positive Action (q.v.) civil disobedience campaign in 1950. In

1951, Edusei was elected to the legislative assembly, becoming Minister of Justice in Nkrumah's (q.v.) first government. For a time he was Propaganda Secretary of the CPP. He became Minister of Interior in 1957, and in that position he played an active role in silencing opposition to the CPP regime. As a member of Nkrumah's government, Edusei became wealthy. His generosity and extravagant life style made him one of the best known of Nkrumah's circle. Between 1952 and 1966 he made over 40 trips to Europe. In England in 1955 he married Mary Jackson, who later created a sensation by buying a gold-plated bed. Edusei also served terms as Minister of Industries and as Minister of Agriculture.

After the fall of Nkrumah in 1966, Edusei was imprisoned. He was charged with holding illegal assets, but acquitted in May 1970 after spending many months in prison. He was banned from politics in the 1979 elections. Edusei, however, was a member of the Central Committee of the People's National Party (PNP) (q.v.) and Chairman of the Asante Region branch of the PNP. After the fall of the Third Republic in 1981, Edusei found himself in prison again. In October 1982 he was sentenced to 11 years for accepting a large loan in the Chiavelli case, but he was released in 1983 due to poor health.

EFUTU (Fetu, Afutu, Fetu). 5°12'N, 1°19'W. A Central Region town not far from Cape Coast (q.v.). It was originally settled by Guan (q.v.) people. In James Anquandah's *Rediscovering Ghana's Past*, the town of Efutu was identified as one of the sites where rare archaeological ornaments of gold and pottery have been retrieved. Efutu was also known for its salt and fishing industries.

EGALA, IMORU. 1914-1981. Wealthy Muslim politician from the Tumu (q.v.) area of the Upper West Region. Egala was elected to Parliament in 1954 and he served as a minister in Nkrumah's (q.v.) first all-African Cabinet. He was defeated in the 1956 elections, but was appointed to the chairmanship of the Cocoa Marketing Board (q.v.). Egala was reelected to

Parliament in 1959, and in 1966, when the military ended Nkrumah's administration, Egala was Minister of Industries.

Even though Imoru Egala was banned from running for political office in both the Second and Third republics, he was politically active, especially in keeping the Nkrumah movement alive. He was thought of as a founding father of the People's National Party (PNP) (q.v.), and he was instrumental in the choice of Hilla Limann (q.v.) as the PNP candidate for President. After the election of Limann, Egala became an adviser to the new President of the Third Republic. He died suddenly in April 1981.

EGUAFO. Guan (q.v.) coastal group known to the Europeans as Comany or Great Komenda. Shama, at the mouth of the Pra (qq.v.), was an Eguafo village. At one time the Eguafo controlled trade through Elmina (q.v.), and they were important middlemen in the gold and slave trade. In time they became part of the Fante (q.v.) alliance.

EGWIRA (Igwira, Igwijra). An area in the extreme western part of what is today the Western Region. It was shown on a 1629 Dutch map, which noted that the land was rich in gold. Egwira overlaps the Aowin and Sefwi lands west of the Tano (qq.v.).

EJISU. 6°43'N, 1°06'W. A town in the Asante Region just east of Kumasi on the highway and railroad to Accra (qq.v.). Some of the most bitter fighting of the Asante-British war took place here in 1900. The Queen Mother of Ejisu, Yaa Asantewa, was leader of the Asante cause against the English.

EJURA. 7°23'N, 1°22'W. A town on the Great Northern Highway north of Kumasi and between Mampong and Atebubu (qq.v.). It is at the northern edge of the Asante (q.v.) Region. A road branches off to the west from Ejura and crosses the Pru valley to the Techiman-Kintampo (qq.v.) road. The Akyem Bosome believe that they originated in Ejura (qq.v.). The town is known today for its grassland agricultural production.

EKUANA. One of the principal Akan (q.v.) clans.

ELECTIONS OF 1992.   After 11 years of Provisional National Defense Council (PNDC) rule, the ban on party politics was lifted in May and, by November, presidential elections had been held. This was followed in December by parliamentary elections which were boycotted by many opposition groups. When the dust settled, Rawlings (q.v.) had emerged as the President of the Fourth Republic, and his National Democratic Congress (q.v.) had won 190 of the 200 parliamentary seats.

The opposition (q.v.) blamed their poor showing in the November presidential elections and their subsequent boycott of the December parliamentary elections on Rawlings's manipulation of the rules of the game to his advantage. Events cited in support of their argument included the circumstances under which the Constitution of the Fourth Republic was written (see CONSULTATIVE ASSEMBLY). Of particular concern to the opposition were Sections 5 (1, 2, and 3) of the Constitution. These sections barred parties from holding public meetings until final certificates of registration had been approved by the Interim National Electoral Commission. While it was not until August when most opposition groups completed the certification process, the opposition accused Rawlings and the National Democratic Congress of using the state machinery to propagate their party's position. According to the opposition, it was also through the apparatus of the state that Rawlings's victory in the November elections was guaranteed when he received over 60 percent of the votes compared to the total of 40 percent by the four other parties.

Notwithstanding   opposition   accusations, Commonwealth observers described the November presidential elections as relatively free and fair.   Some commentators attributed the poor showing of the opposition candidates to factors ranging from inadequate organization to popular recognition of PNDC economic achievements and thus support of Rawlings's National Democratic Congress.

ELIZA CARTHAGO, FORT.   4°53'N, 2°17'W. A post started by the Dutch on a hill overlooking the left bank of the Ankobra (q.v.) in 1702. A. W. Lawrence described this fort as one of two built by the Dutch purely for military purposes--"to defend the approach to Axim by the Brandendurg (qq.v.) and their African allies."

ELLIS, ALFRED BURDON. 1852-1894. Soldier, colonial administrator, and author. He served as a lieutenant in the First West India Regiment under Sir Garnet Wolseley in the 1874 Asante (qq.v.) campaign. From 1878 to 1879 he was District Commissioner at Keta (q.v.), where he carried on a spirited campaign against smugglers. An attempt against his life by Geraldo de Lima and the Anlo (qq.v.) was almost successful. The year 1881 found him back in the army. In 1884 he was in the South African Zulu campaign, and in 1889 he was in the Bahamas. By 1893 he was a Lt. Colonel, fighting Samori's Sofas on the borders of Sierra Leone. Here he contracted a fever from which he died in 1894.

Ellis was the author of a number of books including his *West African Sketches* (1881), *The Land of Fetish* (1883), *The Tshi-Speaking Peoples of the Gold Coast of West Africa* (1887), *West African Stories* and the *Ewe-Speaking Peoples of the Slave Coast of West Africa* (1893), and *The Yoruba-Speaking Peoples of the Slave Coast* (1894).

ELMINA (Edina, Ednaa). 5°05'N, 1°20'W. A town at Elmina Point where a small stream drains the Benya Lagoon into the Gulf of Guinea. It is in the Central Region and was once called the "village of two parts" because of the Efutu and Eguafo (qq.v.) composition of the local population. The town is dominated by the San Jorge Castle (q.v.), built by the Portuguese in 1482. This impressive structure was captured by the Dutch in 1637 and for over two hundred years was the Dutch headquarters on the Gold Coast. In 1872 the English purchased the Castle. Across town from the Castle is San Iago Fort, also an imposing reminder of the colonial era. In earlier days the town was a key outlet for gold, ivory, and slaves from Asante (q.v.). Today the town is surrounded by coconut groves, salt evaporation pans, and beautiful beaches. Elmina is an important port for African fishing canoes. Within sight of Cape Coast (q.v.)--about 8 miles to the east and on the main coastal highway--the town is one of the most popular tourist attractions in Ghana.

ENCASSAR or ENCASSE see SEFWI

ERSKINE, EMMANUEL A. Born 1935. Former commander of the Ghana army. In 1974, he was assigned as Chief of Staff to the United Nations Truce Supervision Organization (UNTSO) forces in Lebanon. After the Israeli invasion of that country in 1978, the United Nations set up an interim force (UNIFIL) as a control mechanism to prevent the breakup of Lebanon. Lieutenant-General Erskine was made first Commander of UNIFIL, a position he held until 1986. Accounts of General Erskine's experiences in the Middle East and his personal opinions about the UNIFIL mission in Lebanon appeared in his *Mission with UNIFIL: An African Soldier's Reflections.*

Back in Ghana, General Erskine was called upon by the Provisional National Defense Council (q.v.) government to head a committee that was charged with the responsibility of making recommendations for military reforms. General Erskine was also known to have spoken out against military involvement in government. Retired from the army and from service with the United Nations, he ran unsuccessfully in the November 1992 presidential elections (q.v.) as the People's Heritage Party candidate.

ETSI (Ati, Atti, Etsu). A small Guan group located just north of the Fante (qq.v.). These were among the earliest people known along the coast. The state was shown on a Dutch map in 1629. In time it became a part of Assin (q.v.).

EVEGBE. The Ewe (q.v.) language. The chief Evegbe dialect used in Ghana is Anlo (q.v.).

EVENING NEWS. An Accra newspaper founded by Kwame Nkrumah (q.v.), with the first edition appearing on 3 September 1948. It became the chief voice of the Convention People's Party (q.v.), and it was through this paper that

Nkrumah first launched his Positive Action program for independence. K. A. Gbedemah (q.v.) was the first editor.

EWE. One of the major groups of people in Ghana. Most of the Ewe live east of the Volta River (q.v.) in Ghana and Togo. Tradition ties them to the Oyo, Yoruba, Ketou in Benin (Dahomey), and Notsie (Nouatja, Nuatja) in Togo. They probably moved into their present locations soon after 1600. Eweland is the area between the Mono River in Togo and the Volta in Ghana. It runs west to east about 80 miles (129 km) and is about the same distance north to south. From 1885 to 1914 the Ewe were divided between British and German rule. Then during World War I (1914-1919) most of the Ewe were under British rule. Under a League of Nations mandate, the eastern part of Eweland became part of French-ruled Togo. The rest was administered by the British, either as a mandate or as part of the Gold Coast (q.v.). In 1956 a plebiscite was held in the British mandate, and a majority voted to cast their lot with the new country of Ghana. Ho, Krepi, and Anlo (qq.v.) are three of the main divisions of the Ewe in Ghana.

EXPORT PROMOTION. Since the colonial era, Ghana's export commodities have included cocoa (q.v.), timber, and minerals. These traditional export items, especially cocoa, yielded much of the nation's foreign exchange. A national program to diversify the economy led in 1969 to the establishment of the Ghana Export Promotion Council (GEPC). Since it was not provided with adequate support, the Council could not function effectively in its early periods of operation. According to the Council's own journal, *The Exporter*, "the highest ever earning of $61.6 million was recorded in 1982." Thus, it was not until the Provisional National Defense Council (PNDC) planned its Economic Recovery Program (ERP) (qq.v.), that increasing attention was paid to export promotion in Ghana.

As a result of this new focus, the number of exportable commodities rose from 124 in 1980 to 345 by 1985. This was accompanied by a rise in the number of exporters from 100 in 1984 to about 280 in 1986. Included in the non-traditional export commodities were pineapples, cola nuts, shrimps, lobsters, and tuna. According to a report published in the January 1988 issue of *West Africa*, the GEPC recorded earnings of about $12 million from tuna export alone. The Council was also able to inform its constituency that the United Kingdom and Switzerland had expressed interest in Ghanaian medicinal plants. Better packaging and labeling of non-traditional products, the GEPC reported, could lead to greater income for exporters. See also INVESTMENT CODE.

-F-

FANTE (Fanti, Fantyn). A coastal Akan (q.v.) group. According to their traditions, their ancestors migrated from Techiman (q.v.) in the Akan hinterlands to their present location in the Central Region. The Fante states were well and long established by the time the Portuguese arrived on the Guinea coast in the fifteenth century. Their original coastal settlement was at Kwaman, which they later called Mankesim (qq.v.). Abora, Abease, Nkusukum, Kwanyako, and Anomabo (q.v.) were other early Fante towns. By 1800 the Fante dominated the coast from Winneba to the Pra River (qq.v.). Unlike Asante (q.v.), the Fante never united as one polity, but they came together on occasions when they were threatened. The Fante often found themselves allied with the British against Asante and Dutch interests on the coast.

FANTE CONFEDERACY, 1868. The Fante Confederacy was an attempt on the part of a number of coastal peoples to unite for protection and for development in the nineteenth century. Delegations from Fante, Denkyira, Wassa, Assin, and Twifo towns met in Mankesim (qq.v.) and reached a basic agreement to form a confederation. Mankesim would be the seat of government. Executive and legislative authorities were to be selected, taxes were provided for, and the mobilization of an army began. The Confederacy denounced Dutch and English plans to exchange posts on the coast without consultation with local chiefs. For a time, prospects looked bright for the organization and enthusiasm spread. New groups applied for admission to the alliance, but it was dead by 1873. The most important cause for the failure of the Confederacy was the British opposition to the whole plan. The British then decided to set up a protectorate over the coastal region. The union has often been referred to by historians of Ghana as a forerunner of the nation's modern nationalism.

FANTE NATIONAL SOCIETY (Mfantsi Amanbuhu Fekuw). A society formed in 1889 at Cape Coast by John Mensah Sarbah, J. W. de Graft-Johnson, J. P. Brown (qq.v.), and others to build national consciousness and pride among the Fante (q.v.). It was the precursor of the Aborigines' Rights Protection Society (q.v.).

FELLI, ROGER JOSEPH ATOGETIPOLI. Born 1938. Soldier and member of the National Redemption Council (NRC) (q.v.). Born at Navrongo in the Upper West Region, near the border with Burkina Faso. Felli enlisted in the army in 1960, was sent to Sandhurst in England, and thereafter advanced rapidly through the ranks. He was a member of the NRC from its formation in 1972 and was one of those closest to Acheampong (q.v.). He rose to be Commissioner of Foreign Affairs in the Supreme Military Council (q.v.). He was executed by the Armed Forces Revolutionary Council (q.v.) in June of 1979.

FERGUSON, GEORGE EKEM. 1864-1897. Colonial officer, geographer, and explorer. Born in Anomabo, trained in London as a surveyor, George Ferguson joined the British Civil Service in 1881. From 1884, he was engaged in mapping the interior behind the Gold Coast (q.v.), and in 1886 he served on the commission that determined the boundaries between the Gold Coast and German Togo territories. After 1890 he conducted missions into the north, as far as Ouagadougou, establishing British control over as much of the territory as he could. *The Papers of George Ekem Ferguson (1890-1897)* give a vivid picture of conditions in what is now the Northern, Upper East and Upper West regions. On 7 April

1897 Ferguson was killed by forces of Samori near the town of Wa (qq.v.).

FETISH. From the Portuguese word "feitiço," meaning "something made." Applied to religion, the term described African traditional religion as devotion to inanimate objects. Many modern scholars of African religion have commented that the early European perception of African religion was inaccurate. The traditional African, it has been argued, did not worship inanimate objects, rather he propitiated the spirits that took residence in those objects.

FEYIASE, BATTLE OF (Feyiasi). 6°36'N, 1°34'W. Situated about 8 miles (13 km) southeast of Kumasi, where, in November 1701, a unified Asante force under Osei Tutu defeated the Denkyira army under Ntim Gyakari (qq.v.). This defeat marked the emergence of the Asante nation.

FIA. The Ewe word for "chief." Fiaga is a paramount chief.

FLAG. The flag of Ghana is a tricolor of red, gold, and green, with a black star in the center of the gold stripe. In 1964 Nkrumah (q.v.) had the colors of the flag changed to a tricolor of red, white, and green, with the black star on the center white. After the coup of 1966, the old flag was returned.

FOMENA. 6°17'N, 1°31'W. The capital of Adansi (q.v.).

FOMENA, TREATY OF. In February 1874, after the British under Wolseley had destroyed Kumasi, the Asante (qq.v.) agreed to a peace treaty. The Asantehene (q.v.) signed a treaty at Fomena on 14 March 1874. The Asante renounced claims to Denkyira, Assin, Akyem, Adansi, and Elmina (qq.v.), and gave up rents for coastal forts. They agreed to pay a large indemnity, and the Asantehene promised to do his best to stop human sacrifice.

FOREIGN EXCHANGE BUREAUS (FOREX). Licensed currency dealers authorized by the Bank of Ghana to buy and sell foreign currency. As part of the Provisional National Defence

Council's (PNDC) (q.v.) Structural Adjustment Program (SAP), the central bank of Ghana introduced a weekly currency auction in 1986. By November of 1987, treasury bills were also being traded. The authorization of individuals and financial institutions to sell and buy foreign currencies was, therefore, part of a broader plan by the central government to stabilize the fiscal condition of the nation and, in particular, to undercut an existing black market in currency trading. The first foreign exchange bureaus opened on 1 February 1987 in Accra. Many such operations now exist in various parts of the country.

FORESTRY ORDINANCES.   The British colonial government began to consider forestry conservation controls as early as 1883, but regulations were postponed because of African opposition. A Forestry Department was created in 1909, and it introduced legislation to create reserves in 1910 and 1911. The bills were bitterly opposed by the Aborigines' Rights Protection Society (q.v.) and many Africans, fearing that the reserves were a subterfuge by the British to take native land. The Forest Ordinance of 1919 gave chiefs responsibility to set aside forest reserves, but few were established. Finally, the Forestry Ordinance of 1927 empowered the government in Accra to form forest reserves, with title and control of the reserves in the native stool authority.

FORT WILLIAM see WILLIAM, FORT

FRAFRA.   Name of a small group of people in the Upper East Region. Most of them reside to the east of Bolgatanga (q.v.) near the border with Burkina Faso.

FRANÇOIS, CURT VON.   1852-1931.   Member of a Prussian military family. He served in the German army during the Franco-Prussian War. Afterwards he was a member of the Grenfell-Wissmann Expedition to the Congo. In 1888 the German Foreign Office sent him to explore the hinterland of the Togo area, and between March and June of that year he visited Salaga, Yendi, Karaga, and Gambaga (qq.v.), crossing into Burkina Faso territory before returning to the coast. He signed agreements with Yendi, Karaga, and Salaga. In 1889 he was assigned to Southwest Africa, where he remained until 1895. He wrote several books about his African experiences.

FRASER, ALEXANDER GORDON. 1873-1962. The first principal of Achimota College (q.v.). Born in Scotland and educated at Oxford, he did missionary educational work in Uganda before he was appointed to run the school at Achimota. He was principal of Achimota from 1924 to 1935.

FREDERIKSBORG (Fort Royal). An old Danish fort built in 1660 just east of Cape Coast (q.v.). It was purchased by the British, who began to remold it about 1699. It was renamed Fort Royal. This property was abandoned about fifty years later.

FREEMAN, THOMAS BIRCH. 1809-1890. Missionary, writer, and government official. Freeman was born in Hampshire, England, of an African father and an English mother. In 1838 he went to Cape Coast (q.v.) as a Methodist missionary, and he played an important role in the expansion of that denomination in the Gold Coast (q.v.) and Nigeria. He kept a journal of three trips from Cape Coast to Kumasi (q.v.), and one trip to Dahomey and Nigeria between 1839 and 1843. He served some time as Civil Commandant of the Accra District, and lived the last twenty years of his life mostly in Accra or at Mankesim (qq.v.). His correspondence with the mission head office in England can be found among papers at the Methodist Archives, London.

FRONT FOR THE PREVENTION OF DICTATORSHIP. Group organized to oppose the Union Government (q.v.) campaign of 1978.

FULLER, FRANCIS. 1866-1944. British official and author. He was the British Chief Commissioner in Asante (q.v.) from 1902 to 1920. He had entered the Colonial Service in 1884 and had served in Nigeria and other places before coming to Kumasi (q.v.). His *Vanished Dynasty: Ashanti* was published in 1921.

FURLEY, J. T. A member of the Colonial Service of the Gold Coast (q.v.) from 1902 to 1923, the last six years of which he was Secretary for Native Affairs. He retired in 1924 and began to collect materials on the history of the Gold Coast from Portugal, the Netherlands, Denmark, and England. Furley's collections were donated to the Balme Library at the University of Ghana (q.v.), Legon.

FYNN, JOHN KOFI. Born 1935. Historian, politician, and professor. Fynn was born in Abura-Dunkwa in the Central Region and was educated at Mfantsipim, the University of Ghana (qq.v.), and the University of London, where he received his doctorate in 1964. He is the author of many articles and a book, *Asante and Its Neighbors 1700-1807* (1971). Though a permanent member of the history department at the University of Ghana (Legon), he has spent time in a number of overseas institutions as visiting scholar. In the period of the Second Republic he was a leading member of the Progress Party (q.v.) and served in the National Assembly, 1969-1972. Later in the Third Republic, he was again active in the Popular Front Party (q.v.).

-G-

GA. Traditional people of Accra, Osu, Labadi, Nungua, Teshi, and Tema (qq.v.). The Ga of Accra are called Gamashie. According to their traditions, the Ga came to the Accra Plains (q.v.) from Nigeria in the sixteenth century under the leadership of Okai Koi (q.v.). They never united under one leader, and so were frequently at the mercy of other people. Between 1677 and 1681 they were conquered by the Akwamu (q.v.). They have a patrilineal society, and traditionally they have supported themselves as fishermen, but their location on the coast also gave them advantages as traders with the Europeans. The Ga are closely related to the Adangbe (q.v.), who share common traditions and customs.

GA MANCHE. The principal Ga chief of Accra (qq.v.).

GAMBAGA. 10°32'N, 0°26'W. The ancient Mamprusi (q.v.) capital. Located in the Northern Region just below the Gambaga Scarp, it is 80 miles (128 km) northeast of Tamale (qq.v). Gambaga was occupied by a British force under Captain Donald Stewart on Christmas Eve in 1896. It became a popular hill station for the English and from 1897 to 1907 it served as their seat of government for the Northern Territories (q.v.). At one time Gambaga was an important commercial town, and the Mole-Dagbani (q.v.) have always looked upon it as their spiritual home.

GARDINER, ROBERT KWEKU ATTA. Born 1914. Government and United Nations official. Gardiner received his first degree in economics from Cambridge in 1941, and an M.A. also in economics from Oxford in 1942. He was a lecturer in economics in Sierra Leone from 1947 to 1949 before being employed in the UN Trusteeship Department. From the UN he moved to Nigeria to become the Extramural Studies Director at the University of Ibadan. He returned home to Ghana to be Director of Social Welfare and Community Development, 1953-1955, Secretary to the Ministry of Housing, 1955-1957, and Head of the Ghana Civil Service, 1957-1959. Gardiner joined the Economic Commission for Africa from 1959 to 1961. He served twice in the UN operation in the Congo, 1961 and again from 1962 to 1963. From 1963 to 1975 he was Executive Secretary of the UN Economic Commission for Africa. Robert Gardiner returned to Ghana in 1975 to become Commissioner for Economic Planning for the Supreme Military Council (q.v.), a position he held until his resignation in May 1978.

GBANYA (Gbanyito). Guan language spoken in Gonja (qq.v.).

GBEDEMAH, KOMLA AGBELI. Born 1912. Journalist, businessman, politician. He attended secondary school in Cape Coast, and then attended Achimota (qq.v.), 1929-1933. After years of teaching in Akuapem and Accra (qq.v.), he went into business. In 1948 he was Chairman of the Committee on Youth Organizations (q.v.). He joined the United Gold Coast Convention (q.v.) and became a founding member of the

Convention People's Party (CPP) (q.v.) in 1949. While Nkrumah (q.v.) was in prison, Gbedemah ran the CPP and edited the *Evening News* (q.v.). He was the organizer of the CPP election victory in 1951 in which he won a seat in the Legislative Assembly. He was Minister of Health and Labour from 1951 to 1952, and from 1952 to 1954 he headed Commerce and Industry, before assuming the position of Minister for Finance, 1954-1961. As Nkrumah moved toward the left politically, he and Gbedemah became estranged. Gbedemah was fired by Nkrumah in September 1961.

From September 1961 until the coup in 1966, Gbedemah live in exile. He devoted himself to business interests until the 1969 elections, when he organized the National Alliance of Liberals (q.v.) and was elected to the National Assembly as leader of the opposition. Denied his seat, he returned to his business activities. After the coup of January 1972 the National Redemption Council (q.v.) appointed Gbedemah a roving ambassador. By 1977 Gbedemah had broken with the military authorities and came out in opposition to the SMC's (q.v.) referendum on Union Government (q.v.). He was arrested by the military in 1978, but soon released. He was banned from taking part in the 1979 elections. In the November 1992 elections, however, Gbedemah was Chairman of the Alliance for Democratic Forces, an umbrella organization of seven parties that opposed the rules and regulations established by the Interim National Electoral Commission for civil elections.

GBEHO, PHILIP. Born 1905. Teacher, musician. Former teacher at Achimota (q.v.), Philip Gbeho is known in Ghana as the composer of the national anthem, "God Bless Our Homeland Ghana." During the colonial period he was active in the struggle for Ewe (q.v.) unification. He served as Director of the Ghana Art Council during Nkrumah's (q.v.) regime.

GBEWA (Bawa, Nedega). Grandson of Tohajie, and son of Kpogonumbo, he founded a Mole-Dagbani state at Pusiga, near Bawku (qq.v.). His daughter Yennenga (Nyennega, Yanataure) started the Mossi (q.v.) dynasties; his son and grandson Sitobu and Nyagse founded Dagomba; another son, Tohogo, founded Mamprugu or Mamprusi; a further son, Nnantombo (Yantambo), founded Nanumba (qq.v.); and other children founded lesser Mole-Dagbani states.

GBUGBLA. The people of Prampram, an Adangbe (qq.v.) coastal town.

GBUIPE. The Gonja Division whose chief town was Buipe, a town just above the Black Volta on an old trade route from Kumasi and Kintampo to Daboya (qq.v.), and ultimately Jenne in modern Mali.

GHANA. An ancient Mande kingdom located in the Sahel north of the Niger on the edge of the Sahara. The kingdom began to decline after it was conquered by the Almoravids in 1076. By 1235 it was replaced by Mali as the chief power in the Sahel. In the 1920's a popular tradition developed in the Gold Coast (q.v.) that remnants of the people of ancient Ghana had moved south from the Sahel after the destruction of that ancient kingdom. It is generally agreed that J. B. Danquah (q.v.) deserves credit for the suggestion that the Gold Coast be named Ghana when independence came in 1957.

GHANA COLLEGE. A school organized in the Oddfellows Hall, Cape Coast, by Nkrumah (q.v.) in July 1948 for secondary school boys who had been dismissed from their regular institutions for participating in a strike in February of that year. For the Convention People's Party (q.v.), the students had participated in the nationalist movement and, therefore, needed to be protected from reactionary forces. Today, Ghana National College in Cape Coast is a co-ed institution.

GHANA CONGRESS PARTY (GCP). A political party formed in 1952 by J. B. Danquah (q.v.) and other intelligentsia. In 1954 the GCP was replaced by the National Liberation Movement (q.v.), and this in turn was followed by the United Party (q.v.) in 1957. Each of these parties was an attempt to check the power of Nkrumah (q.v.).

GHANA PATRIOTIC MOVEMENT (GPM). A group organized by Alex Quaison-Sackey in 1977 in support of the Supreme Military Council's Union Government (qq.v.).

GHANA PEACE AND SOLIDARITY COUNCIL (GPSC). One of the groups that was organized in 1977-1978 to campaign in support of the Supreme Military Council plan for Union Government (qq.v.).

GHANA PEOPLE'S REPRESENTATIVE ASSEMBLY. A meeting called by Nkrumah (q.v.), at the West End Arena in Accra in November 1949, to oppose changes in the government suggested by the Coussey Committee (q.v.).

GHANABA, KOFI. Born 1923. Musician. Born in Accra, christened Warren Gamaliel Akwei, and formerly known in the music world as Guy Warren, this jazz drummer officially changed his name to Kofi Ghanaba in July of 1974. Ghanaba's music career began at the Government Elementary in Accra where he was a member of the school band. Later, in 1940, he played with the Accra Rhythmic Orchestra. The following year (1941), he won a government teacher training scholarship to Achimota College, but he soon left for a brief stay in the United States. He returned in 1943 as a reporter for the *Speculator Daily*. In 1944, Ghanaba joined the Tempos (a group described by its contemporaries as the greatest African jazz band of all time).

In the field of radio, Ghanaba is known to have introduced disc-jockeying to the Gold Coast Broadcasting Service. He also organized a series of jazz programs for the British Broadcasting Corporation in London. By the mid-1950s, Ghanaba was in Liberia, where he worked in radio for a few more years before traveling to Chicago to join Gene Esposito's Band as co-leader. While in the United States, he played with such renowned jazz artists as Art Blakey, Duke Ellington, and Louis Armstrong. It was, however, via his association with the Esposito Band as co-leader and arranger that Ghanaba produced his famous album *Africa Speaks, America Answers* (1955). His 1958 recording, *Themes in*

African Drums is a classic and his *I Have a Story to Tell* (1966) is a mini-autobiography. He was the first African musician to be admitted as a member of the prestigious American Society of Composers, Authors, and Publishers in 1957.

Notwithstanding his many accomplishments overseas, Kofi Ghanaba returned home in the 1970s disenchanted. It has been argued that many failed to understand his genius. The many articles written about him in national newspapers by both admirers and detractors testify to the continuing arguments about the works and personality of this great Ghanaian drummer. Ghanaba continues to be an active performer. His 1981 interpretation of Handel's "Hallelujah Chorus" earned him the title of Odomankoma Kyrema, or Divine Drummer. He was, in 1990, president of the Ghana Musicians Association (MUSIGA).

GHARTEY IV (also known as Kwamim Akyempong). Ca. 1820-1897. President of the Fante Confederacy (q.v.), 1868-1873; King of Winneba, 1872-1897. Ghartey was also an important merchant on the coast during the second half of the nineteenth century.

GLOBAL 2000 FOUNDATION. A philanthropic organization based in Atlanta, Georgia. Chaired by former American President Jimmy Carter, the organization aims at helping developing nations to find new strategies to improve and increase production levels of small-scale farmers. Global 2000 projects were first introduced in Ghana in 1986. The first projects of the foundation were officially launched by ex-President Carter in July of 1986 at Besease, near Ejura in the Asante (qq.v.) Region. In its first year of operation, about 500 small-scale farmers in Ghana benefited from Global 2000 activities. These included the provision of improved seedlings, credit facilities, and extension services. Activities of the organization assumed a national character during the 1987 farming season. The five growing areas in the country targeted for Global 2000 activities were included Somanya district in the Eastern Region; Sekyeredumase, Offinso, Ejura, Nkoranza, and Kintampo in the

Asante and Brong Ahafo regions; Ho and Kpandu in the Volta Region; Swedru (qq.v.) and Ajumako in the Central Region; and Damango district in the Northern Region. These areas were targeted for maize production while a sixth location, Wa in the Upper West Region, was the target for sorghum production.

Global 2000 established its technical committee in Ghana by July 1986. Extension officers with on-farm demonstrations became a hallmark of the Ghana experiment. See also AGRICULTURE.

GOKA, F. K. D. Born 1921. Goka was from the Volta (q.v.) Region. He was a member of the assemblies from 1954 to 1966 and a leading participant in Nkrumah's Convention People's Party (q.v.). He was a teacher before entering political life. He was a Regional Commissioner of the Volta Region, 1959-1960. In 1960 he became Minister of Trade, and in the following year he became K. A. Gbedemah's (q.v.) successor as Finance Minister. He implemented the unpopular economic austerity program before the coup of 1966.

GOLD COAST. European name for the coastal area between the Ivory Coast and Togo. Derived from the original Portuguese Costa d'Mina, the English adopted the name in 1874 for the area under their "protection," and as their rule extended over Asante (Ashante) and the Northern Territories (qq.v.) the name came to be applied to those areas as well. The Gold Coast became Ghana in 1957.

GOLD COAST NEWSPAPERS. A number of newspapers published along the coast incorporated the Gold Coast name in their titles. The *Gold Coast Aborigines* was published at Cape Coast from 1898. Its motto was "For the safety of the Republic, and the welfare of the Race." Its first editor was a Methodist minister named F. Egyir-Asam, an early Gold Coast nationalist. The *Gold Coast Chronicle* began in Accra in September 1890, edited by J. Bright Davies. The *Gold Coast Echo* was successor to another paper called the *Western Echo*. *The Gold Coast Echo* appeared between 1888 and 1890 at

Cape Coast, and was edited by J. E. Casely-Hayford (q.v.). The *Gold Coast Express* and *Gold Coast Free Press* were both newspapers that appeared in the 1890s as was Dr. F. V. Nanka-Bruce's (q.v.) *Gold Coast Independent*. J. E. Casely-Hayford's *Gold Coast Leader* was a Cape Coast paper from 1902 to 1929. The *Gold Coast Methodist Times* was a Cape Coast journal edited by Methodist ministers. The *Gold Coast Nation* was the Aborigines' Rights Protection Society (q.v.) paper, published during the World War I period by such able men as J. D. Abraham and J. P. Brown (qq.v.). The *Gold Coast News* was published by an English lawyer, W. C. Niblett, but it survived only a few months in 1885. Mensah Sarbah's (q.v.) *Gold Coast People,* promising to be a "mouthpiece" for the people, began in 1891. The *Gold Coast Spectator* and the *Gold Coast Times* round out the list. The latter paper was founded in 1874 by Prince James Brew (q.v.). It became a weekly in 1881, and for many years it was the voice of merchant opinion at Cape Coast.

GOLD COAST YOUTH CONFERENCE. A nationalist movement organized by J. B. Danquah (q.v.) and others in 1929. It held its first conference at Achimota (q.v.) in April 1930. In 1948 the Gold Coast Youth Conference was absorbed by the United Gold Coast Convention (q.v.).

GOLDEN STOOL (Sika Dwa). The symbol of Asante (q.v.). Originating in the times of Osei Tutu and Okomfo Anokye, the Golden Stool is believed by the Asante to embody the soul of their nation.

GOLD WEIGHTS. Objects made from bronze or other metals by the lost-wax method. At one time the weights were used in a balance to weigh gold, but they are also prized as art objects. Many gold weights represent African proverbs.

GOMOA (Gomua). The Akan who live between the Ga and Fante in the Winneba (qq.v.) area. They were once called the Akraman.

GONJA (Gongya, Gonya).   The western part of the Northern Region. The state of Gonja was founded by people said to have come from Mali in the seventeenth century. Yagbum was the capital, and Buipe (qq.v.) the most important commercial center.   Ndewura Jakpa is the traditional founding father. Headmen use the name of their town with the suffix "-wura" added. In time Salaga (q.v.) became the major trade city, and today the paramount chief of Gonja lives at Damongo (q.v.). The mass of the people use the Vagala language, which belongs to the Gur or Grusi (qq.v.) classification. Guan (q.v.) is also spoken in the area. During the seventeenth century the Gonja were said to have expanded eastward at the expense of Dagomba (q.v.).   The Asante (q.v.) conquered Gonja in the eighteenth century and placed it under heavy tribute.   The Asante call Gonja "Ntafo." The French, Samori's forces, the Zabrama (q.v.), and the British all arrived at the end of the nineteenth century. When the scramble ended, Gonja was part of the Northern Territories of the Gold Coast (qq.v.).

GOULDSBURY, VALÉSIUS SKIPTON.   British Surgeon-Major and colonial administrator.   Dr. Gouldsbury visited Yendi (q.v.) in 1876 as a British Commissioner, becoming the first Englishman to reach the middle Volta Basin.

GRANT, FRANCIS CHAPMAN. 1825-1908. Merchant. Son of a Scottish father and an African mother, he was educated in England. By the 1860s he was one of the leading merchants at Cape Coast (q.v.). He played a role in the organization of the Fante Confederacy (q.v.), 1868-1873, and he served several terms on the Gold Coast Legislative Council.

GRANT, "PA" GEORGE ALFRED.   1878-1956.   Merchant. Grandson of Francis Chapman Grant (q.v.), he became wealthy as a timber merchant during the first four decades of the twentieth century. In 1947 he was one of the founders of the United Gold Coast Convention (q.v.), of which he was the first president.

GREAT AKANNY (Akanni). This area is shown on a 1629 Dutch map as Great Acanij, and on the 1729 Anville map as Akanni, "formerly very powerful." The territory overlaps the Adansi-Assin (qq.v.) area of today.

GREAT KOMENDA. 5°03'N, 1°29' W. The capital of the Eguafo polity, on the coast west of Elmina (qq.v.).

GRIFFITH, WILLIAM BRANDFORD, SR. 1824-1897. British Governor. Born in Windsor, Barbados, where he was a member of the Legislative Assembly from 1861 to 1874. By 1880 he arrived in the Gold Coast (q.v.) as Lieutenant-Governor, a position he held until he became Governor. As Governor from 1885 to 1895 he did much to extend British responsibility over the Gold Coast. Boundaries with the Germans and French were defined, departments of roads, education, telegraph, and prisons were created, the first African joined the Legislative Assembly, and the first census was taken. Griffith was interested in the diversification of agriculture, but had little success in this area. It was during his administration that much of the Northern Territory (q.v.) began to recognize British control.

GRIFFITH, WILLIAM BRANDFORD, JR. 1858-1939. Colonial administrator. Like his father the governor, William Brandford Jr. was born in Barbados. Following his father to the Gold Coast (q.v.), he became Queen's Advocate, then District Commissioner, then Attorney-General, and finally Chief Justice of the Gold Coast Colony in 1887, 1898, and 1903. In 1934 he published the *Digest of Gold Coast Law Reports*. This publication was followed in 1935 by his *Note on the History of Courts and Constitution of Gold Coast Colony*.

GROSS FRIEDRICHSBURG (Princestown). 4°47'N, 2°08'W. This fort was built in 1683 by the Brandenburgers (q.v.). From 1717 to 1725 it was held by John Konny (q.v.), and the Dutch then took over the fort.

GRUSI. A general term used for several small groups in the Northern and Upper regions. The Kasena, Mo (qq.v.), Nunuma, Sisala (q.v.), Tampolense, and Vagala (q.v.) are usually identified under this rubric, but the term is of doubtful value. In the 1880s these people were often raided by the forces of Samori and of Babatu (q.v.). In some sources Grusi appears as Gourounsi, Grunshi, Grunsi, Gurunsi, etc. The Grusi live also in Burkina Faso.

GUAN (Guang, Gwan). An ancient group of people who now live in a great curve from Gonja in the Northern Region to Krakye, to Larteh in the Eastern Region, and to Senya Bereku and Efutu (qq.v.) in the Central Region. The Guan language is related to the language of the Akan.

GUGGISBERG, FREDERICK GORDON. 1869-1930. Governor of the Gold Coast (q.v.). Born in Toronto, Canada, he joined the army in 1889. He did survey work in the Gold Coast, 1902-1908, then he became Surveyor-General of Nigeria, serving there from 1910 until the outbreak of World War I. During the war he served in France. After the war he was appointed Governor of the Gold Coast, a position he held with great distinction from 1919 to 1927. He was later Governor of British Guiana, 1928-1930.

At the beginning of his tenure as Governor of the Gold Coast, Guggisberg presented a Ten-Year Development Program to the Legislative Council. He suggested first the improvement of transportation in the Gold Coast--harbors, railroads, and roads. Then, in order of priority, he listed water supply, drainage, hydroelectric projects, public buildings, town improvements, schools, hospitals, prisons, communication lines, and other improvements. He also set a goal of having half the technical departments staffed with Africans as soon as they could be trained. It was the most ambitious program ever proposed in West Africa to that time. Takoradi Harbor, Achimota College, Korle Bu Hospital, completion of the Accra-Kumasi railroad, the return of the Asantehene from exile, the Constitution of 1925, and the Provincial Councils of Chiefs (qq.v.) were achievements of Governor Guggisberg.

GUR. The Voltaic language category of the Gurma, Mole-Dagbane, Grusi, Lobi (qq.v.), and other Ghanaian groups in the northern section of the country.

GURENSE see GRUSI

GURMA. People who live in northeastern Ghana near the Togo border. Basare, Kyamba, Bimoba (q.v.), Moaba, and Konkomba (q.v.) are some of the groups in this classification.

GYADAM (Jedem). 5°56'N, 1°02'W. The old capital of Akyem Kotoku (q.v.) from 1824 to 1860. It was located in the Birim (q.v.) gap. In 1860 the capital was moved to Nsuaem after the old capital was destroyed in a war with Akyem Abuakwa (q.v.).

GYAKARI, NTIM. Ca. 1670-1701. Ruler of the Denkyira from about 1692 to 1701, when he was killed in the battle of Feyiase (q.v.). Gyakari's death and the defeat of the Denkyira marked the rise of the Asante (q.v.).

GYAMAN. An Akan Abron (qq.v.) group who founded the kingdom about 1690. They fell under Asante (q.v.) domination about 1740 and did not free themselves until 1875. Gyaman, however, revolted against Asante rule on numerous occasions. In July 1893 England and France divided the area, with the principal town, Bonduku, going to the French and being incorporated into the Ivory Coast. Samori (q.v.) and his forces occupied the region for a time in 1895.

GYASEHENE (Gyaasehene or Gyaasewahene). The head of the palace personnel of an Akan (q.v.) chief.

- H -

HAMARI see AMARIA

HANO, ALFA DAN TADANO. The first Zerma or Zabrama (q.v.) (Zaberma) leader. About 1860 Hano led a group of horsemen and footmen from Zerma, in modern Niger, to Dagomba (q.v.). Tradition has it that Hano was deeply religious, that he had made a pilgrimage to Mecca, and that he studied in a Quranic school at Salaga. Some time after the Zabrama arrived in the

Volta area they began a series of raids northwards into the lands between the Black and White Voltas (qq.v.). After the death of Hano, about 1870, Alfa Gazare dan Mahama became the leader of the Zabrama and consolidated the power of these people over a wide area of what is today northern Ghana and western Burkina Faso.

HANSEN, JOHNNY. Radical politician. During the Second Republic, Hansen emerged as leader of the People's Popular Party (PPP), a left-wing socialist group with ties to Nkrumah's old Convention People's Party (qq.v.). This close connection to former supporters of Nkrumah got the PPP banned in 1971. By March 1975 Hansen was in trouble with the Supreme Military Council (q.v.) when he and the Ghana Peace and Solidarity Council (q.v.) were accused of "organizing people for subversion." The Supreme Military Council kept Johnny Hansen in prison for some time, but he was released in 1978. In January 1979 he was leader of the People's Revolutionary Party (PRP) (q.v.), a militant socialist group. The PRP merged into the People's National Party (q.v.) by the time elections were held later in the year. During the Third Republic Hansen headed a movement called the Kwame Nkrumah's Revolutionary Guard. At the end of 1981 a coup ended the Third Republic and established the Provisional National Defense Council (PNDC) (q.v.). Hansen became Secretary of Internal Affairs in the PNDC. In March 1983 he became Secretary of Labor and Social Welfare, a position he held for only three months before parting with the PNDC. Hansen and his Kwame Nkrumah Revolutionary Guard were ideological critics of the PNDC administration. Later, in the mid-1980s, he became first Vice-Chairman of the Movement for Freedom and Justice, an organization that criticized the PNDC approach to constitutional rule in Ghana. Hansen was arrested in late 1992 for having knowledge of bomb explosions in Accra during the elections of the Fourth Republic.

HANTE see AHANTA

HARE, WILLIAM FRANCIS. Born 1906. Earl of Listowel. Hare was appointed as the Governor-General of the new country of

Ghana on 23 June 1957, and took his oath 13 November. He was the second and last Governor-General of Ghana, a position he lost when Ghana became a republic in July 1960. Earlier, Hare had served as the last Secretary of State for India and Burma. From 1948 to 1950 he was Minister of State for Colonial Affairs.

HARLEY, JOHN WILLIE KOFI. Born 1919. Policeman and politician. He was born into an Ewe (q.v.) family at Akagla, near Akwamu (q.v.), in the Eastern Region, and attended Presbyterian schools, Accra Academy, and the Metropolitan Police College in England. He joined the Gold Coast Police in 1940, and advanced through the ranks until he became Inspector-General of Police in 1966. Shortly thereafter he became Deputy Chairman of the National Liberation Council (q.v.), 1966-1969, and Deputy Chairman of the Presidential Commission in 1969. He retired after the Second Republic was established.

HARMATTAN. The dry, tropical, continental air mass that blows from the northeastern corner of the continent across the Sahara. The dry northeast trade winds affect climatic conditions in the country, especially from December through February.

HAUSA. According to one tradition, the ancestors of the Hausa people came from Arabia to settle the area of northern Nigeria. Some Hausa people reside in Niger. Even though the Hausa settlements in Nigeria were brought under Islamic/Fulani control in the early nineteenth century, the Hausa language remained the lingua franca of the region and, in fact, the language was spoken at the various markets between Nigeria and the Volta area in northeastern Ghana which Hausa traders frequented. Many Hausa live permanently in Ghana. Hausa is also a general term for any soldier or member of the constabulary who came from the north and served in the British colonial force.

HENDERSON, FRANCIS B. 1859-1934. British naval officer. In November 1896 Lt. Henderson commanded the forces charged with the responsibility of saving the area above Asante (q.v.)

from French, German, and Samori (q.v.) influence. After several engagements with the forces of Samori, he was captured and later allowed to return to the coast.

-HENE.   An Akan (q.v.) suffix signifying chief or ruler. It is equivalent to -wura in Gonja, -na in Dagomba, and -manche in Ga (qq.v.).

HERALD.   The Accra *Herald* was founded in September 1857 by Charles Bannerman (q.v.). After the publication was moved to Cape Coast (q.v.) the following year, it became the *West African Herald.*

HO.   6°36'N, 0°28'E. The chief town of the Volta Region (q.v.). It is located in the Kaba hills about 45 miles (72 km) northeast of the Adomi (q.v.) Bridge across the Volta. This Ewe (q.v.) town was once the German headquarters in the region. It was also an important missionary town during the colonial era.

HODGKIN, THOMAS LIONEL.   1910-1982.   Marxist-Leninist scholar and supporter of Nkrumah (q.v.). Professor at the University of Ghana (q.v.) beginning 1958, he became the first Director of the Institute of African Studies (q.v.) at Legon in 1962. He often published articles under the pseudonym of Kwasi Robinson. His wife, Dorothy Mary Crowfoot, won the Nobel Prize for chemistry in 1964.

HODGSON, FREDERIC.   1851-1925.   Colonial officer. He joined the British Colonial Service in 1869, was Colonial Secretary of the Gold Coast (q.v.) in 1888, Acting Governor in 1889, and Governor from 1898 to 1900. He then became Governor of Barbados from 1900 to 1904, and Governor of British Guyana, 1904-1911. He retired in 1911, and was appointed to the West African Lands Committee.

HODSON, ARNOLD WIENHOLT.   1881-1944.   Colonial officer. Hodson saw service in Transvaal, Bechuanaland, Somaliland, and Ethiopia before being appointed Governor of the Falkland Islands, 1926-1930. He was Governor of Sierra Leone, 1930-

1934, and Governor of the Gold Coast, 1934-1941. He retired at the end of his administration of the Gold Coast (q.v.).

HOMOWO FESTIVAL. A Ga-Adangbe (qq.v.) homecoming festival in which people return to their hometown to be tc gether, greet new members of the family, and remember the dead.

HORTON, JAMES AFRICANUS BEALE. 1835-1883. Army physician. Born in Sierra Leone of Ibo ancestry, Horton went to the British Isles in 1853 and studied medicine there. Returning to West Africa as an army physician, he finally retired from British service as a Lieutenant General. From 1859 to 1881 he was often stationed on the Gold Coast (q.v.). He published many books about West Africa. His *Political Economy of British West Africa* (1865) and *West African Countries and Peoples* (1868) influenced the people who tried to form the Fante Confederacy, 1868-1873. He had suggested the division of the British-controlled territories on the Gold Coast into a Fante Kingdom and an Accra Republic.

HUTTER, PAUL. Missionary, merchant, and hermit. Hutter started his career as a Swiss missionary at Ada (q.v.) in 1892. In 1896 he became a trader on the Volta, exchanging salt from Ada for guinea corn, Mossi blankets, and shea butter at Krakye (qq.v.). In 1903 he settled near Krakye and became famous as a hermit.

HUTTON-MILLS, THOMAS. 1865-1931. Lawyer and nationalist leader. Born in Accra, his African name was Korle Na. He was a grandson of James Bannerman (q.v.), a former Lieutenant-Governor of the Gold Coast. Hutton-Mills studied law in England, 1891-1894. He was an active member of the Aborigines' Rights Protection Society (q.v.) and first President of the National Congress of British West Africa (qq.v.). He was a member of the Legislative Council, 1898 to 1904, and again from 1909 to 1919.

HUTTON-MILLS, THOMAS. Lawyer and politician. He was active in the campaign for independence from colonial rule during the

1940s. In 1951 he was elected from Accra with Nkrumah as Convention People's Party (qq.v.) members of the Legislative Assembly. He served in Nkrumah's first government as Minister of Commerce, Industry, and Mines and then as Minister of Health and Labour. He was dropped from the Cabinet in 1954, and was replaced by Imoru Egala (q.v.).

HWELA (Huela, Vuela, Weela). Dyula farmers who live along the Black Volta (qq.v.).

- I -

IGWIJRA see EGWIRA

INDIRECT RULE. System of government introduced into British colonies which employed traditional rulers as agents of the colonial government. The native states became provinces under the administration of Regional Commissioners (RC). These provinces were further divided into districts under District Commissioners (DC). The Governors of the colonies were the supreme authorities in the colonies for Britain. Historians agree that Lord F. D. Lugard, in *The Dual Mandate in British Tropical Africa* (Edinburgh, 1922), outlined what became the standard British policy in Africa, of which the Gold Coast (q.v.) was a part.

INFUMA. 4°48'N, 1°57'W. Town in the Western Region, Ahanta, on the coast west of Sekondi (qq.v.). It is also known as Dick's Cove or Dixcove (q.v.). The English established a base here about 1691 and built Fort Metal Cross.

INHERITANCE LAW. Provisional National Defense Council (PNDC), (q.v.) legislation that regulated legal rights to the inheritance of property in Ghana. The four laws were the Intestate Succession Law (PNDCL 111); the Customary Marriage and Divorce (Registration) Law (PNDCL 112); the Administration of Estate (Amendment) Law (PNDCL 113; and the Head of Family (Accountability) Law (PNDCL 114). The legislation that recognized the nuclear family as the prime economic unit became law on 17 August 1985. According to a government statement, the laws were necessary because they brought traditions of inheritance in line with changes in the country.

INKORANZA see NKORANZA

INSTITUTE OF AFRICAN STUDIES. The Institute of African Studies at the University of Ghana, Legon, was formally opened in October 1963 by President Kwame Nkrumah (qq.v.). Thomas Hodgkin (q.v.), an Englishman, was the first Director. The Institute was created to study, preserve, and protect African culture.

INVESTMENT CODE. The investment code of the Provisional National Defense Council (PNDC) (q.v.) administration was announced on 15 July 1985 as part of the government's Economic Recovery Program (ERP) (q.v.) initiated since coming to power in 1981. In an effort to provide guidance to its privatization plans the PNDC outlined in the code the areas of the national economy where it was ready to attract investments. Food production and industries that used local resources (timber processing, fisheries, furniture production) were particularly targeted for tax breaks. Subsequent to the implementation of the investment code, the government held a number of public seminars at which the effects of the investment policy on local industries were discussed. See also AGRICULTURE; EXPORT PROMOTION.

INSUTA see NSUTA

ISALA see SISALA

- J -

JAKPA LANTA (Sumaila Ndewura). Ca. 1622-1666. Ruler of Gonja (q.v.). According to Gonja tradition, Jakpa was the grandson of Nabaga (q.v.), the founder of Gonja. Jakpa expanded Gonja to include all the area between the Black and White Voltas (qq.v.). He established the administrative divisions of Gonja under Nbanya (q.v.) chiefs. Jakpa was mortally wounded at Brumasi, south of the confluence of the Black and White Voltas, while fighting the Brong (q.v.). According to tradition, he was buried at Buipe (q.v.).

JAMAN see GYAMAN

JAMES, CYRIL LIONEL ROBERT. 1901-1989. Marxist historian who was born in Trinidad and was a long time friend of George Padmore (q.v.). They founded the International African Service Bureau (IASB) to advance the cause of African nationalism. James and Padmore had great influence on Kwame Nkrumah (q.v.). James was author of many books about Black heroes and revolutions. One of them was *Nkrumah and the Ghana Revolution*, 1977. Occasional reporter on sports for the *Manchester Guardian*, James lived in England until 1938. Between 1938 and 1953 he lived in the United States. After 1953 he lived in England, except for two years, 1958-1960, when he returned to the West Indies. James died in London in 1989 and was returned to Trinidad for burial.

JAMES FORT (Accra). The English established themselves at this location in the Accra (q.v.) area about 1650. The structure was almost destroyed in the July 1862 earthquake. Today it is a prison.

JIBOWU REPORT. A Commission of Inquiry into the Affairs of the Cocoa Purchasing Company established under the chairmanship of Olumuyiwa Jibowu. The committee's report issued on 21 June 1956 showed that there was gross misuse of public funds by members of the Convention People's Party (q.v.). This was one of the earliest signs of corruption in Nkrumah's (q.v.) party.

JIMAN. 8°37'N, 0°06'E. Site on the Oti River above Lake Volta and just south of Bimbila (qq.v.) where evidence of habitation as early as 10,450 B.C. has been found. This Middle Stone Age site is the earliest reported habitation in Ghana.

JOB 600 (also known as State House). Built as the venue for the 1965 Organization of African Unity (OAU) meeting in Accra (q.v.). The huge complex off Castle Road in Accra was built and furnished in less than ten months at immense expense.

JUABEN see DWABEN

JUDICIAL COUNCIL. After much criticism in 1988 from the Ghana Bar Association that the judicial system under the administration of the Provisional National Defense Council (q.v.) created room for corruption, the government established a Judicial Council. Membership of the new Judicial Council, which was chaired by the Attorney-General, included the following: i) a judge each from the Supreme Court, the Court of Appeal, and the High Court; and representative of the Association of Circuit Court Judges and Magistrates. The council also had as its members: ii) a Judge Advocate-General from the Ghana Armed Forces; iii) a representative each from the Committee for the Defense of the Revolution (q.v.), the Judicial Services, and the Board of Public Tribunals; iv) the Ghana Bar Association was to present two representatives. The Judicial Council was charged with making recommendations for the appointment of justices of the superior courts, proposing judicial reforms, investigating complaints about the conduct of judges and magistrates, submitting quarterly reports to the government, and acting as the disciplinary authority for all judges and magistrates. Justices to the superior courts were, however, to be appointed by the government upon consultation with the Judicial Council.

JUKWA. 5°16'N, 1°20'W. A village in the Central Region 14 miles (23 km) north-northwest of Cape Coast (q.v.). Jukwa was the chief Denkyira (q.v.) town from 1824 to 1873. Here on 5 June 1873 the Asante army defeated the Fante (qq.v.) and Denkyira armies. Jukwa was destroyed by the Asante, but later rebuilt.

JUNE 4TH MOVEMENT. A group formed in 1980 to provide moral support to Jerry Rawlings and other ex-Armed Forces Revolutionary Council (qq.v.) members harassed by the administration of the Third Republic. The movement derived its name from the date (4 June 1979) when a group of junior officers, led by Jerry Rawlings, seized control of government and engaged in an intensive program of ridding the army of corruption. Members of the June 4th Movement called for similar levels of accountability in the civil sector under the Limann (q.v.) administration of the Third Republic.

JUSTICE PARTY (JP). One of the opposition parties in the Second Republic. Its leader, Erasmus R. T. Madjitey (q.v.), supported the 1972 military coup. The Justice Party was an outgrowth of a merger of the National Alliance of Liberals, the People's Action Party, the United Nationalist Party (qq.v.), and the All People's Republican Party in 1970.

JUULA see DYULA

- K -

KABES, JOHN. Died 1734. Merchant. By 1680 Kabes was one of the leading merchants in Komenda (q.v.). He was engaged in the production of maize and also operated a fleet of canoes along much of the Gold Coast (q.v.). Like many African merchant princes operating between the coast and the interior as middlemen, Kabes, like John Konny (q.v.), Thomas Ewusi, and Noi, had large bands of armed persons under their command, many of them being slaves. J. K. Fynn in his *Asante and Its Neighbors* described these African merchant princes as brokers with considerable influence who did business with the various European companies that operated on the coast in the late seventeenth and early eighteenth centuries (Fynn, pp. 25-26). John Kabes was known to have dealt with the Dutch and the British.

KADE. 6°05'N, 0°50'W. Town in the Eastern Region near the Birim River (q.v.). It is a diamond-mining area and is the terminal of the central railroad. Kade is, however, known for its match factory.

KAKA, BATTLE OF. 8°10'N, 1°36'W. At this small village just northeast of Kintampo in what is now Brong-Ahafo (qq.v.) Region, Osei Bonsu in 1801 crushed forces of Gyaman and Gbuipe (qq.v.) which were working to restore Osei Kwame to the Golden Stool of Asante (qq.v.).

KANJIGA see BUILSA

KARAGA. 9°55'N, 0°26'W. One of the divisional Dagomba (q.v.) towns in the Northern Region. It was destroyed in 1898 in a battle between the British and the Zabrama (q.v.).

KARAMO (Kramo). The term "karamo" is used among the Akan generally to refer to a Muslim (qq.v.). The word "Karamoko" has been used to refer to a Muslim scholar or cleric.

KARITE see SHEA

KASENA. A Grusi (q.v.) group who live in the Paga and Navrongo (q.v.) area of the Upper West Region and across the border from Paga.

KATAMANSO (Akantamasu). 5°44'N, 0°05'W. Place in the Accra plains some 15 miles (24 km) northeast of Accra where the great battle of 7 August 1826 took place between Asante (qq.v.) and British forces and their local allies. The battle is sometimes also called the Battle of Dodowa (q.v.). Asante suffered heavy losses in this engagement.

KENTE CLOTH. Vertical woven cloth strips of about four inches' width per strip. These are sewn together to form a cloth worn by men as a toga. The patterns are colorful, and each design has its own name. Kente cloth has become one of the symbols of Ghana. Both the Ewe and Asante (qq.v.) pride themselves on their Kente weaving. Kpetoe, near Ho (qq.v.), is the Ewe center of Kente weaving. Bonwire, near Kumasi (qq.v.), is the Asante center.

KETA (Quita, Quittah). 5°55'N, 0°59'E. Anlo-Ewe commercial town in the Volta Region on an isthmus between the Keta Lagoon (qq.v.) and the Atlantic. It is often threatened by the sea, and in September of 1983 a major project was launched to prevent the town from being washed away.

Keta was founded in the seventeenth century by Togbi Wenya. The Danes established a post in the early eighteenth century, only to be replaced by the Dutch. The Danes returned in 1737 and built a fort in 1784. This was bought by the British. The area is rich in seafood, vegetables, pineapples, coconuts, plantain, poultry, goats, and pigs. Sixty-five thousand gallons of palm oil were exported from Keta in 1855. Erosion caused by lagoon flooding and the powerful sea waves continues to be the major problem faced by the town.

KETA LAGOON. Large lagoon in the Volta Region near the sea which is up to 8 miles (13 km) wide and 20 miles (32 km) long. A narrow spit, on which Anloga, Keta, and other Anlo (qq.v.) towns are located, separates it from the ocean.

KETE-KRAKYE (Krachi). 7°46'N, 0°03'W. The old towns were located about a mile apart. Krakye was a Volta River port, located just above the Oti confluence with the Volta (qq.v.), and across from where the Sene entered the Volta. Located above the Dabunga-Gyimator Cataracts of the Volta, Krachi became the terminal for canoes coming up the river with salt for the north. A ferry also crossed the river here to Nsunua on the west bank. Kete and Krachi have been described as early twin-towns, with Kete serving in the early centuries as the "slave-market village" usually filled with traders from faraway places.

Krakye was also home of the famous Dente shrine which was located in a cave on the wooded bluff overlooking the river. Krakye was a chief city and for a time it was the capital of the Brong (q.v.) Confederation.

The Volta River Project doomed old Kete-Krakye. The rapids, the Dente's cave, and the towns disappeared beneath Lake Volta in 1966. Kete-Krakye was the largest settlement in the flooded area. The twin-towns had to be resettled a short distance back, at Kantankufri. A new town emerged. In 1970 the new town overlooking Lake Volta had a population of 5,097. And the oracle was hard at work again, a scant 2 miles from his old site.

KIBI (Kibbi, Kyebi). 6°10'N, 0°33'W. The capital of Akyem Abuakwa (q.v.) since about 1815. It is located in the Atewa Hills in the Eastern Region, 15 miles (24 km) northwest of Koforidua, 60 miles (96 km) above Accra (qq.v.). A Basel Mission (q.v.) was opened here in 1861.

KINTAMPO. 8°03'N, 1°43'W. Market town in Brong-Ahafo on the western route from Kumasi (qq.v.) to the north. It is about 25 miles (40 km) from the Black Volta (q.v.). It was once an important market for the Asante commerce with Hausa (qq.v.) traders. The first Englishman reached Kintampo in 1884. Krause, a German, was there in 1887. Louis Binger, a Frenchman, spent five days there in November 1888.

KINTAMPO CULTURE. Archaeological name of an early culture which developed in Ghana as early as 1300 B.C. Sites have been unearthed by archaeologists from Christian's Village (5°38'N, 0°13'W), near Accra, to Ntereso (9°07'N, 1°12'W), in the Northern Region (qq.v.). The sites are concentrated around Kintampo. Evidence found at these places points to domesticated animals and early agriculture.

KITAB GHUNJA. Arabic documents of local authorship that chronicled the early history of Gonja (q.v.) from its creation in the mid-sixteenth century by Malian conquerors, through its consolidation, and its later conquest and incorporation into the Asante (q.v.) empire in the mid-eighteenth century.

KOBINA AMAMFI (Kwabia Amanfi). Ca. 1600-1630. Younger brother and successor to Twum Antwi (Chu Mientwi), traditional founder of the Oyoko (q.v.) royal line. Kobina Amamfi was succeeded by Oti Akentin, who was followed by

Obiri Yeboa, and then Osei Tutu (qq.v.) (the founder of the Asante nation).

KOFI KAKARI (Karikari). Ca. 1600-1884. Asantehene, 1867-1874. His reign began with campaigns east of the Volta, 1867-1871. In 1873 the Asante invasion of the south ended in the Sagrenti War (qq.v.), 1873-1874, and the British destruction of Kumasi (q.v.). Kofi Kakari was destooled in 1874. He conspired to regain the Golden Stool (q.v.) in 1883, but died suddenly on 24 June 1884.

KOFORIDUA. 6°05'N, 0°15'W. Capital of the Eastern Region, and chief town of New Dwaben (qq.v.) (Juaben). It is located on the highway and railroad from Accra to Kumasi (qq.v.). The railroad reached Koforidua in 1912.

KOKOFU. 6°30'N, 1°32'W. Village in the Asante Region near Lake Bosumtwi, and few miles from Bekwai (qq.v.). It was one of the founding villages in the Asante Confederacy (q.v.).

KOLA (cola, cola nitida, gora, bese). A nut grown on trees in the forest zone of West Africa and therefore in modern Ghana as well. This pinkish-purple and occasionally white nut is about the size of a chestnut. Its caffeine is a mild stimulant with a crisp, bitter taste that can cut hunger and thirst. Kola nuts were popular items of trade between the western coast and the Islamic regions to the north of the forest and even to the northern coasts of Africa, a commercial activity in which Ghana played an important part. In the West African environment, kola nuts are also valued for their medicinal purposes and for religious activities.

KOMENDA (Commendo, Guoffo, Kommani, Kommenda, Coomendah). 5°03'N, 1°29'W. A town in the Central Region just west of Elmina (q.v.). It was the chief town of the old Eguafo (q.v.) polity. The English established a base in 1663, the Dutch built Vredenburg there in 1688. Despite the brief presence of the French in 1688, it was the Dutch and English whose operations dominated the town.

KONKOMBA (Komba). A Gurma (q.v.) group who live along the Oti River on the Togo border in northeastern Ghana. They are a stateless group who have often been subjects of the Dagomba (q.v.). They call themselves the Bekpokpam, their language is Lekpokpam, and their territory Kekpokpam. Conflicts between them and the Nanumba have been numerous.

KONNY, JOHN (Counie, Kony, Couny). Ca. 1660-1732. Merchant prince. Konny was one of the great merchants on the Gold Coast (q.v.) in the early eighteenth century. For some time he was an ally of the Brandenburg African Company (q.v.), and from 1711 to 1724 he was Commander of the Prussian fort of Gross Friedrichsburg (q.v.) at Pokoso or Prince's Town (q.v.), some 27 miles (43 km) southwest of Takoradi (q.v.). He is sometimes called the "Last Prussian Negro Prince," and sometimes the "Brandenburg Caboceer." For over a decade he was the chief go-between for the Asante-German trade. After the Germans pulled out of Ahanta (q.v.), Konny held off the Dutch for over six years, but the Dutch took Gross Friedrichsburg away from him in 1724.

KONONGO. 6°37'N, 1°13'W. Town on the Accra-Kumasi highway in Asante Region (qq.v.). It is a twin-town of Odumasi. The railroad reached there in 1923. Konongo is known for its gold mines.

KONOR. The paramount chief of the Krobo (q.v.).

KORANTENG-ADDOW COMMITTEE. A committee set up by the Supreme Military Council in January 1977 to draw up the Union Government (qq.v.) proposals. The committee presented its report on 4 October 1977. It recommended an Executive President selected by adult suffrage from a list presented by an electoral college. It also suggested a 140-member legislature of people who would run as independents without connection to a political party because party politics would be prohibited. The Chairman of the committee was Dr. Gustav G. Koranteng-Addow, who at the time was Attorney-General and Commissioner of Justice.

KORLE BU. The General Hospital of Accra. Founded in 1925, during the administration of Governor Gordon Guggisberg (q.v.), it was the first teaching hospital in the country.

KORMANTIN (Kormantan, Kormanti, Great Kromanti, Cormantyne). 5°12'N, 1°05'W. A coastal village in the Central Region between Anomabo and Saltpond (qq.v.). The Dutch were here before 1600, but by 1638 the English were building a fort on a hill nearby. In 1665 the Dutch captured the English fort and named it Fort Amsterdam. The British held it again from 1782 to 1785. The Asante (q.v.) took the fort and plundered it in 1807, and the people of Anomabo destroyed it in 1811. By then the Europeans had already outlawed the Atlantic slave trade. The ruins were regained by the British in 1868. In the 1950s a restoration project began, but it has not been completed.

KORSAH, KOBINA ARKU. 1894-1967. Lawyer, judge, nationalist leader. Born in Saltpond, educated at Mfantsipim, Fourah Bay College, and the Universities of Durham and London, Korsah became one of the more distinguished early nationalist leaders. He was active in the Aborigines' Rights Protection Society and the National Congress of British West Africa (qq.v.). He was the municipal member of the Legislative Council from Cape Coast (q.v.) from 1928 to 1940. In 1942 he was a member of the Executive Council. Appointed a judge in 1945, he became Chief Justice of the Gold Coast in 1956, and first Chief Justice of Independent Ghana in 1957. In 1963 he presided over the treason trials of Tawia Adamafio and others charged in the attempted assassination of Nkrumah (qq.v.). When the defendants were acquitted, President Nkrumah removed Korsah from office. Korsah died three years later.

KOTEI, R. E. A. Died 1979. Soldier. One of the leaders of the military government from 1972 to 1979. He was Commissioner of Works and Housing from 1972 to 1975 and of Information in 1975. He then became Chief of the Defence Staff. He was executed by the Armed Forces Revolutionary Council (q.v.) in June 1979.

KOTOKA AIRPORT (Accra). Ghana's International Airport, located on the northeastern end of Accra (q.v.) just off Liberation Road. It is only a 15-minute drive to Tema (q.v.) via the Nkrumah Freeway. The airport was named for General Emmanuel K. Kotoka (q.v.), who was killed at the airport in April 1967 during an attempted military coup.

KOTOKA, EMMANUEL KWASI. 1926-1967. Soldier. Kotoka was born in the little village of Alakple, near Keta, in the Volta Region (qq.v.). He enlisted in the Gold Coast Regiment in 1947 and attended Infantry School at Teshie. By 1951 he was a Sergeant-Major. Commissioned in November 1954, he served for a time in England and Germany. By 1959 he was a Captain. In 1960 and 1962 he went to the Congo (Zaire) as a member of the UN Emergency Force. By 1965 he was Commander of the First Brigade of Infantry at Kumasi. There he helped plan the coup which removed Nkrumah (q.v.) from power, on 24 February 1966. He was 39 years old and a Colonel by then. After the coup, Kotoka became a member of the National Liberation Council and Commander of the Ghana Armed Forces (qq.v.), with the rank of Major-General, soon to be Lieutenant-General, and Minister of Defence, Health, Labour, and Social Welfare. He was killed during an unsuccessful countercoup on 17 April 1967 by Lt. Moses Yeboah in front of the Accra airport. A statue of General Kotoka was erected on the spot where he fell, and in 1969 the airport was named for him.

KOTOKO. The Privy Council of Asante (q.v.). It was made up of the Asantehene, the Queen Mother, the chiefs of Dwaben, Bekwai, and Mampong, and selected nobles of Kumasi (qq.v.). It was the court of last resort. It could also declare war.

KOTOKO UNION SOCIETY. An organization formed by educated Asante (q.v.) in 1916 to foster Asante pride and interests.

KOTOKU AKYEM (Akyem Oda). One of the branches of the Akyem (q.v.). Most of the Kotoku Akyem live in the Eastern Region near the Birim River (qq.v.).

KPANDU. 7°00'N, 0°18'E. An Ewe town on the left or east bank of Lake Volta (qq.v.) about 90 miles (144 km) inland from the coast and 20 miles (34 km) from the Togo border. It is now an administrative unit of the Volta Region, but it was once the center of German kola plantations. It has become a busy port since Lake Volta was finished.

KPEMBE (Pembi). 8°33'N, 0°30'W. Gonja divisional capital which is located just 2 miles (3 km) east of Salaga (qq.v.). It was captured by the Asante (q.v.) about 1744. Europeans began to arrive from 1876, and the chief of Kpembe signed a treaty with British Agent G. E. Ferguson (qq.v.) in September 1894. A German force under von Zech occupied the town in 1896.

KPESI (Kpeshi). Guan people along the coast in the Tema (qq.v.) area. These people were believed to have settled the Accra Plains before the Ga and Adangbe (qq.v.) arrived.

KPETOE. 6°33'N, 0°42'E. Village in the Volta Region near the Togo border and 17 miles (27 km) southeast of Ho (qq.v.). It is famous as a center for the production of Ewe Kente cloth (q.v.).

KPONG (Pong). 6°09'N, 0°04'E. Manya Krobo town in the Eastern Region on the Volta River between Senchi and Akuse (qq.v.). It is 18 miles (30 km) downstream from Akosombo Dam and about 50 miles (80 km) northeast of Accra (qq.v.). The town was burned in the Anlo-Ada (qq.v.) War in 1865. It became an important emporium for the palm oil trade during the early days of European commerce. In 1880 Governor Ussher (q.v.) described the town as "a receptacle for all the rascals in the eastern division." Both the Basel (q.v.) and Wesleyan missionaries organized schools in the area. It also served as headquarters for some of the early exploration of the Volta River (q.v.). Today the University of Ghana (q.v.) has an agricultural station at Kpong, and it is a veterinary center. In November 1977 a power project was started on the river nearby, and the first unit of this enterprise went into operation in 1981.

KRAMO see KARAMO

KRAUSE, GOTTLOB ADOLF. 1850-1938. German explorer. He made his first trip to Africa in 1869, and between 1879 and 1881 he explored the Sahara and North Africa. On 12 May 1886 he left Accra to follow a route to the Niger. He was in Salaga (q.v.) from 18 June to 7 July, when he joined a caravan which was taking kola (q.v.) nuts to Timbuktu. The caravan followed the left bank of the White Volta northward, passing through Dagomba (qq.v.) to Walewale, and on into what is today Burkina Faso. Krause reached the Mossi (q.v.) capital at Ouagadougou on 24 September, and remained there almost a month before heading north again. In December he returned to the Mossi capital, not having gone all the way to the Niger. Early in 1887 he returned south again, visiting Wa, Bole, and Kintampo (qq.v.), before reaching Salaga again in April. After this trip he settled in Togo for several years as a merchant, but returned to Germany as a result of World War I.

KREPI. An Ewe group who live in the Volta Region between Ho (qq.v.) and Asikuma. Peki is their chief town. Their ruler is called the Fia. At one time they were dominated by the Akwamu (q.v.), but they broke away in 1833. The English purchased a claim to the area from Denmark in 1850, but during the scramble for Africa by the Europeans it ended in German hands. In 1914 the British got the area again.

KROBO (Klo). Adangbe group who live along the right bank of the Volta (qq.v.). Odumase, Kpong, and Akuse (qq.v.) are their chief towns. The two major Krobo groups are the Manya and the Yilo (qq.v.), each under a chief called the Konor. The area was at one time subject to Denmark, but the British dominated the region after 1850.

KROBO HILL. 6°05'N, 0°03'E. Famous Krobo position just southwest of Akuse, near the Tema-Akosombo (qq.v.) highway. It was almost impregnable, except for lack of good water supplies. The Krobo often held out here against their enemies.

KRONTIHENE (Kontihene). The commander of an Akan (q.v.) military force. In Asante the Bantama (qq.v.) stool had priority for the position.

KUHNE, JOHANNES see RAMSEYER, FRIEDRICH AUGUST

KUMASI (Kumase, Coomassie). 6°41'N, 1°37'W. The capital of Asante (q.v.). Founded about 1680 by Asantehene Osei Tutu near an earlier village of Tafo in the old Kwaman (qq.v.) district. In the 1930s Kumasi was called the Garden City of West Africa. Kumasi was and continues to be the commercial and transportation center of the middle belt of Ghana.

The first half of the nineteenth century was the golden age of Kumasi, which was the capital of the richest and most powerful nation in that part of West Africa. By 1850 the population may have been more than 30,000, and visitors reported on the vitality of the city. But the city was occupied by the British in 1874. The palace of the Asantehene (q.v.) was destroyed and much of the city was burned. Recovery was not complete before the English returned in 1896. Once again much of the town was destroyed, and this time the Asantehene, Prempe I (q.v.), was carried away into exile. By 1897 the British had built a fort in the center of the town, and foreign troops patrolled the streets. Kumasi had reached its nadir. The population was less than 3,000. In 1900 the Asante revolted and laid siege to the British in their fort. Once again the city suffered, and the Asante lost the last of their claims to independence. In 1901 Asante became a part of the Gold Coast administration.

The British connection brought modern transportation to Kumasi. Highways to Accra, the Cape Coast, and Obuasi and Dunkwa (qq.v.) in the south were improved. The Great Northern Road--through Mampong, Atebubu, Salaga, and Tamale to Bolgatanga and Navrongo (qq.v.)--was also improved. The railroad (q.v.) from Sekondi (q.v.) arrived in 1903, and the tracks from Accra in 1923. A railroad to the north was planned, but never built. By 1911 the population of Kumasi was 18,853, and in 1921 the city was a thriving metropolis of almost 24,000. Prempe I was allowed to return in 1924, the same year that Wesley College opened. The

Central Market was established in 1925 just across Zongo Road from the Catholic Cathedral and the Railroad Station. Electricity was installed in 1927, and piped water came in 1934. The census in 1931 showed the population to be almost 36,000. A Town Council was established in 1943 that became a Municipal Council in 1954. The University of Science and Technology (q.v.) opened in 1952, and in 1953 Kumasi acted as host to the Sixth Pan-African Conference. In 1948 there were nearly 78,000 citizens in the Garden City. The population of Kumasi, the second-largest city in Ghana, was estimated in 1988 to be about 385,192.

KUMAWU. 6°54'N, 1°17'W. A town in the Asante Region some 10 miles (16 km) southeast of Nsuta or 30 miles (48 km) northeast of Kumasi (qq.v.). By tradition the town was founded by people from the village of Asantemanso and according to one oral tradition, the settlement competed against Kumasi for the capital of Asante (qq.v.).

KUSASI (Kusase, Kusae). A Mole-Dagbani (q.v.) group who live in the Upper East Region of Ghana and in Burkina Faso and Togo. Bawku (q.v.) is their chief town. Their language is Kusal.

KUSI OBODUM (Kusi Bodum, Kwesi Bodom). Asantehene, 1750-1764. He was an old man when his reign began. His predecessor, Opoku Ware (q.v.), had selected a prince named Dako as his heir. Kusi Obodum was enstooled and Dako began a civil war. Dako was ultimately defeated and executed. Later, a campaign in the east against Oyo and Dahomey turned out to be a disaster, and Kusi Obodum, old and almost blind, abdicated. He died a short time later. His body was not placed in the royal mausoleum at Bantama (q.v.).

KWA. Niger-Congo language classification which includes the languages of the Akan, Guan, Ewe, and Ga-Adangbe (qq.v.).

KWAHU (Kwawu, Quahoe). An Akan people who live between the Afram River to the north, the Onyim River on the northwest, the Pawnpawn on the east, and the Accra-Kumasi railroad on the south. Abetife, Mpraeso (qq.v.), and Nkawkaw are important Kwahu towns. During the eighteenth and nineteenth centuries Kwahu was counted in the Asante (q.v.) sphere. The Kwahu area was fertile ground for the Presbyterian missionaries.

KWAHU ESCARPMENT. The watershed between the Afram and its tributaries to the north and the tributaries of the Tano, Pra, and Densu (qq.v.). The fall line runs roughly from Wenchi, through Mampong to Koforidua (qq.v.).

KWAKU ADUSEI see OPOKU WARE II

KWAKU DUA I (Fredua Agyeman). Ca. 1797-1867. Asantehene, 1834-1867. He took part in the Gyaman campaign in 1818-1819 and was a division Commander in the battle of Katamanso (qq.v.) (Akantamansu or Dodowa) in 1826. He was elected Asantehene (q.v.) in 1834 without opposition. After his reign began he adopted a policy of peace, trade, and open roads. He persuaded the Dwaben (q.v.) refugees to return to their old homes in 1841. In that same year he sent troops north into Gonja and Dagomba (qq.v.) in a campaign that lasted until 1844. In 1863 his armies occupied considerable territories in the south, which was under British protection. Relations with the British steadily declined from 1863 until Kwaku Dua died on 27 April 1867.

KWAKU DUA II (Kwaku Dua Kuma, Agyeman Kofi, Quacoe Duah). Ca. 1860-1884. Asantehene, 27 April-10 June 1884. He was enstooled during a period of great turmoil in Kumasi (q.v.), and during his short reign he tried to eliminate all his enemies. He died of smallpox after a reign of six weeks. An interregnum followed his death, 1884-1888.

KWAKU DUA III see PREMPE I

KWAMAN (Kwaaman). The capital of the Kumasi traditional area in the reigns before Osei Tutu (qq.v.) and the establishment of Kumasi.

KWAME MENSA see MENSA BONSU

KWAME NKRUMAH IDEOLOGICAL INSTITUTE (Winneba).
An institute established by Nkrumah (q.v.) to produce
Ghanaian Nkrumahist socialists and African freedom fighters.
The cornerstone was laid on 18 February 1961. The first
Director was Kwodwo Addison, a former trade union official
and friend of John Tettegah (q.v.). A collection of theorists
from Communist countries were appointed to the Institute's
first faculty. On 5 November 1965 Nkrumah assumed personal
charge of the administration after the Director was fired. The
coup a few weeks later in 1966 ended ideological training at
the Institute and the facilities turned into the Advanced
Teacher Training College of Winneba (q.v.). The program is
now part of the School of Education at the University of Cape
Coast (q.v.).

KWAWU see KWAHU

KYEBI see KIBI

KYEREPONG (Cherepong). A Guan (q.v.) group. Most of the
Kyerepong live in the Eastern Region. They have several
villages in the Akuapem (q.v.) hills around Adukrom.

- L -

LABADI (Labade). 5°33'N, 0°09'W. Ga (q.v.) coastal town which
was one of the original seven Ga settlements. It appeared on
a Dutch map in 1629. Today it is an eastern suburb of Accra
(q.v.).

LADOKU. A coastal Adangbe state which once existed east of
Accra and between the Dodowa and Volta rivers (qq.v.). The
state was also known as Ningo. The town of Ladoku was
conquered by the Akwamu (q.v.) in 1679, and it was destroyed
in 1702. The area supplied fish, salt, and livestock to Gold
Coast (q.v.) markets.

LAMPTEY, EMMANUEL ODARQUAYE OBETSEBI. 1902-1963. Ga (q.v.) attorney and politician. A native of Accra, he graduated in law from the University of London in 1939 and returned home to practice law and be elected as municipal member of the Legislative Council. Lamptey was one of the founders of the United Gold Coast Convention (q.v.) and was one of the famous Big Six arrested after the riots of 1948. He was a member of the Coussey Committee (q.v.), which drew up plans for constitutional reform in 1949, but he was defeated in the 1951 elections. As one of the leading opponents of Nkrumah (q.v.), he helped form the Ghana Congress Party in 1952, the National Liberation Movement in 1956, and the United Party in 1957 (qq.v.). In 1961 he went into exile in Togo, where he plotted against the Convention People's Party (q.v.) and Nkrumah. After Nkrumah offered an amnesty to his opponents, Lamptey returned home, but was arrested on 5 October 1962 and sent to Nsawam prison, where he died the following January of cancer.

LAMPTEY, JONATHAN KWESI. Born 1909. A native of Sekondi (q.v.). He attended Mfantsipim School at Cape Coast, Wesley College at Kumasi, Achimota, the University of Exeter (England), and the University of London. Returning to the Gold Coast, he became a science teacher at Mfantsipim (q.v.). He was also an early member of the Convention People's Party (CPP) (q.v.). He acted as Deputy Chairman of the (CPP) in 1950 and was elected to the Legislative Assembly in 1951 on the party's ticket. He became Junior Minister of Finance in Nkrumah's (q.v.) first government. Before 1951 was over, Lamptey broke with Nkrumah and returned to teaching, this time in Sekondi. He soon entered politics as a member of the Ghana Congress Party (q.v.). In September 1954 he followed K. A. Busia into the National Liberation Movement, and then into the United Party (qq.v.). After the coup of 1966 he became Head of the State Gold Mining Corporation. When political parties were allowed again in 1969, he became a lieutenant of Busia in the Progress Party (q.v.). He won a seat in the National Assembly of the Second Republic, 1969-1972. He was a member of Busia's Cabinet, first as Minister of Defence and then as Minister of Parliamentary Affairs. He acted as Prime Minister on several occasions while Busia was out of the country. He retired from politics after the coup of 1972.

LANDS BILL OF 1894. A measure introduced in the Legislative Council on 14 November 1894. The bill would have vested wastelands, forestlands, and minerals in the Crown of England. The object was to control exploitation of the timber and mineral resources in areas under British protection. Opposition developed at once, and the measures never became law.

LANDS BILL OF 1897. A bill introduced in the Legislative Council on 10 March 1897. It gave the British Crown rights of administration of public lands, but did not claim Crown ownership. Africans could make land grants to Europeans only with the Governor's express permission. Opposition to the bill developed at once, and the Gold Coast Aborigines' Rights Protection Society (q.v.) grew out of the agitation. The bill was withdrawn in 1898. A Concessions Ordinance was enacted in 1900 which accomplished most of what the British wanted to do in the land acts, namely, give security to titles for concession-holders and give protection against fraud to the African landowners.

LAND TITLE REGISTRATION LAW. Enacted in 1986 to enforce compulsory registration of land throughout the country. In a memorandum to the enactment, the new law was said to be replacing a Land Registration Act of 1962. The government of the Provisional National Defense Council (q.v.) argued that the 1962 law encouraged litigation, as there was no systematic proof that a person in occupation of land had obtained rights in respect thereof. Another major weakness of the 1962 law was that there were no maps or plans that determined scientific and accurate boundaries. While addressing these weaknesses, the 1986 land registration law would also make agricultural tenancies and credit less complicated.

LANTA see JAKPA LANTA

LEAGUE OF GHANA PATRIOTS. Inner circle of Nkrumah's lieutenants in the Convention People's Party (qq.v.).

LEGISLATIVE COUNCIL. In 1850 when the Gold Coast (q.v.) was established as a separate dependency of the British Crown, the Legislative Council was created to advise the Governor. Members were appointed by the Governor for the first 75 years of the history of the Council. Africans were appointed from the beginning, James Bannerman (q.v.) serving on the first Council. Guggisberg's (q.v.) reforms of 1925 provided for the election of a member each by Accra, Cape Coast, and Sekondi (qq.v.) as well as six members to be elected by councils of chiefs. The Burns Constitution of 1946 (q.v.) provided for an African majority for the first time and gave representation to Asante (q.v.). The 1950 changes provided for an assembly of 75, plus six special members. This body would select its own Speaker. The Northern Territories (q.v.) were also represented.

LEGON. 5°39'N, 0°11'W. Some 8 miles (13 km) north of Accra (q.v.). The University of Ghana is located at Legon.

LEGON OBSERVER. Bi-weekly journal of the Legon Society on National Affairs. It began publication in July 1966 and has been published intermittently as political conditions have allowed.

LENNOX-BOYD CONSTITUTION, 1957. The compromise constitution which was supported by the British Secretary of State for the Colonies, Rt. Hon. A. T. Lennox-Boyd. This was the constitution under which the Gold Coast (q.v.) became independent Ghana.

LEVER BROTHERS (Unilever). Trading firm which was founded by William Leverhulme (1851-1925) in 1884. It entered the West African market in 1896, with special interest in palm oil and cocoa (q.v.). By 1929 it was diversified into mines, timber, and almost every area of commerce. In 1929 the Unilever interests created the United Africa Company (q.v.). The company's operation continues today in the soap business.

LEWIS REPORT. In 1953 the Gold Coast (q.v.) government requested W. A. Lewis of Manchester University to investigate the possibilities of industrialization in the Gold Coast. Lewis suggested creating a favorable climate for industry, improvements in agriculture, expansion of basic services, and gradual expansion of exports.

LIBERATOR. National Liberation Movement (q.v.) newspaper which began publication in 1955 and lasted only to 1957. It opposed Nkrumah's Convention People's Party (qq.v.).

LIGBI (Ligby). One of the earliest Dyula groups of merchant to trade along the Black Volta (qq.v.). Ligbi were involved in the kola (q.v.) and gold trade at one time.

LIJDZAAMHEID, FORT. (Fort Patience), 5°17'N, 0°44'W. A fort started by the Dutch at Apam, just west of Winneba (qq.v.), in 1697. The fort was said to have been taken over by the British in 1868 but returned to the Dutch by a treaty. The name of the fort (Lijdzaamheid or Patience), according to A. W. Lawrence, came from the Dutch perception of their endurance to hostilities from local groups. Today the building is used as a police station.

LIMANN, HILLA. Born 1934. President of the Third Republic--24 September 1979 to 31 December 1981. A native of the Sisala district where he was enskinned as the Paramount Chief of the Gwolu traditional area in 1990. Dr. Limann had earned an economics degree from the University of London, and a doctorate in political science and law from the Sorbonne in France. In Ghana, Limann taught school before joining the diplomatic service. He was a member of the Convention People's Party (q.v.) and called himself an Nkrumahist before the coup of 1966. Later he was a member of the commission which wrote the Constitution for the Second Republic. In April 1979 he was nominated by the People's National Party (PNP) (q.v.) as their candidate for President. This was due in part to his being a nephew to Imoru Egala (q.v.), chief founder of the PNP, but by his own right, Hilla Limann was a highly qualified candidate. His Vice-Presidential candidate, J. W. de Graft-Johnson (q.v.), was also an attractive candidate. They easily defeated their opposition, and were sworn in on 24 September 1979. The administration of the Third Republic, which Limann headed was criticized by opposition groups as ineffective in addressing the nation's political and economic problems. To the PNP government, however, their rule was one guided by cautious and pragmatic considerations necessary for the long-term redress of the situation in which the country found itself.

On 31 December 1981 Jerry Rawlings and the Provisional National Defence Council (qq.v.) seized power for a second time. Limann was arrested and held in protective custody until September 1983. Not much was heard of Dr. Limann until 1992 when the People's National Convention (q.v.) unsuccessfully ran him as their Presidential candidate in the Fourth Republic.

LITTLE KOMENDA see KOMENDA

LOBI (Lo, Lober). A Mole-Dagbani (q.v.) group who inhabit the extreme northwestern section of Ghana. Some also live in Burkina Faso and in northwestern Ivory Coast. The Birifor, Miwo, Lo Dagaba, Lowili, and Yangala are related groups.

LOCAL GOVERNMENT ORDINANCE, 1951. A CPP-sponsored ordinance which was enacted by the Legislative Assembly in November 1951. It provided for local councils, with two-thirds of the members selected by popular vote and one-third appointed by the chiefs. The Chairman of the local council would be an elected member, and he would be the real authority at the local level.

LONGORO. 8°11'N, 1°53'W. A small village on the Black Volta in the Brong-Ahafo Region which used to be the limit to which canoe traffic could come until the Volta dam (qq.v.) was built. Goods were once unloaded here for Kintampo (q.v.).

LONSDALE, RUPERT LA TROBE. A British officer who traveled widely in the Gold Coast colony, Asante, and the Northern

Territories (qq.v.) during the 1880s. In October 1881 he left Accra for Kumasi, and from Kumasi he went to Salaga, Yendi, Krakye, and Krepi (qq.v.), before returning to Accra. In a report of 18 March 1882, he outlined the commercial possibilities of trade in the north. From April to August 1882 he went on a mission to Asante and Gyaman, returning through Sefwi and Denkyira to Cape Coast (qq.v.). He made several trips to Kumasi in 1887. Lonsdale reported at the time on the internal dissensions within Asante. He died in 1888.

- M -

MACCARTHY, CHARLES. 1768-1824. Governor of the Gold Coast (q.v.), 1822-1824. British general and administrator of French and Irish parentage. Serving in the French army during the revolution, MacCarthy joined the British service and in 1812, he was placed in charge of British forces in the Senegal. He became the first acting Governor in 1814 and in 1816 he was made Governor of Sierra Leone. When the Company of Merchants (q.v.) was dissolved in 1821, he became responsible for the British settlements on the Gold Coast as well. He is remembered as one of the better administrators of Sierra Leone.

In the Gold Coast MacCarthy quickly developed an antipathy to the Asante (q.v.), and he formed the coastal peoples into an alliance against the Asante. In 1823 the Asante executed a Fante (q.v.) in British service, and MacCarthy, anxious to silence the Asante, moved against them. On 21 January 1824 he was killed in a skirmish near Bonsaso (q.v.). The Africans call the engagement Insamankow or Nsamankow.

MACLEAN, GEORGE. 1801-1847. British administrator. He went to Africa as a lieutenant in the Royal African Colonial Corps in Sierra Leone in 1826. On 19 February 1830 and with the rank of Captain, George Maclean of the Royal African Colonial Corps became President of the Council of Merchants at Cape Coast (qq.v.). In this position, Maclean was also Governor of the Gold Coast (q.v.) colony from 1830 through 1836, and again from 1838 through 1843. From 1843 until his death in 1847 he was Judicial Assessor. As Governor of the Gold Coast, Maclean managed, through negotiations, to maintain peaceful relations with Asantehene Osei Yaw Akoto and with Asantehene Kwaku Dua (qq.v.) in the earlier part of that monarch's reign. As a result of this peace initiated by the Treaty of Peace and Commerce (1831), trade with the Akan (q.v.) interior considerably increased. In later decades of the nineteenth century, the varying interpretations by both the Asante and the British of the 1831 treaty, according to Ivor Wilks (q.v.), was fundamental to the conflicts that developed between the two powers.

MADJITEY, ERASMUS (ERIC) RANSFORD TAWI. Born 1920. He was Commissioner of Police under Nkrumah (q.v.), 1958-1964, but was sacked when a constable tried to kill the President. From then until the 1966 coup he was held in prison under preventive detention (q.v.). He was Ghana's High Commissioner to Pakistan, 1966-1969, during the National Liberation Council (q.v.) period. When political parties were allowed again he was one of the leaders of the National Alliance of Liberals (q.v.), and was elected to the National Assembly for Manya Krobo (q.v.). He was leader of the Opposition to Busia (q.v.) in the Parliament. He was arrested in April 1978 by the Supreme Military Council, but was released by the coup of the Armed Forces Revolutionary Council (qq.v.).

MAKOLA. The three major markets of Accra located between Independence Avenue and Liberation Avenue. These markets were respectively referred to as Makola 1, 2 and 3. On 18 August 1979, the markets were razed by Armed Forces Revolutionary Council (q.v.) troops for the reason that the market women had gained too much economic power and had been party to widespread black marketing in the country.

MAMPELLE. The language of Mamprusi (q.v.).

MAMPONG AKUAPEM (Mampon Akwapim). 5°55'N, 0°08'W. Town in the hills of Akuapem where the Basel missionaries experimented with cocoa (qq.v.) seedlings first in 1859. Tetteh

Quashie (q.v.) planted his first cocoa near here in 1878 and had his first harvest in 1883. The hospital of Mampong is named for Tetteh Quashie.

MAMPONG ASANTE (Mampon Ashanti). 7°04'N, 1°24'W. Town on the Great Northern Road from Kumasi to Tamale, 30 miles (48 km) northeast of Kumasi (qq.v.). It is one of the founding states of the Asante Union, and the Mamponghene is second only to the Asantehene (q.v.) in importance in the Union. He occupies the Silver Stool while the king of Asante occupies the Golden Stool (qq.v.). The Bretuo clan of Mampong migrated from Adansi (q.v.).

MAMPONG ESCARPMENT. The southern elevated edge of the Volta basin is the principal watershed of Ghana. The line runs from Wenchi in the northwest to Koforidua (qq.v.) in the southwest. The watershed is referred to by some as the Mampongtin Range and as the Kwahu Escarpment (q.v.) by others.

MAMPRUGU. This is the old capital of Mamprusi (q.v.). It was located in the area of Gambaga and Nalerigu (qq.v.), the present chief city of the Mamprusi. The name of the old capital is sometimes used as the name of the Mamprusi people.

MAMPRUSI. One of the Mole-Dagbani (q.v.) states in the Northern Region. It was founded by conquerors who came from the east in the fourteenth century. The dynasty was founded by Gbewa of Pusiga (qq.v.). His son Tohogo (Tohagu, or Tohugu) founded the town of Mamprugu. Gambaga and Naleregu (qq.v.) are the chief villages of Mamprusi. The Mamprusi are Muslim in theory, but they do not follow traditional Muslim practices. They signed a treaty of friendship with the British on 28 May 1894.

MANCHE (Mantse). A paramount chief of the Ga and Adangbe (q.v.).

MANCHESTER PAN-AFRICAN CONGRESS. The Congress of 1945 that took place at Manchester brought together nationalists such as Kwame Nkrumah, Joe Appiah, and J. C. de Graft-Johnson (qq.v.). It was at this Congress that Nkrumah first came into contact with many of those who soon would become leaders in the movement for African independence. Nkrumah organized his West African National Secretariat (q.v.) at Manchester in order to promote the idea of a West African Federation. George Padmore (q.v.) served as Joint Secretary with Kwame Nkrumah.

MANHYIA (Menhia). The section of Kumasi (to the northeast of the current central market) where the palace of the Asantehene (qq.v.) is located. The meeting hall of the Asanteman Council is also located here.

MANIFESTO, THE RURAL. A Provisional National Defense Council (PNDC) (q.v.) statement on rural development was made public on 4 April 1984. The document was the theoretical framework for an integrated rural development in Ghana. In this manifesto, the features and causes of rural underdevelopment were evaluated. Also, in this document, strategies for the eradication of rural underdevelopment were presented. The document directly linked the nation's economic problems to rural underdevelopment. The PNDC, therefore, planned strategies that concentrated on the provision of facilities, infrastructures, and organizational structures to aid rural development. The goal was to improve and increase food production, food storage, and food processing in the rural sectors. Programs for the provision of improved health services, housing, roads, and rural electrification were also mentioned. See also AGRICULTURE.

MANKESIM (Mankessim, Mankesemu). 5°16'N, 1°01'W. Important Fante "Great Town" in the Central Region about 20 miles (32 km) northeast of Cape Coast on the highway towards Accra (qq.v.). It is the location of the great Fante Oracle, Nananom Mpow. The Fante Confederacy (qq.v.) was started here in 1867.

MANKUMA. 9°11'N, 2°29'W. A small village on the Bole-Wa road in the Northern Region, just east of the Black Volta and

12 miles (19 km) north of Bole (qq.v.). It is the location of the mausoleum of the chiefs of Yagbon (Gonja).

MANSO (Mansu). 5°31'N, 1°10'W. The Assin (q.v.) Apemanim capital, on the Cape Coast-Kumasi (qq.v.) highway in the Central Region. Located some 30 miles (40 km) north of Cape Coast, it was once an important collection point for slaves being brought down from Asante (q.v.) for sale on the coast.

MANYA KROBO. A branch of the Adangbe. These Eastern Krobo live in the Volta Plains and have a capital at Odumasi (qq.v.).

MATE KOLE, EMMANUEL. 1860-1939. Konor, or Paramount Chief, of the Manya Krobo, he was born at Odumasi (qq.v.). Once a teacher in Basel mission (q.v.) schools. He was elected Konor in 1892. During his rule he advocated agricultural development, and he built many miles of roads. In 1911 he became the first Paramount Chief to be appointed to the Gold Coast Legislative Council, on which he served several terms.

MAWU. The supreme deity of the Ewe (q.v.), creator of the world, and source of all power.

MENSA BONSU. Ca. 1840-1896. Asantehene (q.v.). He became king after Kofi Kakari (q.v.) was deposed in September 1874. Among his immediate tasks was the restoration of the power of Kumasi (q.v.). He defeated Dwaben (q.v.) in November 1875, and tried to regain control of trade to the north. Despite efforts at reorganizing the civil administration and the military to secure his power, he was deposed in March 1883. The British arrested Mensa Bonsu in early 1896, and he died a short time later.

MENSAH, JOSEPH HENRY. Born 1928. Economist, politician. Educated at Achimota (Legon), London School of Economics, and Stanford University. He was a teacher and did research at the University of Ghana (q.v.) in Legon, 1953 to 1958, then was an economist for the UN from 1958 to 1961. He returned to Ghana to work for the National Planning Commission, 1961-1965. From 1965 to 1969 he was with the Economic

Commission for Africa. In 1969 he joined Busia's Progress Party (qq.v.), was elected to the National Assembly, and was Minister of Finance, 1969-1972. The National Redemption Council (q.v.) sent him to prison in 1975 for causing disaffection from their rule. Released in 1978, he was banned from politics the following year, but was an active supporter of the Popular Front Party (q.v.), the old Busia coalition, in the 1979 elections. He went into exile in London in 1983 where he headed the Ghana Democratic Movement, a London-based opposition group to the administration of the Provisional National Defense Council (PNDC) (q.v.). Mensah was believed to have been associated with a 1984 plan to overthrow the PNDC. Later, in 1985 Mensah and two other persons were arrested in the United States for violating U.S. customs laws in a conspiracy to buy missiles, anti-aircraft guns and other weapons, ostensibly to be sent to Ghana to destabilize the administration of the PNDC. Even though his two associates were convicted in 1986, J. H. Mensah was freed on grounds of a mistrial.

METAL CROSS (Metaal Kruis, "Brass Cross"). The Dutch name for Dixcove (q.v.) Fort. The post was built by the English at the end of the seventeenth century, but the Dutch held it from 1868 until 1872, when the Dutch sold it to the British. The English called it Metal Cross. The fort was restored in the 1950s and is now used as government offices.

MFANTSE (Fante). The language of the Fante-Akan (qq.v.) people, spoken in the central and western coastal areas of Ghana.

MFANTSIPIM. One of Ghana's most prestigious secondary schools. It was started in 1876 as a Wesleyan mission at Cape Coast (q.v.). It became a secondary school in 1909. Many of Ghana's most distinguished sons are products of this boys' school.

MILNER-SIMON AGREEMENT. The agreement between the British and French over the boundary of their areas of Togoland. It was concluded on 10 July 1919. England gained control of eastern Dagomba and part of the Ewe (qq.v.) territory. This was confirmed by a League of Nations mandate in 1922.

MINA COAST. The West African coastal area that became the Gold Coast (q.v.) in the seventeenth century. The Portuguese were the first Europeans to arrive here about 1471. Compared to the grain and the ivory coasts to the west, the Mine (Da Mina or the Gold Coast) was preferred by the Portuguese as they exchanged European goods for gold and gold ornaments. By 1482, the location of Elmina (q.v.) on the Mina coast had become the favorite Portuguese port of call as they built the fortress, Castle of San Jorge (q.v.). Portuguese monopoly of the Gold Coast was challenged when other Europeans, such as the English and the Dutch, organized their respective East India companies in the early seventeenth century.

MINING. Prospecting for minerals in the Gold Coast (q.v.) was an important economic occupation in pre-colonial times. It was, however, not until the creation of the Ashanti Goldfield Corporation (AGC) (q.v.) in 1897 that large-scale commercial prospecting became a factor in Ghana's economy. Prospecting for diamonds, bauxite, and manganese accelerated in the first half of the twentieth century.

In the late 1960s, Ghana was a major world producer of these minerals--contributing from 5.6 to 7.3 percent of world diamond production in 1965-1968 and ranking fifth in free-world gold production. Like the entire national economy, the mining industry suffered in the decade of the 1970s, and by the beginning of the 1980s, output had declined. The ailing condition was due in part to the pursuit of obsolete mining policies, application of poor technology and techniques, and use of outmoded machinery. For production to increase and make a significant contribution to the national economy when the world price for cocoa (q.v.) was on the decline, there was a need for substantial new investments in the mining sector. Machinery had to be updated, and management improved.

These were the challenges that faced the mining industry in the 1980s when the government, as part of its Economic Recovery Program (q.v.), engaged in negotiations with donor countries and institutions. As a result of these arrangements, the State Gold Mining Corporation (SGMC), in 1986, was able to sign a $30-million management agreement with the Ghana-Canada Mining Group for the rehabilitation of the Tarkwa and Prestea (qq.v.) gold mines. Also in 1990, the AGC received a syndicated loan totaling $115 million from the International Financial Corporation and about $34 million from the Standard Charted Merchant Bank. The United Nations and the International Bank for Reconstruction and Development (World Bank) also aided the mining industry by initiating regulations to address health and safety problems of mine workers. A closer relationship between workers, mining management, and the government was also highlighted through a series of seminars at which mutual concerns were discussed. Not only was attention paid to redressing problems in the mining sector, but by 1986, about 50 new companies had been licensed to operate in Ghana. Under the Minerals and Mining Law (PNDCL 153) of 1986, private citizens were for the first time licensed to prospect for minerals, and the Precious Minerals Marketing Corporation was established as an avenue through which small-scale miners could sell their find.

These changes resulted in increased mineral production from 1984 onwards--the 279,280-carat output of diamonds in 1983 increased to 339,352 carats in 1989, and similar increases were reported for manganese and bauxite. And, for the first time in the history of Ghana, gold surpassed cocoa (q.v.) as the nation's chief foreign exchange earner, in 1992.

MISORE. The founder of the Mole-Dagbani Talensi (qq.v.) group. He came from Mamprugu to settle in the Tongo Hills, above Mamprusi (q.v.). He was succeeded by his son, Seyene.

MO. Descendants of Grusi Sisala (qq.v.) who migrated to both the Bamboi region on the Black Volta and the area around Wa (qq.v.).

MOABA see BIMOBA

MOINSI HILLS (Adansi Hills). The hills running from Lake Bosumtwi southwest to Obuasi and Dunkwa (qq.v.), between the Fum and Oda rivers (q.v.).

MOLE GAME RESERVE. Ghana's largest and best-developed game reserve. The area covers some 900 sq. miles (2,331 sq. km). It is located 92 miles (148 km) west of Tamale, and the entrance is near the Gonja (qq.v.) village of Larabanga. It is named for the Mole River, which begins in the park. Baboon, antelope, and monkeys are the most common animals found in the park.

MOORE, GEORGE EDWARD. 1879-1950. Nationalist. A treasury clerk and Asafo captain in Cape Coast (qq.v.). He was one of the more radical members of the Aborigines' Rights Protection Society (q.v.). In 1940 he was elected as Municipal Member of the Legislative Council and served there until he died in 1950.

MØRCH, FREDERIK SIEGFRIED. 1800-1839. Danish Governor who was in the Gold Coast (q.v.) from 1834 to 1839. He founded a plantation, called Frederiksgave, in Akuapem (q.v.), where he hoped to demonstrate the agricultural potential of the Gold Coast in order to attract Danish settlers.

MOSHI see MOSSI

MOSSI (Moshi). Mole-Dagbani people who have common traditions with Nanumba, Dagomba, Mamprusi, Builsa, Talensi (qq.v.), and other groups in the Northern and Upper regions of Ghana and in Burkina Faso. The Mossi were also known to have established one of the few states in the Niger basin that was not brought under the control of the Songhay empire.

MOURI (Moure, Mouree, Moree, Mori). 5°08'N, 1°12'W. An Asebu (q.v.) village on the coast in the Central Region just east of Cape Coast. The Dutch started trading here around 1594 and began Fort Nassau in 1612. This was the Dutch headquarters and the earliest of their possessions until they moved to Elmina (q.v.) in 1637. Fort Nassau was abandoned after 1815 and transferred to Britain in 1868.

MPANYIMFO. The council of elders of an Akan (q.v.) village, town, or polity.

MRAMMUO. Akan (q.v.) for gold weights.

MUNICIPAL CORPORATIONS ORDINANCE, 10 May 1858. An ordinance which provided for municipal elections of mayors and councillors and the establishment of municipal courts in the Protectorate. The corporation was authorized to assess house taxes. This law was repealed in 1861, after corporations had been established in James Town and Cape Coast (q.v.).

MUNICIPALITIES ORDINANCE OF 1889. An ordinance which provided for municipal councils, to be elected by qualified voters. The councils would deal with municipal services, and could levy a house tax to pay for these services. Opposition to the tax kept the ordinance from ever being used.

MUSLIM ASSOCIATION PARTY (MAP). A Gold Coast Muslim Association was formed in 1932 as a welfare and social society. By 1953 the Association was involved in politics, and in 1954 it became the Muslim Association Party. Most of the leaders were anti-CPP. The Party was strong among immigrant peoples in the Zongo (q.v.) areas of the larger towns. They joined the United Party in opposition to the Convention People's Party (q.v.) in November 1957.

MUSLIMS. About 12 percent of the population of Ghana were considered Muslim in the first post-independence census in 1960. In the 1970 and 1984 enumerations information on the religious distribution of the population was not represented. It was, however, estimated in 1988 that about 15 percent of the nation's population were Muslim. Most Ghanaian Muslims are Sunni, following the Maliki version of Islamic law. Sufism, involving the organization of mystical brotherhood (tariqa) for the purification and spread of Islam, is not widespread in the country. The Tijaniya and the Qadiriya brotherhood are, however, represented. The Ahmadiyyah, a Shiite sect originating in nineteenth-century India, is the only non-Sunni order in the country. Islamic education (among orthodox Muslims) in Ghana, for the most part, had remained at the Quranic level. The Ahmadiyyah (q.v.) order has, however, been running schools along the lines of the Western model and has also been active in the organization of vocational institutions.

-N-

NA, NABA (pl. Nabdema, Nanamse). Title or honorific among the Mole-Dagbani (q.v.) for secular rulers or chiefs.

NABAGA (Wadh Naba). The traditional leader of the Mande who established Yagbum near Bole (qq.v.) about 1550. He was the grandfather of the great Gonja leader Jakpa Lanta (qq.v.) (Lante).

NABTE. Language of the Namnam (Nabdom), one of the Mole-Dagbani (qq.v.) groups of the Upper East Region.

NALERIGU. 10°32'N, 0°22'W. Mamprusi capital in the Northern Region a short distance from Gambaga (qq.v.).

NAMNAM (Nabdom). A Mole-Dagbani (q.v.) group in the Upper East Region. Their language is Nabte (q.v.), they call their land Nabrug, and by their traditions they came from Nalerigu (q.v.).

NANA. An honorific or term of respect. Used for grandparents and chiefs among the Akan (q.v.).

NANAANOM MPOW. The sacred grove of the Fante at Mankesim (qq.v.). Here are buried the patriarchs of the Fante, who are said to have come to the coast from Techiman (q.v.).

NANKA-BRUCE, FREDERICK VICTOR. 1878-1953. Medical physician, journalist, and Secretary of the National Congress of

British West Africa (q.v.). He studied medicine at Edinburgh University. In addition to his medical practice in Accra (q.v.), he was a planter and shipper of cocoa (q.v.) and actively involved in politics. He was a member of the Aborigines' Rights Protection Society (q.v.), and was a Municipal Member of the Legislative Council for a time.

NANUMBA (Nanum, Nanune). A Mole-Dagbani group in the Northern Region (qq.v.), with the Daka River on their western border and the Oti on the east. Their kingdom is related to Mamprusi and Dagomba (qq.v.). It was founded by Nnantombo, son of Na Gbewa and brother of Sitobu (qq.v.). Their principal town is Bimbila (q.v.).

NAPOLEON. An experimental farm begun by Col. George Torrane (q.v.) in 1807. It was revived in the 1830s by James Swanzy, and later continued by T. B. Freeman (qq.v.) in the 1840s. The Wesleyans changed the name to "Beulah" after they took over the operation. Cotton, coffee, grapes, limes, oranges, guavas, and mangoes were all tried out here. The farm was operated until about 1860. It was located near Cape Coast (q.v.).

NASA, BATTLE OF. 10°09'N, 2°21'W. The battle took place in the Upper West Region northeast of Wa (q.v.) in 1890. Babatu and his Zabrama defeated the Wala (qq.v.) army. Afterwards the Wa Na (q.v.) committed suicide. Nasa was destroyed; Wa was taken and its elders were all executed.

NASSAU, FORT see MOURI

NATHAN, MATTHEW. 1862-1939. Governor of the Gold Coast (q.v.). Nathan was a graduate of the Royal Military Academy at Woolwich, and he was commissioned into the Royal Engineers in 1880. He was Acting Governor of Sierra Leone in 1899 and Governor of the Gold Coast, 1900-1904. Before retiring from colonial service in 1930, he had worked also in Hong Kong and Queensland.

NATIONAL ALLIANCE OF LIBERALS (NAL). The chief opposition to the Busia (q.v.) government during the Second Republic. Influential members of this group included K. A. Gbedemah (q.v.). Eric Madjitey (q.v.) was its leader in the National Assembly, 1970-1972. The NAL held only 29 seats in the National Assembly compared to Busia's Progress Party's (q.v.) 105 seats.

NATIONAL ANTHEM. The anthem played at the independence celebrations in March 1957 was entitled "Ghana Arise." It was written at the request of Nkrumah by an English Labour member of Parliament. On 14 March 1958 the government approved a new national anthem taken from nine entries in a national competition. The music was composed by Philip Gbeho (q.v.). It starts "God bless our homeland, Ghana."

NATIONAL ASSOCIATION OF SOCIALIST STUDENTS ORGANIZATIONS (NASSO). An organization formed in 1957 by Tawia Adamfio (q.v.) for radical Ghanaian students. The organization was abolished in 1961 after Nkrumah decided to establish the Kwame Nkrumah Ideological Institute (q.v.) at Winneba.

NATIONAL BOARD FOR SMALL-SCALE INDUSTRIES (NBSSI). Inaugurated April 1985. The creation of the small-scale industrial board was in recognition that the "informal sector," especially the indigenous private sector, was essential to the Provisional National Defense Council (PNDC) Economic Recovery Program (ERP) (qq.v.). This attempt to encourage small-scale enterprises was made with the dismal history of parastatals in Ghana in mind. The establishment of the NBSSI was, therefore, a strategy that was intended to relieve the central government of certain responsibilities while ensuring more participation from the people in a national industrial program. To encourage more people from the local private sector to participate in industrial development, it was necessary that the new enterprises be small since private capital accumulation in Ghana has been minimal.

    In early 1990, the NBSSI drew up a program--the Entrepreneurship Development Program--under which local entrepreneurs were to be trained. World Bank support for the program was declared in November 1989. Also in 1989, the PNDC administration set aside a revolving fund amounting to about \$25 million to assist 3,500 small-scale industrialists. About \$2 million of the amount appropriated in 1990 for projects under the Program of Action for the Mitigation of the Social Consequences of Adjustment for Development (q.v.) were loans to aid small-scale enterprises in the Asante Region alone. Furthermore, the Bank of Ghana earmarked about \$30 million to aid small-scale enterprises in the form of loans in 1990. Elaborate guidelines were outlined by the NBSSI to explain the various forms of assistance for its programs.

NATIONAL COMMISSION FOR DEMOCRACY (NCD). A Provisional National Defense Council (q.v.) agency organized in 1982 to educate the people politically on government programs. The NCD was also charged with keeping the government informed of conditions in the country. In September 1984, Mr. Justice Daniel F. Annan was appointed to the chairmanship of the NCD. This appointment, according to a government statement, was an affirmation of its ultimate commitment to provide a viable democratic structure. The NCD, therefore, became the organ through which necessary discussions on concepts and institutions of democracy were to take place. In other words, the NCD was assigned three roles-- to provide civic education of citizens, to elaborate on the constitutional process, and ultimately to supervise public elections.

NATIONAL CONGRESS OF BRITISH WEST AFRICA. An organization formed largely as a result of the efforts of J. E. Casely-Hayford (q.v.). In March 1920 six representatives from Nigeria, three from Sierra Leone, one from Gambia, and over forty from the Gold Coast met in Accra (qq.v.) and created the National Congress of British West Africa. The group was created to work for cooperation among Britain's West African peoples and for increased local autonomy. Meetings were held during the 1920s, but by 1930 the movement had become inactive.

NATIONAL DEFENCE COMMITTEE (NDC). The national coordinating committee established by the Provisional National Defence Council (PNDC) (q.v.) government in 1982. The committee was charged with the responsibility of directing activities of the Peoples' and Workers' Defence Committees (qq.v.) so as "to advance the cause of the PNDC revolution." The government, however, announced the dissolution of the People's and Workers' Defence Committees on 31 December 1984. These organizations were replaced by Committees for the Defence of the Revolution (CDRs).

NATIONAL DEMOCRATIC CONGRESS (NDC). Organized in 1992. The NDC symbol was an umbrella, and its colors were black, red, green, and white. The party's platform was to continue and consolidate the achievements of the Provisional National Defence Council (PNDC) (q.v.). With Rawlings (q.v.) as its presidential candidate, opposition parties argued that the NDC was the (P)NDC in disguise, and hence a free and fair election could not be carried out. The NDC candidate for President, J. J. Rawlings, won about 60 percent of the votes cast in the November 1992 election (q.v.). While the opposition parties (q.v.) cried foul, Commonwealth observers at the election reported a relatively free and fair election. With many opposition candidates boycotting the December 29 parliamentary elections, the NDC won 190 of the 200 parliamentary seats in the Fourth Republic. The Fourth Republic was inaugurated on 7 January 1993.

NATIONAL DEMOCRATIC PARTY (Demos). A party organized to contest the elections of 1951 against both the United Gold Coast Convention and the Convention People's Party (qq.v.). Dr. F. V. Nanka-Bruce (q.v.) was the chief force in the organization of this conservative party.

NATIONAL DEVELOPMENT COMPANY (NADECO). A company formed and controlled by Nkrumah and the Convention People's Party (CPP) (q.v.) in October 1957 as a means of acquiring funds to finance CPP activities. This was done through "commissions" on government contracts.

NATIONAL LIBERATION COUNCIL (NLC). The military group which staged the overthrow of Nkrumah (q.v.) and which ran Ghana from 1966 to 1969. J. A. Ankrah, A. A. Afrifa, A. K. Ocran, and J. W. Harley (qq.v.) were the leaders of the NLC. Emmanuel Kotoka (q.v.) was also a member of the NLC until his death in 1967.

NATIONAL LIBERATION MOVEMENT (NLM). Political movement formed in Asante in September 1954 under the leadership of K. A. Busia and made up of those in favor of a federal decentralized form of government as opposed to the centralized power which the Convention People's Party (qq.v.) proposed. In October 1957 it joined other opposition parties in the United Party (q.v.).

NATIONAL REDEMPTION COUNCIL (NRC). The military group which overthrew the Second Republic. Col. I. K. Acheampong (q.v.), J. H. Cobbina, Major A. H. Selormey, and Major R. M. Baah were leaders of the group. In 1975 Acheampong organized a Supreme Military Council (q.v.), to which the NRC was subordinated.

NATIONAL UNION OF GHANA STUDENTS (NUGS). Early members of the former National Union of Gold Coast Students included Dr. Kwame Nkrumah (q.v.), first President of Ghana. Formed by the nation's students studying abroad, many members returned home to play active roles in the independence movement. In 1958, a year after the Gold Coast gained independence and became Ghana, the organization consequently became the National Union of Ghana Students (NUGS). Though initially created as a non-governmental and non-political group with the purpose of offering a common forum for the discussion of students' problems, the organization by the end of the 1960s had attained a radical militant character. It opposed attempts by the government of the Second Republic to introduce tuition payment by university students. Between 1972 and 1978, the NUGS was active in opposing the policies of the National Redemption Council military government, especially its attempt to introduce a Union Government (qq.v.) (military-cum-civil administration) in Ghana. The NUGS, also on numerous occasions, opposed certain Provisional National Defense Council (q.v.) policies. While some leaders of the organization were arrested and persecuted by various governments, others graduated to become active members of government.

NATIVE ADMINISTRATION ORDINANCE OF 1927. This act of the Legislative Council contained 129 sections. The positions of native rulers and councils were defined, and procedures for elections and destoolment were outlined. Jurisdiction of native government under customary law was specified. Provincial Councils (q.v.), established in 1925, were established as courts. The ordinance expanded the powers of chiefs, recognized the Oman (state) councils as the highest authority within each jurisdiction to decide stool (q.v.) disputes, and made Provincial Councils the appeal court in stool and inter-tribal disputes. The Governor retained power as the final authority.

NATIVE AUTHORITY ORDINANCE OF 1944. This ordinance required that all organs of local authority had to be recognized by the Central Government in Accra.

NATIVE JURISDICTION ORDINANCE OF 1883. The power of chiefs in civil and criminal affairs was defined and decisions of native tribunals were subject to appeal to British courts. The British maintained the right to dismiss recalcitrant chiefs. The 1883 ordinance was the basis of native jurisdiction until 1927. But it was amended in 1910 and 1924.

NATIVE JURISDICTION ORDINANCES (NJO). There were several NJOs approved by the Legislative Councils of the Gold Coast (q.v.). In 1878 an ordinance attempted to define the relation of the British government to chiefs in the Protectorate (q.v.), and to define the powers of chiefs and their councils in civil and criminal matters. It was never implemented and was replaced in 1883.

NATIVE STATES. This is the term used after the Native Administration Ordinance of 1927 (q.v.) for traditional states or kingdoms in the Gold Coast (q.v.). They often were used as districts for administrative purposes. In 1946 there were 13 native states in the Northern and Upper regions, 24 in Asante, and 71 in the Eastern, Central, and Western regions, for a total of 108 native states. In 1957 there were 63 in the three southern regions, 25 in Asante, and 21 in the north, for a total of 109 native states.

NAVRONGO. 10°54'N, 1°06'W. Town on the Great Northern Road in the Upper West Region northwest of Bolgatanga (q.v.) and near the border of Burkina Faso. It is a Kasena (Grusi) (qq.v.) village. The White Fathers of Burkina Faso opened a school here in 1907 and built a cathedral in 1920.

NAYIRI. Paramount Chief of the Mamprusi (q.v.).

NBANYA. The Dyula conquerors who established Gonja (qq.v.). The descendants of the Malians who founded Yagbum (q.v.).

NDEBUGRE, JOHN. Former Provisional National Defence Council (PNDC) (q.v.) Secretary for Agriculture. Educated at the University of Science and Technology (q.v.), Kumasi, John Ndebugre was a prominent student leader (1976-77). He belonged to the radical wing of the National Union of Ghana Students (q.v.). Like most students of his ideological persuasion, Ndebugre opposed the government of the Supreme Military Council (q.v.) which it perceived as "reactionary and capitalistic." He was a supporter of the radical political changes that took place in the late 1970s. In 1981, when Rawlings (q.v.) and the PNDC took power, Ndebugre was appointed Northern Regional Commissioner. Later, he became PNDC Secretary for Agriculture and held the position till his dismissal in May 1985.

Although Ndebugre was accused by the PNDC of becoming too involved in local conflicts in the region of his stewardship, political observers attributed his 1985 dismissal to possible ideological differences with certain members of the council. Thereafter, Ndebugre became active in opposing the PNDC, especially through such organizations as the Movement for Freedom and Justice (see OPPOSITION POLITICS). John

Ndebugre was arrested and detained by the PNDC on a number of occasions during the PNDC's tenure.

NEDEGA. The Mossi name for Gbewa or Bawa, the ancestor of the Mole-Dagbani (qq.v.) peoples. Traditions say that he came from Gurma, in modern Burkina Faso, and that he settled in Pusiga (q.v.) in what is now the extreme northeast of the Upper East Region.

NEW DWABEN. On 21 October 1875 Asante invaded Dwaben (qq.v.). Many of the people of Dwaben emigrated to Koforidua in Akyem (qq.v.), where they founded the new oman (state) of New Dwaben.

NEW PATRIOTIC PARTY (NPP). One of the four major parties that participated in the November 1992 presidential elections (q.v.). Professor Adu Boahen (q.v.), the NPP candidate for President, came in a distant second with about 30 percent of the votes cast compared to Rawlings, the National Democratic Congress (NDC) (qq.v.) candidate, who won about 60 percent of the votes. This ruled out any hope for a runoff election between the two leading candidates as election rules required that the winner receive at least 50 percent of the total votes. The NPP charged the government of the Provisional National Defence Council (q.v.) and Rawlings with electoral irregularities and boycotted the parliamentary elections that followed in December.

Observers of the elections that launched the Fourth Republic in Ghana described the NPP as composed of people who subscribed to the political philosophies of J. B. Danquah and K. A. Busia (qq.v.). Thus, the NPP claimed to stand for freedom and the rule of law as opposed to the NDC call for continuity and accountability in government.

NIFA. The right wing of an Akan (q.v.) army. It is under the command of a Nifahene.

NII BONNE, KWABENA III. Wealthy merchant who was also a sub-chief of Accra (q.v.). In January of 1948, he organized an anti-inflation committee which boycotted European goods for a period of about a month. The boycott was accompanied by a march to Christiansborg (q.v.), joined in by ex-servicemen who protested about the impact of inflation on their pensions and the broken promises of the colonial government. In an effort to contain the demonstrations, shots were fired by government troops killing two protestors. This touched off one of Ghana's most remembered pre-independence riots.

NINGO, GREAT (Old Ningo, Nigo, Nungo). 5°45'N, 0°11'E. A coastal village where the Danes built a fort, Fredensborg (Friedensborg), about 1736. The British gained the area in 1850. The old fort is in ruins.

NKETIA, JOHN HANSON KWABENA. Born 1921. Musicologist, folklorist, poet, and playwright. Former Director of the Institute of African Studies (q.v.) at Legon. Born at Mampong-Asante, he attended the Teacher Training College at Akuropon-Akuapem, the University of London, Columbia University, Northwestern University, and Juilliard School of Music. He has taught on the faculty of several universities, including the University of London, University of Ghana (q.v.), University of California at Los Angeles, and University of Pittsburgh. He is one of the world's greatest authorities on African music.

NKONYA. Guan people who live mostly in the Volta Region (qq.v.).

NKORANZA (Nkoransa). 7°34'N, 1°42'W. Town in the economic heart of the Brong-Ahafo (q.v.) area. It was located 60 miles (96 km) north of Kumasi (q.v.) and was one of the leading Brong towns. Nkoranza was one of the leaders of the Brong rebellion against the Asante (q.v.), 1892-1893.

NKRAMO (sing. Kramo). Muslims (q.v.).

NKROFUL (Nkrofo, Nkrofro). 4°58'N, 2°19'W. Nzema village in the Western Region (qq.v.). It is located some 10 miles (16 km) northwest of Axim (q.v.). The birthplace of Kwame Nkrumah (q.v.) and the place of his burial on 9 July 1972.

NKRUMAH, FATHIA HALEN RITZK. Egyptian wife of Kwame Nkrumah (q.v.).

NKRUMAH, FRANCIS KWESI. Born 21 April 1935 in Elmina. Educated at St. Augustine's, Cape Coast, Wurtzburg and Berlin universities in Germany, and Harvard. He received the medical degree from Berlin, and a Master of Public Health degree from Harvard. He is a Ghanaian physician and son of President Nkrumah (q.v.).

NKRUMAH, KWAME (Osagyefo, Kantamanto, Mbrantsehene, Show Boy, Black Star of Africa). 1900-1972. First Prime Minister and President of Ghana. He was born at Nkroful (q.v.), in the Western Region, and educated at the Roman Catholic School at Half-Assini, Achimota, Lincoln University, the University of Pennsylvania, the University of London, and the London School of Economics. In London he was active in the West African Students' Union (q.v.), and he attended the fifth Pan-African Congress at Manchester in 1945. It was about this period that Nkrumah came to know George Padmore, T. R. Makonnen, W. E. B. Du Bois, Bonkole Awooner-Renner (qq.v.), and others who would help in Ghana's march towards independence. One of his companions in Pennsylvania and in London was Ako Adjei (q.v.).

Nkrumah became General-Secretary of the United Gold Coast Convention (UGCC) (q.v.) in 1947 after he returned to the Gold Coast. His tenure as General-Secretary of the UGCC was a stormy one. In March 1948 he was arrested and detained as one of the Big Six. After his release, he was increasingly at odds with the pace of the intelligentsia who had founded the UGCC. All of the Big Six except Nkrumah were invited to join the Coussey Committee (q.v.) to make recommendations for a new form of government. Nkrumah, K. A. Gbedemah, Kojo Botsio (qq.v.), and their followers demanded "Self-Government Now" as opposed to the gradual position advocated by the UGCC, with which he had broken relations.

On 12 June 1949, the Convention People's Party (CPP) (q.v.), with Nkrumah as Chairman, was born at the Arena in Accra. "Positive Action" (q.v.) and civil disobedience, strikes, boycotts, and non-cooperation with the colonial government became the program of the CPP. On 21 January 1950 Nkrumah was arrested again for promoting an illegal strike. He was sentenced to a total of three yea.s' imprisonment. He spent a year in prison before being elected to the CPP-dominated Legislative Assembly in February 1951. He was released from prison 12 February 1951, and on 23 February he became Leader of Government Business in the Assembly. A year later his title was changed to Prime Minister. On 10 July 1953 he made his "Motion of Destiny," calling for independence within the British Commonwealth. In June 1954 the CPP consolidated its position. During 1955 and 1956 there was bitter debate over the form an independent government would take, but Nkrumah was firmly in control. On 15 November 1956 the Assembly endorsed Nkrumah's plan for a unitary constitution. Ghana was born less than four months later.

From the beginning Nkrumah conceived of himself as more than just the leader of Ghana. Seeing Ghana's independence as linked to the liberation of Africa, Nkrumah thought of himself as the leader of all Africa and thus became very much involved in liberation movements all over the continent. At home, his desire for rapid economic developments and Ghana's central role in African liberation generated criticism. The establishment, in July 1958, of the Preventive Detention Act (q.v.) gave Nkrumah the power to imprison those who questioned his actions. By April 1959, the opposition began to be expelled from the National Assembly.

In 1960, Ghana under Nkrumah became a republic. In the presidential election, Nkrumah overwhelmed J. B. Danquah by 1,016,076 to 124,623 and two years later the CPP-dominated National Assembly proclaimed Nkrumah President for Life. In February 1964 Ghana became a one-party state under CPP rule. Nkrumah was overthrown in a military coup on 24 February 1966 at a time when he was out of the country. He returned to Guinea, where President Sekou Toure proclaimed Nkrumah to be co-president of Guinea. Nkrumah lived long enough to hear that Busia's (q.v.) republic had also been overthrown in a military coup. Then in April 1972 he died in a Bucharest, Romania, hospital. His body was returned to Ghana, where he was given a state burial at Nkroful, his hometown, in July 1972. The body was, however, removed from Nkroful, and on 1 July 1992, the government of the Provisional National Defense Council (q.v.) conducted another state burial of Nkrumah, this time at a specially built mausoleum at the old Polo Grounds (now Nkrumah Memorial Park) in Accra.

NKRUMAHIST PARTIES. While the New Patriotic Party (NPP) claimed to represent the political philosophies of J. B. Danquah and K. A. Busia, and the National Democratic Congress (NDC) was the party of the Provisional National Defense Council (PNDC), so other political parties perceived or claimed to represent the political ideology of Ghana's first President, Dr. Kwame Nkrumah (qq.v.). By election time in November 1992, the Nkrumahists had splintered into various parties--including the People's Heritage Party (PHP), the People's National Convention (PNC), and the People's Independent Party (PIP). Other breakaway parties were the Popular Party for Democracy and Development (PPDD) and the National Convention Party (NCP). Presidential candidates for the three leading Nkrumahist parties were Rtd. General Erskine (q.v.) (PHP), Dr. Limann (q.v.) (PNC), and Mr. Kwabena Darko (PIP).

Although leaders of the Nkrumahist groups were influential in Ghanaian society, political observers attributed their poor showing in the November presidential elections (q.v.) to their inability to unite in a single party. Even with the Busia/Danquah group's (NPP) boycotting of the December elections that followed, the best the Nkrumahist parties could do was for the NCP to win a mere six of the 200 seats in the new parliament.

NNANTOMBO. Son of Gbewa of Pusiga, Nnantombo was the traditional founder of the Mole-Dagbani state in Nanumba (qq.v.).

NORTHCOTT, HENRY. Died 1899. British officer. He was the first British Commissioner and Commandant in the Northern Territories (q.v.). Appointed in September 1897, Northcott was to occupy any place in the hinterland of the Gold Coast (q.v.) not occupied by some other European power. He established his headquarters at Gambaga (q.v.) in June 1898, and accompanied by a former Mossi king, he marched with an English force into the area that is now Burkina Faso. On 30 June 1898 he was met by a French force at Kombissiri, and he turned back with the news that an agreement had ceded the area to France. During the rest of 1898 and early 1899 Northcott organized local government in the Northern Territories and planned a transportation network for the region. Later in 1899 he went to South Africa to take part in the war there. He was killed shortly after arriving in South Africa.

NORTHERN PEOPLE'S PARTY (NPP). A political group organized under the leadership of Simon Diedong Dombo (q.v.). Its purpose was to protect the interests of northerners. It contested the 1954 and 1956 elections and then merged with other opposition parties against the Convention People's Party (q.v.) in November 1957.

NORTHERN REGION. The Gonja, Mamprusi, and Dagomba savanna lands between the Volta borders of Brong-Ahafo and the Upper Regions (qq.v.). Houses are generally round, with grass-thatch roofs, and they are formed into compounds. Tamale (q.v.) is the administrative center. It included the Upper Regions until they were separated 29 June 1960.

NORTHERN TERRITORIES. The hinterland of the Gold Coast north of the Asante lands of the Ahafo and Brong (qq.v.). Following the defeat of Asante in 1896, the Northern Territories of Asante were administratively organized, and by 1906, they had fully been incorporated into the Gold Coast (q.v.). The headquarters was at Gambaga from Christmas 1896, but it was moved to Tamale (qq.v.) in 1907. The area was not represented in the Legislative Council until 1950. When the Gold Coast became independent in 1957, the Northern Territories became the Northern and Upper regions (qq.v.) of Ghana.

NSAKI, BATTLE OF. On a stream just north of Accra (q.v.) a
    coalition of people under the leadership of Frimpon Manso,
    ruler of Akyem Kotoku, defeated the Akwamu (qq.v.) in 1730.
    This forced the Akwamu to retreat across the Volta (q.v.) to
    the area they now occupy east of that river.

NSAMANKOW (Nsamanko, Insamakow) see BONSASO

NSAWAM. 5°48'N, 0°21'W. City on the highway and railroad from
    Accra to Koforidua on the Densu River (qq.v.). The town is
    known in post-independence Ghana for its prison.

NSUAEM (5°55'N, 0°59'W) see ODA

NSUMANKWAAHENE. Akan (q.v.) corps of royal physicians.
    Among the Asante, the office of Nsumankwaahene (head of
    the royal physicians) was believed to have been created during
    the reign of Asantehene Osei Tutu (qq.v.). The preoccupation
    of the nsuamankwaafo (members of the nsumakwaa unit) is the
    active search for the best and most powerful charms or
    medicine for the king of Asante. Muslims were believed to
    have been recruited into this Kumasi agency during the reign
    of Asantehene Osei Kwame (qq.v.) in about the seventh decade
    of the eighteenth century.

NSUTA (Insuta). 7°01'N, 1°23'W. One of the major Asante (q.v.)
    metropolitan towns. It was founded about the same time as
    Kumasi (q.v.). The town submitted to the British on 30
    January 1896.

NTAFO. Asante name for Gonja (qq.v.) and the people north of
    Asante. The ancestors of the Akan, said to have come down
    the Volta (qq.v.) from the north.

NTERESO (Nterso). 9°07'N, 1°13'W. Place in the Northern
    Region just west of Yapei and the White Volta (qq.v.). An
    archaeological site near here seems to have been occupied by
    1300 B.C. Oliver Davies excavated a Kintampo culture (q.v.)
    site here, showing evidence of early pastoralism.

NUNGUA (Nungwa). 5°36'N, 0°04'W. Coastal village between Teshi and Tema (qq.v.). It was one of the seven original Ga (q.v.) towns.

NYAGSE. The first Ya Na of Dagbon or Dagomba (qq.v.). He was the son of Sitobu and grandson of Gbewa (qq.v.).

NYAMASI. The subject people or common people of Gonja (q.v.).

NYAMAWASE (Nyanaoase). 5°47'N, 0°23'W. The old Akwamu capital before 1730, when the Akyem drove the Akwamu out of the Akuapem (qq.v.) area.

'NYAME see ONYAME

'NYAME AKUMA. God's axes. Stone relics dated from Neolithic times which have been found all over Ghana. They may have been used as hoes in ancient times. They have been associated with the Kintampo culture (q.v.).

NYANOA (Nyanga, Nyango, Yagbum). 9°15'N, 2°23'W. Place in the Northern Region a few miles northeast of Bole which was the home of the Yagbumwura, Paramount Chief of the Gonja from about 1700 to 1942, when the Gonja headquarters was moved to Damongo (qq.v.).

NYANTROBI, BATTLE OF. In 1660 the armies of Akwamu defeated Okai Koi of Accra (qq.v.), who committed suicide after the battle.

NYARKO KWEKU (Nyanko Eku). Omanhene (Paramount Chief) of the Agona state (qq.v.) who was believed to have briefly allied himself with the Akyem in the early years of the eighteenth century. Had the Agona alliance with the Akyem held, the latter could have had an unlimited supply of guns and powder from the coast. Agona's retreat from the alliance generated hostilities from the Akyem.

NYENDAAL, DAVID VAN. Dutchman who was the first known European to go to Kumasi (q.v.). He was believed to have arrived at the Asante capital in 1701, soon after the Asante defeated Denkyira at Feyiase (qq.v.). He stayed about a year and died in 1702, shortly after his return to the coast. He never had the chance to write an account of his experiences in Asante.

NZEMA (Nzima). Coastal people in the Western Region between the Tano and Ankobra rivers (qq.v.). Europeans often called the area Apollonia (Apolonia) (q.v.). Kwame Nkrumah was an Nzema from Nkroful (qq.v.), just a short distance above the coast. The British built fort Apollonia at Beyin (q.v.), in Nzema territory about 1768.

- O -

OBIRI YEBOA MANU. Ca. 1660-1693. A leader of the Asante Oyoko (qq.v.) matriclan. He was a nephew of Oti Akenten (q.v.). The uncle had moved the Asante into the Kwaman area around the old trading town of Tafo (qq.v.). Obiri Yeboa was followed as head of the Oyoko matriclan by his nephew, Osei Tutu (q.v.), who established the Asante Union and created Kumasi (q.v.) as its capital.

OBOSOM (pl. Abosom) see ABOSOM

OBUASI. 6°12'N, 1°40'W. City in the Asante Region about 39 miles (63 km) south of Kumasi (qq.v.). It is located in the richest mining area of Ghana. Gold mining began there in 1897. Gold mining at Obuasi remains the largest production field in Ghana. The operations are run by the Ashanti (Asante) Goldfields Corporation (q.v.), a joint private-Ghana government venture.

OCANSEY, ALFRED JOHN. 1879-1943. Born in Ada, he became a leading merchant, journalist, and nationalist. As a merchant he introduced electric generators, motion pictures, record players, radios, and automobiles to the Gold Coast (q.v.). As the owner of the *African Morning Post* he brought Nnamdi

Azikiwe to Accra (qq.v.) as his editor. He was an admirer of Marcus Garvey and an advocater of Gold Coast nationalism. He was described as one of the forces behind the cocoa holdup of 1930-1931.

OCRAN, ALBERT KWESI. Born 1929 in Brakwa, Central Region, he was educated at the Roman Catholic School in Accra. He joined the army in 1947 and went to Officers' Training School, Teshi. He then went to England and attended Eton Hall, several military programs, and the British Staff College at Camberley. Commissioned in 1954, he was attached to the British army in West Germany for a time in 1955. After service in Kumasi and Accra (qq.v.), he was sent to the Congo. Ocran was one of the officers who overthrew the Nkrumah (q.v.) administration in 1966. His book *A Myth Is Broken* (1968) recounted the author's views about the 1966 coup; his *Politics of the Sword* (1977) discussed the military government of which he was a part. While a member of the National Liberation Council (q.v.), Ocran was responsible for the Works, Housing, Transport, and Communications ministries. In May 1967 he became Commander of the Ghanaian army, and in November 1968 he was Acting Chief of the Ghanaian Defence Staff. In 1969 he joined Afrifa and L. W. K. Harley (qq.v.) on the Presidential Commission. He retired to lead a quiet private life since 1969.

ODA (Insuaim, Nsuaem). 5°55'N, 0°59'W. Capital of Akyem Kotoku (q.v.). Founded in 1863 as Nsuaem, the name was changed to Oda in 1922. It is a commercial and administrative center on the railway from Sekondi to Kade (qq.v.). Oda is one of the important diamond-producing regions on the Birim River (q.v.).

ODEKURO (pl. Adekurofo). The headman of a village.

ODUMASI (Odumase). 6°8' N, 0°01' W. The capital of the Manya Krobo (q.v.) after 1892. It is 50 miles (80 km) northeast of Accra (q.v.). The Basel Mission (q.v.) opened a school here as early as 1857.

ODWIRA. The national purification festival of the Akan (q.v.). It is the most important day of the year in Asante (q.v.). The Odwira is held in September at the time of the harvest of the new yams. It is a day of purification in which allegiance to authority is renewed. The spirits of ancestors are propitiated, and the Asantehene (q.v.) visits the royal mausoleums. In the past many people were sacrificed on this day.

OFFICE OF REVENUE COMMISSIONERS (ORC) see CITIZENS' VETTING COMMITTEE (CVC)

OFORI ATTA I (Aaron Eugene Boakye Danquah). 1881-1943. Omanhene of Akyem Abuakwa (qq.v.), 1912-1943. Half brother of J. B. Danquah. Educated in Basel Mission (q.v.) schools and the Basel Mission Theological Seminary at Akuropon (q.v.), he spent several years as a clerk. He then joined the West African Frontier Force in 1900. Returning to clerical jobs in Accra and Kibi (q.v.), he was elected Omanhene of Akyem-Abuakwa in 1912. From then until his death he was the most influential traditional ruler in the Gold Coast (q.v.). From 1916 he was a member of the Legislative Council, and just before his death he was appointed to the Executive Council of the Colony.

OFORI ATTA II (Daniel Opoku Akyempon). 1899-1973. Paramount Chief of Akyem Abuakwa (q.v.). Educated in Basel Mission schools in Kibi and Begoro (qq.v.) and Albert Academy in Sierra Leone. From 1928 to 1943 he was an employee of the Akyem Abuakwa Native Authority, and in September 1943 he was selected to succeed his uncle, Ofori Atta I (q.v.), as Paramount Chief of Akyem Abuakwa. He was President of the Joint Provincial Council of Chiefs from 1948 to 1954 and a member of the Legislative Assembly from 1951 to 1954. He was a member of the Coussey Committee (q.v.). His opposition to Nkrumah (q.v.) resulted in an investigation of his administration of Akyem Abuakwa. The government then destooled Oforo Atta II, and forcibly brought him to Accra in September 1958. Only after the National Liberation Council (q.v.) came to power was he allowed to return to Kibi. Once again he was allowed to become ruler of Akyem Abuakwa.

OFORI ATTA, JONES. Born 1937. Economist and politician. Educated at Kibi, Achimota, Legon, and the University of Ottawa, Canada. He worked for a time as teacher and journalist. Elected to the National Assembly for the Second Republic, he also served in the Ministry of Finance and Economic Planning, and in the Prime Minister's office. After the coup of 1972 he spent some time in prison. After his release he became a professor in the economics department at the University of Ghana (q.v.), Legon. In 1978 he was arrested again by the Supreme Military Council (SMC), for opposition to the Union Government (qq.v.) plans. He was released after the SMC was toppled. During the Provisional National Defence Council (q.v.) administration, he spent time in exile but returned home before the November 1992 elections.

OFORI ATTA, WILLIAM (Paa Willie). 1910-1988. Lawyer, teacher, politician. Son of Ofori Atta I of Akyem Abuakwa (qq.v.). He was educated at Kibi, Mfantsipim, Achimota (qq.v.), and Cambridge. He taught at Achimota, 1933-1943, worked for the Akyem Abuakwa Native Authority for several years, and was Headmaster of Abuakwa State College (1947-1952). He was one of the founding members of the United Gold Coast Convention (UGCC) (q.v.), and one of the "Big Six" held in detention after the riots of 1948. The members of the Big Six were J. B. Danquah, Kwame Nkrumah, Obeshebi Lamptey, Edward Akufu Addo, and Ako Adjei (qq.v.). William Ofori Atta, affectionately called Paa Willie, was elected to the National Assembly in 1951, but was defeated for reelection in 1954. He became one of the leaders of the opposition to the Convention People's Party, being associated with the Ghana Congress Party in 1952, the National Liberation Movement in 1954, and the United Party (qq.v.) in 1957. After the overthrow of Nkrumah, the National Liberation Council (qq.v.) military government made him a member of their Political Committee, the Constitutional Commission, and he was made Chairman of the Cocoa Marketing Board (q.v.). He was a member of the Constituent Assembly in 1968, and was elected to the National Assembly as one of the leaders of the Progress Party (q.v.). In the

Second Republic he was first Minister of Education, Culture, and Sports and then Minister of Foreign Affairs. He was arrested by the Supreme Military Council (q.v.) in April 1978, but released after the coup in June of that year. He retired from active politics in 1979 when his candidacy for President on the United National Convention (q.v.) party's ticket was defeated. William Ofori Atta was given a state burial when he died in 1988 at the age of 78.

OFORI KUMA I (Kwao Safori, Sakyiama Tenten). Died 1731. Ruler of Akuapem (q.v.). A member of the royal family of Akyem Abuakwa, he was the leader of a coalition which helped the Guan in their rebellion against Akwamu (qq.v.), 1728-1730. After the Akwamu were forced across the Volta (q.v.), the Guan made Ofori Kuma their Paramount Chief. He died shortly thereafter.

OFORI KUMA II (Bernard Ofosu Apea Koranteng). 1879-1954. Controversial Paramount Chief of Akuapem (q.v.) from 1914 to 1919 and from 1932 to 1941. His contempt for traditions frequently got him into trouble with his subjects, and he was twice destooled. Between tours as Okuapemhene (q.v.) he practiced law.

OFORI PANIN. Died 1727. The fourth Paramount Chief of Akyem Abuakwa (q.v.). Ofori Panin established the rule of Akyem Abuakwa in the Birim River (q.v.) valley.

OGUAA. The Fante name for Cape Coast (qq.v.).

OGUAA FETU AFAHYE. The major festival at Cape Coast (q.v.). It commemorates the purification of the fishing shrines. It occurs the first week of September, climaxing on the first Saturday of the month.

OHEMAA (pl. Ahemaa). Queen mother.

OHENE (pl. Ahene). King, ruler, paramount chief, etc. The head of an Akan (q.v.) political unit. Akan chiefs belong to particular clans, and they trace descent through the female line.

They are "father" to their people and responsible for their people's secular and religious welfare. Their person is sacred, but their duties are strictly defined at the time of enstoolment. Abuse of power may result in destoolment.

OKAI KOBINA. 1922-1985. Pioneer highlife composer and singer. Born at Abura in the central region, he completed his primary education in 1943. Okai went to Accra (q.v.) to study tailoring under the tutelage of Appiah-Agyekum, a tailor-guitarist. Okai and Appiah-Agyekum's compositions were heard on station ZOY, the radio station of the Gold Coast (q.v.). In 1947 Okai joined E. K. Nyame's band and was the leading soprano voice of the band till 1977 when E. K. Nyame died.

OKAI KOI. Ca. 1610-1660. Chief of Great Accra (q.v.). His capital was at Ayewaso (q.v.), a few miles inland from the coast. He was the Ga (q.v.) ruler who allowed the English, Danes, Dutch, and Swedes to build trading posts along the coast at Accra (q.v.). He was defeated by the Akwamu at Nyantrobi (qq.v.), north of Accra, in 1660. He was said to have committed suicide shortly after the battle.

OKOMFO (pl. Akomfo). Priest.

OKUAPEMHENE. The Paramount Chief of Akuapem (q.v.) (Akwapim).

OKYEAME. Linguist or spokesman of an Akan (q.v.) ruler.

OKYEAME (The Spokesman). A Ghanaian literary quarterly which was started by the Ghana Society of Writers in 1961. Kofi Awooner and Christina Ama Ata Aidoo (qq.v.) have each served a turn as editor.

OKYEHENE. The Paramount Chief of Akyem Abuakwa (q.v.).

OKYEMAN COUNCIL. The council of chiefs of Akyem Abuakwa (q.v.).

OLLENNU, NII AMAA. 1906-1986. Teacher, author, lawyer. A Ga from Labadi (qq.v.), he was educated at the Presbyterian Mission School in Labadi, at Accra High School, and studied law in England. He was a teacher at Accra High School from 1929 to 1937 and a member of the Accra Council, 1944-1950; of the Legislative Council, 1946-1950; and of the Coussey Committee (q.v.) on Constitutional Reform in 1949. He became a High Court Judge in 1956 and a member of the Supreme Court in 1962. He was Speaker of the National Assembly of the Second Republic, 1969-1972, during which time he was briefly the Acting President of the republic due to the precarious health of the then President, the late Edward Akufu Addo (q.v.). In the early 1980s, Ollennu acted as principal adviser to the Consultative Council of the Greater Accra Regional Secretary, especially on chieftaincy affairs. Ollennu was author of several law books. His *Principles of Customary Law in Ghana* (1962) and his work on *Intestate Succession in Ghana* (1966) have been considered great contributions to the study of customary law in Ghana. Ollennu was given a state burial upon his death in 1986.

OMAN (pl. Aman). The Akan (q.v.) state.

OMANHENE (pl. Amanhene). Headman of an Oman (q.v.).

ONYAME ('Nyame). The Supreme Being of the Akan (q.v.). 'Nyame is perceived to be "God of the Sky." Akan mythology describes a former golden age when 'Nyame was closer, but moved away into the skies when man fell from grace. The lesser gods are considered by the Akan to be the children of 'Nyame. Asase Yaa (q.v.) is the earth goddess.

OPERATION FEED YOURSELF (OFY). The policy of food self-sufficiency launched by Acheampong and the National Redemption Council (qq.v.) in 1972. It was initially successful, but ultimately a failure.

OPOKU FOFIE. Ca. 1775-1803. Asantehene (q.v.). He was the successor to Asantehene Osei Kwame (q.v.), who was destooled about 1803. Opoku Fofie died shortly after becoming king and was succeeded by Osei Tutu Kwame Asibe Bonsu (q.v.) as Asantehene.

OPOKU FREFRE. Ca. 1760-1826. Royal Treasurer and Gyasewahene of Asante (qq.v.) during the first quarter of the nineteenth century; he was one of the closest advisers of Asantehene Osei Bonsu (q.v.), 1804-1823. He also commanded part of the Asante army in campaigns against the Fante and Gyaman (qq.v.). He was killed at Katamanso (q.v.) in the great defeat of 1826.

OPOKU, THEOPHILUS. 1824-1913. A native of Akuropon in Akuapem, he was the first African to be ordained a minister in the Gold Coast by the Basel Mission (qq.v.).

OPOKU WARE I. Ca. 1700-1750. Asantehene (q.v.) from around 1720 to 1750. He was the grandnephew of Asantehene Osei Tutu (q.v.). Historians of Asante (q.v.) disagree on the date of Opoku Ware's ascension to the throne. This is because they are uncertain of the year of Osei Tutu's death (1712 and 1717 have been suggested). By 1720, however, Opoku Ware was the Asantehene. His reign was a period of great expansion at the expense of all his neighbors. He defeated the armies of Sefwi, Aowin, Gonja, Dagomba, Techiman, Gyaman, and Akyem (qq.v.). By the time of his death he had established Asante hegemony over much of what is today Ghana, but he never crushed the Fante and Wassa (qq.v.) which kept his victories from being complete, and aided rebellions in outlying provinces.

OPOKU WARE II (Barima Kwaku Adusei, J. Matthew Poku). Born 1918. Asantehene (q.v.), 1970- . He was a nephew of Asantehene Prempe II (q.v.). He was educated at Adisadel College (Cape Coast), and he studied law in England. He served as Commissioner of Communications in the National Liberation Council (q.v.), 1968-1969, and was Second Republic Ambassador-designate to Rome when elected Asantehene. He was crowned Asantehene Opoku Ware II on 6 July 1970.

OPON ENIM. The traditional founder of the Adansi (q.v.) state, sometime after 1500. The Adansi claim to be the senior Akan (q.v.) state. The first capital was Adansimanso (q.v.) in the Kwisa and Moinsi Hills (q.v.).

OPON, SAMPSON. Ca. 1884-1960. Evangelist. A native of the Brong-Ahafo Region (q.v.), near the Ivory Coast border, who was converted to Christianity in 1920 and became a famous preacher who claimed prophetic powers.

OPPOSITION POLITICS. For information on opposition politics during the First Republic, see BUSIA, KOFI; DANQUAH, JOSEPH; UNITED GOLD COAST CONVENTION; and UNITED PARTY. An entry under APPIAH, JOSEPH, provides additional information on opposition to both the First and Second republics. See also NATIONAL UNION OF GHANA STUDENTS. While challenges to the Third Republic came from labor groups and among student organizations, it was the Popular Front Party (q.v.) that acted as the parliamentary opposition to the administration of President Limann (q.v.). See also OWUSU, VICTOR.

Opposition to the Provisional National Defence Council (PNDC) administration (1981-1992) came from groups based at home and abroad. Among those based in London was the Ghana Democratic Movement (GDM) in which such figures as J. H. Mensah, Jones Ofori-Atta, and Jones de Graft-Johnson (qq.v.) were active. There was also the Ghana Movement for Freedom and Justice (GMFJ). These right-wing groups opposed the PNDC as being unconstitutional. While the GDM and the GMFJ were the better-organized opposition groups abroad, others, such as the left-wing United Revolutionary Front and the Campaign for Democracy in Ghana, accused the PNDC of betraying the radical stand of the June 4th Revolution (q.v.).

Even though party politics were banned under the PNDC, there existed groups in Ghana that opposed the government. These included the Kwame Nkrumah Revolutionary Guard, whose members were often detained for anti-PNDC activities. Professor A. Adu Boahen, presidential candidate on the New Patriotic Party (NPP) (qq.v.) ticket in

1992, was most vociferous in his criticism of the PNDC. Before emerging as leader of the NPP, he served as Chairman of the local Movement for Freedom and Justice. Occasionally, PNDC policies were also criticized by the Ghana Council of Bishops, the National Union of Ghana Students, and certain members of the Ghana Bar Association. When the ban on party politics was lifted in 1992, many of these groups organized themselves into parties. See also ELECTIONS OF 1992; NEW PATRIOTIC PARTY.

ORANGE, FORT. Fort built by the Dutch at Sekondi (q.v.) about 1640. It was plundered by the Ahantas (q.v.) in 1694 but later rebuilt. It serves as a lighthouse today.

OSEI BONSU see OSEI TUTU KWAME

OSEI KWADWO (Osei Kojo, Osei Kuma). Ca. 1735-1777. Asantehene (q.v.) from 1764 to 1777. In 1765 he joined the Fante in fighting the Wassa, Twifo, and Akyem (qq.v.). The Akyem were defeated, and all their leading chiefs committed suicide. The Asante and Fante soon fell out, and the Akyem renewed their war with the Asante. The Akyem were defeated again, but when the Asante attacked the Krobo, the Krobo forced the Asante to retreat. Campaigns were conducted in Gyaman and Banda, and the Asante army attacked Dagomba (qq.v.) in 1772 and brought back many slaves. Osei Kwadwo surrounded himself with a powerful bodyguard, and he sent Asante commissioners to keep an eye on conquered peoples. Ivor Wilks (q.v.) credited Asantehene Osei Kwadwo with the development of bureaucracy in Asante government.

OSEI KWAME. Ca. 1764-1803. Asantehene (q.v.) from 1777 to 1798. Son of a Mamponghene, he was forced on the electors in Kumasi (qq.v.) when he was hardly 13 years old. An attempted coup against Osei Kwame in 1790 was crushed. In 1797 opposition to his reign forced him to leave Kumasi, and when he did not appear for the Odwira (qq.v.) festival in 1798 he was destooled. Another reason given for the removal of Osei Kwame from power was that he surrounded himself with Muslims (q.v.), and hence it was feared that he might introduce

Islamic law in Asante. There were movements for his restoration, but in 1803 he was executed by strangulation.

OSEI TUTU. Ca. 1660-1712 or 1717? Asantehene (q.v.), ca. 1680-1712 or 1717. Nephew of Obiri Yeboa, Oyoko (qq.v.) leader and Kwamanhene. Osei Tutu completed the pacification of the peoples around Kwaman (q.v.) which was begun by his uncle. With the aid of his friend Okomfo Anokye, he established Kumasi, the Odwiri festival, the tradition of the Golden Stool (qq.v.), and the Asante Union. He also established the precedents that came to stand as the Asante constitution. Around 1698 he began the campaign against Denkyira which climaxed in 1701 with Asante victory over Denkyira at Feyiase (qq.v.). This left Asante the most powerful Akan (q.v.) state. The defeat of Denkyira also opened the way to the coastal trade for Asante. Osei Tutu was killed in a campaign against Akyem Kotoku at a crossing of the Pra River (qq.v.).

OSEI TUTU KWAME (Osei Bonsu, Osei Tutu Kwamina Asibe). Ca. 1779-1823. Asantehene (q.v.) from about 1804 to 1823. At the start of his reign he halted a rebellion in the northern part of Asante (q.v.). In 1807 he led his army against the Fante (q.v.) in the south. He returned again in 1811 and in 1816. He came to be called "Bonsu," signifying "whale," the master of the seas and therefore the coastal Fantelands. Had it not been for the Europeans, particularly the British, Osei Tutu Kwame would have established firm Asante control over the coastal regions. The British saw Asante as a threat to their coastal interests. During this monarch's reign, Asante maintained cordial relations with the Dutch. In 1817 the British sent T. E. Bowdich to Kumasi (qq.v.) to negotiate with Osei Bonsu. In 1819 Joseph Dupuis (q.v.) also visited the Asantehene. Notwithstanding efforts at negotiating trade with the British, at the time of Osei Bonsu's death in 1823, Asante relations with the British were under severe strain.

OSEI YAW AKOTO. Ca. 1800-1834. Asantehene (q.v.) from 1824 to 1834. Half brother of Asantehenes Osei Bonsu and Opoku Fofie (qq.v.). He inherited a war with the British and their local allies in which the Asante had just defeated a British force under the command of Governor Charles MacCarthy, who was killed, at Nsamankow (qq.v.) (Bonsaso or Insamankow) on 21 January 1824. Then in 1826, Asante forces under Osei Yaw Akoto faced European forces and their local allies in the battle of Katamanso (near Dodowa) (qq.v.). Asante was dealt a costly defeat. The Asante Union, especially relations with Dwaben (q.v.), was shaken. Tremendous pressure was brought on Osei Yaw Akoto to abdicate. In his determination to hold on to power, Osei Yaw Akoto eliminated some of the powerful opposition such as Okyeame Adusei and Dwabenhene Kwasi Boaten. In 1831 Osei Yaw Akoto signed a treaty of peace with the British at Fomena (q.v.). British priorities in the south were recognized. The claims of Asante over Akyem, Wassa, Denkyira, Assin, Fante, and Ga (qq.v.) were renounced. In return the British guaranteed the Asante free access to coastal trade.

OSU (Orasky, Christiansborg). One of the original Ga coastal villages, it is today an Accra (qq.v.) neighborhood. The Swedes were trading here as early as 1652. In 1661 the Accra ceded a spot to the Danes, who began to build a castle which they named for Christian IV of Denmark. The Castle changed hands several times over the years. The Portuguese called it St. Francis Xavier, 1679-1683. Christiansborg Castle (q.v.) was bought from the Danes by the English in 1850. They moved their headquarters from Cape Coast to the Castle in 1874, and in 1957 it became the seat of government for Ghana. It came to be called Government House.

OTI AKENTEN. Ca. 1630-Ca. 1660. The third-generation Oyoko Royal of the Asante (qq.v.).

OTU, KWESI. Died 1852. Ruler of Abora, one of the Fante (q.v.) states, from 1820 to 1852. He was a friend of Thomas Birch Freeman (q.v.) and other missionaries, and he became a convert who promoted Christianity and Western ways among the Fante.

OWUSU, VICTOR. Born 1923. Lawyer and politician. Native of Agona Asante (q.v.). He was educated at the Universities of Nottingham and London and was called to the English Bar, Lincoln's Inn, in 1952. During the Nkrumah (q.v.) years Owusu developed a reputation as an outstanding lawyer. He was president of the Ghana Bar Association from 1964 to 1967. After the coup of 1966 the National Liberation Council (q.v.) made him both Attorney General and Commissioner of Justice. He helped organize the Progress Party (PP) (q.v.) and became its national Vice-Chairman. In the 1969 elections he was elected to the National Assembly from the Agona Kwabre district; during the Second Republic he was first the Minister for External Affairs and then Minister of Justice and Attorney General. The coup of 1972 resulted in his detention along with many of the PP leaders, but in 1978 he helped organize the Front for the Prevention of Dictatorship to campaign against the Union Government plans of the Supreme Military Council (qq.v.). The movement was banned and Owusu found himself in prison again. After Acheampong (q.v.) was forced out in July 1978, Owusu was released, but he was disqualified from standing for election or holding office because of "abuse of office." In spite of this, he joined other former Progress Party members in forming a new party, the Popular Front Party (PFP) (q.v.), and he was the presidential candidate of that party. He came in second in the first round of voting, but was defeated by Hilla Limann (q.v.) in the second vote. During the Third Republic, Owusu continued as the leader of the PFP. He worked hard to combine all the opposition parties in preparation for the 1983 and 1984 elections. By early December 1981 he had put together the All People's Party. But at the end of the month the Provisional National Defense Council and Jerry Rawlings (qq.v.) ended the Third Republic. Victor Owusu was arrested a few times by the PNDC.

OYOKO. One of the principal Akan clans. Osei Tutu (q.v.), founder of the Asante Union, was a member of this clan, so it is the royal clan of Kumasi (q.v.).

OYOKO STATES. These are the Asante (q.v.) states which are ruled by members of the Oyoko matriclan. Kumasi, Dwaben,

Bekwai, Kokofu, and Nsuta (qq.v.) all were ruled by members of the Oyoko matriclan. This gave a sense of fraternity and cohesion to the Asante Union. Mampong (q.v.) was an exception. Its leader was always a member of the Beretuo (q.v.) or Bretuo matriclan.

- P -

PADMORE, GEORGE (Malcolm Nurse). 1903-1959. A native of Trinidad; he attended Fisk, New York, and Howard universities in the United States. He became a member of the Communist Party and adopted the name of George Padmore. He was in the Soviet Union in 1929. Padmore was in Germany in 1931 where he was the editor of the *Negro Worker*. In a short time, though, he was deported, going to England. In England, Padmore made contact with many radicals from Commonwealth countries and emerged as a leader in the Pan-African movement. It was in London in 1945 that he met Kwame Nkrumah (q.v.), and they began the collaboration that continued until Padmore died fourteen years later. After Kwame Nkrumah returned to the Gold Coast (q.v.), Padmore frequently visited him. In 1953 Padmore published *The Gold Coast Revolution*. In 1957 George Padmore was an honored guest at the independence ceremonies. Shortly thereafter his friend appointed him head of Ghana's new African Bureau to advance the cause of African unity. When Padmore died in 1959, he was buried at Christiansborg Castle (q.v.).

PEKI. 6°32'N, 0°14'E. The chief town of the Krepi (q.v.) people. It is in the Volta Region some 70 miles (112 km) northeast of Accra and near Lake Volta (qq.v.).

PEOPLE'S ACTION PARTY (PAP). A political party which contested the election of 1969 under the leadership of Imoru Ayarna. The PAP won only two seats in the 1969 National Assembly.

PEOPLE'S DEFENCE COMMITTEE (PDC). The basic unit in the government structure set up in 1982 by the Provisional National Defence Council (q.v.). These committees were to maintain national discipline and supervise national resources. All PDCs were under a National Coordinating Committee.

PEOPLE'S HERITAGE PARTY (PHP) see NKRUMAHIST PARTIES

PEOPLE'S INDEPENDENT PARTY (PIP) see NKRUMAHIST PARTIES

PEOPLE'S MOVEMENT FOR FREEDOM AND JUSTICE (PMFJ). A group organized in January 1978 to oppose the Supreme Military Council's Union Government (qq.v.) proposals. Some of its members were Jones Ofori-Atta, William Ofori-Atta, A. A. Afrifa, Adu Boahen, and Komla A. Gbedemah (qq.v.). It was banned after a few months.

PEOPLE'S NATIONAL CONVENTION (PNC) see NKRUMAHIST PARTIES

PEOPLE'S NATIONAL PARTY (PNP). The dominant political party of the Third Republic. Membership included such persons as Kojo Botsio and Imoru Egala, who had once been close to Nkrumah (qq.v.). Most of the members had been in opposition to Busia (q.v.) during the Second Republic. Their executive candidates, Hilla Limann (q.v.), nephew of Imora Egala, and Joseph William Swain de Graft-Johnson (q.v.), were elected in June 1979. The PNP won 71 of the 140 seats in the National Assembly at the same time.

PEOPLE'S POPULAR PARTY (PPP). One of the small parties organized in 1969. Its leaders were Willie Lutterodt and Johnny Hansen (q.v.). It was left-wing socialist in political orientation. At first it was disqualified as an attempt to revive Nkrumah's Convention People's Party (qq.v.), but the ban was later lifted. In 1979 it became the People's Revolutionary Party (PRP) (q.v.).

PEOPLE'S REVOLUTIONARY PARTY (PRP). A political party organized in 1979 by Johnny Hansen (q.v.) and others to advance the cause of radical socialism. The same group had called themselves the People's Popular Party (q.v.) in 1969. The party was disqualified before the balloting in 1979.

PETROLEUM. In mid-1983 Ghana was producing small amounts of oil from a field 10 miles (16 km) offshore from Saltpond (q.v.). Prospecting was under way in the Gulf of Guinea off Keta (q.v.) and Half Assini. The cost of petroleum since 1972 has been a major cause of Ghana's balance-of-payments problems. Ghana operates a refinery at Tema (q.v.).

PIONEER. A private newspaper started in Kumasi (q.v.) in 1939. The publishers of this newspaper have often come into conflict with governments because of their independent stands on issues.

POLL TAX OF 1852. On 19 April 1852 an assembly of chiefs and elders meeting at Cape Coast (q.v.) Castle with the British Governor and his Council agreed to an ordinance establishing a poll tax of a shilling on every man, woman, and child in the area under British protection. The proceeds were to be used as salaries for the chiefs and for public services. A similar plan was worked out with chiefs at Accra, but chiefs around Keta (qq.v.) refused to agree to a tax. By 1854 general opposition to the tax had developed. The ordinance was amended in May 1858, but after 1862 there was no longer any real attempt to collect the tax.

POPULAR FRONT PARTY (PFP). A political party organized in 1979 under the leadership of Victor Owusu, Joseph H. Mensah, Jones Ofori-Atta, and other former colleagues of K. A. Busia from the Progress Party (qq.v.) of the Second Republic. The party was in favor of free enterprise, and was pro-West. The PFP won 42 seats in the June 1979 elections, and their candidate for President came in second. Victor Owusu, the candidate, came in first in Asante, Brong-Ahafo, and the Northern Regions (qq.v.), and went into the runoff with

Limann (PNP) (qq.v.), who won. In the July runoff the PFP got 38 percent of the vote. In late 1981 the PFP merged into the coalition called the All People's Party (APP). A few days later the Provisional National Defense Council (q.v.) seized political power in a military coup.

POSITIVE ACTION. In October 1949 Kwame Nkrumah (q.v.) published a pamphlet, "What I Mean by Positive Action," calling for strikes, boycotts, and non-cooperation unless the British granted immediate self-government to the Gold Coast (q.v.). He announced that the campaign was beginning in January 1950.

POST. A bi-monthly publication started by the Ghanaian government Information Services on 2 January 1980. At that time the Information Services also published *The Ghana Review*, a quarterly pictorial magazine, and *Today in Ghana*, a booklet on aspects of life in Ghana. In addition to these, in 1980 the Information Service published eight Ghanaian language newspapers each month.

PRA. River which, with its tributaries, the Ofin, the Oda (q.v.), the Fum, and the Birim (q.v.), drains much of southern Ghana. It flows into the Gulf of Guinea near Shama, about 8 miles (13 km) east of Sekondi (qq.v.). It is crossed by a suspension bridge 6 miles (10 km) inland, near Beposo. The river serves as a boundary between Asante (q.v.) and three other regions. Asantehene Osei Tutu was killed in the second decade of the eighteenth century while crossing the river in a campaign against Akyem (qq.v.).

PRAMPRAM (Gbugbla). 5°42'N, 0°07'E. Coastal Adangbe (q.v.) village in the Eastern Region a short distance east of Tema (q.v.). It is about 30 miles (48 km) east of Accra (q.v.). The Dodowa River (q.v.) enters the Gulf just east of the town. The British built Fort Vernon here at the start of the nineteenth century, but abandoned it by 1820.

PRANG. 7°59'N, 0°53'W. Town in the Brong-Ahafo Region (q.v.) on the Great Northern Road, and about halfway between Atebu and the ferry across Lake Volta at Yeji (qq.v.). It is close to the Pru branch of Lake Volta (qq.v.). It was a major stopping place on the cattle drives from Burkina Faso to Kumasi (q.v.).

PRASU (Praso). 5°56'N, 1°22'W. The name means "Pra water." It is a key town, located on the Pra River, mid-way on the Cape Coast-Kumasi (qq.v.) highway. For many years this was the border between Asante (q.v.) and British-protected territories.

PRATT, KWESI, Jr. Journalist and political activist. Born in 1953, Kwesi Pratt received secondary school education at Tema and graduated from the Ghana Institute of Journalism in Accra. Between 1974 and 1975, Pratt worked as a *Ghanaian Times* reporter. He later moved to the Ghana News Agency. By 1981 when the Provisional National Defence Council (PNDC) (q.v.) ended the Third Republic, Pratt was the public relations officer for the National Youth Council.

Though detained after the 31 December 1981 coup, Kwesi Pratt was briefly kept as secretary to the reconstituted National Youth Organizing Commission. Later, he was moved rapidly from one position to another. He worked at the Ministries of Youth and Sports, Fuel and Power, and Information, as well as at the National Association of Local Councils. While some in government saw Pratt as a "security risk," he endeared himself to many anti-PNDC factions for his criticism of the government. Between 1982 and 1992, Kwesi Pratt was detained eight times. During that period, he joined the anti-PNDC Movement for Freedom and Justice (see OPPOSITION POLITICS). After the ban on party politics was lifted in 1992, Pratt co-founded the Popular Party for Democracy and Development but was unable to participate in the elections that followed for lack of money to register his party.

PREMPE I (Kwaku Dua III, Agyeman Prempe). Ca. 1873-1931. Asantehene (q.v.), 1888-1931. Exile, 1896-1924. He was a brother of Kwaku Dua II, who died in 1884, beginning an interregnum of four years. In March 1888, at fifteen, he became Asantehene-designate as Kwaku Dua III. Kokofu, Mampong, and Nsuta (q.v.) objected, and civil war resulted. The rebels appealed to the British for support. Prempe was finally enstooled in June 1894, with Mampong and Kokufu taking part in the ceremony, but there was much discontent in Asante (q.v.) territories, and frequent campaigns were necessary to maintain order. The British used the turmoil as justification for intervention into Asante affairs, and in January 1896 the British invaded Asante and occupied Kumasi (q.v.). Prempe was arrested, and the Asante state was declared dissolved by the British. Prempe and his family were taken first to Elmina (q.v.), then to Sierra Leone, and finally to the Indian Ocean's Seychelles Islands, from which Prempe I was not allowed to return until 1924. At first the British treated him as a private citizen, but in 1926 they did recognize him as Kumasihene. He died in 1931.

PREMPE II. (Edward Prempe Owusu, Kwame Kyeretwie, Osei Agyeman Prempe). 1892-1970. Kumasihene, 1931-1935. Asantehene (q.v.), 1935-1970. He was a nephew of Prempe I (q.v.). Before he became Kumasihene he was a storekeeper in Kumasi (q.v.), but he was one of the founders of the Asante Kotoko Union Society in 1916, and he played an active role in the campaign for the return of his exiled uncle to the Gold Coast (q.v.). After the death of Prempe I in 1931, he became Kumasihene, and in 1935, after the British allowed the restoration of the Asante Union, he became the Asantehene. From that time until his death in 1970 he was an important influence in Gold Coast affairs. He often was opposed to British policy, but he was also opposed to moves that might create disorder and revolution. He never trusted Kwame Nkrumah and the CPP Veranda Boys (qq.v.), and his relations with Nkrumah were strained. After independence Nkrumah quickly centralized power over Ghana in his own hands. Half of Asante was sliced away as the Brong-Ahafo Region (q.v.). From that time on Prempe II withdrew from national politics, though he was elected President of the National House of Chiefs in 1969 a short time before his death.

PREMPEH COLLEGE. A Presbyterian-affiliated boys' secondary school founded in Kumasi (q.v.) in 1949. It is located in the western outskirts of the town, just off the Western By-Pass and Sunyani roads.

PRESIDENT'S OWN GUARD REGIMENT (POGR). This military group was first established on 1 October 1960 as an honor guard, but within a year it had become a private army, supervised in part by officers from Communist countries. By 1965 the POGR had two battalions with 50 officers, 1,100 men, and the most modern equipment in the Ghanaian army. It was directly responsible to the President rather than the regular military commanders. The POGR was abolished after the 1966 coup.

PRESTEA. 5°26'N, 2°09'W. Mining town located 20 miles (32 km) northwest of Tarkwa (q.v.)in the Western Region.

PREVENTIVE DETENTION ACT (PDA). One year after independence, the Convention People's Party (q.v.) government introduced the Preventive Detention Act (PDA) which initially allowed Nkrumah (q.v.) to imprison enemies of the state for up to five years (and later ten years). According to the law, persons charged under the PDA may not have recourse to a trial. By empowering the government to arrest and detain any enemy of the state or any person who was a threat to state security, the PDA, as early as 1958, set the course of dictatorship in Ghana. The PDA was renewed in June 1962 and in May 1964. It ended with the coup of 1966. It was under the PDA law that J. B. Danquah (q.v.) was arrested and kept in jail till his death in 1965 in prison.

PRINCE'S TOWN (Princestown, Polesu, Pokoso). 4°47' N, 2°08' W. Ahanta coastal town in the Western Region just west of Cape Three Points and some 47 miles (76 km) west of Sekondi-Takoradi (qq.v.). It was an outpost of Brandenburg (q.v.) by 1682, and they built Friedrichsburg Castle here about 1684. This was acquired by the Dutch by 1725, who called it Fort Hollandia. Some restoration has been done on the fort in recent times.

PRINSENSTEN, FORT (Prinzenstein). The Danes established a post at Keta (q.v.) in the early eighteenth century. The Dutch soon replaced the Danes, but in turn were forced out by Akwamu (q.v.) in 1731. The Danes returned in 1737, but Prinsensten was not built until 1784. It was purchased by the British in 1850.

PROGRAM OF ACTION FOR THE MITIGATION OF THE SOCIAL CONSEQUENCES OF ADJUSTMENT FOR DEVELOPMENT (PAMSCAD). On 22 February 1988, the Provisional National Defence Council (PNDC) (q.v.) Secretary for Finance and Economic Planning, Dr. Kwesi Botchwey (q.v.), chaired a PAMSCAD conference in Geneva (Switzerland). The conference was attended by twelve multinational agencies and sixteen nongovernmental organizations with interests in Ghana's economic development. Dr. Botchwey discussed with the participants the social and political cost of Ghana's Economic Recovery Program (ERP) (q.v.) and Structural Adjustment Programs (SAPs) initiated in the early 1980s with the support of the World Bank and the IMF. Under these recovery plans, the PNDC government instituted various austerity programs which included the introduction of fee-paying medical and educational services, worker redeployment and various attempts at streamlining the nation's bureaucratic institutions. According to an argument by Dr. Botchwey, the achievements of the SAPs and ERPs, which had resulted in a sustained 6 percent economic growth for Ghana by 1988, could not be maintained if the social and political implications of economic recovery were not addressed. He, therefore, called on donor countries and agencies to make funds available to Ghana to specifically address those problems. According to reports, Dr. Botchwey's appeal was positively received by the participants of the Geneva conference. Much of the social mobilization programs of PAMSCAD, especially the worker-redeployment and the technical, vocational education and training, were handled through the Ministry of Mobilization and Social Welfare during the tenureship of David Sapong Boaten (q.v.). See also MINING, AGRICULTURE, INVESTMENT CODE.

PROGRESS PARTY (PP). The dominant political party of the Second Republic, 1969-1972. The party was organized in 1969, mostly of people who had once been members of the United Party (q.v.). Kofi Abrefa Busia, Victor Owusu, William Ofori-Atta (qq.v.), and much of the Akan (q.v.) middle class belonged to the PP. The PP won an impressive victory in August 1969, with 105 seats in the National Assembly to 29 seats for the opposition National Alliance of Liberals (q.v.), and 5 other seats for minor parties. Busia became Prime Minister in the Second Republic. The coup of 1972 ended his administration.

PROTECTORATE. After 1902, territory under protection of the British. It was used to refer to different geographical locations at different times. Before 1874, "the protectorate" was a reference to the coastal areas. Asante and the Northern Territories were outside British political influence until after 1902.

PROVINCIAL COUNCILS OF CHIEFS. In March 1918 the chiefs of the Eastern Province of the Gold Coast (q.v.) began to meet for mutual consultation. The 1925 constitutional changes provided for three Provincial Councils of Chiefs. The Western Council (with 20 paramount stools) could elect one member of the Legislative Council; the Central Council (with 27 paramount stools) could have two members of the Legislative Council; and the Eastern Council (with 13 paramount stools) was allowed three members of the Legislative Council. The Provincial Councils gave chiefs a chance to consult together and to make their positions known to the British. The first meetings under the 1925 provisions were held in May 1926.

PROVISIONAL NATIONAL DEFENCE COUNCIL (PNDC). The central committee of the government established by Flight Lieutenant Jerry J. Rawlings (q.v.) following the coup of 31 December 1981. It was initially made up of three soldiers, three civilians, and a student leader. Membership of the PNDC changed over the eleven-year duration that the government was in power. In November/December 1992, democratic elections (q.v.) were held in Ghana. Former PNDC chairman J. J.

Rawlings was elected to the presidency of the Fourth Republic. See also J. J. RAWLINGS.

PUBLIC TRIBUNAL. Public tribunals were established by the Provisional National Defence Council (PNDC) (q.v.) in 1982. A law providing for the establishment of a national public tribunal to hear and determine appeals from and decisions of regional public tribunals was passed in August of 1984. Sections 3 and 10 of the PNDC Establishment Proclamation, however, limited public tribunals to hear only cases of political and economic nature. The government reserved to itself the right to refer to a public tribunal offenses under any other enactment.

A public tribunal board which consisted of not less than five individuals and not more than fifteen members was also appointed by the PNDC. At least one board member was to be a lawyer with a minimum of five years' experience in the legal profession.

During its 1984 annual meeting, the Ghana Bar Association condemned the establishment of public tribunals as undemocratic and called on its members not to participate in them. The PNDC, on the other hand, defended the tribunals as "fundamental to a good legal system." According to a government statement, the tribunals were established in response to a growing legal consciousness on the part of the people.

PUSIGA. 11°05'N, 0°07'W. Village in the Upper East Region some 8 miles (13 km) east of Bawku (q.v.) and near the borders of Togo and Burkina Faso. It is here that Gbewa founded the Mole-Dagbani (qq.v.) dynasty that founded many states in northern Ghana and Burkina Faso. The Kusasi (q.v.), who live in Pusiga, are one of these Mole-Dagbani peoples. The Mossi, Mamprusi, Dagomba, Nanumba (qq.v.), etc., all trace their origins to Pusiga.

- Q -

QUAHOE (Quahu) see KWAHU

QUAISON-SACKEY, ALEX.   Born 1924.   Attorney, politician, diplomat, author.   A native of Winneba, Quaison-Sackey was educated at Mfantsipim, Achimota, Exeter, Oxford, the London School of Economics, and Tours, and he read law at Lincoln's Inn.   He was employed in the Gold Coast-Ghana Civil Service until appointed Ghana's representative to the United Nations (UN), 1959-1965, during which time he was also Ghana's ambassador to Cuba and Mexico.   He was Africa's first President of the UN General Assembly, 1964-1965.   He was Foreign Minister of Ghana in 1965 and until the 1966 coup. In 1963 he published *Africa Unbound.*   In 1977 he organized the Patriotic Movement to support the Union Government plan of the Supreme Military Council (SMC) (qq.v.).   In January 1978,   Alex   Quaison-Sackey   was   appointed   Ghana's ambassador to Washington by the SMC.

QUAQUE, PHILIP (Quacoe).   1741-1816.   A native of Cape Coast (q.v.), he was sent to England to be educated by the Society for the Propagation of the Gospel in 1754.   He was ordained an Anglican priest while still in London in 1765, and he married an Englishwoman.   In 1766 he returned to Cape Coast as a missionary and schoolmaster.   He also served as chaplain at Cape Coast Castle until he died in 1816.

QUASHIE, TETTEH (Tete Kwashi, Tetti Quashi, Tetteh Kwashi, Tetteh Quarshie).   1842-1892.   Born at Osu, he was trained as a blacksmith at a Basel Mission (qq.v.).   In 1870 he went to Fernando Po (Bioko, Equatorial Guinea) and worked on a cocoa (q.v.) plantation for eight years.   Returning home in 1878, he brought some cocoa pods, which he planted at Mampong in Akuapem (qq.v.).   He made his first harvest in 1883.   The Basel Mission had planted cocoa pods in Akuapem two decades earlier, but little developed from their efforts. The Ghanaian cocoa industry developed from Tetteh Quashie (Quarshie) and his efforts.

QUIFORO see TWIFO

QUIST, EMMANUEL CHARLES. 1880-1959. A native of Christiansborg who was of Ga-Dutch extraction; he was educated at Basel Mission schools at Christiansborg and Akuropon (qq.v.). He went on to England and read law at the Middle Temple. Returning to Accra (q.v.), he served on the Town Council there from 1919 to 1929. He became the first African to be a Crown Counsel in 1914. He was a member of the Legislative Council in 1925 and 1934, and served as President of the Legislative Council from 1949 to 1950. He then became the first Speaker of the Gold Coast-Ghana National Assembly, 1951-1957.

- R -

RAILROADS. Ghana has a rail system with a route length of just under 600 miles (966 km). The Western Line from Sekondi to Kumasi (qq.v.) is the oldest, built between 1898 and 1903 and partly rebuilt between 1919 and 1926. A branch from Tarkwa to Prestea (qq.v.) was added, 1908-1911. The track from Sekondi to Kumasi covers just under 170 miles (274 km). The Eastern Accra-Kumasi line was started in 1909 and not finished until 1923. The distance for the Eastern is 188 miles (303 km). A Central line was run 99 miles (160 km) from the Huni Valley junction with the Western line to Kade (q.v.) between 1922 and 1927. In 1956 the triangle from Accra to Sekondi to Kumasi was completed with a line from Achiasi, below Oda, to Kotoku, below Nsawam (qq.v.). This tied the Western and Eastern lines. A final rail line from Achimota to Tema and the Shai Hills (q.v.) was opened in 1954. There were elaborate plans for lines north of Kumasi in 1927. Plans were for a great circle from Kumasi to Tamale to Naga to Navrongo, from Naga to Wa to Bole (qq.v.), and back to Kumasi. The depression of the 1930s and World War II ended all such dreams. A northern line has been discussed by various governments but no plan has been implemented.

RAMSEYER, FRIEDRICH AUGUST, and JOHANNES KUHNE. Two Germans who were captured by the Asante at Anum in 1869 and held as hostages in Kumasi, with M. J. Bonnat (qq.v.), until 1874. Their experience in captivity was published in 1875 as *Four Years in Ashantee.*

RATTRAY, ROBERT SUTHERLAND. 1881-1938. Colonial officer, anthropologist, folklorist, and ethnographer. Rattray was a Scotsman, born in India. In 1906 he joined the Gold Coast Customs Service on the Volta River (q.v.). In 1911 he became Assistant District Commissioner at Ejura, on the Great Northern Road, above Mampong in Asante (qq.v.). By 1914 he had learned both Mossi and Akan (Twi) (qq.v.). He went on to become a DC, but administration had lost its appeal, and in 1921 he was appointed the one and only head of the Anthropological Department of Asante. He retired from that position nine years later, and he was killed while flying a glider in 1938. All told, he published twelve volumes of ethnography and folklore. His books on the Asante and the people of the Asante hinterland are masterpieces.

RAWLINGS, JERRY JOHN. Born 1947. Flight Lieutenant, Chairman of the Armed Forces Revolutionary Council (AFRC), Chairman of the Provisional National Defense Council (PNDC) (qq.v.), and President of the Fourth Republic. Born in Accra on 22 June 1947 to a Ghanaian mother and a Scottish father, J. J. Rawlings attended Achimota and Ghana Military Academy at Teshi. Commissioned in 1969 as Lieutenant, Rawlings took flight training at Takoradi, and by 15 May 1979, when he led an abortive coup to overthrow the government of the Supreme Military Council (SMC) (q.v.), he was a Flight Lieutenant. Released from prison on 4 June 1979 by another coup, Rawlings was made Chairman of the AFRC, which ruled Ghana only until September that year when he turned the reins of power over to an elected government of the Third Republic. In the brief period of four months, Rawlings and the AFRC purged the army and executed officers accused of corrupting the forces as well as three former heads of state, namely I. K. Acheampong, A. A. Afrifa, and F. W. K. Akuffo (qq.v.).

Retired from the military by the administration of the Third Republic, Rawlings's relations with the government became strained as he and members of the June 4th Movement (q.v.) accused the Limann (q.v.) administration of relaxing the code of accountability established by the AFRC. The poor performance of the civilian administration in enforcing both political and economic discipline led to the return of Rawlings to power in December 1981 as head of the Provisional National Defence Council (q.v.). During the early 1980s, Rawlings and the PNDC applied to the civilian sector the same enthusiasm with which the AFRC purged the armed forces. The constitution of the Third Republic was suspended, public tribunals (q.v.) were established to investigate abuses, and policies were put in place to remedy the ailing national economy.

The economic policies implemented in phases by Rawlings and the PNDC restored international confidence in Ghana's development (see ECONOMIC RECOVERY PROGRAM). During this period, those who opposed the recovery programs accused the government of selling out to the World Bank and the International Monetary Fund (IMF). The signs of economic recovery under Rawlings and the PNDC, however, showed that the ERP had yielded positive results. Even more important were the policies of Rawlings and the PNDC in the domestic political arena. Moving away from the use of defense committees to regulate civil and political societies, the government created a National Commission for Democracy (q.v.) which was charged with setting in motion the process of democratization. The result was the 1988 district assemblies (q.v.) elections. The democratization process further led to the 1992 presidential elections (q.v.) from which Rawlings emerged as President of the Fourth Republic. His party, the National Democratic Congress (q.v.), won 190 seats in the 200-member parliament. See also OPPOSITION POLITICS.

REGIONS. Before 1951 the Gold Coast was divided into the Gold Coast Colony, Ashanti (Asante), and the Northern Territories Protectorate (qq.v.). The three provinces were respectively administered from Accra, Kumasi, and Tamale (q.v.). The Colony had been created in 1874, with part of Togo Trust Territory added to it in 1919. Ashanti (Asante) was created in 1901, and the Northern Territories Protectorate was also organized in 1901. In 1919, parts of the Togo Trust were included in the Northern Territories. After 1951, a new system of provincial divisions began to emerge. The Trans-Volta-Togo region was created in 1952 to be managed from Ho (q.v.). It would become the Volta Region (q.v.). The Colony was divided into Eastern, Western, and Greater Accra regions. Brong-Ahafo was separated from Ashanti (Asante) in 1958. The Regions of Ghana Act of 29 June 1960 adjusted all the boundaries and created the Central Region out of the Western Region, and the Upper Region from the Northern Region (qq.v.). In 1982, further adjustments were made in the Upper Region to create the Upper East and Upper West regions. From the three major divisions of the colonial era, the country was divided into ten regions by the end of the 1980s.

REINDORF, CARL CHRISTIAN. 1834-1917. Son of a Danish father and Ga mother, Reindorf was born at Prampram (qq.v.). He became a minister and teacher with the Basel Mission (q.v.). He participated in the project to translate the Bible into Ga, published in 1912. His greatest work, however, was the *History of the Gold Coast and Asante*, completed in 1889 and published by the Basel Mission in 1895. This work, which was the first major written history by an African, was very much based on local traditions.

RELIGION. According to the first post-independence population census of 1960, 41 percent of Ghanaians described themselves as Christians and 38 percent Traditionalists. Twelve percent of the population described themselves as Muslims (q.v.) while the remaining 9 percent affiliated themselves with no religious denomination. Further distribution of the 1960 census according to the Christian sects showed the following statistics: 25 percent Protestants (non-Pentecostal), 13 percent Catholics, 2 percent Protestant (Pentecostal) and about 1 percent Independent African Churches.

In both the 1970 and 1984 population counts, no distribution of the people along religious lines was indicated. A 1985 estimate, however, showed a sharp rise in the Christian population to about 62 percent of the people. But, while the percentage of Protestants (non-Pentecostal) remained at 25 percent, the ratio of Catholics rose to 15 percent, and Protestants (Pentecostals) were about 8 percent. The greatest rise occurred among the Independent African Churches--about 14 percent compared to their 1 percent in 1960. The Muslim population of Ghana was estimated in 1985 to be about 15 percent. While the dramatic increase in the population described as Christian may be attributed to the spread of Western education, the success of Independent African Churches may be attributed to the ability of that denomination in adjusting Christian doctrines to suit local cosmologies. Also, while most Muslims in Ghana are orthodox Sunnis, the Ahmadiyyah (q.v.) movement, which has adopted the Western system of education, has become well rooted.

RELIGIOUS BODIES LAW (PNDCL 221). The Religious Bodies (Registration) Law 2989 (PNDCL 221) took retroactive effect from 1 June 1989. According to a government statement, the law was passed to serve as a regulatory and control framework for religious organizations operating in the country. Under the law, no religious organization existing in Ghana was to operate three months from 1 June 1989 unless it had been duly registered. Registration for operation was to be sought from a government-created Religious Affairs Committee of the National Commission for Culture. As part of the application for certification, the following items were to be submitted: the constitution of the religious organization, address and location of its headquarters, information on the spread of membership in the country, places of worship or activity, and financial statements and intended sources of funds. While the government argued that the law was intended to protect citizens from corrupt individuals, the law was criticized as an infringement upon religious rights.

ROWE, SAMUEL. 1835-1888. Governor of the Gold Coast (q.v.), 1881-1884. He was an army surgeon who was posted to Lagos in 1862. He took part in the Asante (q.v.) campaign of 1873, was Lieutenant-Governor of the West African Settlements in 1875, Administrator of the Gambia, 1875-1877, Governor of the West African Settlements, 1877-1881, Governor of the

Gold Coast 1881-1884, and Governor of Sierra Leone from 1885 until he died in office, 1888.

ROYAL AFRICAN COMPANY. A joint-stock company chartered in 1672. On the Gold Coast it operated Cape Coast (qq.v.) Castle and a number of subordinate trade posts. After 1751 the African Company of Merchants (q.v.) took over control of Gold Coast trade, even though the Royal African Company continued to own its properties until the properties were assumed by the Crown in 1821.

ROYAL WEST AFRICAN FRONTIER FORCE (RWAFF). A West African military force created by the Colonial Office in 1897. It was called the West African Frontier Force until 1928. During World War I (q.v.), the Gold Coast Regiment of the WAFF saw service in Togo, the Cameroons, and East Africa. In 1943 the Gold Coast Regiment went to Burma. The WAFF was originally created to act as a constabulary force. Most of the recruits, especially in the Gold Coast, were Muslims from the Northern Territories, hence the occasional reference as the Hausa corps (q.v.). By 1957, when the RWAFF became the Ghanaian army, only about 10 percent of the officers were Africans.

RUYGHAVER, FORT. A Dutch base built in 1653 some 60 miles (96 km) up the Ankobra River (q.v.) to trade in gold. It was named for the then Dutch Director-General of the Gold Coast (q.v.), Jacob Ruyghaver. Unable to maintain a garrison so far from the coast, the Dutch destroyed the base in 1658.

-S-

SABARI (Sabare). 9°17'N, 0°16'E. Village in the Northern Region 23 miles (37 km) southeast of Yendi on the old Hausa caravan route to Salaga (qq.v.). It was near a crossing of the Oti (q.v.) or Sabram River. Muhammad Zangina had a mosque built here, and it became a Muslim (q.v.) center.

SABOE see ASEBU

SAFORI see OFORI KUMA I

SAGBADRE WAR. The struggle between Anlo (q.v.) and Denmark in 1783 caused by an Anlo attack on a Danish trader. Anlo was defeated, and a peace treaty was signed in 1784. The Danes built several forts near the mouth of the Volta (q.v.) to maintain the peace.

SAGRENTI WAR. The Asante (q.v.) name for the campaign between the British and Asante in 1873-1874. Sagrenti was the Akan pronunciation for name of the British Commander, Sir Garnet Wolseley (qq.v.).

SAHWI see SEFWI

SALAGA (Saharah). 8°33'N, 0°31'W. A village in the eastern Gonja area of the Northern Region (qq.v.) which flourished from around 1800 to 1874. Its reason for existence was the slave and kola (q.v.) trade between the Asante (q.v.) and peoples along the Niger. It started as a small Nanumba (q.v.) village, grew into a busy Gonja trade center, and declined rapidly as Asante withered from British attacks. Dr. V. S. Gouldsbury (q.v.), an Englishman, was the first European to see Salaga. He reached it in 1876, shortly after the town began to decline. There were still traces of the former prosperity. The Frenchman Louis Binger (q.v.) arrived twel e years later, after the decline was far advanced. Binger described Salaga as a ruined city. The Germans actually did destroy the place in 1896, but the British made a feeble attempt to restore it after 1898. Salaga remains today as a small town.

SALLAH CASE. In 1970 the Busia (q.v.) government dismissed E. K. Sallah from his position as a manager of the Ghana National Trading Corporation. The courts ruled that Sallah was illegally dismissed and ordered the government to reemploy Sallah. Busia refused. The opposition used the case to denounce the Progress Party (q.v.) and Busia's regime.

SALTPOND. 5°12'N, 1°04'W. Coastal town in the Central Region Fante area between Anomabo and Ankoful (qq.v.). The town was a focal point for political meetings in the period just before independence. Today, the town is known for its offshore oil drill.

SAM, ALFRED. Ca. 1880-Ca. 1934. An Akyem mercha..t who started a movement to encourage African-Americans to move to the Akyem area of the Gold Coast during the period just before and during the early part of World War I (qq.v.). The movement was not a success.

SAMORI (Samori Toure, Samory). Ca. 1830-1900. Dyula (q.v.) leader who came originally from Guinea. In the 1860s he built a state around Bisandugu in Guinea and began to expand into the area of modern Mali. His state had elements of an Islamic theocracy. By the late 1880s the expansive designs of Samori clashed with those of the French. So in 1894 Samori moved his center of operations to Dabakala in modern Ivory Coast. From there he planned to build a new nation by expanding north and east. To make his position stronger, he offered an alliance to Prempe I of Asante (qq.v.). In reply, in October 1895, Prempe asked Samori to help the Asante reestablish their former power in the Gold Coast (q.v.). The British moved quickly to head off such an association. In January 1896 a British expeditionary force occupied Kumasi (q.v.), and Prempe was sent into exile. Samori's forces, under his son Sarankenyi-Mori, crossed the Black Volta and moved freely back and forth in the area between Bole and Tumu (qq.v.). For a time there was even a possibility of cooperation between Samori and Babatu (q.v.) against the Europeans. In November 1896 the British sent forces toward Wa (q.v.) to clear the east bank of the Black Volta of the forces of Samori. In fighting during March and April 1897 Samori's troops had the upper hand. They captured the English commander, Francis Henderson (q.v.). But by May Samori had moved his army further north and the threat to what is today the Northern and Upper West regions of Ghana diminished. Months later Samori was captured by the French and exiled to Gabon, where he died in 1900.

SAMPSON, MAGNUS JOHN. 1900-1958. Teacher and writer. He was member of the Coussey Committee (q.v.) on Constitutional Reform in 1949, and the Legislative Assembly, 1951-1954. His *Gold Coast Men of Affairs*, published in 1937, is his best-known work. *A Political Retrospect of the Gold Coast, 1860-1930* (n.d.) and *West African Leadership: Public Speeches Delivered by J. E. Casely-Hayford* (1940) were examples of the growing interest in local history in the Gold Coast in the period shortly before independence.

SAN ANTONIO (Santo Antonio de Axem). This fort was the second base established by the Portuguese on the Gold Coast. The Portuguese were first here in 1503, but the triangular fort was started about 1515. It was taken by the Dutch in 1642 and became British in 1872. The structure was restored in the 1950s, and today it is used by the town of Axim (q.v.) as council and police offices.

SAN JAGO (San Jago, Conradsburg). The Portuguese first built a structure here on a hill in Elmina (q.v.) at the start of the sixteenth century. A. W. Lawrence has described this structure as "the oldest purely military work." The Dutch fort was built in the 1650s and enlarged in 1671. San Jago or Conradsburg, as the Dutch called it, became British in 1872. Today it is maintained by the Museum and Monuments Board.

SAN JORGE (Sao Jorge de Mina, St. George's, Elmina Castle). Located at Elmina (q.v.), this is the oldest and most impressive of all the structures standing in Ghana today. The location and some of the site preparation took place at Edina in 1480 or 1481. In December 1481 more than 600 men sailed from Portugal under the command of Diogo de Azambuja for the Gold Coast. Bartholomew Diaz was one of those with the fleet. The fleet brought much of the building material from Portugal. The Castle served as the Portuguese headquarters from 1482 to 1637; then it served the Dutch as their trade center from 1637 to 1872, when it became British. It remains today as one of the most impressive monuments to the presence of Europeans on the Guinea Coast.

SAN SEBASTIAN. Fort San Sebastian was built by the Portuguese at Shama (q.v.) around 1560. This was east of modern Sekondi, and near the mouth of the Pra (qq.v.). It was soon taken by the Dutch, who enlarged it between 1640 and 1642. It was acquired by the English in 1872 and restored in the 1950s. It is used for offices today.

SANTEMANSO see ASANTEMANSO

SARBAH, JOHN MENSAH (Kofi Mensah). 1864-1910. He was born at Cape Coast and was the son of one of the outstanding merchants of the Fante coast. He was educated in law at Lincoln Inn in London, and he became the first Gold Coaster to be licensed to practice law. He founded the *Gold Coast People*, which he published from 1891 to 1898. He was one of the founders of the Gold Coast Aborigines' Rights Society (q.v.) in 1897. He published his *Fanti Customary Law* in 1897, *Fanti Law Reports* in 1904, and the *Fanti National Constitution* in 1906. He was most interested in education, was active in founding and supporting the Collegiate School at Cape Coast, and helped create Mfantsipim School (q.v.) in 1904. He was a member of the Legislative Council (q.v.) from 1901 until his death. Mensah Sarbah Hall at the University of Ghana (q.v.) at Legon is named in his honor.

SASRAKU ANSA I. Died 1689. The seventh Paramount Chief of Akwamu (q.v.). He was the ruler of Akwamu at its point of greatest expansion. He conquered the Ga and began the subjection of Ladoku (q.v.).

SAVELUGU. 9°37'N, 0°49'W. Farm center in the Northern Region on the Great Northern Road some 20 miles (32 km) north of Tamale (q.v.). It is one of the three chief divisional towns of Dagomba (q.v.).

SEDITION ORDINANCE, 1934. This expansion of the definition of sedition by the Legislative Council in 1934, during the depression, stirred up a great protest in Accra and Cape Coast (qq.v.).

SEFWI (Sahwi, Segwi, Encassar, Inkassa). Anyi-Bawle Akan group which once covered much of what is today the Western Region north of the Aowin and Wassa (qq.v.). Today they are mostly located between Wiawso and Bibiani between the Tano and Ankobra rivers (qq.v.). They were dominated by Denkyira during the latter part of the seventeenth century and by Asante (qq.v.) after 1717. In 1717 the Sefwi invaded Asante and sacked Kumasi (q.v.). Members of the royal family, including the Asantehene Opoku Ware's (q.v.) mother, were murdered. The royal mausoleums were plundered. In response the Asante conquered all of Sefwi and annexed it to Asante. Sefwi continued to be a part of Asante until 1887. There are three divisions of Sefwi today: Sefwi Anwiawso (Anhwiaso), located near the source of the Ankobra River at 6°20'N, 2°16'W; Sefwi Bekwai, the smallest division, located at 6°11'N, 2°19'W; and Wiawso, on the Tano River at 6°12'N, 2°29'W.

SEKONDI. 4°56'N, 1°42'W. A coastal city in the Ahanta part of the Western Region (qq.v.). It is the twin city of Takoradi (q.v.). At one time Sekondi was regarded as a major port, but after the modern port was opened at Takoradi the Sekondi docks were no longer important. The Dutch built Fort Orange at Sekondi in 1640. Today the fort is a lighthouse. The town is the terminus of the railroads to Kumasi and Accra (qq.v.). In 1988, the population of Sekondi-Takoradi was estimated to be about 107,650 people. See also TAKORADI.

SEKYERE. A district of Asante north and northeast of Kumasi (qq.v.) between the upper Ofin River and the Afram River. Dwaben and Mampong (qq.v.) of Asante are in this area.

SEKYI, WILLIAM E. (Kobina Sekyi). 1892-1956. He was born in Cape Coast, where his father was Headmaster of the Wesleyan School. He attended Mfantsipim and the University of London and became a lawyer in 1919. He was President of the Aborigines' Rights Protection Society (q.v.) for many years and was a staunch nationalist who advocated the ideas of Marcus Garvey and was active in the National Congress of British West Africa (q.v.). He was a member of the Coussey

Committee (q.v.) on constitutional reform in 1949. In 1918 he wrote *The Anglo-Fante*, the first English language novel written in the Gold Coast. His play, *The Blinkards*, a satire on Africans who try to act like Europeans, was published posthumously in 1974.

SENCHI RAPIDS. 6°12'N, 0°05'E. This was the limit of navigation on the Volta (q.v.) in the wet season. The Senchi Ferry, operated by the United Africa Company (q.v.) from 1920 to 1956, was once a famous institution. The Ferry closed in 1956 when the Adomi Bridge (q.v.) opened to traffic. Since the construction of the dam at Akosombo to the north of Senchi, navigation on the resulting lake extends as far north as Tamale Port (qq.v.).

SENYA. A Guan group who live on the coast in the Gomoa district at Senya Beraku (qq.v.).

SENYA BERAKU (Bereku). 5°23'N, 0°29'W. A Gomoa coastal village east of Winneba (qq.v.) in the Central Region. The Dutch built a post here in 1667 and started to build Fort Good Hope in 1706. From time to time the British took over the Dutch post, and it was transferred to the British in 1868. The village was long famous for its iron and gold smiths who produced fine jewelry, chains, weapons, and metalwork.

SHAI. An Adangbe group who are related to the Ada and Krobo (qq.v.). Most of the Shai live in the Accra District of the Greater Accra Region.

SHAMA. 5°01'N, 1°38'W. Eguafo coastal town in the Western Region near the mouth of the Pra River and about 6 miles (10 km) to the east of Sekondi (qq.v.). The Portuguese bought gold here in 1472, and reported that the village had 800 inhabitants. For a decade, until Elmina (q.v.) Castle was finished, Shama was the chief Portuguese trade post. San Sebastian (q.v.) was started around 1560. The Dutch took the place in 1640 and rebuilt San Sebastian in the 1660s. It became British in 1872.

SHEA TREE (Karite). The *Butyrospermum parkii* is the most important tree in the Northern and Upper regions (qq.v.). The fruit resembles a yellow plum and contains a sweet pulp which is edible when ripe. Shea butter is obtained from oil in the kernels of the nuts. Shea oil is used for cooking, as an ointment, and as a hairdressing.

SHIENE HILLS see ZABZUGU HILLS

SIKA DWA see GOLDEN STOOL

SILK COTTON TREE (kapok). The *Ceiba pentandra* is one of the monarchs of Ghanaian forests. It can grow to a height of 200 feet (60 m) and is highly regarded for making canoes.

SILVER STOOL. Stools of Mampong, Techiman, and the Asante (qq.v.) Queen Mother.

SISALA (Isala, Sissala, Pasala). A Grusi (q.v.) group in the Upper West Region on the Burkina Faso border and between the Kulpawn and Sisili rivers. Dr. Hilla Limann (q.v.), President in the Third Republic, came from this group. The Vagala and Kasena (qq.v.) are closely related to the Sisala.

SITOBU (Sitobo). One of the sons of Gbewa of Pusiga and the father of Nyagse of Dagomba (qq.v.). Sitobu probably lived in the fifteenth century. One brother, Tohogo, founded Mamprusi (qq.v.). Another brother, Nnantombo, founded Nanumba (qq.v.). Sitobu settled awhile at Gambaga, and then lived at Savelugu, north of Tamale (qq.v.). He is buried at Bagale at the mausoleum of the Dagomba Nas. His son Nyagse (q.v.) was the first ruler of Dagomba.

SKIN. Symbol of authority in the Northern and Upper regions of Ghana comparable to the stool among the Akan (qq.v.) or a throne in Europe.

SLATER, ALEXANDER RANSFORD. 1847-1940. Governor of the Gold Coast. He attended the King Edward's School in

Birmingham and Emmanuel College, Cambridge. He was Colonial Secretary of the Gold Coast (q.v.) from 1914 to 1922. During this period he was Acting Governor several times. He was Governor of Sierra Leone, 1922 to 1927, and of the Gold Coast from 1927 to 1932. During his administration he was most interested in expanding the transportation system of the Gold Coast, but little was accomplished be use of the depression. After he left Accra he served as Governor of Jamaica, 1932-1934.

SLOAN, PATRICK. English Marxist who joined the staff of Kwame Nkrumah's Ideological Institute at Winneba (qq.v.) in 1961. He became an adviser to Nkrumah. Late in 1964 he suggested that all materials critical of socialism be purged from Ghana. This resulted in the establishment of a committee of nine, under Professor William E. Abraham of the University of Ghana (qq.v.), Legon, in November 1964. The committee began work on a system to identify and remove anti-socialist literature.

SMITH, JOHN HOPE. The last Chief Agent of the Company of Merchants Trading to Africa at Cape Coast (qq.v.). He replaced Joseph Dawson in January 1817, and he held the position as President of the Council of Merchants at Cape Coast until the charter of the company was revoked by the Crown. He was replaced by Governor Charles MacCarthy (q.v.) of Sierra Leone in March 1822. During Smith's stay at Cape Coast the Bowdich mission to Kumasi (qq.v.) in 1817 and the Dupuis mission of 1820 opened direct contact between the British and Kumasi for the first time. Asantehene Osei Bonsu (q.v.) agreed to allow a British Resident at Kumasi and to recognize the British as mediators in Asante-Fante (qq.v.) relations. The English were to guarantee Asante trade on the coast. Misunderstandings persisted throughout the period. Osei Bonsu was willing to improve relations with the British so long as the latter would recognize Asante sovereignty over the coastal people. Smith and his council at Cape Coast refused to even deal with the Asantehene's ambassadors and began to prepare for a showdown. Meantime the English Parliament abolished the company and placed the Gold Coast settlements under the Governor of Sierra Leone. War between the Asante and the British soon followed.

SOCCO see BEGHO

SOCIAL DEMOCRATIC FRONT (SDF). A political party in the 1979 elections. The party was a merger of trade union people and social democrats who during the Second Republic had been members of the National Alliance of Liberals and the Justice Party (qq.v.). The party called for the creation of a socialist state. Their candidate for President in the 18 June 1979 election was Dr. Ibrahim Mahama. Alhaji M. A. Issifu was the party leader. The SDF won three seats in the Assembly and their candidate for President came in fifth.

SOCIÉTÉ COMMERCIALE DE L'OUEST AFRICAIN (SCOA). Swiss commercial firm which purchased cocoa in Gold Coast (q.v.) for the Swiss chocolate industry from 1914 until after 1957.

SOGAKOFE (Sogakope, Sogakorpe). 6°00'N, 0°36'E. Town on the Volta River about 25 miles (40 km) north of Ada (qq.v.). It is at the bridge over the Volta, on the Accra-Lome highway, some 50 miles (80 km) from the Togo border.

SOMANYA. 6°06'N, 0°01'W. The chief village of the Yilo Krobo; it is located on the Accra-Akosombo highway near Kpong and Akuse (qq.v.).

SONGAW LAGOON. 5°49'N, 0°28'E. Salt marshes and lagoon west of the Volta near Ada (qq.v.). The area is famous for its birds.

SONGO HILLS. 10°55'N, 0°30'W. The watershed between the Red and White Voltas in the Upper East Region above Gambaga (qq.v.).

SOPHIE LOUISE, FORT. Trade post built at Cape Three Points or Takrama, on the coast, Western Region (qq.v.). It was built by the Brandenburgers (q.v.) in 1690. The Dutch took over the place in 1717, calling it Fort Maria Luisa. Not much remains of the building today.

SORLIYA. Believed to be the original Paramount Chief and founder of Wa (q.v.).

SOUTHWEST MONSOON. The winds from the South Atlantic that blow to the coast of Ghana. These winds are also called the tropical maritime or equatorial air mass. Their currents are generally cool and moist. The Southwest Monsoon is opposed by the Northeast trades or the Harmattan (q.v.), which blow down from the Sahara, and are dry. The movement of the fronts of these winds affect the climate of the country.

SPARK. A fortnightly journal started by Nkrumah (q.v.) in December 1962 in imitation of Lenin's *Iskra*. It carried articles on socialist themes.

SPOKESMAN. An opposition newspaper to Busia and the Progress Party (qq.v.) government during the Second Republic. It was edited by Kofi Badu (q.v.).

SRI, TOGBI (Cornelius Kofi Kwakume). 1862-1956. Paramount Chief of Anlo, 1907-1956. He modernized Anloga, promoted the Bremen Missions and Western ideas, and was an advocated of Ewe (qq.v.) unification. He was a member of the Gold Coast Legislative Council, 1916-1938.

STANDARD. Catholic weekly published from 1938. The paper has been banned on several occasions for being critical of the government of the day.

STAR. The newspaper of K. A. Busia and the Progress Party (qq.v.) during the Second Republic.

STEWART, DONALD. 1860-1905. British officer. He entered the British army in 1879 and served in Afghanistan, the Transvaal, and the Sudan. He was the political officer with the Asante expedition in 1864 and served as British Resident at Kumasi (qq.v.), 1896-1902, and Chief Commissioner of Asante, 1902-1904. In December 1896 he made a trip northward to occupy Gambaga (q.v.) for the British. From there he went to Tenkodogo, in modern Burkina Faso, where he met Lieutenant Paul Voulet (1866-1899) of the French army. They agreed upon a temporary border between British and Fr nch interests. In 1904 Stewart went as Commissioner to Britis. East Africa.

STOOL. The Akan (q.v.) symbol of authority, the office of chief or king.

SUHUM. 6°02'N, 0°27'W. Town in the Eastern Region on the Accra-Kibi (qq.v.) highway. It was the center of the 1937 and 1938 cocoa boycotts.

SUMAN (pl. Asuman). A charm, talisman, fetish (q.v.), or totem believed to have magical power for good or evil.

SUNYANI. 7°20'N, 2°20'W. The capital of the Brong-Ahafo Region (q.v.). The population for the Sunyani local authority area was recorded in the 1984 census to be 98,183.

SUPREME MILITARY COUNCIL (SMC) (I). I. K. Acheampong came to power in January 1972 as head of the National Redemption Council (qq.v.). On 9 October 1975 he reorganized his government and created the Supreme Military Council (q.v.). This group ruled Ghana under Acheampong until Acheampong's forced resignation on 5 July 1978.

SUPREME MILITARY COUNCIL (SMC) (II). On 5 July 1978 Acheampong's (q.v.) associates in the SMC persuaded him to resign. He was replaced as head of state by Lt. Gen. Frederick W. K. Akuffo (q.v.). The second SMC ruled Ghana until 4 June 1979, when it in turn was ousted by the Armed Forces Revolutionary Council of Jerry John Rawlings (qq.v.).

SUTHERLAND, EFUA THEODORA. Born 1924. She was born at Cape Coast and her maiden name was Morgue. She is one of Ghana's most famous poets and playwrights. She was one of the first African women to attend Cambridge in England,

and she married an American, William Sutherland, in 1954. She is the author of many plays, and she has been connected with the University of Ghana's (q.v.) School of Drama for many years. *Edufa* and *Foriwa* are two of her better-known plays.

SUTRI RAPIDS. The falls of the Tano River (q.v.). The rapids are located between the villages of Tanoso and Asuaso near Sunyani in the Brong-Ahafo Region (qq.v.).

SWANZY COMPANY, F. AND A. A mercantile business founded by Frank and Andrew Swanzy in the middle of the nineteenth century. By the 1890s it operated stores in almost every village in the Gold Coast (q.v.). In 1919 it became part of the Eastern Trade Corporation, which in turn was consolidated into the United Africa Company (q.v.).

SWEDISH AFRICA COMPANY. A company organized by a group of Dutch merchants in the seventeenth century. They financed Henry Caerlof, a native of Poland, in trade activities on the Gold Coast (q.v.). Caerlof had formerly worked for the Dutch West India Company. He was instrumental in establishing several stations along the coast in the 1640s and 1650s. Caerlof later betrayed his Dutch supporters and worked for the Danes.

SWEDRU (Agona Swedru). 5°32'N, 0°42'W. The chief commercial center of the Agona (q.v.) area of the Central Region. It is located on the road between Oda and Winneba (qq.v.), about 15 miles (24 km) north of Winneba and the coast.

SWINTON, LORD (Philip Lloyd-Greame to 1924, Philip Cunliffe-Lister to 1935). 1884-1972. Member of the British Parliament, 1918-1935. President of the Board of Trade of England, 1922-1923, 1924-1929, 1931. Secretary of State for Colonies, 1931-1935. Secretary of State for Air, 1935-1938. Cabinet Minister Resident in West Africa, 1942-1944. Minister for Civil Aviation, 1944-1945. Secretary of State for Commonwealth Relations, 1952-1955. In 1942 the British government recognized the necessity of coordinating all allied war activities in West Africa at one place. Lord Swinton was appointed Cabinet Minister Resident in West Africa and established his headquarters at Achimota College in the Gold Coast (qq.v.) in July 1942. For the next three years Achimota became the central command post for all West Africa. Swinton was replaced by Harold Harington Balfour in 1944, and Balfour held the responsibilities at Achimota until the end of World War II (q.v.). Swinton's memoirs of his public life, *I Remember*, were published in 1948.

SWISS AFRICAN TRADING COMPANY (SAT). A small Swiss trading company which had its headquarters at Kumasi from 1922 to purchase cocoa (qq.v.) for the Swiss chocolate industry. It was bought out by the United Africa Company (q.v.) in 1936.

SWOLLEN SHOOT. A virus carried by the mealie bug which attacks and eventually kills cocoa (q.v.) trees. The disease was first reported in the Gold Coast (q.v.) in 1936. Since the best-known remedy was cutting out infected trees, the practice aroused resentment among cocoa growers in the 1930s.

- T -

TAFI. A small Volta-Togo group located between the Avatime (qq.v.) and the Nyangbo.

TAFO, NEW. 6°13'N, 0°22'W. Town in the Eastern Region on the railroad northwest of Koforidua (q.v.). It is the home of the Cocoa Research Institute.

TAFO, OLD. 6°44'N, 1°37'W. A very old town on the ancient trade route from Begho through Adansi (q.v.) to the Guinea coast. It was near here that the Asante founded Kwaman and then Kumasi (qq.v.).

TAKORADI. 4°53'N, 1°45'W. Twin city of Sekondi, located on the coast in Western Region (qq.v.). The Swedes were trading here as early as 1650. The beach was contested by the Swedes, Danes, Dutch, and English, and in 1659 the Dutch built Fort Witzen here. They abandoned Witzen in 1818. The Brandenburgers (q.v.) also tried once to establish a base in Takoradi around 1684. The major port of the Gold Coast (q.v.) was opened there in 1928. The headquarters of the Gold Coast railroads (q.v.) was moved there in 1934, and an airport was built a short time later. The Bureau of African Industries was located there in 1934, and the city became an important industrial center, with cocoa processing and lumber, paper, tobacco, plywood, and salt production. See also SEKONDI.

TAKRAMA. A place on Cape Three Points on the Ahanta coast of the Western Region where the Brandenburgers (qq.v.) built a fortified lodge in 1690. It was called Fort Sophie Louise (q.v.). It was sold to the Dutch in 1717, and the Dutch called it Fort Maria Luisa. Only a trace of the foundations was left in 1960.

TAKYIMAN see TECHIMAN.

TALENSI (Talene, Tallensi). A Mole-Dagbani group who live in the Upper East Region above the Mamprusi and below the Frafra (qq.v.). Their society is called Tale, their country is Taleland, and their language is Talene or Talen.

TAMAKLOE, EMMANUEL FORSTER. British clerk. He began his career as a German interpreter at Kete Krakye (q.v.), 1897-1907, but then joined the British service and was a census clerk in 1910. Later he was a clerk at Yendi (q.v.), where he collected local history and folklore. In 1931 his *Brief History of the Dagbamba People* was published by the government printer in Accra. That same year his "Mythical and Traditional History of the Dagomba" appeared as a chapter in *Tales Told in Togoland*, edited by Allan Cardinall (q.v.). Tamakloe also collaborated with H. A. Blair in producing a Dagbane (q.v.) dictionary and grammar.

TAMALE. 9°24'N, 0°50'W.   Regional capital of the Northern Region (q.v.). It is the administrative, financial, commercial, and transportation center for all the northern part of Ghana. It is on the Great Northern Highway from Kumasi to Bolgatanga, has one of Ghana's better airports, and is only 27 miles (43 km) from Yapei or Tamale Port, located on Lake Volta (qq.v.). Tamale became the British administrative headquarters of the Northern Territories (q.v.) in 1907.   At that time the population was 1,435. A primary school opened there in 1909, and a secondary school was established in 1927. Trade schools and mission schools were created in the 1920s. Lloyd Shirer and his wife, of Pennsylvania, operated a school here for many years to train teachers. By 1970 Tamale had five secondary schools and two teacher training colleges. The average annual rainfall in Tamale is 43 inches (109 cm), most falling from June to October. The dry season is from November to June. February and March are the hottest months, and the rainy season, especially August, is the coolest time. The population of Tamale was estimated to be 151,069 in 1988.

TAMALE PORT (Yapei).   9°10'N, 1°10'W.   A port on the northern end of Lake Volta (q.v.). It was first established as the terminus for river traffic on the White Volta in 1908. It is 27 miles (43 km) from Tamale (q.v.). A bridge crosses the lake at this point. One road goes on to Damongo, and another road turns south and goes to Kintampo, Techiman, and Kumasi (qq.v.).

TANO OBOASE (Tano beneath the rock). A place near the source of the Tano River, not far form Techiman in Brong Ahafo (qq.v.). It is the center of worship of the Tano (Ta Kora) shrine.

TANO RIVER. The most sacred river of the Akan (q.v.). It rises in the Brong Ahafo Region near Techiman and flows in a southwesterly direction into the Western Region, by Wiawso (qq.v.), to the border of the Ivory Coast, and through the Juen Lagoon to the ocean. It is navigable to the falls near Tanoso (7°17'N, 2°15'W), where the Bechem-Sunyani road crosses the river.   The Bain, Suhien, Samre, Yoyo, Suraw, Famuna

(Pamunu), Srani, Amama, and other tributaries drain the section of Ghana which has the greatest rainfall.

TARKWA (Tarquah). 5°18'N, 1°59'W. Mining, commercial, and administrative center on the railroad in the Western Region about 50 miles (80 km) north of Dixcove (qq.v.). Governor Ussher (q.v.) reported a population of above 7,000 in 1880. It was one of the first two interior towns where the British stationed a District Commissioner (DC). The town is surrounded by low hills where today there are many derelict mines, but a gold refinery is located in Tarkwa. The town operates also as a lumber center.

TECHIMAN (Takyiman). 7°35'N, 1°56'W. A town in the Brong Ahafo Region some 18 miles (29 km) southeast of Wenchi (qq.v.). It was an important kola (q.v.) market for many years. The Fante (q.v.) have a tradition that their ancestors came from Techiman. The town is very old and once played an important part in the trade with the Dyula (q.v.). It was taken by the Asante (q.v.) in 1722-1723.

TECHNOLOGY CONSULTANCY CENTER (TCC). Founded in 1972. Located at the University of Science and Technology in Kumasi (qq.v.). The center was created to promote small-scale informal industries, using appropriate technology. The TCC began designing equipment for use in the formal sector in 1973. It was the TCC that established the Intermediate Technology Transfer Unit (ITTU) in the midst of informal areas to encourage innovation by local craftsmen in order to upgrade existing craft industries.

TEKYIMAN see TECHIMAN

TEMA. 5°37'N, 0°01'W. One of the original seven Ga (q.v.) coastal towns. It has been turned into Ghana's most modern port and industrial city. It is 17 miles (27 km) east of Accra (q.v.) and is part of the Greater Accra Region. Tema is still an important fishing harbor, but today it is also home of the Valco plant, an oil refinery, the home docks of the Black Star Line (q.v.), car assembly plants, meat processing plants, cocoa (q.v.) processing plants, and many other industries built to take advantage of the power from the Akosombo Volta (qq.v.) Electric Project, located some 45 miles (72 km) to the north. Tema also boasts one of the largest planned industrial communities in Africa. It is connected to Accra by a coastal road, a freeway, and a railroad. The 1988 population of the city was estimated to be about 109,975 people.

TENDAANA (pl. Ten'dama). Earth priest in the Northern and Upper regions of Ghana. The term "tendaanba," derived from the same root, has been used to mean landowners, while "tendaanlun" has been used generally to refer to priestly authority.

TENZUGU SHRINE. A famous religious shrine in the Tong Hills of the Upper Region (q.v.) near Zuarungu and Bolgatanga (q.v.). The British destroyed the shrine in 1911 and again in 1915, but people continued to make pilgrimages there. The shrine is a large natural temple in a rock cavern. R. S. Rattray (q.v.) visited the shrine in May 1928, and he wrote an account of a service there.

TESHI (Teshie). 5°35'N, 0°06'W. One of the seven original Ga (q.v.) coastal settlements. It is 10 miles (16 km) east of Accra (q.v.), and it is part of Greater Accra. The Dutch were trading here by the 1730s, and the Danes built Fort Augustaborg at Teshi in 1787. It was bought by the British in 1850. The British established the Royal West African Frontier Force (q.v.) Training School at Teshi, and many of West Africa's leading military men were trained at this school. The Ghanaian military academy is located here.

TETTEGAH, JOHN KOFI BARKU. Born 1930. He was born at Denu, near the Togo border, in the Volta Region. He attended Catholic schools and Secretarial College in Accra. For a time he was employed with G. B. Ollivant, where he became active in trade union activities. By 1954 he was General-Secretary of the Gold Coast Trades Union Congress (TUC) (q.v.) and a member of the general board of the International Conference of Trade Unions. In the meantime he became a member of the

Central Committee of the Convention People's Party (CPP) and a close associate of Tawia Adamafio (qq.v.) and the radical wing of the CPP. In 1959 Tettegah headed Nkrumah's (q.v.) Workers' Brigades (q.v.) for a brief period. Then in July 1960 he was appointed a Roving Ambassador. While an employee of the government, he continued his connection with the TUC, and was Secretary-General of the All-African Trades Union Federation, 1964-1966. After the fall of Nkrumah he left Ghana, not returning until the coup that ended the rule of Busia (q.v.). Later, in 1973, Tettegah was arrested by the National Redemption Council (q.v.), along with Kojo Botsio (qq.v.), and charged with plotting to overthrow the government. The original sentences of death were commuted to life in April 1974 and he remained in prison until November 1978. The Provisional National Defence Council (q.v.) government, in 1983, appointed Tettegah Ambassador to the Soviet Union. Later, in the 1980s, he was transferred to represent Ghana in East Africa, but returned home before the November 1992 elections to help plan Rawlings's (q.v.) presidential campaign.

THIRD FORCE (TF). This was a political organization created in 1969 in opposition to Busia's Progress Party and Gbedemah's National Alliance of Liberals (qq.v.). The *Legon Observer* (q.v.) supported the "middle of the road" position of the TF. Some of the Third Force supporters organized the All People's Congress (APC). John Bilson, M.D., of Kumasi was leader of the APC. The Third Force appeared again in 1979, when Bilson ran for President as candidate of the party. He came in a poor sixth.

THOMAS, SHENTON WHITELEGGE THOMAS. 1879-1962. Governor of the Gold Coast, 1932-1934. He was educated at St. John's School, Leatherhead, and Queen's College, Cambridge. He served the Colonial Service in Kenya, Uganda, and Nigeria, and was Colonial Secretary of the Gold Coast (q.v.) before becoming Governor of Nyasaland, 1929-1932, of the Gold Coast, 1932-1934, and of Malaya, 1934-1942. He was then interned by the Japanese during World War II (q.v.) and retired in 1946.

THOMPSON, AUGUSTUS WILLIAM KOJO (Kojo Thompson). 1880-1950. Accra lawyer and politician. He was born at Winneba and educated at Mfantsipim and Wesleyan schools in Accra and Nigeria. He then went to London and qualified for the bar at Lincoln's Inn in 1914. He spent the rest of his life practicing law in Accra (q.v.). He became active in Accra politics, being active in the Youth Conference and the Mambii political group. Among his close associates in the 1930s were Alfred Ocansey, Nnamdi Azikiwe, and I. T. A. Wallace Johnson (qq.v.). In the 1920s he failed in campaigns for election to the Legislative Council from Accra, but in 1935 his radical attacks on the British government helped him defeat the more conservative F. V. Nanka-Bruce (q.v.). As a member of the Legislative Council he became famous for his attacks on colonial rule, traditional rulers, and European businesses, especially the United Africa Company (q.v.). In 1941 he was member of a committee, with J. B. Danquah (q.v.), which recommended reforms in the Legislative Council which were partly incorporated in the Burns (q.v.) reforms of 1946. In 1944 Thompson was convicted in an extortion case. This ended his political career.

TINDANA (pl. tindamba) see TENDAANA

TINTEINTINA. The Tendaana, or earth priest, among the Sisala (qq.v.). There are many variations to the title: Tendagena among the Dagomba (q.v.) and Tegatu among the Awuna (Grusi) (q.v.).

TOGOLAND, BRITISH. After World War I (q.v.) the League of Nations entrusted or mandated the western part of the former German colony of Togoland to England. The total area placed under British control amounted to 13,041 square miles (33,777 sq km). The northern part of this area was 7,196 square miles (18,638 sq km), and it was placed under the jurisdiction of the Northern Territories of the Gold Coast (qq.v.). The southern section of 5,845 square miles (15,139 sq km) was governed as part of the Trans-Volta-Togoland Region (q.v.). In 1945 the whole Togoland Mandate of the British became a United Nations Trust Territory. The southern section held a plebiscite in May 1956 over the question of joining Ghana when independence came. This created much bitterness between the Ewe (q.v.), who favored an independent Ewe nation, and those people who favored union with Ghana. Those who wanted union in a free Ghana won, and in 1957 the southern section of the Togoland Trust Territory became the Volta Region (q.v.) of Ghana.

TOGOLAND CONGRESS PARTY (TCP). A political party active in the 1950s. The TCP wanted unification of the Ewe (q.v.) in the British and French Trust Territories as a separate Ewe state. The party was defeated in the May 1956 plebiscite over unification with the Gold Coast (Ghana). It won two seats in the July 1956 Gold Coast elections, but did not last long after that.

TOGOLAND REMNANTS. The many small groups who were the original inhabitants of the lands which the Ewe (q.v.) occupied. These inhabitants were pushed into the remote mountain areas to the east of the Volta River in what after 1957 became the Volta Region (qq.v.). They are collectively referred to at times as the Central Togo tribes (q.v.). The Avatime, Buem (qq.v.), Adele, Nyangbo, and Logba are examples of Central Togo groups.

TOGOLAND UNION. Ewe (q.v.) group created in 1943 to work for the unification of the Ewe, and an independent Ewe nation to be formed from the British- and the French-mandated territories of Togoland.

TOHAJIE (Tohajiye). The legendary progenitor of the Mole-Dagbani (q.v.) peoples. Traditions vary, but Tohajie was called the "Red Hunter." He lived in what is now modern Niger. He and a wife named Pagawolga had a son named Kpogonumbo. This son migrated to Gurma, in what is now Burkina Faso. Kpogonumbo and a wife, Soyini or Solyini, had a son named Gbewa in some traditions, Bawa in the Mamprusi traditions, and Nedega in the Mossi (qq.v.) traditions. Gbewa (Bawa, Nedega) in turn moved west again, to Pusiga, in the modern Kusasi (qq.v.) country of Ghana. Gbewa had a daughter and many sons, and these children created a number of Mole-Dagbani states.

TOHOGO (Tohugu, Tohagu, Tusugu). Son of Gbewa of Pusiga. Probably lived in the middle of the fifteenth century. After his brother Zirile disappeared on a campaign in Gurma, the council at Pusiga selected Tohogo as their leader. This touched off a bitter fight between the sons of Gbewa, and Tohogo fled to his mother's town of Mamprugu, where he founded the Mamprugu or Mamprusi (qq.v.) state.

TON TON. Dyula reference for the Brong-Ahafo area around Wenchi (qq.v.).

TORRANE, GEORGE. President of the Council of Merchants at Cape Coast 1805 to 1807. He experimented with coffee and other crops at Cape Coast (q.v.) in an attempt to develop the economy. He also adopted a policy of collaboration with the Asantehene Osei Bonsu (q.v.) which recognized Asante claims to suzerainty over the Assin and the Fante (qq.v.) that amounted to a betrayal of people who were British friends. Torrane was convinced that peace and trade were likely if the Asante were allowed to control the coast.

TOWN COUNCILS. In 1858 Municipal Councils were elected at James Town (Accra) and Cape Coast (qq.v.). Support for the idea collapsed when the Councils tried to collect taxes. Councils were established in Accra in 1896, at Sekondi in 1904, at Cape Coast in 1905, and at Kumasi (qq.v.) in 1943. The Municipal Corporations Bill of 1924 provided for a majority of elected members on the Councils and broadened the vote to allow all who owned or rented houses taxed at five pounds to cast a ballot for members of the Councils.

TRADES UNION CONGRESS (TUC). Workers' unions began to be organized in the Gold Coast (q.v.) in the 1930s. In September 1945, various unions came together at Sekondi (q.v.) to form the TUC. This congress collapsed after the general strike of January 1950. It was not until 1953 that the movement reunited, and in September 1954, John Tettegah (q.v.) was elected full-time Secretary-General of the group. From then until the fall of the Nkrumah (q.v.) administration in 1966, the TUC was an important adjunct of the Convention People's Party (CPP) (q.v.) and every person employed in the public sector was required to pay union dues.

The government of the Second Republic (1969-1972) restricted the influence of the labor union and abolished the payment of compulsory dues as TUC leaders were suspected of having closer ties to the CPP. The strained relationship between the government and the TUC improved only in the early years of the administration of the National Redemption Council (q.v.). As of 1974, however, as the nation's economy became depressed, standards of living fell, and TUC relations with the then Supreme Military Council (q.v.) deteriorated.

In the years that follow--from the time of the Third Republic through the early years of the Provisional National Defence Council (PNDC) (q.v.) administration--the national labor union maintained antagonistic relations with the government. There was a feeling that the Limann (q.v.) administration was inept in finding solutions to the national economic crisis, while the conditions inherent in the PNDC's Economic Recovery Program (q.v.) were viewed by the union as too harsh for workers to endure. With the creation of workers' defense committees (q.v.) to ensure management accountability, and with the establishment of tripartite committees through which workers, management, and the government could negotiate their differences, relations improved. By the end of the PNDC administration in 1992, the tripartite committee had successfully negotiated three wage adjustments with the Trades Union Congress.

TRANS-VOLTA-TOGOLAND REGION (TVT). A region established in 1952 to administer the area now called the Volta Region.

TSETSE. There are 21 species of African bloodsucking flies. They transmit several diseases, especially sleeping sickness. Animal and human population density in the affected areas is sparse.

TSHI see TWI

TSHIKAPA MUTINY. A January 1961 uprising of the Third Battalion of the Ghanaian Army stationed at Tshikapa in Kasai, Congo (Zaire). The rebelling troops severely beat their Commander, David Hansen.

TSIBOE, JOHN WALLACE. 1904-1963. A native of Assin Attandaso who was educated at Wesleyan in Kumasi. He then opened a store in Kumasi (q.v.) and became a wealthy merchant. He founded the Abora Printing Company, and in 1939 he founded the *Ashanti Pioneer*. The paper became a major mouthpiece for Asante (q.v.) interests. Tsiboe was an early member of the United Gold Coast Convention (q.v.). In 1949 he briefly joined the Convention People's Party (CPP), but was soon in the opposition to Nkrumah (qq.v.). In 1950 he failed in an attempt to organize the Gold Coast Labour Party. He then joined the Ghana Congress Party (GCP) and then the National Liberation Movement (NLM) in 1954. In the 1956 elections he was the NLM candidate for the Legislative Assembly from his home Abora (q.v.) district, but he was defeated. In 1957 he helped organize the United Party (UP) (q.v.). After independence the *Ashanti Pioneer* became the leading critic of the CPP government. Nkrumah banned the paper in 1962. John Tsiboe's wife, Nancy Tsiboe, worked closely with her husband. She was a candidate of the GCP in 1954. She joined the NLM in 1954, and she was later the National Treasurer of the UP.

TSIKATA, KOJO. A former captain in the Ghanaian army whom Kofi Awoonor once described as "a student of world revolution." He was arrested by the Supreme Military Council (SMC) (q.v.) in November 1975 and tried for his connection with the "Ewe Plot" to kill SMC leaders. He was sentenced to death, but released in August 1978. During the period of the

Third Republic he was a constant critic of President Hilla Limann (q.v.) and he claimed that he was arrested and tortured by Military Intelligence. He was one of the founders of the June 4th Movement of Rawlings (qq.v.) supporters. After the coup that ended the Third Republic, Tsikata became a special adviser to the Provisional National Defence Council (PNDC) (q.v.) and head of state security. There were rumors in 1982 that Kojo Tsikata had knowledge regarding the murders of three judges and a retired military officer but that was not proven. Many observers of the PNDC administration saw Kojo Tsikata as the brains behind the security apparatus that guaranteed the continuity of the PNDC in office.

TUSUGU see TOHOGO

TWI (Tshi). Language of the Akan (q.v.). The variations of the Twi language include Akuapem, Asante, Akyem (Akim), and Fante (qq.v.).

TWIFO (Twifu, Cuifferoe). One of the Akan states in the Pra valley on the trade route between the Asante and the Fante (qq.v.).

- U -

UNILEVER. The conglomerate which started as Lever Brothers (q.v.) in 1884. Lever Brothers entered the West African trade in 1896 and rapidly bought out many smaller companies. By 1925, when the founder, William Leverhulme, died, Unilever was made up of more than two hundred firms. Unilever had controlling interest in the United Africa Company (UAC) (q.v.) by 1932. Since independence, UAC and Lever Brothers operated as independent companies until 24 July 1992 when they merged again under the company name of Unilever.

UNION GOVERNMENT (Unigov). A proposal of the Supreme Military Council (SMC) (q.v.) in 1977 to combine civilian and military rule as the sole administration of the country. Justice Koranteng-Addow (q.v.) was chairman of the committee that wrote the plan. The idea was to create an elected government of military and civilian officials who would hold office without alliances in political organizations. A referendum on the plan was held in March 1978, and the SMC claimed that the electorate had approved Union Government by large margins. But opposition was so great that the plan was never put into operation.

UNITED ACTION FRONT (UAF). A coalition of dissident political factions put together by Frank G. Bernasko (q.v.) at the end of 1981. It was stillborn because political parties were outlawed by the Provisional National Defence Council (q.v.) shortly thereafter.

UNITED AFRICA COMPANY (UAC). In March 1929 the African Association, the Eastern Company, and the Niger Company merged to form the United Africa Company (UAC). By 1932 Unilever (q.v.) had gained controlling interest in the stock of UAC. The United Africa Company was the most important business firm in the Gold Coast (q.v.) at independence.

UNITED GHANA FARMERS' COUNCIL. A farmers' group founded in 1953 and recognized by the Convention People's Party (q.v.) as the sole representative of the farmers in September 1957. It was banned after the coup of 1966. Martin Appiah-Danquah was the Secretary-General of the United Ghana Farmers' Co-operative Council.

UNITED GOLD COAST CONVENTION (UGCC). The first true political party in the Gold Coast (q.v.) to talk of self-government "in the shortest time possible." It was founded on 4 August 1947. The key founders were A. G. Grant (chairman), R. S. Blay, J. B. Danquah, R. A. Awoonor-Williams, William E. Ofori Atta, E. A. Akufo Addo, J. W. de Graft-Johnson, and Obetsibi Lamptey (qq.v.). Its immediate aim was to replace chiefs on the Legislative Council with educated people. The UGCC employed Kwame Nkrumah (q.v.) as its General-Secretary at the suggestion of Ako Adjei (q.v.). The UGCC was defeated by the Convention People's Party (q.v.), a party Nkrumah organized in June 1949 after he broke away from the UGCC. Nkrumah had served as UGCC

General-Secretary from January to September 1948. The general election in which Nkrumah defeated the UGCC was in February 1951. The UGCC was dissolved in 1952.

UNITED NATIONAL CONVENTION (UNC). A political party formed in 1979 by William Ofori Atta and other former supporters of K. A. Busia and the Progress Party (qq.v.). The UNC was the moderate party of academics, professional people, and businesspeople. The party won 13 seats in the 1979 National Assembly elections; the UNC candidate for president, William Ofori Atta, came in a poor third behind Hilla Limann of the People's National Party (PNP), the winner, and Victor Owusu of the Popular Front Party (qq.v.). At the beginning of the Third Republic the PNP and UNC agreed to cooperate, but the alliance lasted only a short time. In August 1980 the UNC walked out of the National Assembly in a dispute over the appointment of judges. At the end of 1981 the UNC was negotiating for a merger of opposition parties when the Provisional National Defence Council (q.v.) coup ended political activities and the Third Republic.

UNITED NATIONALIST PARTY (UNP). A small political party which contested the 1969 elections. Its leader was Joe Appiah (q.v.). The UNP won only two seats in the National Assembly. The next year it merged into the Justice Party (q.v.).

UNITED PARTY (UP). A coalition of groups opposed to the Convention People's Party (CCP) (q.v.) which was organized on 3 November 1957 in Accra at a rally presided over by K. A. Busia (qq.v.). T. Hutton-Mills, J. A. Braimah, Nancy Tsiboe, S. D. Dombo, Joe Appiah, and J. B. Danquah (q.v.) were among the leaders of this anti-Nkrumah movement. The Preventive Detention Act (q.v.) of 1958 wreaked havoc on the UP. Busia went into exile in June 1959, leaving S. D. Dombo as leader of the opposition in the Assembly. In the 1960 elections the UP ran J. B. Danquah as their candidate for President against the CPP leader, Nkrumah (q.v.). Nkrumah got 1,016,076 to only 124,623 for Danquah. In 1961 Danquah and many of the last UP leaders were sent to prison. By the following year, for all practical purposes, Ghana was a one-party state.

UNIVERSITY OF CAPE COAST (UCC). The youngest of Ghana's universities, it was founded in 1961 to train teachers for secondary schools and teachers colleges. It has Faculties of Education, Physical Education, Arts, Science, Social Science, Business, and Agriculture.

UNIVERSITY OF GHANA (UG). The University College of the Gold Coast was founded in 1948 near Achimota (q.v.) around Legon Hill. It had a special relationship with the University of London, and all degrees were issued in the name of the University of London until 1961. From 1948 to 1957 the principal of the university was David M. Balme (q.v.), a classical scholar, who was a graduate of Cambridge. He played a key role in organizing the university along Cambridge lines, with residence halls, faculty rule, and an intellectual tradition. At independence in March 1957 the name changed to the University College of Ghana. Then in October 1961 it became the University of Ghana, granting its own degrees and breaking its ties with the University of London. The institution has Schools of Administration, Law, and Medicine and Faculties of Agriculture, Home Science, Arts, and Social Science. The country's only Program of African Studies is at the university.

UNIVERSITY OF SCIENCE AND TECHNOLOGY (UST). The University of Science and Technology at Kumasi (q.v.), started in 1952 as the Kumasi College of Technology. Renamed the Kwame Nkrumah University of Science and Technology, it attained full university status in August 1961. After the coup in 1966, the name of Dr. Nkrumah was removed from the university's description. It has Faculties of Agriculture, Engineering, Pharmacy, Science, Art, Medicine, Architecture, and General Studies.

UPPER REGIONS. The Upper Region was created from the Northern Region on 29 June 1960. It was made up of many small Grusi, Mole-Dagbani, and Gurense (qq.v.) peoples. In

1982 the Provisional National Defence Council (q.v.) divided the Upper Region into the Upper West and Upper East regions.

USSHER, HERBERT TAYLOR. Died 1880. Governor of the Gold Coast (q.v.). Ussher's first experience in West Africa was as private secretary to the Governor of Lagos in 1864. In 1866 he became Collector of Customs for the Gold Coast and from that position he was promoted to Administrator of the Gold Coast, 1867-1872. These were turbulent years during which the Dutch and English tried to exchange posts on the Gold Coast; the Asante army threatened the coastal regions, and the Fante (qq.v.) tried to organize a federation. In 1872 the decision was made that England would take over all Dutch possessions on the Gold Coast. Ussher was transferred to Tobago (near Trinidad) as Governor from 1872 to 1875. Then he was sent to the other side of the world, to Labuan (off Malaysia), as Governor from 1875 to 1879. In 1879 he returned to the Gold Coast as Governor. He died at Christiansborg Castle on the first day of December 1880, and he was buried at James Town, Accra (qq.v.).

USSHER FORT. The Dutch opened a lodge in 1642 at Accra (q.v.) which within a decade they enlarged and named Fort Crevecoeur. This structure was badly damaged by an earthquake in 1862. Six years later it was turned over to the British. They rebuilt it and named it after the administrator of the Gold Coast at the time, Herbert Taylor Ussher (qq.v.). It became a prison, but in 1975 it was turned over to the Museum and Monuments Board for historical preservation.

- V -

VAGALA (Vigala, Vagele). Grusi group related to the Mo, Sisala (qq.v.), and Tampolensi. They live in the Gonja area northeast of Bole (qq.v.).

VERANDA BOYS (Verandah). Men in the urban areas who lounge on the porches of patrons, waiting to run errands for the boss. The term was used by the Convention People's Party (CPP) to refer to early supporters of Nkrumah (qq.v.). By implication, Nkrumah's CPP was depicted as the party of the ordinary people.

VICTORIA, FORT (Phipp's Tower). An early structure was started about 1702 at Cape Coast (q.v.) by the British that was called Phipp's Tower. It was rebuilt in 1837 and called Fort Victoria; it served as a combined barracks and lookout post.

VODZA. 5°57'N, 1°0'E. Anlo town on the Keta Lagoon where Geraldo de Lima (qq.v.) carried on slave trade in the 1850s and 1860s. On 13 May 1871 the British bombarded de Lima's deserted residence at Vodza. The Anlo promised to turn de Lima over to the British if he showed himself. He stayed away for many years, but on 7 January 1885 he was lured back to Vodza and captured.

VOLTA. The Volta River begins as three branches--the Black, Red, and White Voltas--in Burkina Faso. A fourth branch begins in Benin as the Pendjari, which becomes the Oti (q.v.) after it enters Togo. From the source of the Black Volta to the Gulf of Guinea at Ada (q.v.) is a distance of about 1,000 miles (1609 km). The entire system drains an area of 150,000 square miles (388,500 sq km) in Benin, Togo, Burkina Faso, Ivory Coast, and Ghana. Within Ghana the Volta drains 61,000 square miles (157,990 sq km), which is 67 percent of the country.

The African name for the river after it becomes one stream below Kete-Krakye (q.v.) is Firao (Frao) or Atirri. "Volta" was the name given the river in the fifteenth century by the Portuguese on account of its meandering course. For four centuries Europeans were blocked from the Volta by the dreaded bar near Ada. Finally, in 1861, an English expedition under Edward Bullock Andrew crossed the bar in surf boats and ventured upstream, portaging around rapids, for a distance of almost 120 miles (193 km). In 1868 the *Eyo* became the first steamer to cross the Ada bar. From the bar it is possible to move up the river to the tidal limit at Akuse (q.v.), which was 55 miles (88 km) above Ada. This was the end of navigation in the dry season save for canoes. In the wet season small-draft vessels ventured a few miles more to the Senchi Rapids (q.v.). Here portage was required even for canoes. The river is at its lowest in March and at its highest at the end of September.

The Volta is about a mile wide at Ada. A ferry crosses at this point to Anyanui, on the left bank from Ada. Bridges cross the river at Tefle and at Adomi (q.v.). Hydroelectric projects were completed across the river at Kpong (1981) and the Ajena Gorge (1964) (qq.v.). On 19 May 1964 the gates of the dam across the Ajena Gorge were closed, and Lake Volta began to form. See VOLTA DAM.

VOLTA ALUMINUM COMPANY (VALCO). A consortium of aluminum interests created by Edgar Kaiser of Kaiser Aluminum in 1959. By an agreement reached with Nkrumah in 1960, the consortium agreed to build an aluminum smelter at Tema (qq.v.). VALCO was given special electric and tax rates in exchange for a commitment to purchase up to 74 percent of the current produced at the Akosombo Dam (q.v.) for a period of 30 years. This guaranteed payments on the loans made to build the dam. The smelter was completed in 1966 and full production was reached by 1968. An expansion project was added in 1976. Hopes that VALCO would use Ghanaian bauxite were not realized by 1983 because bauxite could be imported from Jamaica at a lower cost.

On 10 July 1984, the government of Ghana and VALCO announced that, after eighteen months of negotiations, a new agreement that was satisfactory to both parties had been signed.

VOLTA BASIN. The Volta Basin in Ghana is the area between the Gambaga (q.v.) Scarp on the north, the Konkori Scarp on the west, the Mampong or Kwahu Scarp (qq.v.) on the south, and the Togo border on the east.

VOLTA DAM. The Volta or Akosombo Dam (q.v.) was started in 1961 and the gates to the dam were first closed in May of 1964. The dam is an earth and rockfill structure 370 feet (113 m) high and 2,100 feet (640 m) long at its crest. The dam is rockfill rather than concrete as a protection against earthquakes.

VOLTA DELTA. In the extreme southeastern corner of Ghana is a flat, featureless area with many lagoons which pushes out into the Gulf of Guinea. Sandbars block the exit of the river and create several channels. The Songaw and Keta lagoons (qq.v.) are both saltwater. The Avu and Ke lagoons are freshwater. The lagoons and rivers are a source of fish and salt. Coconut and oil palms grow well in the delta, and shallots, cassava, maize, and other truck crops are cultivated. There are large areas of tidewater grass.

VOLTA REGION. Before the Gold Coast became Ghana, this region was named the Trans-Volta-Togoland Region (qq.v.). It consisted of small areas which had once been part of the Gold Coast Colony (q.v.), plus the southern part of the old Togo Trust Territory. It became the Volta Region in 1954. Ho (q.v.) is the administration center for the region, which is divided into North and South Anlo, Keta (qq.v.), Tongu, Ho, Kpandu, and Buem-Krakye (qq.v.).

VOLTA RIVER see VOLTA

VOLTA RIVER AUTHORITY (VRA). The agency established in 1961 to manage the Volta River Hydroelectric Project (q.v.). It succeeded the Volta River Project. The first responsibility of the VRA was to move the 80,000 people living in the area to be flooded by Lake Volta and resettle them in new homes and villages. In a 12-18 February 1990 *West Africa* article (pp. 216-217), Kofi Diaw and Einhard Schmidt-Kallert commented on many of the hardships caused the people as a result of the resettlement program.

From 1966 the VRA has directed the operations of the Akosombo and the Kpong (qq.v.) hydroelectric stations and their distribution networks. Transmission lines to Togo and Benin were opened in 1972. It was, however, not until the late 1980s that major cities in the northern part of Ghana were supplied with electricity from the project. Burkina Faso could now be supplied from Ghana.

VOLTA RIVER PROJECT (VRP). Planning on the project to develop the Volta River began years before the dam of the Ajena Gorge (qq.v.) was actually built. Albert Kitson, head of the Gold Coast Geological Survey Department, marked the Gorge as an excellent place for a dam on 24 April 1915. Later, Kitson also spotted Bui (q.v.), on the Black Volta, as another place that could be developed. Planning on the project began in earnest in 1951. The Volta Dam was started in 1961, finished in 1965, and dedicated by President Nkrumah (qq.v.) just before he was deposed in 1966. Lake Volta, created by the Volta Dam, covers 3,276 sq mi (8,485 sq km), is 250 miles (402 km) long, and has a shoreline of 4,500 miles (7,241 km).

VOLTA RIVER TRANSPORT SERVICE. In 1902 the British organized a fleet of canoes to transport supplies from Ada up the Volta to Longoro, on the Black Volta near Kintampo, and Yeji, on the White Volta below Salaga (qq.v.). After Tamale became the administrative center in the north in 1907, the canoe transport was extended to Yapei or Tamale Port (qq.v.). By 1930 improvements in the road network of the Gold Coast made canoe traffic obsolete. Today, pontoons and barges travel the lakes, carrying people and goods.

VREDENBURG, FORT (Vreedenburgh). Both the English and Dutch built bases at Komenda (q.v.) in the seventeenth century. Even the French were interested in the location for a while. The Dutch began Vreedenburgh about 1688. Almost a century later the fort was taken and destroyed by the British. The Dutch rebuilt it in 1785. In 1872 the Dutch ceded the place to the English.

- W -

WA. 10°03'N, 2°29'W. Important early trade depot of the Dyula (q.v.) on the western route from the coast to Jenne. The Black Volta (q.v.) and the border with the Ivory Coast are just a short distance to the west. It is the administrative capital of the Upper West Region of Ghana. Southward the road goes to Bole (q.v.), northward to Lawra, eastward to Yagaba or Daboya (q.v.). The city today is a cosmopolitan town of many peoples: the Wala (q.v.), the Dagaba (Dagarte), the Lobi, and many Muslims (qq.v.). There are two impressive mosques, and the most important festival, the Damba (q.v.), celebrates the birthdate of Muhammad, the prophet of Islam.

WADH NABA see NABAGA

WALA (sing. Walo, Oule, Walba, Wile). People of the Wa (q.v.) state. Their language is Wale or Wali. They are a Mole-Dagbani group who came from Mamprusi (qq.v.) in the seventeenth century and established their rule over the Dagaba and Lobi (q.v.) who were already in the area. The traditional leader of the journey to Wa was Soalia. Power was divided between groups that settled in several small places in and around Wa. The Wala have often been attacked by other peoples. The Gonja (q.v.) have attacked them several times. In the late 1880s Babatu's Zabrama (qq.v.) attacked the Wala, destroyed a mosque in Wa, and executed many of the local Muslim leaders. The Wa Na committed suicide after a bloody defeat at Nasa (q.v.). The Wala, searching for security, signed a treaty for protection with the British in 1894, and with the French the following year. These treaties initially did them little good because the area was soon devastated by Samori's (q.v.) forces. Only after Samori left the area did the British venture back.

WALEMBELE. 10°30'N, 1°58'W. Sisala (q.v.) town on a branch of the Kulpawn in the Upper West Region. It is 27 miles (43 km) south of Tumu (q.v.). The region came under the rule of the Zabrama (q.v.) in the late nineteenth century.

WALEWALE. 10°21'N, 0°48'W. Town in the Northern Region on the Great Northern Highway, 28 miles (45 km) due south of Bolgatanga and about the same distance southwest of Gambaga (qq.v.). Louis Binger (q.v.), the French explorer, reported being here from 10 August to 17 September 1888.

WANGARA. Mande merchants who were attracted to the Black Volta area from Mali in search of gold and kola (q.v.). They made important settlements at Begho and at Wa (qq.v.). They are often called the Dyula (q.v.).

WANKE see WENCHI

WARD, WILLIAM ERNEST FRANK. Born 1900. After attending Lincoln College, Oxford, and Ridley Hall, Cambridge, Ward became a member of the first faculty at Achimota (q.v.) in 1924. He remained in the Gold Coast (q.v.) until World War II, spending his spare time in the study of African music, folklore, and history. In 1935 he published *A Short History of the Gold Coast*. In the seventh edition this became *A Short History of Ghana*, 1957. In 1940 William Ward finished a fuller account of the history of the Gold Coast. This was just before he left the Gold Coast to go to Mauritius. That second book was not published until after the war, in 1948; it appeared as *A History of the Gold Coast*. After independence this was revised and became *History of Ghana*, 1958. Both these books have gone through many editions. In 1940 Ward went to Mauritius as Director of Education. After the war he returned to England as Educational Adviser to the Colonial Office, 1945-1956, and editor of *Overseas Education*, 1946-1963. He continued to write. *Educating Young Nations* appeared in 1959; *Fraser of Trinity and Achimota* and *Government in West Africa* both were published in 1965. *The Royal Navy and the Slavers: The Suppression of the Atlantic Slave Trade* followed in 1969. In addition he helped with a history of East Africa, a history of Africa, and publications on education in the non-European world.

WARSHAS see WASSA

WASIPE. 8°32'N, 2°12'W. Village in the Northern Region on the western road between Bamboi and Bole, and just a short distance from the Black Volta (qq.v.). Alluvial gold was once found in the area. Old pits can be found between Wasipe and Bole. At some point the Wasipe-wura moved from Wasipe to

Daboya (qq.v.). Daboya is the divisional capital of the Gonja Wasipe division.

WASSA (Warshas, Wasa, Wasaw, Wasswa). One of the major groups of the Akan (q.v.). They are shown on a 1929 map as Wassa and on a 1729 map as Warshas or Wassa. Wassa today is in the Western Region. The Nzema and Ahanta are their southern neighbors, Aowin and Sefwi are on the west and north, and the Denkyira and Fante (qq.v.) are in the east. Wassa is divided into two divisions, the upper, or Amanfi, and the lower, or Fiaso. Wassa was conquered by Denkyira (q.v.) in the latter half of the seventeenth century. Throughout the eighteenth and nineteenth centuries, it was with the Asante (q.v.) that Wassa came into conflict due to the latter's effort to keep the routes to the coast open. The Wassa tried to ally with the coastal people to ensure their protection. In 1871 they were associated with the Fante (q.v.) confederacy movement.

WATER WORKS ORDINANCE, 1934. An ordinance that would have required citizens of towns that had been supplied with modern water systems to pay for it. This ordinance was suggested at the same time the Sedition Ordinance (q.v.) was proposed in the Legislative Assembly. A delegation under J. B. Danquah (q.v.) was sent to England to protest. The Aborigines' Rights Protection Society (q.v.) also sent a separate delegation. Both groups demanded that people in the Gold Coast (q.v.) be given more participation in the government of the Gold Coast, but they did not entirely agree on how this would be done.

WATSON REPORT. Economic and political conditions in the Gold Coast created much discontent after World War II (qq.v.). Early in 1948 a Ghanaian merchant, Nii Kwabena Bonne III (q.v.), organized a boycott of European goods. On 28 February unarmed veterans were fired on as they marched toward Government House. Two men died. Rioting and looting spread across Accra (q.v.) and into a number of towns, and before order was restored some thirty persons were dead, many were injured, and much property destroyed. Six leaders of the United Gold Coast Convention (q.v.) were arrested and detained at distant places in the north. These men became the famous "Big Six." Governor Gerald Hallen Creasy (q.v.) then asked that the Secretary of State for the Colonies appoint a commission to come out from England to investigate the causes for the riots and discontent. Andrew Aiken Watson was chairman of the Watson Commission. The Commission remained in the Gold Coast several weeks conducting hearings, and the Watson Report was released in August 1948. It recommended a greater role for educated Africans in the government of the Gold Coast by expanding the legislative branch of the government and by including five African ministers on the Executive Council, with departments responsible to the legislature. It also suggested that chiefs should take no part in political affairs, but should be limited to their traditional roles. The government then decided to test African opinion, so an all-African committee was appointed under the leadership of Sir Henley Coussey (q.v.). There were 38 members, including five of the "Big Six" who had been sent into detention a few months before.

WELBECK, NATHANIEL A. Born 1915. Teacher and politician who was one of the original members of the Central Committee of the Convention People's Party (CPP) (q.v.). He went on to be one of Nkrumah's (q.v.) most trusted lieutenants. He was propaganda secretary of the CPP (q.v.), and after being elected to the Legislative Assembly in 1954 he became Minister of Works. Over the years until Nkrumah's fall he held various posts in the Cabinet and the party. He supervised the initial stages of the organization of the Workers' Brigades (q.v.) in 1957. He was also the Minister of Information, and last of all the Minister of State for Party Propaganda. He served briefly as Ghana's representative to Guinea in 1958, and to the Congo (Zaire) in 1960. After the 1966 coup, he spent some time in prison.

WENCHI (Wanque). 7°44'N, 2°06'W. Important town in Brong Ahafo 18 miles (29 km) northwest of Techiman and 95 miles (152 km) northwest of Kumasi (qq.v.). It is on one of the old caravan routes from the coast to Begho (q.v.) and beyond, and the whole area attracts archaeology buffs in search of the past.

Wenchi was the hometown of the late Prime Minister Dr. Kofi Abrefa Busia (q.v.).

WEST AFRICAN AIRWAYS CORPORATION (WAAC). A joint project of the English-speaking countries of West Africa organized in 1947. The British Gambia, Sierra Leone, Gold Coast, and Nigeria cooperated in the airline.

WEST AFRICAN COCOA RESEARCH INSTITUTE. An institute established at Tafo (q.v.) (Eastern Region) in 1938 to do research on cocoa (q.v.). After Ghanaian independence it became the Cocoa Research Station.

WEST AFRICAN CONFERENCE. A movement which developed at the end of World War I to try to get the West African English-speaking colonies to work together for self-determination. J. E. Casely-Hayford, T. Hutton Mills, W. E. G. Sekyi, and F. V. Nanka Bruce (qq.v.) were the Gold Coast leaders. The head office at first was at Sekondi (q.v.). In March 1920 the West African Conference evolved into the National Congress of British West Africa (q.v.).

WEST AFRICAN FRONTIER FORCE (WAFF) see ROYAL WEST AFRICAN FRONTIER FORCE (RWAFF)

WEST AFRICAN NATIONAL SECRETARIAT (WANS). Group formed in London after the Manchester Pan-African Congress (q.v.) in 1945. The object was to follow up on the ideas of the Manchester Congress and to work for self-determination and a federation of West Africa. Isaac Theophilus Akunna Wallace Johnson was chairman, Kwame Nkrumah (q.v.) was the secretary. George Padmore and Bankole Awooner-Renner (qq.v.) were members.

WEST AFRICAN PRODUCE BOARD. An agency created by the British in 1942, during World War II (q.v.), to push for an increase in the production of materials considered necessary for the war. In the Gold Coast (q.v.) the Produce Board encouraged production of food products, rubber, cocoa (q.v.), minerals, palm kernels, and timber.

WEST AFRICAN STUDENTS' UNION (WASU). An organization of Africans in London founded in 1925. J. B. Danquah and Edward O. Asafu-Adjaye of the Gold Coast (qq.v.) were early leaders. Almost every Gold Coast student in London after 1925 was affiliated with the WASU. Marcus Garvey gave the WASU a hostel in 1928. He also helped finance WASU publications. Blacks from all over the world were brought together at WASU meetings. The WASU was a union of the Gold Coast Students' Union, the Nigerian Progress Union, and the Association of Students of African Descent.

WEST AFRICAN TIMES (later the *Times of West Africa.*) Newspaper started in Accra by J. B. Danquah (qq.v.) in 1931.

WEST AFRICAN YOUTH LEAGUE (WAYL). An organization founded in 1934 by Isaac Theophilus Akunna Wallace Johnson, a communist and Pan-Africanist from Sierra Leone who moved to the Gold Coast in 1933, and Bankole Awooner-Renner (q.v.), also an active communist. The WAYL's goal was to advance the cause of self-determination and the overthrow of British rule. Nnamdi Azikiwe used the *African Morning Post* in Accra (qq.v.) as a mouthpiece for the WAYL. The colonial authorities expelled I. T. A. Wallace Johnson from the Gold Coast in 1938 and the League soon collapsed. This was the first radical movement organized in the Gold Coast to call for complete freedom from the British.

WEST INDIA COMPANY, DUTCH. A Dutch company created in 1621 to trade in the West Indies and on the coast of Africa. It was reorganized in 1674 and continued to operate until it went bankrupt and had to be dissolved in 1791. It took Elmina from the Portuguese in 1637 and Axim (qq.v.) in 1642. For many years after that it dominated all the trade west of Elmina, and for a few years, from 1642 to 1674, came close to dominating all the trade on the Gold Coast (q.v.). In 1717 it acquired the property of the Brandenburgers (q.v.), but the company had already lost its commanding edge to the British by then. After 1791 the Netherlands' government assumed control of Dutch interests along the Gold Coast, and trade continued until all the posts were sold to the British in 1872.

WEST INDIA AND GUINEA COMPANY (WIGC). A Danish Company which traded with West Africa in the seventeenth and eighteenth centuries. The company resulted from the union of the Gluckstadt and Copenhagen trading groups and was never very successful. It was abolished in 1754 and the Danish crown took over its assets. The British purchased all Danish claims in 1850.

WESTERN ECHO. A Cape Coast newspaper founded by James Brew (qq.v.) in 1885. It pushed the idea of representative government for the Gold Coast (q.v.). Its last issue appeared in December 1887, but it was soon replaced by the *Gold Coast Echo*, edited by a nephew of James H. Brew--J. E. Casely-Hayford (q.v.).

WESTERN REGION. The southwestern part of the old Gold Coast Colony (q.v.). It includes Sefwi, Aowin, Nzema, Ahanta, and Wassa (qq.v.). The administrative center is at Sekondi (q.v.). The present boundaries were established in 1960.

WHITE VOLTA. Tributary of the Volta that rises in the Yatenga section of Burkina Faso. It flows east of Ouagadougou about 30 miles (48 km), and crosses into the Upper East Region of Ghana some 12 miles (19 km) west of Bawku (q.v.). At the Gambaga Scarp it turns sharply west to join the Red Volta near the village of Gambaga, continuing on west for some 38 miles (61 km) more, and then turning sharply southward, to travel down the center of Ghana until it enters Lake Volta above Yapei (qq.v.).

WIAWSO (Weoso). 6°12'N, 2°29'W. An important town in the Sefwi area of the Western Region (qq.v.). It is on the Tano River (q.v.). The British opened an agricultural station here in 1915. This encouraged cocoa (q.v.) cultivation in the area.

WILKS, IVOR G. H.   Born 1928.   A native of Coventry, United Kingdom, and an outstanding scholar and researcher.   He has authored over a hundred articles and short papers in recognized scholarly journals.   His *South Wales and the Rising of 1839: Class Struggle as Armed Struggle* (1984) won the 1985 Welsh Arts Council Non-Fiction Prize for books published in Welsh studies.   But Wilks is better known for his research and writings on Asante (q.v.) history.   His *Asante in the Nineteenth Century: The Structure and Evolution of a Political Order* (1975) won the 1976 African Studies Association Herskovits Award for the best book in African studies published or distributed in the United States.   As evident from the discussions in the "Preamble" to the 1989 reprint of the book, Wilks's conclusions and findings on Asante have served as points of departure for many other researchers.   Apart from his presentations on the structure of political authority in nineteenth-century Asante, Wilks has also written on the presence of Islam in the Asante center and periphery.   Two such works are his *Wa and the Wala: Islam and Polity in Northwestern Ghana* (1989) and *Chronicles from Gonja: A Tradition of West African Muslim Historiography* (1986, co-authored with Nehemiah Levtzion and Bruce Haights).   Some of Wilks's field interviews in Ghana are deposited at the Institute of African Studies at the University of Ghana, where he was a staff member from 1953 through 1966.   Herskovits Professor of African Studies, Ivor Wilks retired from his appointment at Northwestern University at Evanston, Illinois, at the end of the 1992-93 academic year but remains an Honorary Senior Member of the Centre for Research and Scholarship, St. David's University College, University of Wales.

WILLIAM, FORT.   One of the out-forts in the fortifications around Cape Coast (q.v.) Castle.   It was first built around 1820 and called Smith's Tower.   It was refurbished in 1831 and the name was changed to Fort William.   After 1835 it was used as a lighthouse.

WINNEBA (Winnebah, Simpa). 5°20'N, 0°37'W. Important coastal town in the Central Region some 35 miles (56 km) west of Accra. The traditional founder was Simpun. It is an important Efutu (q.v.) center. The English were trading there by 1633 and built a fort from which to trade in 1694, but no trace of Winneba Fort is left today. In the 1920s it was an important resort and residence for Europeans. It was the third most important port on the coast and an outlet for the cocoa (q.v.) and palm oil produced in the interior. Winneba was once famous for the canoes made on its beaches and for its fishermen, but the port was closed in 1961. When Kwame Nkrumah laid the foundation stone for the Kwame Nkrumah Institute of Ideology (qq.v.) on 18 February 1961 the President of the USSR attended the ceremonies. The Institute lasted less than six years. The buildings became the Winneba Advanced Teachers' College. The National Academy of Music, the Physical Education College, and the Advanced Teacher Training College have maintained the town's importance.

WINNIETT, WILLIAM. Died 1850. Naval officer who was Lt. Governor at Cape Coast, 1846-1849, and Governor in 1850. His first major act on the Gold Coast was to conduct an expedition against the Chief of Apollonia (qq.v.), who had killed many people and had offered gold for the heads of strangers brought to him. Winniett imprisoned the Chief at Cape Coast (q.v.) Castle. In September 1848 he became the first British Governor to go to Asante, visiting with Asantehene Kwaku Dua (qq.v.) until 26 October. He kept "a Journal of a Visit to Ashanti" (Winniett to Earl Henry George Grey, 15 November 1848). He took part in the negotiations with the Danes to buy their rights on the Gold Coast, and in March 1850 he toured the newly acquired territory. Winniett became full Governor after the Gold Coast was separated from Sierra Leone in 1850. He also selected James Bannerman (q.v.), a Scottish-African, to be Civil Commandant at Christiansborg (q.v.) in 1850. That Castle was acquired from Denmark. When Winniett died at the end of December 1850, Bannerman became Lt. Governor of the British colony.

WLI FALLS (Afegame, Agumasato). 7°08'N, 0°36'E. Spectacular waterfalls east of Hohoe in the Volta Region (q.v.) and on the Togo border at Mount Agumasato. The falls are nearly 1,000 feet (305 m) high.

WOLSELEY, SIR GARNET JOSEPH. 1833-1913. Military Commander. Commissioned in 1852, he served in Burma, the Crimea, India, China, Canada, Zululand, and Egypt before being sent to the Gold Coast (q.v.). In 1873 Wolseley was vested with supreme civil and military command in the Gold Coast. He reached Cape Coast on 2 October 1873 and quickly prepared to march against Asante (qq.v.). He entered Kumasi (q.v.) on 4 February 1874, and two days later the city was destroyed. The Asantehene was forced to renounce the allegiance of Denkyira, Assin, Akyem, Adansi, and Elmina (qq.v.) with its allies. An impossible indemnity was imposed on the Asante. Many of the provinces of Asante declared their freedom from Asante. Wolseley soon departed from the Gold Coast and returned to England the conquering hero (he was made a Major-General at the age of 40). The Asante (Sagrenti) campaign made Wolseley famous.

WORK AND HAPPINESS. A plan introduced by President Nkrumah (q.v.) in 1961. It declared Socialism to be the national objective of Ghana. Nkrumah promised self-sustaining industral growth by 1967. Nkrumah's government was overthrown in 1966.

WORKERS' BRIGADES. Organized as Builders' Brigade in December 1957, they were units to provide work for unemployed youth and to mobilize political support for the Convention People's Party (CPP) (q.v.). Base camps were set up in each region of Ghana. In 1964 the Brigades began to receive training as paramilitary units. They were often assigned security duties and were used to swell crowds at CPP functions and public affairs. They were also involved in agricultural production. They were dissolved after the 1966 coup.

WORKERS' DEFENCE COMMITTEE (WDC). On 1 January 1982, the morning after the Provisional National Defence Council (PNDC) seized power, Jerry John Rawlings (qq.v.) announced that "Power belongs to the people." PNDC policy guidelines provided for a strategy to single out ordinary citizens for leadership roles. These guidelines stated that "The December Revolution aims at ensuring that power is exercised by the people organized from the grassroots." The PNDC promised to radically transform the socioeconomic institutions of Ghana. To offer those at the bottom of society a chance to participate in making decisions, the PNDC created the Peoples' Defence Committees (PDCs), Workers' Defence Committees (WDCs), Citizens' Vetting Committees (CVC) (qq.v.), Regional Defence Committees (RDC), and National Defence Committees (NDC) (q.v.). All these organizations were to be involved in community projects and community decisions, and individual members were to expose corruption and anti-social activities. Mawuse Dake was made Secretary to the National Defence Committee, charged with making the whole structure work. Activities of the WDCs brought them into conflicts with management in private and public corporations. In 1982 many such clashes were reported at Unilever Soap, Valco, Ghana Textiles Printers, and Juapong Textiles. Since the activities of some WDCs adversely affected the management of companies, the PNDC announced the dissolution of both the NDC and the WDC in December 1984 and replaced them with Committees for the Defence of the Revolution (CDRs) in which both management and workers were to cooperate.

WORLD WAR I, 1914-1919. Britain declared war on Germany on 4 August 1914. The following day Major von Doering, Acting Governor of Togoland, offered neutrality to the Gold Coast (q.v.) and to the French in Dahomey. France and England declined the German offer and immediately crossed into German territory. The Togo capital at Lome, just across the border from Aflao (q.v.), was occupied without bloodshed. Lome was occupied on 7 August, Yendi on the 14th, and Ho (qq.v.) on the 17th. The only real fighting took place as the British and French moved to take the German wireless station at Kamina. But that campaign was brief, and German forces in Togo surrendered on 26 August. The two allies divided Togo between themselves.

At the start of the war the Gold Coast Regiment of the West African Frontier Force (q.v.) consisted of 49 British and 1,584 African troops. The Northern Territories Constabulary had two British officers and 321 African troopers. Recruitment of Africans into British service was voluntary throughout World War I. From 1914 to 1918 over 3,000 men of the Gold Coast Regiment and more than a thousand auxiliary personnel were sent to the Cameroons and East Africa for service outside the Gold Coast. Many more joined the colonial military and police services for duty within the Gold Coast. Troops sent to the Cameroons in September 1914 remained there until May 1916. The Gold Coast Regiment embarked for East Africa in July 1916, took part in the campaigns in both the German and Portuguese areas, and returned to the Gold Coast in September 1918.

Wartime licensing, inflation, shortages, and strenuous economy in government expenditures caused serious problems. Muslim unrest and sympathy for their fellow Muslims in Islamic areas allied to Germany caused apprehension among colonial officials. There were some disorders in Asante (q.v.) and the Central Province in 1914; at Bongo, near the Burkina Faso border, in 1916; and at Great Ningo and in Gonja (qq.v.) in 1917, but at no time was there danger of a major revolt in the Gold Coast during World War I. Generally, most of the people sided with the Allied cause. But there was a sharp rise in national consciousness in the Gold Coast during World War I. Allied rhetoric about democracy and self-determination did not go unheeded in Africa. People in the Gold Coast began to hear W. E. B. Du Bois (q.v.) and Marcus Garvey. And for the first time the Colony, Asante, and the Northern Territories (qq.v.) began to develop a sense of unity.

WORLD WAR II, 1939-1945. World War II weakened the British Empire and the élan of the British. With the fall of France in June 1940, and hegemony of Europe began to disintegrate. The Gold Coast (q.v.) found itself completely surrounded by territory ruled by Vichy France. The very existence of Britain was threatened, and Britain would have collapsed in 1941 had it not been for the United States and Russia. This had profound repercussions on the British Empire everywhere. The Gold Coast Brigade of the Royal West African Frontier Force (q.v.) was sent off to Kenya to drive the Italians out of East Africa at the beginning of World War II. With that mission accomplished, the troops were returned home, reorganized, and in June 1943 sent off to Burma. Conscription was resorted to in 1941, and during World War II some 65,000 persons from the Gold Coast saw service in one of the various Allied units.

In 1942 the British began a program of appointing Africans to senior positions in the government. A new constitution with majority representation in the Legislative Assembly was promised after the war. The British launched major campaigns for increased production of food, oils, minerals, timber, and rubber. Income taxes were introduced. And obligations were incurred by the British that would make concessions inevitable after the war.

Accra and Achimota (qq.v.) became the command center for the allies in West Africa. The US Air Force opened a major air base at Accra Airport in 1941 to ferry planes and supplies to North Africa and the Middle East. An auxiliary base was established at Takoradi (q.v.). During 1942 and 1943 an average of 200 to 300 planes refueled each day at Accra. Headquarters for West Africa were established at Achimota in July 1942 to coordinate war efforts for the British, Free French, Belgians, and Americans in that theater of operations. Lord Swinton (q.v.) (Phillip Cunliffe-Lister), with the title of Cabinet Minister Resident in West Africa, commanded at Achimota from 1942 to 1944, when he was replaced by Harold Balfour.

WULOMO. The Ga (q.v.) high priest who presides over Ga communities. He exercises both political and religious authority. The Wulomo of Accra was the commander of the Ga military confederation in the early days.

WURA. The suffix for "chief" in Gonja (q.v.). It is equivalent to *na* in Dagbani areas, *hene* among the Akan, and *manche* among the Ga.

- X - Y -

YAA ASANTEWAA (Ya Asantiwah). Died 1921. Edwesohemma. The Queen mother of Ejisu (q.v.) (Edwese). She was a leader of Asante (q.v.) opposition against the British in a war in 1900. She was sent into exile in the Seychelles Islands after the war, in May 1901, and she died in exile in 1921.

YAA ASANTEWAA WAR, 1900-1901. The last conflict between the Asante and the British started as a result of demands by British Governor Frederic Hodgson for the Golden Stool (qq.v.). The British quickly gained the upper hand. Yaa Asantewaa (q.v.) and fourteen others were sent into exile, and Asante was placed under a British Chief Commissioner.

YAGBUM see NYANOA

YAGBUMWURA. The Paramount Chief of Gonja whose seat of government was formerly at Nyanoa or Yagbum, northeast of Bole (qq.v.).

YAKUBA. The twenty-seventh Ya Na of Dagomba (qq.v.). He was the son of Na Andani, and he ruled in the middle of the nineteenth century. He was the ruler of Dagomba at the time the Zabrama (q.v.) horsemen came to Dagomba under Alfa dan Tadano Hano from Zerma (modern Niger).

YA NA. The Paramount Chief of Dagomba (q.v.).

YANKEY, AGUSTUS KWESI. Born 1936. Labor leader. He served several years as General-Secretary of the General Transport, Petroleum, and Chemical Workers' Union. At the Ghana Trades Union Congress (TUC) at Kumasi (qq.v.) on 16

December 1983 he was elected to replace A. M. Issifu (who had resigned earlier) as Secretary-General of the TUC.

YANTAMBO see NNANTOMBO

YANTAURE see YENNENGA

YAPEI (Tamale Port) 9°10'N, 1°10'W. Village in the Northern Region on the northern end of Lake Volta just sou.h of where the Mole River enters the Volta (qq.v.). Yapei is some 28 miles (45 km) southwest of Tamale (q.v.). The northern port of Lake Volta is located here, and a bridge crosses the Volta at this location. The population was just 233 in 1948, and by 1970 it was only 1,203. Jakpa and the Gonja defeated the Dagomba (q.v.) here in the early seventeenth century. The Ya Na at the time was Dariziegu (qq.v.), the eleventh of his line.

YAW AKOTO see OSEI YAW AKOTO

YEJI. 8°13'N, 0°39'W. Village in the Brong-Ahafo Region where the Great North road from Kumasi to Tamale crosses the Lake Volta (qq.v.) Ferry. Before the impoundment of the lake, the river was about 600 yards (549 m) wide at this point. Today the ferry crosses a wide lake. The road from Yeji through Salaga (q.v.) to Tamale was paved in 1907. Yeji is located just above where the Pru River (q.v.) enters Lake Volta. It is about 20 miles (32 km) to Salaga, and 85 miles (136 km) to Tamale.

YENDI. 9°26'N, 0°01'W. The capital of the Dagomba, Yendi is in the Northern Region, 55 miles (88 km) east of Tamale, and 45 miles (72 km) north of Bimbila (qq.v.). It was once a Konkomba (q.v.) town, named Chare, but the Dagomba established themselves here in the early seventeenth century. From 1745 to 1873 the Dagomba owed tribute to Asante (q.v.). The Europeans began to arrive in Yendi shortly after the Dagomba began to free themselves from Asante. For several hundred years Yendi was an important depot on the trade routes to Hausaland (q.v.). Dupuis in 1824 reported on Yendi on the basis of information he received from travelers arriving in Kumasi (qq.v.). Dr. Gouldsbury visited Yendi in 1876, followed by Lonsdale (qq.v.) a few years later. The German Von François was there in 1888, followed by Von Carnap. G. A. Ferguson was in Yendi in August 1894. Yendi almost got destroyed by the Germans on 5 December 1896, and after the British and Germans divided Dagomba, Yendi fell to the Germans. It became British in August 1914.

YENDI DABARI (Dapali, Dipali). 9°48'N, 0°57'W. The "Ruins of Yendi" are located near the modern village of Dapali, in the Northern Region, 30 miles (48 km) north of Tamale (qq.v.). The first Ya Na of Dagomba, Nyagse (qq.v.), established his capital here. About 1713 the Gonja threatened Dagomba, and the capital was moved eastward to modern Yendi (qq.v.).

YENDI SKIN AFFAIRS. Since the mid-nineteenth century, the position of Paramount Chief, or Ya Na, of Yendi has been passed back and forth between two descendants of Ya Na Yakuba (qq.v.). Upon this Ya Na's death, his son Abdulai was enskinned as Ya Na, and upon Abdulai's death, his brother Andani became the next Ya Na. That seemed to have set the precedent--the next Ya Na being chosen from whichever side of the royal family was currently not holding the skin. This tradition, however, was broken in 1954 when Mahama III was succeeded by Abdulai III from the same line of the royal family. Notwithstanding the obvious dissatisfaction of the Andani family, the colonial administration did not interfere.

Following Ghana's independence, both factions in the Yendi chieftaincy dispute have influenced various political regimes to rule in their favor, hence the politicization of the Yendi skin dispute. This is evident from the numerous legislation and decrees existing on the conflict.

In an attempt to find a lasting answer to the dispute, the government of the Provisional National Defense Council (PNDC) (q.v.) in 1984 promulgated a law that removed from the political arena the solution of the conflict and placed it in the courts. According to the "Yendi Skin Affairs Appeal Law of 1984," aggrieved individuals in the conflict were to present their cases at the Court of Appeals. The law also stipulated that, were individuals in the conflict dissatisfied with appeals court decisions, a case could be filed at the Supreme Court. As was expected, both parties to the conflict submitted applications to the Supreme Court in 1984 following the enactment of the PNDC law. The Supreme Court's decision on the case in 1986 was unanimously in favor of Abdulai IV of the Abdulai line.

YENNENGA (Kachiogo, Yantaure, Yalanga, Yenenga, Nyennega). Daughter of Na Gbewa (Nedega) of Pusiga (qq.v.). Gbewa is the traditional progenitor of all the Mole-Dagbani peoples of the Volta Basin (qq.v.). Gbewa's oldest child was his only daughter, Yennenga. Tradition says that Gbewa did not want her to marry, so she ran away and mated with a Busansi hunter named Rialle (Riale). Their son, Ouedraogo (Ouidiraogo, Wedraoge, Widiraego, etc.), is the ancestor of the Mossi (q.v.) nobility.

YILO KROBO. One branch of the Krobo Adangbe (qq.v.). Their chief town is Somanya, located just west of Akuse and the Volta River (qq.v.). They once lived on Krobo (q.v.) Mountain with the Manya Krobo. They still live in the eastern part of the Accra Plains (q.v.). They are closely related to the Ada and Shai (qq.v.) people. All the Adangbe believe that they first came from near Lolove Hill.

YIRI. A family compound in the Upper and Northern regions of Ghana.

YOGGO (Yogo, Yoggu). 9°29'N, 1°06'W. Village in the Northern Region northwest of Tamale (qq.v.). This was the head village for the Dagomba before the descendants of Gbewa, Sitobu and his son, Nyagse (qq.v.), arrived. Na Nyagse, first ruler of Dagomba, died here. It is still the home of the head animist priest of Dagomba.

YO NA. The Chief of Savelugu (q.v.). He is an important figure in the hierarchy of the Dagomba because Savelugu was in the center of the Dagomba realm before the Dagomba were forced eastward to Yendi (q.v.) in the seventeenth century. Savelugu was near Yendi Dabari and Yoggo (qq.v.).

YOUNG PIONEER MOVEMENT (YPM). A youth organization established by the Convention People's Party and Kwame Nkrumah (qq.v.) in 1961 to replace the Boy Scout Movement in Ghana. It was disbanded after the 1966 coup.

YOUTH STUDY GROUP (YSG). A group founded in 1948 by K. A. Gbedemah, Kojo Botsio, and others who broke away from the United Gold Coast Convention (UGCC) and began to support Kwame Nkrumah (qq.v.) as their leader in opposition to the lawyers who ran the UGCC. The YSG organized mass meetings for Nkrumah. One of these mass meetings at the West End Arena in Accra organized the Convention People's Party (q.v.), on 12 June 1949.

- Z -

ZABRAMA (Zabarima, Zaberma, Zaberawa, Djerma, Zerma, Songhai). People who speak the Djerma dialect of the Songhai language. In the 1860s a group of horsemen came from the area of modern Niger to serve the ruler of Dagomba (q.v.). The leader of this group of Zerma was Alfa dan Tadano Hano (q.v.). Tradition says that Hano was a very religious Muslim and that he spent some time in a Quranic school in Salaga (q.v.). In time these men began to raid into the animist areas between the White and Black Voltas (q.v.). Trade in captives from these raids was so profitable that Hano determined to establish an Islamic state in the area. Hano died about 1870, and he was followed by Alfa Gazari dan Mahama. Gazari consolidated the power of the Zerma (now known as the Zabrama) in a large area north of the Kulpawn in what is today the Upper West Region of Ghana and the western part of Burkina Faso. Gazari was succeeded by Babatu (q.v.) in 1883. Gazari encountered rebellion among his followers, a threat from the troops of Samori (q.v.), and encroaching white men. In 1897 the French defeated Babatu at Gandiaga in March and at Doucie in June. Babatu retreated into Dagomba, where he joined his former allies, the Dagomba, in resistance to British advances. Babatu died about 1900. Hamma Zaza, a son of Gazari, was the last leader of the Zabrama.

ZABZUGU HILLS. 9°17'N, 0°22'E. Also called the Shiene Hills. These low hills are between the Oti River and the Togo border in the Konkomba area of the Northern Region southeast of Yendi (qq.v.). There is iron ore in this area.

ZANGINA, MUHAMMAD. The seventeenth Ya Na of Dagomba (qq.v.). He was a nephew of his predecessor, Gungobili. He converted to Islam during his reign and invited many mallams into Dagomba. Before he was converted his name was Wumbei. He ruled at the beginning of the eighteenth century, when many Hausa and Dyula Muslims (qq.v.) were trading in Dagomba. Gonja invaded Dagomba near the end of the reign of Zangina, and the Gonja came within 20 miles (32 km) of Yendi (qq.v.) before they were halted and defeated at Sang. Zangina was son of Na Tutugri and grandson of Na Luro, who had moved the Dagomba capital to Yendi. When Zangina's uncle, Na Gungobili died, there was a dispute over the succession. The ruler of Mamprusi (q.v.) was invited to settle the dispute and selected Zangina. The method of solving the succession created bitterness that divided Dagomba during the war with Gonja. According to one tradition, Zangina abdicated in 1713 to allow his cousin, Andani Sigili (Zighli), to unite Dagomba against Gonja. Zangina died a short time later at Agbandi, a short distance southeast of Yendi near the Oti River.

ZAZA, HAMMA. A son of Alfa Gazari, who became leader of the Zabrama in Dagomba about 1900 after the death of Babatu (qq.v.). He lived in the part of Dagomba over which the Germans had established control.

ZERILE see ZIRILE

ZERMA see ZABRAMA

ZIRILE (shirili, Zerile, Zirili, Zitiri). Son of Na Gbewa of Pusiga (qq.v.). Brother of Yennenga (Kachiogo), Tohogo, Sitobu, Nnantombo (qq.v.) (Ngamtambo), and Kufogo. Zirile was the oldest son of Gbewa, but Gbewa wanted Kugogo to rule after him. Zirile killed his brother and took the skin of Pusiga. The children of Na Gbewa founded the Mole-Dagbani (q.v.) states.

ZONGO. The strangers' quarters or section of a town.

ZULANDE. The second Ya Na of Dagomba (qq.v.). He was a great-grandson of Na Gbewa, a grandson of Sitobu, and son of Nyagse (qq.v.).

BIBLIOGRAPHY

CONTENTS

A.	Bibliographies and Guides	259
B.	General Information	265
C.	Serials	268
D.	Government Publications	271
E.	Archaeology	273
F.	General History	278
G.	History before 1840	280
H.	History, 1840-1956: Colonialism	284
I.	History Since Independence	298
J.	Regional Studies	311
K.	Travel	327
L.	Geography	333
M.	Arts	335
N.	Literature and Press	340
O.	Language	347

258 / Bibliography

P.   Culture and Social Life   351

Q.   Economics   360

R.   Religion and Philosophy   369

S.   Education   374

A. BIBLIOGRAPHIES AND GUIDES

Afre, S. A. *Ashanti Region of Ghana: An Annotated Bibliography, from Earliest Times to 1973.* Boston: G. K. Hall, 1975. 494 p.

Aguolu, Christian Chukwuedu. *Ghana in the Humanities and Social Sciences, 1900-1971: A Bibliography.* Metuchen, N.J.: Scarecrow Press, 1973. 469 p.

Agyei, Samuel Kwasi. *A Guide to Records Relating to Ghana in Repositories in the U.K. Excluding the Public Record Office.* Hebden Bridge, West Yorkshire: Altair Publishing, 1988. 391 p.

Agyemang, H. D., comp. *Legon Theses: A Checklist of Theses and Dissertations Accepted for Higher Degrees by the University of Ghana, Legon, 1964-1977.* Legon: Balme Library, 1978. 33 p.

Amanquah, S. N. *A Bibliography of University of Ghana Staff Publications, 1948-73.* Legon: University of Ghana, 1974. 256 p.

Amedekey, E. Y. *The Culture of Ghana: A Bibliography.* Accra: Ghana Universities Press, 1970. 215 p.

Amoabeng, Kwaku. "The English Language in Ghana: A Comparative Annotated Bibliography." Ph.D. Dissertation, State University of New York at Stony Brook, 1986. 852 p.

Amoako, Samuel Kwadwo. "Education Financing: A Case of the Boarding Scholarship System in Ghana." Ed.D. Dissertation, Columbia University Teachers' College, 1986. 266 p.

Asiedu, Edward Seth. *Public Administration in English-Speaking West Africa, 1945-1975: An Annotated Bibliography.* Boston: G. K. Hall Reference Books, 1977. 366 p.

Ayensu, Edward S. *Medical Plants of West Africa.* Algonac, Mich.: Reference Publications, 1978. 330 p.

Boyo, Osmanu Eshaka, Thomas Hodgkin, and Ivor Wilks, comps. *Check List of Arabic Works from Ghana.* Legon: Institute of African Studies, University of Ghana, Dec. 1962.

Brand, Richard Robert. *A Selected Bibliography of Accra, Ghana, a West African Colonial City (1887-1960).* Monticello, Ill.: Council of Planning Librarians, 1970. 27 p.

Brokensha, David, and S. I. A. Kotei. "A Bibliography of Ghana: 1958-1964." *African Studies Bulletin,* 10, 2 (1967), 35-79.

Burt, Eugene, C., ed. *African Art; Five Years' Cumulative Bibliography, Mid-1983 through 1988.* Seattle, Wash.: Data Art, 1988. 170 p.

Cardinall, Allan Wolsey. *A Bibliography of the Gold Coast.* (Issued as a companion volume to the Census Report of 1931.) Accra: Government Printer, Gold Coast Colony, 1932. 384 p.; rpt. Westport, Conn.: Greenwood Press for Negro Universities Press, 1970; and Ann Arbor, Mich.: University Microfilms-Xerox, 1970.

Carson, Patricia. *Materials for West African History in the Archives of Belgium and Holland.* Oxford: Athlone Press, 1962. 86 p.

Cochrane, T. W. *Preliminary Bibliography of the Volta River Authority Programme.* Accra: Volta River Authority, 1971. 83 p.

___. *Supplementary to Bibliography of the Volta River Project and Related Matters*. Accra: Volta River Authority, 1972. 6 p.

Dadson, Theresa. *Index to the Legon Observer, vols. 2-9 (1967-1974)*. Boston: G. K. Hall, 1979. 180 p.

Darko, Samuel Fordjour. "An Historical Inquiry into the Development of Higher Education in Ghana, 1948-1984: A Study of the Major Factors That Controlled and Inhibited the Development of the University of Ghana." Ph.D. Dissertation, North Texas State University, 1985. 510 p.

De Heer, A. N., comp. *A List of Ghanaian Newspapers and Periodicals*. Accra: Ghana Library Board, 1970. 16 p.

Dumett Raymond E. *Survey of Research Materials in the National Archives of Ghana*. Basler Afrika-Bibliographien: Schwäbisch Gmund: Afrika Verlag Der Kreis, 1974. 48 p.

Ewens, Graeme. *Africa O-Ye! A Celebration of African Music*. London: Guinness, 1991. 224 p.

Fage, John Donnelly. "Some General Considerations Relevant to Historical Research in the Gold Coast." *Transactions of the Gold Coast and Togoland Historical Society*, 1 (1952), 24-29.

___. "Some Notes on a Scheme for Investigation of Oral Tradition in the Northern Territories of the Gold Coast." *Journal of the Historical Society of Nigeria* (Ibadan), 1, 1 (Dec. 1956), 15-19.

Garrard, T. F. *Gold of Africa: Jewellery and Ornaments from Ghana, Côte d'Ivoire, Mali and Senegal in the Collection of the Barbier-Musller Museum*. Munich: Prestel, 1989. 247 p.

Ghana Information Service. *Ghana: A Brief Guide*. Accra: Ghana Information Service Department, 1991. 95 p.

Ghana, University of. *Early Africana (1556-1900) in the Balme Library*. Legon: University of Ghana Press, 1972. 70 p.

Gray, Carl. *African Music: A Bibliographical Guide to the Traditional, Popular, Art and Liturgical Music of Sub-Saharan Africa.* London and New York: Greenwood Press, 1991. 499 p.

Havinden, M. A. *The History of Crop Cultivation in West Africa: A Bibliographical Guide.* Exeter: Department of Economic History, University of Exeter, 1970. 20 p.

Henige, David P. *Correspondence from the Outforts to Cape Coast Castle, 1681-1699.* Madison, Wis.: University of Wisconsin, 1972. 64 p.

___. "The National Archives of Ghana: A Synopsis of Holdings." The *International Journal of African Historical Studies* (Boston), 6, 3 (1973), 475-486.

Hogg, Peter C. *The African Slave Trade and Its Suppression.* London: Frank Cass, 1973. 409 p. A classified and annotated bibliography of the slave trade.

Hunwick, J. O., ed. *Proceedings of a Seminar of Ghanaian Historiography and Historical Research.* Legon: University of Ghana, 1977. 290 p.

Johnson, Albert F. *A Bibliography of Ghana, 1930-1961.* Accra: Longman, Green for the Ghana Library Board, 1964. 210 p.; Evanston, Ill.: Northwestern University Press, 1964. 210 p.

Jones, Adam. "Ghana National Archives: A Supplementary Note." *History in Africa,* 15 (1988), 385-388.

Kafe, Joseph Kofi. *Ghana: An Annotated Bibliography of Academic Theses, 1920-1970 in the Commonwealth, the Republic of Ireland, and the United States of America.* Boston: G. K. Hall Reference Publications, 1973. 219 p.

Kaplan, Irving, et al. *Ghana: A Country Study.* 4th ed. Area Handbook Series. Washington, D.C.: U.S. Government Printing Office, 1981. 447 p.

Kotei, S. I. A. *Dr. W.E.B. DuBois, 1868-1963: A Bibliography.* Accra: Ghana Library Board, 1964. 39 p.

___. *Library Resources for African Studies in Ghana.* Legon: Department of Library and Archival Studies, 1974. 76 p.

Kropp-Dakubu, M. E. ed., *The Languages of Ghana.* London: Kegan Paul International for the IAI, 1988. 181 p.

Lawrence, A. W. *Fortified Trade-Post: The English in West Africa, 1645-1822.* London: Jonathan Cape, 1969.

___. *Trade Castles and Forts of West Africa.* Stanford, Calif.: Stanford University Press, 1964. 389 p.

Lems-Dworkin, Carol. *A Pan-African Annotated Bibliography.* London and New York: Hans Zell, 1991. 382 p.

Makepeace, Margaret. "English Traders on the Gold Coast, 1657-1668: An Analysis of the East India Company Archives." *History in Africa*, 16 (1989), 237-284.

Matthews, Noel. *Materials for West African History in the Archives of the United Kingdom.* Guides to Materials for West African History, European Archives, 5. London: Athlone Press, 1973. 225 p.

Petterson, David K. *Health in Colonial Ghana: Disease, Medicine, and Socio-Economic Change, 1900-1955.* Waltham, Mass.: Crossroads Press, 1981. 187 p.

Pitcher, G. M., comp. *Bibliography of Ghana, 1957-1960.* Kumasi: Library of the University of Science and Technology, 1962. 111 p.

Reindorf, Jor. *Scandinavians in Africa: A Guide to Materials Relating to Ghana in the Danish National Archives.* New York: Columbia University Press, 1980; Oslo: Universitets-forlaget, 1980. 140 p.

Ryder, Alan Frederick Charles. *Materials for West African History in Portuguese Archives.* London: Athlone Press, 1965. 92 p.

Rydings, H. A. *The Bibliographies of West Africa.* Ibadan: Ibadan University Press, 1961. 36 p.

Saha, Santosh C. *A History of Agriculture in West Africa: A Guide to Information Sources.* Lewiston, N.Y.: Edwin Mellen Press, 1990. 127 p.

Schmidt, Nancy J. *Sub-Saharan African Films and Filmmakers: An Annotated Bibliography.* London and New York: Hans Zell, 1988. 401 p.

Silverman, Raymond, and David Owusu-Ansah. "The Presence of Islam among the Akan of Ghana: A Bibliographic Essay." *History in Africa,* 16 (1989), 325-339.

Smit, H. M. *Hidden Items on Ghana in the Monograph Collection of the Balme Library.* Legon: The Balme Library, University of Ghana, 1981-1982. 2 volumes.

___ comp. *Ghana in Non-Ghanaian Serials and Collective Works 1974-1977: A Bibliography.* Legon: Balme Library, University of Ghana, 1981. 90 p.

Tetty, Charles, comp. *Medicine in West Africa, 1880-1956: An Annotated Bibliography.* Accra: University of Ghana Medical School Library, 1975. 547 p.

Travis, Carole, ed. *Periodicals from Africa: A Bibliography and Union List of Periodicals Published in Africa.* Boston: G. K. Hall Reference Books, 1977. 620 p.

Witherell, Julian W., and Sharon B. Lockwood, comps. *Ghana: A Guide to Official Publications, 1872-1968.* Washington, D.C.: Library of Congress General Reference and Bibliography Division, 1969. 110 p.

Wolfson, Freda. "Historical Records on the Gold Coast." *Bulletin* (Institute of Historical Research, London University), 24, 70 (1951), 121-240.

B. GENERAL INFORMATION

Ahuma, S. R. *Memoirs of West African Celebrities: With Special Reference to the Gold Coast.* Liverpool: Marples, 1905. 260 p.

Ajayi, J. F. A., and Michael Crowder. *History of West Africa.* 2 vols. New York: Columbia University Press, 1972. Reprint, New York: Longman, 1985.

Amonoo, Reginald F. *Languages and Nationhood: Reflections on Language Situation with Particular Reference to Ghana.* Accra: Sedco Publishing, 1985. 56 p.

Anin, T. E. *Gold in Ghana.* Accra: Selwyn Publishers, 1987. 273 p.

Ayitey, Sackey Albert. *The Politics of Poetry in West Africa.* Ph.D. Dissertation, New York University, 1984. 501 p.

Boahen, Adu A. *Africa under Colonial Domination, 1880-1935.* London: Heinemann; Berkeley, Calif.: University of California Press, 1985. 865 p. Abridged and published in London by J. Cuorey; at Berkeley, Calif.: University of California Press; and in Paris: UNESCO, 1990. 357 p.

Chazan, Naomi. *Development, Underdevelopment, and the State in Ghana.* Boston: African Studies Center, 1982. 41 p.

___, and Timothy M. Shaw. *Coping with Africa's Food Crisis.* Boulder, Colo.:, Lynne Rienner, 1987. 225 p.

Collins, John. *Musicmakers of West Africa.* Washington, D.C.: Three Continents Press, 1985. 177 p.

Dodds, Maggie, ed. *Ghana Talks: Ghana Past and Present.* Washington, D.C.: Three Continents Press, 1976. 241 p.; First published in Accra in 1974 as *History of Ghana--a Series of Lectures.*

Elias, Taslim Olawale. *Ghana and Sierra Leone: The Development of Their Laws and Constitutions.* Vol. 10 of *The British Commonwealth: The Development of Its Laws and Constitutions.* London: Stevens, 1962. 334 p.

Ephson, Isaac S. *Gallery of Gold Coast Celebrities, 1632-1958.* Accra: Ilen Publications, 1969. 3 volumes.

Farrar, Vincent K. "Traditional Akan Architecture and Building Construction: A Technological and Historical Study." Ph.D. Dissertation, University of California, Berkeley, 1988. 224 p.

Horton, J. A. B. *West African Countries and Peoples.* Edinburgh: Edinburgh University Press, 1868; rpt. 1969. 281 p.

Lipschutz, Mark R., and R. Kent Rasmussen. *Dictionary of African Historical Biography.* Chicago: Aldine Publishing Company, 1978. 292 p.

MacDonald, George. *The Gold Coast Past and Present: A Short Description of the Country and Its People.* London: Longman, Green, 1898; rpt. New York: Negro Universities Press, 1969. 352 p.

Macmillan, Allister, comp. *The Red Book of West Africa.* 1st ed. 1920; rpt. London: Frank Cass, 1968. Gold Coast section, pp. 139-228.

Mohammed, S. "Human Rights in Ghana." *West Africa*, 1-7 July 1991, 1066-1068.

Ofosu-Appiah, L. H., ed. *Encyclopedia Africana: Dictionary of African Biography.* Vol. 1: *Ethiopia-Ghana.* Algonac, Mich.: Reference Publications, Inc., 1977. 367 p.

Pedler, Frederick J. *The Lion and the Unicorn in Africa: A History of the Origins of the United Africa Company, 1787-1931.* London: Heinemann Educational, 1974. 343 p.

___. *Main Currents of West African History 1940-1979.* London and New York: Barnes and Noble, 1979. 301 p.

Pellow, Deborah, and Naomo Chazan. *Ghana: Coping with Uncertainty.* Westview Profiles of Contemparary Africa Series. Boulder, Colo.: Westview Press, 1986. 238 p.

Rattray, Robert Sutherland. *A Short Manual of the Gold Coast.* n.p., 1924. 88 p.

Ray, Donald I. *Ghana: Politics, Economics and Society.* Boulder, Colo.: Lynne Rienner, 1986. 160 p.

Redmayne, Paul. *The Gold Coast, Yesterday and Today.* London: Chatto and Windus, 1838. 128 p.

Remy, Mylene. *Ghana Today.* Paris and New York: J. A. Editions and Hippocrene Books, 1977. 256 p.

Reynolds, Edward. *Stand the Storm: A History of the Atlantic Slave Trade.* London and New York: Allison and Busby, c. 1985; rpt. 1989. 182 p.

Royal Institute of International Affairs. *Ghana: A Survey of the Gold Coast on the Eve of Its Independence.* London: RIIA, 1957. 62 p.

Sampson, Magnus J. *Gold Coast Men of Affairs: Past and Present.* Ilfracombe: Stockwell, 1937. 224 p.

Sarfoh, Joseph A., comp. *Population, Urbanization, and Rural Settlement in Ghana: A Bibliographic Survey.* New York: Greenwood, 1987. 124 p.

C. SERIALS

Achimota Review. Achimota, 1927-1937.

Africa. Journal of the International African Institute. London. 1928-.

Africa Contemporary Record: An Annual Survey and Documents. Rex Collings, Holmes and Meier. London. 1968.

Africa Index. Oxford. 1976-.

Africa Report. African-American Institute. Washington, D.C., and New York. 1956-.

Africa: South of the Sahara. Europa Publications. 1970-.

Africa Yearbook and Who's Who. Africa Journal. London. 1977-.

African Abstracts. International African Institute. London. 1950-1972.

African Affairs. Journal of the Royal African Society. London. 1901-.

African Library Journal. Africana Publishing Corporation. New York. 1970-.

African Statistical Review. African Studies Association. Ann Arbor, Mich. 1958-.

African Statistical Yearbook. UNECA. Addis Ababa. 1974-.

Akan Studies Council. Newsletter of the Akan Studies Council of the African Studies Association (United States). Raymond Silverman (editor), Michigan State University. 1988-

Asian and African Studies. Journal of Israel Oriental Society. Jerusalem. 1965-

Bulletin of the Ghana Geographical Association. Paris. 1960-

Canadian Journal of African Studies. Montreal. 1967-

Current Bibliography on African Affairs. Greenwood. New York. 1962-

The Ghana Bar Bulletin. Accra. 1988-.

Ghana Bulletin of Theology. Department of Religion, University of Ghana. Legon. 1964-.

Ghana News. Published by the Ghana Information Service Department, P.O. Box 745, Accra. Copies might be obtained from Embassy of Ghana Information Section, 3512 International Drive, N.W., Washington, D.C. 20008.

Ghana Notes and Queries. Historical Society of Ghana. Legon. 1961- (irregular in the 1980s)

Ghana Who's Who. Bartels. Accra. 1972-.

Ghana Year Book. Ghana Graphic Company. Accra. 1958-.

International African Bibliography. Mansell Publishing Company. New York. 1980-.

International Journal of African Historical Studies. Brookline, Mass. 1968-.

Jeune Afrique. Paris. 1962-.

Joint Acquisitions List of Africana. G. K. Hall. Boston. 1978-.

Journal of African History. Cambridge. 1960-.

Journal of African Studies. Washington, D.C. 1974-.

Journal of Modern African Studies. Cambridge. 1963-.

Journal of Religion in Africa. E. J. Brill. Leiden. 1967-.

Journal of West African Languages. Cambridge. 1964-.

Legon Observer. Legon Society on National Affairs. Legon. 1966-. (irregular in the 1980s)

Okyeame. Ghana Society of Writers. Accra. 1960-.

Research Review. Institute of African Studies, University of Ghana. Legon. 1965-.

Talking Drums. Issue No. 1, 12 September 1983-. Talking Drums Publications, Madav House, 68 Mansfield Road, London NW3 2HY.

Tarikh. Ibadan. 1965-.

Transactions of the Gold Coast and Togoland Historical Society. Achimota. 1952-1957.

Transactions of the Historical Society of Ghana. Legon. 1957-

University of Ghana Law Journal. Legon. 1964-

West Africa. London. 1917-

West African Journal of Archaeology. Ibadan. 1971-

D. GOVERNMENT PUBLICATIONS

Committee of Experts (Constitution) on Proposals for a Draft Constitution of Ghana. *Proposals for a Draft Constitution of Ghana.* Accra: Republic of Ghana, Government Printer, 1991. 328 p.

Ghana. Census Office. *Reports of the 1960 Population Census.* 7 vols. Accra: Ghana Publishing Corp., 1964.

___. *1970 Population Census of Ghana.* 8 vols. Accra: Ghana Publishing Corp., 1972.

___. *1984 Population Census of Ghana, Demographic and Economic Characteristics.* 11 vols. Accra: Statistical Services, 1987.

Ghana. Central Bureau of Statistics. *Statistical Handbook of the Republic of Ghana.* Accra: Government Printing Office, 1967- and irregularly thereafter.

___. *Statistical Year Book.* Accra: Government Printing Office, 1961- and irregularly thereafter.

Ghana. Ministry of Information. *Nkrumah's Deception of Africa.* Accra: State Publishing Corp., 1967. 95 p.; also by Judiciary Committee, U.S. Senate, Washington, D.C.: U.S. Government Printing Office, 1972.

___. *Nkrumah's Subversion of Africa: Documentary Evidence of Nkrumah's Interference in the Affairs of Other African States.* Accra: State Publishing Corp., 1967. 91 p.; also by Judiciary Committee, U.S. Senate, Washington, D.C.: U.S. Government Printing Office, 1972.

___. *Your Health Guide.* Accra: Ministry of Information, 1989-.

Gold Coast Colony. *Correspondence Relating to the National Congress of British West Africa.* Accra: Government Press, 1920. 61 p.

___. *Gold Coast Gazette*, 1872-5 March 1957. Accra: Government Printer.

___. *The Gold Coast Handbook*. Accra: Government Printer, 1923, with several editions thereafter.

___. *Report of the Commission of Enquiry into Disturbances in the Gold Coast*. Andrew Aiken Watson, Chairman. London: HMSO, 1948. 103 p.

Gold Coast Colony. Census Office. *Report of the Census, 1891*. Accra: Government Printer, 1891. 201 p.

___. *Report on the Census for the Year 1901*. London: Waterloo and Sons, 1901. 66 p.

___. *Census of the Population, 1911*. 3 parts. Accra: Government Press, 1912.

___. *Census Report, 1921, for the Gold Coast Colony, Ashanti, the Northern Territories, and the Mandated Area of Togoland*. Accra: Government Press, 1923. 185 p.

___. *The Gold Coast, 1931; a Review of Conditions in the Gold Coast in 1931 as Compared with Those of 1921, Based on Figures and Facts Collected by the Chief Census Officer of 1931, Together with a Historical, Ethnographical, and Sociological Survey of the People of the Country*. A. W. Cardinall, Chief Census Officer. Accra: Government Press, 1932. 265 p.

___. *Appendices Containing Comparative Returns and General Statistics of the 1931 Census*. Accra: Government Press, 1932. 246 p.

___. *Census of Population, 1948: Report and Tables*. London: Published on Behalf of the Government of the Gold Coast by the Crown Agents for the Colonies, 1950. 422 p.

Gold Coast Colony. Public Relations Department. *Achievement in the Gold Coast; Aspects of Development in a British West African Territory.* Accra: Government Printer, 1951. 96 p.

Gold Coast Colony. Survey Department. *Atlas of the Gold Coast.* Accra: Government Press, 1927. 24 maps and charts.

___. *Atlas of the Gold Coast.* 5th ed. Accra: Government Press, 1949.

Government of Ghana. *District Political Authority and Modalities for District Level Elections: Blue Book.* Accra: Government Printer, 1987. Contains information on the structure and responsibilities of district assemblies.

Great Britain. *Commission of Inquiry into Disturbances in the Gold Coast, 1948. Report of.* (Watson Report). London: HMSO, 1948. 103 p.

___. *The Ghana Order in Council, 1957* (Constitution of 1957). London: HMSO, 1957. 47 p.

Great Britain. Colonial Office. *Statement by His Majesty's Government on the Report of the Commission of Enquiry into Disturbances in the Gold Coast, 1948.* London: HMSO, 1948. 14 p.

Volta River Preparatory Commission. *The Volta River Project.* 3 vols. London: HMSO, 1956. Includes bibliographies.

E. ARCHAEOLOGY

Ameyaw, Kwabena. "Kwawu: An Early Akan State." *Ghana Notes and Queries*, 9 (November 1966), 39-45.

Anquandah, James. "The Archaeological Evidence for the Emergence of Akan Civilization." *Tarikh* (Ibadan), 7, 2 (1982), 9-21.

___. *Rediscovering Ghana's Past.* Accra: Sedco Publishing; Harlow, Essex: Longman Group, 1982. 161 p.

Bellis, James Oren. "Archaeology and the Culture History of the Akan of Ghana." Ph.D. Dissertation, Indiana University, 1972. 269 p.

Carter, P. L., and P. J. Carter. "Rock-paintings from Northern Ghana." *Transactions of the Historical Society of Ghana,* 7 (1965), 1-3.

Crossland, L. *Pottery from the Begho-B2 Site, Ghana.* Calgary: University of Calgary Press, 1989. 177 p.

___. "Traditional Textile Industry in Northern Brong Ahafo, Ghana: The Archeological and Contemporary Evidence." *Sankofa,* 1 (1975), 69-73.

Davies, Oliver. "The Neolithic Revolution in Tropical Africa." *Transactions of the Historical Society of Ghana,* 4, 2 (1960), 14-20.

___. *Archaeology in Ghana: Papers.* Edinburgh: Nelson and Sons for the University College of Ghana, 1961. 45 p.

___. *Archaeology in the Volta Basin.* Legon: Department of Archaeology, University of Ghana, 1969. 100 p.

___. *Excavations at Sekondi.* Accra: Ghana Universities Press, 1970. 100 p.

___. *The Archaeology of the Flooded Volta Basin.* Occasional Papers in Archaeology, 1. Legon: Department of Archaeology and Volta Basin Research Project, University of Ghana, 1971. 34 p.

___. "The Ntereso Culture in Ghana." In *West African Culture Dynamics: Archaeological and Historical Perspectives,* B. K.

Swartz Jr., and Raymond E. Dumett, eds. The Hague, Paris, and New York: Mouton, 1980, 205-225.

___. *West Africa before the Europeans: Archaeology and Prehistory.* Methuen Handbooks of Archaeology. London: Methuen, 1967. 364 p.

Effah-Gyamfi, E. "Aspects of the Archaeology and Oral Traditions of the Bono State." *Transactions of the Historical Society of Ghana*, 15, 2 (Dec. 1974), 217-227.

___. "Bono Manso: An Archaeological Investigation into Early Akan Urbanism." Ph.D. Dissertation, Calgary, 1985. 229 p.

Flight, Colin. "The Kintampo Culture and Its Place in the Economic Prehistory of West Africa." In *West African Culture Dynamics: Archaeological and Historical Perspectives*, B. K. Swartz Jr., and Raymond E. Dummett, eds. The Hague, Paris, and New York: Mouton, 1980, 91-100.

Kense, F. J. "Daboya: A Gonja Frontier." Ph.D. Dissertation, Calgary University, 1981.

Kiyaga-Mulindwa, David. "Archaeological and Historical Research in the Birim Valley." *Sankofa*, 2 (1976), 90-91.

___. "The Earthworks of the Birim Valley, Southern Ghana." Ph.D. Dissertation, Johns Hopkins University, 1978.

___. "Social and Demographic Changes in the Birim Valley, Southern Ghana, ca. 1450 to ca. 1800." *The Journal of African History* (London), 23, 1 (1982), 63-82.

Kropp-Dakuba, M. E. "Linguistic Prehistoric and Historical Reconstruction of the Ga-Dangbe Migration." *Transactions of the Historical Society of Ghana*, 13, 1 (1972), 87-111.

___. "On the Linguistic Geography of the Area of Ancient Begho." *Mitteilungen der Basler Afrika Bibliographien*, 14 (1976), 63-91.

Nygaard, Signe, and M. R. Talbot. "First Dates from Coastal Sites Near Kpone, Ghana." *Nyame Akuma* (Legon), 11 (1977), 29-30.

___. "Interim Report on Excavation at Asokrochona, Ghana." *West Africa Journal of Archeology* (Ibadan), 6 (1976), 13-19.

Ozanne, P. C. "Ghana." In *The Iron Age in Africa*, ed. P. L. Shinnie. London: Oxford University Press, 1971.

___. "Notes on the Early Historic Archeology of Accra." *Transactions of the Historical Society of Ghana*, 6 (1962), 51-70.

Posnansky, Merrick. "The Archaeological Foundations of the History of Ghana." In *Proceedings of the Seminar on Ghanian Historiography and Historical Research*, ed. J. O. Hunwick. Legon: University of Ghana, 1977. 290 p.

___. Archaeology and the Origins of the Akan Society in Ghana." In *Problems in Economic and Social Archaeology*, ed. G. de Sieveking, I. M. Longworth, and E. K. Wilson, London: Duckworth, 1977, 49-59.

Shaw, C. Thurstan. "Archaeology in the Gold Coast." *African Studies*, 2, 3 (1943), 139-147.

___. *Excavation at Dawu: Report on an Excavation in a Mound at Dawu, Akuapim, Ghana*. London: Nelson for the University of Ghana, 1961. 124 p.

___. "Excavations at Bosumpra Cave, Abetifi." *Prehistoric Society Proceedings* (London: Nelson), 10 (1944), 1-67.

Shinnie, P. L., and P. C. Ozanne. "Excavations at Yendi Dabari." *Transactions of the Historical Society of Ghana.* 6 (1962) 87-118.

Sutton, J. E. G. "Archaeology in West Africa: A Review of Recent Work and a Further List of Radiocarbon Dates." *Journal of African History,* 23, 3 (1982), 291-313.

Swartz, B. K., Jr. "An Analysis and Evaluation of the Yapei Pebble Tool Industry, Ghana." *The International Journal of African Historical Studies* (Boston), 5, 2 (1972), 265-270.

___. "A Stratified Succession of Stone Age Assemblies at Hohoe, Ghana." *West African Journal of Archaeology,* 4 (1974), 57-81.

Wilks, Ivor. "Land, Labour, Capital and the Forest Kingdom of Asante." In M. Rowland and J. Friedmand, eds., *The Evolution of Social Systems.* London: Duckworth, and Pittsburgh: University of Pittsburgh Press, 1977, 487-534.

___. "Portuguese, Wangara and Akan in the Fifteenth and Sixteenth Centuries: I. The Matter of Bitu." *Journal of African History,* 23 (1982), 333-349.

___. "Portuguese, Wangara and Akan in the Fifteenth and Sixteenth Centuries: II. The Struggle for Trade." *Journal of African History,* 23 (1982), 463-472.

York, R. N. *Archaeology in the Volta Basin, 1963-1966.* Legon: University of Ghana, 1967. 45 p.

___. "Excavations at Bui: A Preliminary Report." *Bulletin of the Institute of African Studies* (Legon), 1, 2 (1965), 36-39.

F. GENERAL HISTORY

Agbodeka, Francis. *Ghana in the Twentieth Century.* Accra: Ghana
Universities Press, 1972. 152 p.

Arhin, Kwame. *The Expansion of Cocoa Production in Ghana: The
Working Conditions of Migrant Cocoa Farmers in the Central
and Western Regions.* Legon: Institute of African Studies,
1985. 137 p.

___. *Traditional Rule in Ghana: Past and Present.* Accra: Sedco
Publishing, 1985. 163 p.

___. *West African Trade in Ghana in the Nineteenth and Twentieth
Centuries.* London: Longman, 1979. 146 p.

Boahen, Albert Adu. *Evolution and Change in the Nineteenth and
Twentieth Centuries.* London and New York: Longmans,
1975. 261 p. Paperback, 1979.

___. *Topics in West African History.* London and New York:
Longman, 1966. 174 p. 2nd. edition, with J. A. Ade Ajayi
and Michael Tidy. London and New York: Longman, 1986.
202 p.

Buah, F. K. *A History of Ghana.* London: Macmillan, 1980. 229 p.

Chazan, Noani. "Ghanaian Political Studies in Transition: A
Reflection on Some Recent Contributions." *Development and
Change*, July 1978, 479-503.

Claridge, William Walton. *A History of the Gold Coast and Ashanti
from the Earliest Times to the Commencement of the Twentieth
Century.* London: J. Murray, 1915. 649 p. and 638 p.; rpt.
London: Frank Cass, 1964. 577 p. and 580 p.

Cornevin, Robert. *Histoire du Togo.* 2nd ed. Paris: Berger-Levrault,
1969. 554 p.

Curtin, Philip D. *The Atlantic Slave Trade: A Census.* Madison, Wis.: University of Wisconsin Press, 1969. 338 p.

Decalo, Samuel. *Historical Dictionary of Togo.* Metuchen, N.J., and London: Scarecrow Press, 1976. 243 p.

Dickson, Kwamina B. *A Historical Geography of Ghana.* Cambridge: Cambridge University Press, 1969. 379 p. Paperback, 1971.

Ellis, Alfred Burdon. *A History of the Gold Coast of West Africa.* London: Chapman and Hall, 1893. 400 p.; rpt. New York: Negro Universities Press, 1969; rpt. Totowa, N.J.: Rowman and Littlefield, 1971.

Fage, John Donnelly. *Ghana: A Historical Interpretation.* Madison, Wis.: University of Wisconsin Press, 1959. 122p.

Flint, John E. *Nigeria and Ghana.* Englewood Cliffs, N.J.: Prentice-Hall, 1966. 176 p.

Forde, Daryll, and P. M. Kaberry, eds. *West African Kingdoms in the Nineteenth Century.* Oxford: Oxford University Press, 1967. 289 p.

Foster, Philip, and Aristide R. Zolberg, eds. *Ghana and the Ivory Coast.* Chicago: University of Chicago Press, 1971. 303 p.

Freeman-Grenville, G. S. P. *Chronology of African History.* London: Oxford University Press, 1973. 312 p.

Killingray, David. *Africa and the Second World War.* Basingstoke: Macmillan, 1986. 283 p.

McFarland, Daniel M. *Historical Dictionary of Ghana.* Metuchen, N.J., and London: Scarecrow Press, First Edition, 1985. 296 p.

___. *Historical Dictionary of Upper Volta.* Metuchen, N.J., and London: Scarecrow Press, 1978. 217 p.

Rawley, James A. *The Transatlantic Slave Trade; A History.* New York: W. W. Norton, 1981. 452 p.

Reindorf, Carl Christian. *A History of the Gold Coast.* London and New York: Longman, Green, 1935. 241 p.; in several editions to 1956.

___. *History of the Gold Coast and Asante, Based on Traditions and Historical Facts, Comprising a Period of More Than Three Centuries from about 1500 to 1860.* Basel: Basel Mission, 1895. 384 p.; 2nd ed. Basel: Basel Mission Book Depot, 1951; Accra: Ghana Universities Press, 1966. 349 p.

Wolfson, Freda. *Pageant of Ghana.* West African History Series. London: Oxford University Press, 1958. 266 p.

G. HISTORY BEFORE 1840

Akinjogbin, I. A. "Archibald Dalzel: Slave Trader and Historian of Dahomey." *Journal of African History*, 7, 1 (1966), 67-78. Dalzel was Governor at Cape Coast from March 1792 for ten years.

Bartels, Francis L. "Philip Quaque, 1741-1816." *Transactions of the Gold Coast and Togoland Historical Society* (Achimota), 1 (1955), 153-177.

Curtin, Philip D., ed. *Africa Remembered: Narratives by West Africans from the Era of the Slave Trade.* Madison, Wis.: University of Wisconsin Press, 1967. 363 p.

___. *The Image of Africa; British Ideas and Action, 1780-1850.* Madison, Wis.: University of Wisconsin Press, 1965. 526 p.

Daaku, Kwame Yeboa. "The European Traders and the Coastal States, 1630-1720." *Transactions of the Historical Society of Ghana*, 8 (1965), 11-23.

___. "John Konny: The Last Prussian Negro Prince." *Tarikh* (Ibadan), 1, 4 (1967), 55-64.

Davis, K. G. *The Royal African Company.* London: Longmans, 1956. 396 p.; New York: Atheneum, 1970.

Fage, John Donnelly. "The Administration of George Maclean on the Gold Coast, 1830-44." *Transactions of the Gold Coast and Togoland Historical Society of Ghana* (Achimota), 1, 4 (1954), 104-120.

___. "A New Check List of the Forts and Castles of Ghana." *Transactions of the Historical Society of Ghana* (Legon), 4, 1 (1959), 57-67.

Feinberg, Harvey Michael. "Elmina Town in the Eighteenth Century." Paper read at the African Studies Association (USA) Conference, at Los Angeles, 1984.

___. "New Data on European Mortality in West Africa: The Dutch on the Gold Coast, 1719-1760." *Journal of African History*, 15, 3 (1974), 357-371.

___. "There Was an Elmina Note, But...." *The International Journal of African Historical Studies* (Boston), 9, 4 (1976), 618-630.

Furley, John T. "Notes on Some Portuguese Governors of the Captaincy Da Mina." *Transactions of the Historical Society of Ghana*, 3, 3 (1958), 194-214.

___. "Provisional List of some Portuguese Governors of the Captaincy of Da Mina." *Transactions of the Gold Coast and Togoland Historical Society* (Achimota), 2, 2 (1956), 54-62.

Grove, Jean M., and A. M. Johansen. "The Historical Geography of the Volta Delta during the Period of Danish Influence." *Bulletin d'Institut Français d'Afrique Noire* (Dakar), 30, 4 (Oct. 1968), 1374-1421.

Kea, Ray A. *Settlements, Trade, and Polities in the Seventeenth-Century Gold Coast.* Johns Hopkins Studies in Atlantic History and Culture. Baltimore: Johns Hopkins University Press, 1982. 475 p.

Lawrence, Arnold Walter. *Fortified Trade-posts: The English in West Africa, 1645-1822.* London: Cape, 1969. 237 p.

___. *Trade Castles and Forts of West Africa.* London: Cape, 1963. 390 p.; Stanford, Calif.: Stanford University Press, 1964.

Martin, Eveline Christiana. *The British West African Settlements 1750-1821: A Study in Local Administration.* Imperial Studies Monographs, 2. London: Longman, Green, 1927; rpt. Westport, Conn.: Negro Universities Press, 1970. 186 p.

Meredith, Henry. *An Account of the Gold Coast of Africa, with a Brief History of the African Company.* London: Longman, Hurst, Rees, Orme, and Brown, 1812. 264 p.; rpt. Travels and Narratives series, Cass Library of African Studies, 20. London: Cass, 1967. Meredith was a member of the Cape Coast Council and Governor of Winneba Fort who was killed in 1812.

Norregaard, Georg. *Danish Settlements in West Africa, 1658-1850.* Trans. Sigurd Mammen. Boston: Boston University Press, 1966. 287 p.

Owusu-Ansah, David. "The State and Islamization in 19th Century Africa: Buganda Absolutism versus Asante Constitutionalism." *Journal of the Institute of Muslim Minority Affairs*, 8, 1 (1987), 132-143.

Priestley, Margaret. "The Ashanti Question and the British: Eighteenth-Century Origins." *Journal of African History*, 2, 1 (1961), 35-59.

___. "Philip Quaque of Cape Coast." In *Africa Remembered; Narratives by West Africans from the Era of the Slave Trade,* ed. by Philip D. Curtin. Madison, Wis.: University of Wisconsin Press, 1967, 99-139.

___. "Richard Brew: an Eighteenth-Century Trader at Anomabu. *Transactions of the Historical Society of Ghana*, 4 (1959), 29-46.

___. *West African Trade and Coast Society: A Family Study.* London: Oxford University Press, 1969. 207 p.

Stahl, Ann Brower. "The Kintampo Culture: Subsistence and Settlement in Ghana during the Mid-Second Millennium B.C." Ph.D. Dissertation, University of California at Berkeley, 1985, 334 p.

Van Dantzig, Albert, comp. and trans. *The Dutch and the Guinea Coast 1674-1743: A Collection of Documents from the General State Archive at the Hague.* Accra: Ghana Academy of Arts and Sciences, 1978. 375 p.

___. *Dutch Documents Relating to the Gold Coast and the Slave Coast, 1680-1740.* 2 vols. Legon: University of Ghana, 1971.

___. *Forts and Castles of Ghana.* Accra: Sedco, 1980. 96 p.

___. *Les Hollandais sur la Côte de Guinée à l'époque de l'essor de l'Ashanti et du Dahomey, 1680-1740.* Paris: Société Française d'Histoire d'Outre-Mer, 1980. 329 p.

Varley, William J. "The Castles and Forts of the Gold Coast." *Transactions of the Gold Coast and Togoland Historical Society* (Achimota), 1, 1 (1952), 1-17.

Vogt, John L. "The Early Sao Tome-Principe Slave Trade with Mina, 1500-1540." *The International Journal of African Historical Studies* 6, 3 (1973), 453-467.

___. *Portuguese Rule on the Gold Coast 1469-1682*. Athens, Ga.: University of Georgia Press, 1979. 266 p.

Wartemberg, J. Sylvanus. *Sao Jorge d'Elmina, Premier West African Settlement: Its Traditions and Customs*. Ilfracombe: Stockwell, 1951. 166 p.

Wilks, Ivor. "The Mossi and Akan States, 1500-1800." In *History of West Africa*, vol. 1, ed. J. F. A. Ajayi and Michael Crowder. New York: Columbia University Press, 1972, pp. 344-386.

Yarak, Larry W. *Asante and the Dutch, 1744-1873*. Oxford and New York: Oxford University Press, 1990. 316 p.

H. HISTORY, 1840-1956:
COLONIALISM

Adams, C. D. "Activities of Danish Botanists in Guinea, 1783-1850." *Transactions of the Historical Society of Ghana*, 3, 1 (1957), 30-46.

Adjaye, Joseph Emmanuel Kwesi. *Diplomacy and Diplomats in Nineteenth Century Asante*. New York and London: University Press of America, 1984. 310 p.

Agbodeka, Francis. *African Politics and British Policy in the Gold Coast, 1868-1900: A Study in the Forms and Force of Protest*. Legon History Series. London: Longman; Evanston, Ill.: Northwestern University Press, 1971. 206 p.

___. "The Fanti Confederacy, 1865-69, an Enquiry into the Origins, Nature and Extent of an Early West African Protest Movement." *Transactions of the Historical Society of Ghana*, 7 (1964), 82-123.

___. "Nationalism in the Gold Coast, 1900-45." *Tarikh* (Ibadan), 3, 4 (1971), 22-32.

Ahuma, S. R. B. *The Gold Coast Nation and National Consciousness.* With an introduction by J. C. de Graft-Johnson. 2nd ed. London: Frank Cass, 1971. 63 p.

Allman, Jean M. "The Youngmen and the Porcupine: Class, Nationalism, and Asante's Struggle for Self-Determination, 1954-1957." *Journal of African History*, 31 (1990), 263-279.

___ *The Quills of the Porcupine: Asante Nationalism in an Emergent Ghana.* Madison, Wis.: University of Wisconsin Press, 1993. 263 p.

___, and Richard Rathbone. "The Youngmen and the Porcupine: A Discussion." *Journal of African History*, 32 (1991) 333-338.

Appiah, Joseph Yaw. "Trade, European Influence, and the Colonial Transformation in Ghana, 1400-1929." Ph.D. Dissertation, State University of New York at Albany, 1989. 213 p.

Apter, David Ernest. *Ghana in Transition.* 2nd rev. ed., Princeton, N.J.: Princeton University Press, 1972. 434 p.

Arden-Clarke, Charles. "Gold Coast into Ghana: Some Problems of Transition." *International Affairs* (Oxford), 34 (Jan. 1958), 49-56. Arden-Clarke was the last Governor of the Gold Coast.

Arhin, Kwame, ed. *The Papers of George Ekem Ferguson: A Fanti Official of the Government of the Gold Coast, 1890-1897.* African Social Research Documents, 7. Leiden: Afrika-Studiecentrum; Cambridge: African Studies Centre, 1974. 180 p.

Armitage, Cecil Hamilton, and A. F. Montanaro. *The Ashanti Campaign of 1900.* London: Sands, 1901. 278 p. Armitage was an officer in the campaign and later Chief Commissioner, Northern Territories.

Atz, James R. "The British Colonial Police Service: A Study of Its Organization and Its Operations in Six British African

Colonies, 1937-1966." Ph.D. Dissertation, Temple University, 1988. 328 p.

Austin, Dennis. "The Working Committee of the United Gold Coast Convention." *Journal of African History*, 2, 2 (1961), 273-297.

Baden-Powell, Robert S. *The Downfall of Prempeh: A Diary of Life with the Native Levy in Ashanti, 1895-96.* London: Methuen, 1896. 198 p.

Baesjou, Rene, ed. *An Asante Embassy on the Gold Coast: The Mission of Akyempon Yaw to Elmina, 1869-1872.* African Social Research Documents, 11. Leiden: Afrika-Studiecentrum; Cambridge: African Studies Centre, 1979. 250 p.

Bening, Bagulo Raymond. "The Definition of the International Boundaries of Northern Ghana, 1888-1904." *Transactions of the Historical Society of Ghana*, 14, 2 (Dec. 1973), 229-261.

___. "Internal Colonial Boundary Problems of the Gold Coast, 1907-1951." *International Journal of African Historical Studies* (Boston), 17, 1 (1984), 81-99.

Biss, Harold C. J. *The Relief of Kumasi.* London: Methuen's Colonial Library, 1901. 315 p.

Bittle, William Elmer, and Gilbert Geis. *The Longest Way Home: Chief Alfred C. Sam's Back to Africa Movement.* Detroit: Wayne State University Press, 1964. 229 p.

Blake, John W. *European Beginnings in West Africa, 1454-1578: A Survey of the First Century of White Enterprise in West Africa.* London and New York: Longmans, Green, 1937. 212 p.; Westport, Conn.: Greenwood Press, 1972.

___. *Europeans in West Africa, 1450-1560.* 2 vols. Vol. 1: *Portuguese Discoveries*; Vol. 2: *English Voyages.* London: Hakluyt Society, 1942; Kraus Reprint, 1967.

___. *West Africa: Quest for God and Gold, 1454-1578.* Totowa, N.J.: Rowman and Littlefield; London: Curzon Press, 1977. 246 p.

Bly, Viola Mattavous. "The British Presence and Its Influence on Indigenous Gold Coast Economics, 1865-1902." Ph.D. Dissertation, New York University, 1982. 315 p.

Boahen, Albert Adu. "Politics in Ghana, 1800-1874." In *History of West Africa*, vol. 2, ed. by J. F. A. Ajayi and Michael Crowder. New York: Columbia University Press, 1973. 167-261.

___. "The Roots of Ghanaian Nationalism." *Journal of African History*, 5, 1 (1964), 127-132.

Bonne, Nii Kwabena, III. *Milestones in the History of the Gold Coast: An Autobiography of Nii Kwabena Bonne III.* London: Diplomatist Publications, 1953. 92 p.

Bourret, Florence Mabel. *Ghana: The Road to Independence, 1919-1957.* Rev. ed. Stanford, Calif.: Hoover Institution Press; London: Oxford University Press, 1960. 246 p.

___. *The Gold Coast: A Survey of the Gold Coast and British Togoland, 1919-1951.* Stanford, Calif.: Hoover Institution Press; London: Oxford University Press, 1952. 248 p.

Boyle, Frederick. *Through Fanteeland to Coomassie: A Diary of the Ashantee Expedition.* London: Chapman and Hall, 1874. 411 p.

Brackenbury, Henry. *The Ashanti War, a Narrative.* 2 vols. Edinburgh and London: William Blackwood, 1874, 1884, 1914; rpt. London: Frank Cass, 1968.

Brand, Richard Robert. "A Geographical Interpretation of the European Influence on Accra, Ghana, Since 1877." Ph.D. Dissertation, Columbia University, 1972. 393 p.

Burns, Alan Cuthbert. *Colonial Civil Servant.* London: Allen and Unwin, 1949. 339 p. Burns was Governor, 1941-1947.

Bushoven, Cornelius. "National Law and National Courts in the Political System of the Gold Coast and Ghana, 1874-1966." Ph.D. Dissertation, Duke University, 1971. 305 p.

Cardinall, Allan Wolsey. *In Ashanti and Beyond: The Record of a Resident Magistrate's Many Years in Tropical Africa.* London: Seely Service, 1927; Westport, Conn.: Negro Universities Press, 1970. 288 p.

___. "The Story of the German Occupation of Togoland." *The Gold Coast Review* (Accra), 2, 2 (1926); 3, 1 (1927).

Clifford, Hugh Charles. *The Gold Coast Regiment in the East African Campaign.* London: J. Murray, 1920. 306 p. Clifford was Governor from 1912 to 1919.

Cocking, Roger. "Competition for Traditional Office on the Part of the Western Educated Elite in the Town of Cape Coast, Ghana, during the Colonial Period: The Case of Tufohen Coker." Paper presented at the African Studies Association (USA) Conference, at Los Angeles, 1984.

Coombs, Douglas. *The Gold Coast, Britain and the Netherlands, 1850-1874.* London: Oxford University Press, 1963. 160 p.

Crooks, John Joseph, ed. *Records Relating to the Gold Coast Settlements from 1750 to 1874.* Dublin: Browne and Nolan, 1923; rpt. London: Frank Cass, 1973. 557 p.

Crowther, Francis. *Notes for the Guidance of District Commissioners, Gold Coast Colony.* Accra: Government Printer, 1916. 62 p. Crowther was Secretary of Native Affairs.

Danquah, Joseph Boakye. "Historical Significance of the Bond of 1844." *Transactions of the Historical Society of Ghana*, 3 (1957), 3-29.

___. *Liberty of the Subject: A Monograph on the Gold Coast Cocoa Hold-Up and Boycott of Foreign Goods (1937-38)*. Kibi, Gold Coast: George Boakie, 1938. 63 p.

Edsman, Bjorn M. *Lawyers in Gold Coast Politics, c. 1900-1945: From Mensah Sarbah to J. B. Danquah*. Acta Universitatis Upsaliensia, 111. Uppsala: University of Uppsala, 1979. 263 p.

Ekwelie, Sylvanus Ajana. "The Press in Gold Coast Nationalism, 1890-1957." Ph.D Dissertation, University of Wisconsin, 1971. 335 p.

Eluwa, G. I. C. "The National Congress of British West Africa." *Tarikh* (Ibadan), 3, 4 (1971), 12-21.

Ferguson, Phyllis, and Ivor Wilks. "Chiefs, Constitutions and the British in Northern Ghana." In *West African Chiefs: Their Changing Status under Colonial Rule and Independence*, ed. Michael Crowder and Obaro Ikime. New York: Africana Publishing Corp.; Ile Ife, Nigeria: University of Ife Press, 1970, 326-369.

Frimpong, Kofi. "The Joint Provincial Council of Paramount Chiefs and the Politics of Independence, 1946-58." *Transactions of the Historical Society of Ghana*, 14, 1 (June 1973), 79-91.

Fyfe, Christopher. *Africanus Horton: West African Scientist and Patriot, 1835-1883*. New York: Oxford University Press, 1972. 169 p.

Gailey, Harry A. *Clifford: Imperial Proconsul*. Malabar, Fla.: Krieger Publishing, 1982. 215 p. Biography of Hugh Clifford.

Gann, Lewis Henry, and Peter Duignan. *The Rulers of British Africa, 1870-1914*. Stanford, Calif.: Hoover Institution Press, 1978. 406 p.

Gidea, Roy Y. *Nationalism and Indirect Rule in the Gold Coast: 1900-1950*. New York: William-Frederick Press, 1964. 34 p.

Gillespie, W. H. *The Gold Coast Police, 1844-1938*. Accra: Government Printer, 1955. 89 p.

Gorges, Edmund Howard. *The Great War in West Africa*. London: Hutchinson, 1930. 284 p.

Griffith, William Brandford, Jr. *The Far Horizon: Portrait of a Colonial Judge*. Ilfracombe, Devon: Arthur H. Stockwell, 1951. 319 p.

Grove, Eric. "The First Shots of the Great War: The Anglo-French Conquest of Togo, 1914." *The Army Quarterly and Defense Journal*, 106, 3 (July 1976), 308-323.

Guggisberg, Mrs. Decima Moore, and Major Frederick Gordon. *We Two in West Africa*. London: W. Heinemann; New York: Charles Scribner, 1909. 368 p.

Guyer, David. *Ghana and the Ivory Coast: The Impact of Colonialism in an African Setting*. New York: Exposition Press, 1970. 111 p.

Hailey, William Malcolm. *An African Survey*. London, New York, Toronto: Oxford University Press, 1938, 1957. 1,676 p.

___. *Native Administration and Political Development in British Tropical Africa*. Nendeln, Liechtenstein: Kraus Reprint, 1979. 352 p.

Hatch, John. *The History of Britain in Africa: From the Fifteenth Century to the Present*. New York: Praeger, 1969. 320 p.

Hayford, Casely. *Gold Coast Native Institutions, with Thoughts upon a Healthy Imperial Policy for the Gold Coast and Ashanti.* London: Sweet and Maxwell, 1903. 418 p., rpt. London: Frank Cass, 1970.

Henige, David P. *Colonial Governors from the Fifteenth Century to the Present, a Comprehensive List.* Madison, Wis.: University of Wisconsin Press, 1970. 461 p.

Henty, George Alfred. *The March to Coomassie.* London: Tinsley, 1874. 470 p.

Hetherington, Penelope. *British Paternalism and Africa, 1920-1940.* Totowa, N.J.: Frank Cass, 1978. 196 p.

Hodgson, Mary Alice. *The Siege of Kumassi.* London: C. Arthur Pearson; New York: Longmans, Green, 1901. 365 p. Mary Hodgson was the wife of Governor Frederic Mitchell Hodgson.

Holbrook, Wendell Patrick. "British Propaganda and the Mobilization of the Gold Coast War Effort, 1939-1945." *Journal of African History*, 26 (1986), 315-339.

Horton, James Africanus Beale. *Letters on the Political Condition of the Gold Coast since the Exchange of Territory between the English and Dutch Governments on January 1, 1868.* London: W. J. Johnson, 1870; rpt. London: Frank Cass, 1970. 179 p.

Howard, Rhoda. *Colonialism and Underdevelopment in Ghana.* New York: Holmes and Meier, Africana Publishing Co., 1978. 244 p.

Iliasu, A. A. "The Establishment of British Administration in Mamprugu, 1898-1937." *Transactions of the Historical Society of Ghana*, 16, 1 (June 1975), 1-28.

Jahoda, Gustav. *White Man: A Study of the Attitudes of Africans to Europeans in Ghana before Independence.* London and New York: Oxford University Press, 1961. 144 p.

Johnson, Marion. "M. Bonnat on the Volta." *Ghana Notes and Queries*, 10 (Dec. 1968), 5-17.

___., comp. "Salaga Papers." 2 vols. Legon: Institute of African Studies, University of Ghana, 1966. Mimeographed.

___. "The Slaves of Salaga." *Journal of African History*, 27 (1986), 241-362.

Johnson, Terence J. "Protest, Tradition and Change: An Analysis of Southern Gold Coast Riots, 1890-1920." *Economy and Society* (Oxford), 1, 2 (1972), 164-193.

Jones, Adam. "Four Years in Asante: One Source or Several?" *History in Africa*, 18 (1991), 173-203.

Justesen, O. "The Danish Settlements on the Gold Coast in the Nineteenth Century." *Scandinavian Journal of History*, 4, 1, (1979), 3-34.

Killingray, David. "The Colonial Army in the Gold Coast: Official Policy and Local Response, 1890-1947." Ph.D. Dissertation, London University, 1982.

___. "Military and Labour Recruitment in the Gold Coast during the Second World War." *Journal of African History*, 23, 1 (1982), 83-95.

___. *The Mutiny of the West African.* Oxford: Oxford University Press, 1983. 221 p.

___, and David Anderson, eds. *Policing the Empire: Government, Authority, and Control, 1830-1940.* Manchester (UK) and New York: Manchester University Press and St. Martin's Press, 1991. 260 p.

Kilson, Martin. "The National Congress of British West Africa, 1918-1935." In *Protest and Power in Black Africa*, ed. Robert I.

Rotberg and Ali A. Mazrui. New York: Oxford University Press, 1970, 571-588.

Kimble, David B. *A Political History of Ghana: The Rise of Gold Coast Nationalism, 1850-1928*. Oxford: Clarendon Press, 1963. 587 p.

Knoll, Arthur J. *Togo under Imperial Germany, 1884-1914: A Case Study in Colonial Rule*. African Colonial Studies. Stanford, Calif.: Hoover Institution Press, 1978. 240 p.

Kuklick, Henrika. *The Imperial Bureaucrat: The Colonial Administrative Service in the Gold Coast, 1920-1939*. African Colonial Studies. Stanford, Calif.: Hoover Institution Press, 1979. 225 p.

Lucas, Charles Prestwood. *The Gold Coast and the War*. London: Oxford University Press, 1920. 56 p.

Manns, Andrienne Lynette. "The Role of Ex-Servicemen in Ghana's Independence Movement." Ph.D. Dissertation, Johns Hopkins University, 1984. 304 p.

Mbaeyi, Paul Mmegha. *British Military and Naval Forces in West African History, 1807-1874*. New York: NOK Publishers, 1978. 263 p.

McCarthy, Mary. *Social Change and the Growth of British Power in the Gold Coast: The Fante States, 1807-1874*. Lanham, Md.: University Press of America, 1983. 208 p.

McSheffrey, Gerald M. "Slavery, Indentured Servitude, Legitimate Trade and the Impact of Abolition in the Gold Coast, 1874-1901: A Reappraisal." *Journal of African History* (Cambridge), 24, 3 (1983), 349-368.

Metcalfe, George Edgar. *Great Britain and Ghana: Documents of Ghana History, 1807-1957*. London and Edinburgh: Thomas

Nelson and Sons on behalf of the University of Ghana, 1964. 779 p.

___. *Maclean of the Gold Coast: The Life and Times of George Maclean, 1801-1847.* West African History Series. London: Oxford University Press, 1962. 344 p.

Moberly, F. J. *History of the Great War, Miltary Operations in Togo and the Cameroons, 1914-18.* London: HMSO, 1931. 469 p.

Newbury, Colin W. *British Policy Towards West Africa: Selected Documents, 1786-1914.* 2 vols., *1786-1874* and *1875-1914.* London: Oxford University Press, 1965, 1971. 656 p. and 680 p.

Nikoi, Amon. "Indirect Rule and Government in the Gold Coast Colony, 1844-1954." Ph.D. Dissertation, Harvard University, 1956. 325 p.

Okonkwo, Rina. *Heroes of West African Nationalism.* Enugu, Nigeria: Delta Publishers, 1985. 128 p.

Olorunfemi, A. "The Contest for Salaga: Anglo German Conflict in the Gold Coast Hinterland." *Journal of African Studies,* 11, 1 (Spring 1984), 15-24.

Olusanya, G. O. *The West African Students' Union and the Politics of Decolonization, 1925-1958.* Ibadan: Daystar Press, 1982. 148 p.

Omosini, Olufemi. "The Gold Coast Land Question, 1894-1900: Some Issues Raised on West Africa's Economic Development." *The International Journal of African Historical Studies* (Boston), 5, 3 (1972), 453-469.

Padmore, George. *The Gold Coast Revolution: The Struggle of an African People from Slavery to Freedom.* London: D. Dobson, 1953. 272 p.

Patterson, K. David. *Health in Colonial Ghana: Disease, Medicine, and Socio-Economic Change, 1900-1955.* Los Angeles: Crossroads Press, 1981. 189 p.

___. "The Influenza Epidemic of 1918-19 in the Gold Coast." *Journal of African History* (Cambridge), 24, 4 (1983), 485-502.

Pearce, R. D. *The Turning Point in Africa: British Colonial Policy, 1938-48.* London: Frank Cass, 1982. 223 p.

Person, Yves. *Samori: une révolution Dyula.* 3 vols. Mémoires de l'Institut Fondamental d'Afrique Noire. Dakar: IFAN, 1968-1975. 2,377 p.

Priestley, Margaret. "The Gold Coast Select Committee on Estimates: 1913-1950." *The International Journal of African Historical Studies,* 4 (1973), 543-564.

Ramseyer, Friedrich August. *Dark and Stormy Days at Kumasi.* London: S. W. Partridge, 1901. 240 p.

___, and Johannes Kuhne. *Four Years in Ashantee.* London: J. Nisbet; New York: R. Carter, 1875. 320 p.

___, and Paul Steiner. *Four Years' Captivity in Ashanti.* London: S. W. Partridge, 1901. 119 p.

Reade, William Winwood. *The African Sketchbook.* London: Smith, Elder. 2 volumes.

___. *The Story of the Ashantee Campaign.* London: Smith, Elder, 1874. 433 p.

Ricketts, Henry J. *Narrative of the Ashantee War.* London: Simkin and Marshall, 1831, 221 p.

Rohdie, Samuel. "The Gold Coast Aborigines Abroad." *Journal of African History,* 6, 3 (1965), 389-411.

Rooney, David. *Sir Charles Arden-Clarke.* London: Rex Collings; Melbourne, Fla.: Krieger, 1982. 236 p. Biography of the last Governor of the Gold Coast.

Rubens-Rathbone, R. J. A. "The Transfer of Power in Ghana, 1945-1957." Ph.D. Dissertation, University of London, 1968. 416 p.

Saaka, Yakubu. "The Myth and Reality of Politics in Ghana: The Legacy of Kwame Nkrumah." Paper presented at the African Studies Association Conference (USA), at Los Angeles, 1984.

Sampson, Magnus J. "George Eken Ferguson of Anomabu." *Transactions of the Gold Coast and Togoland Historical Society* (Achimota), 2, 1 (1956), 30-45.

___. *Gold Coast Men of Affairs: Past and Present.* Ilfracombe: Stockwell, 1937; rpt. London: Dawsons, 1969. 224 p.

Shaloff, Stanley. "The Cape Coast Asafo Company Riot of 1932." *International Journal of African Historical Studies* (Boston), 7, 4 (1974), 591-607.

___. "Press Controls and Sedition Proceedings in the Gold Coast, 1933-39." *African Affairs* (London), 71, 284 (July 1972), 241-263.

Silver, Jim. "The Failure of European Mining Companies in the Nineteenth-Century Gold Coast." *Journal of African History*, 22, 4 (1981), 511-530.

Simensen, Jarle. "The Asafo of Kwahu, Ghana: A Mass Movement for Local Reform under Colonial Rule." *The International Journal of African Historical Studies*, 8, 3 (1975), 383-406.

Spitzer, Leo, and La Ray Denzer. "I.T.A. Wallace-Johnson and the West African Youth League." *The International Journal of African Historical Studies*, 6, 3 (1973), 413-452.

Stanley, Henry Morton. *Coomassie: The Story of the Campaign in Africa, 1873-4.* London: Sampson Low, Marston and Co., 1896. 212 p. An account by the explorer.

___. *Coomassie and Magdala: The Story of Two British Campaigns in Africa.* London: Sampson Low, Marston, Low and Searle, 1874; New York: Harper and Brothers, 1874. 510 p.

Tenkorang, Samuel. "John Mensah Sarbah, 1864-1910." *Transactions of the Historical Society of Ghana,* 14, 1 (June 1973), 65-78.

Thomas, Roger G. "Forced Labour in British West Africa: The Case of the Northern Territories of the Gold Coast, 1906-1927." *Journal of African History,* 14, 1 (1973), 79-103.

___. "The 1916 Bongo 'Riots' and Their Background: Aspects of Colonial Administration and African Response in Eastern Upper Ghana." *Journal of African History,* 24, 1 (1983), 57-75.

Tordoff, William. "Brandford Griffith's Offer of British Protection to Ashanti in 1891." *Transactions of the Historical Society of Ghana,* 6 (1962), 32-49.

Twumasi, Yaw. "J.B. Danquah: Towards an Understanding of the Social and Political Ideas of a Ghanaian Nationalist and Politician." *African Affairs,* 77, 306 (Jan. 1978), 73-88.

Walker, Howard Kent. "The Constitutional Debate between Opposition and Government Nationalists in the Gold Coast on the Eve of Independence." Ph.D. Dissertation, Boston University, 1968. 338 p.

Wallerstein, Immanuel. *The Road to Independence: Ghana and the Ivory Coast.* The Hague: Mouton, 1964. 200 p.

Ward, John Paul. "The Journalistic Frontier of Africa: Special Correspondents Covering the Sixth Anglo-Ashanti War, 1873-1874." Ph.D. Dissertation, Boston University, 1971. 441 p.

Ward, William Ernest Frank. "Britain and Ashanti, 1874-1896." *Transactions of the Historical Society of Ghana*, 15, 2 (Dec. 1974), 131-164.

Wight, Martin, ed. *British Colonial Constitutions, 1947.* Oxford: Clarendon Press, 1952. 571 p.

___. *The Gold Coast Legislative Council.* Studies in Colonial Legislature, 2nd. ed., by Margery Perham. London: Faber and Faber, 1947. 285 p.

Willocks, James. *From Kabul to Kumassi. Twenty-four Years of Soldiering and Sport.* London: John Murray, 1904. 440 p.

Wilson, Henry S. *Origins of West African Nationalism.* London: Macmillan, 1969. 391 p.

Wolfson, Freda. *Pageant of Ghana.* West African History Series. London: Oxford University Press, 1958. 266 p.

Wolseley, Garnet Joseph. *The Story of a Soldier's Life.* 2 vols. New York: Scribner's, 1903. Administrator of Cape Coast and British Commander in the Asante campaign, 1873-1874. See vol. 2, 257-370.

Wraith, R. E. "Frederick Gordon Guggisberg: Myth and Mystery." *African Affairs* (London), 8, 318 (Jan. 1981), 116-122.

___. *Guggisberg.* West African History Series. London: Oxford University Press, 1967. 342 p.

Yarak, Larry W. "The 'Elmina Notes' Myth and Reality in Asante-Dutch Relations." *History in Africa*, 13 (1986), 363-382.

I. HISTORY SINCE INDEPENDENCE

Adamafio, Tawia. *By Nkrumah's Side: The Labour and the Wounds.* Accra: Westcoast Publishing House; London: Rex Collings, 1982. 144 p.

Addo-Fenning, Robert. "Gandhi and Nkrumah: A Study of Non-Violence and Non-Cooperation Campaigns in India and Ghana as an Anti-Colonial Strategy." *Transactions of the Historical Society of Ghana*, 13, 1 (1972), 63-85.

Adjei, Mike. "Merger Misconceptions." *West Africa* (London), 3356 (23 November 1981), 2782-2783. Ghanaian politics just before the December 1981 coup.

Afrifa, Akwasi A. *The Ghana Coup, 24th February 1966.* London: Frank Cass; New York: Humanities Press, 1966. 144 p.

Agyeman, Kofi D. *Ideological Education and Nationalism in Ghana under Nkrumah and Busia.* Accra: Ghana University Press, 1989. 81 p.

Agyeman-Badu, Yaw, and Kwaku Osei-Hwedie. *The Political Economy of Instability; Colonial Legacy, Inequality and Political Instability in Ghana.* Lawrenceville, Va.: Brunswick Publishing Co., 1982. 56 p.

Akyeampong, Henry Kwasi. *The Foundations of Self-Government: Selected Historic Speeches on Ghana's Independence.* Accra: George Boakye Publishing Co., 1967. 51 p.

___. *Ghana's Struggle for Democracy and Freedom; Speeches 1957-1969 by Dr. K. A. Busia.* Legon: University of Ghana Bookshop, 1979. 300 p.

Alexander, (Major General) Henry Templer. *African Tightrope: My Two Years as Nkrumah's Chief of Staff.* London: Pall Mall Press, 1965; New York: F. A. Praeger, 1966. 152 p.

Aluko, Olajide. "After Nkrumah; Continuity and Change in Ghana's Foreign Policy." *Issue*, 5, 1 (1975), 55-62.

___. *The Foreign Policies of African States.* London: Hodder and Stoughton, 1977. 243 p.

___. *Ghana and Nigeria 1957-70: A Study in Inter-African Discord.* London: Rex Collings; New York: Barnes and Noble, 1976. 275 p.

___. "Ghana's Foreign Policy under the National Liberation Council." *Africa Quarterly* (New Delhi), 10, 4 (Jan-Mar. 1971), 312-328.

Amamoo, Joseph G. *The Ghanaian Revolution.* London: Jafinit Co., 1988. 243 p.

Ames, Sophia Ripley. *Nkrumah of Ghana.* Chicago: Rand McNally, 1961. 184 p.

Amonoo, Benjamin. *Ghana, 1957-1966; Politics of Institutional Dualism.* Winchester, Mass.: Allen and Unwin, 1981. 242 p.

Anin, T. E., ed. *Essays on the Political Economy of Ghana.* Accra: Selwyn Press, 1991. 238 p.

Appiah, Joseph. *Joe Appiah: The Autobiography of an African Patriot.* New York: Praeger, 1990. 374 p.

___. *The Man, J. B. Danquah.* Accra: Academy of Arts and Sciences, 1974. 51 p.

Arhin, Kwame, *A View of Kwame Nkrumah, 1902-1972: An Interpretation.* Accra: Sedco Publishing, 1990. 47 p.

Armah, Kwesi. *Africa's Golden Road.* London: Heinemann, 1965, 292 p.; Humanities Press, 1966.

Arnold, Guy. "A New Start in Ghana." *African Report*, 24, 6 (Nov.-Dec. 1979), 43-46.

Asamoa, Kofi Vovonyo. "A Comparative Study of the Political Thoughts and Policies of Kwame Nkrumah and Kofi Abrefa Busia." Ph.D. Dissertation, Howard University, 1977. 396 p.

Assensoh, A. B. *Kwame Nkrumah-Six Years in Exile, 1966-1972.*

Assensoh, A. B. *Kwame Nkrumah-Six Years in Exile, 1966-1972.* Ilfracombe, Devon: Stockwell, 1978.

Austin, Dennis. *Ghana Observed: Essays on the Politics of a West African Republic.* New York: Holmes and Meier, Africana Publishing Co., 1976. 199 p.

___. *Politics in Ghana, 1946-1960.* London and New York: Oxford University Press for the Royal Institute for International Affairs, 1964. 459 p.

___, and Robin Luckham. *Politicians and Soldiers in Ghana, 1966-72.* London and Totowa, N.J.: Frank Cass, 1975. 332 p.

Awoonor, Kofi. *Ghana: A Political History from Pre-Colonial to Modern Times.* Accra: Woeli Publishers, 1990. 294 p.

___. *The Ghana Revolution: Background Account from a Personal Perspective.* Bronx, N.Y.: Oases Publishers, 1984. 146 p.

___. "Kwame Nkrumah: Symbol of Emergent Africa." *Africa Report,* 17, 6 (June 1972), 22-25.

Balogun, Kolawole. *Mission to Ghana; Memoir of a Diplomat.* New York: Vantage, 1964. 73 p.

Barker, Peter. *Operation Cold Chop.* 2nd ed. Accra: Ghana Publishing Corp., 1979. 236 p. An account of the 24 February 1966 coup.

Barnor, Ansah. "Opposition Leaders Jockey for Position." *West Africa* (London), 3351 (19 October 1981), 2438-2440. An account of the political situation just before the collapse of the Third Republic.

Bartels, Charles, editor-in-chief. *Ghana Who's Who, 1972-73.* Accra: Bartels Publications, 1972. 454 p.

Baynham, Simon. *The Military and Politics in Nkrumah's Ghana.* Boulder, Colo.: Westview Press, 1988. 294 p.

Bebler, Anton. *Military Rule in Africa: Dahomey, Ghana, Sierra Leone, and Mali.* London: Pall Mall; New York: Praeger, 1973. 267 p.

Bennett, Valerie Plave, and Amos Perlmutter, comp. *The Political Influence of the Military: A Comparative Reader.* New Haven, Conn.: Yale University Press, 1980. 508 p.

Bennion, Francis Alan Roscoe. *The Constitutional Law of Ghana.* London: Butterworth and Co., 1962. 527 p.

Bing, Geoffrey. *Reap the Whirlwind; An Account of Kwame Nkrumah's Ghana from 1950 to 1966.* London: MacGibbon and Kee, 1968. 519 p. Bing was Attorney General and an adviser to Nkrumah.

Boahen, Adu A. *The Ghanaian Sphinx: Reflections on the Contemporary History of Ghana, 1972-1987.* Accra and New York: Ghana Democratic Movement, 1989. 74 p. Paper was originally presented at the J. B. Danquah Memorial Lecture of the Ghana Academy of Arts and Sciences, 1988.

Botchwey, Francis A. *Political Development and Social Change in Ghana: A Study of the Influence of Kwame Nkrumah and the Role of Ideas in Rapid Social Change.* Buffalo, N.Y.: Black Academy Press, 1972. 174 p. Dr. Botchwey was PNDC Secretary for Finance and Economic Planning.

Busia Kofi Abrefa. *Africa in Search of Democracy.* London: Routledge; New York: Praeger, 1967. 192 p.

Card, Emily, and Barbara Callaway. "Ghanian Politics: The Elections and After. What Factors Explain Busia's Electoral Victory and What Are His Regime's Prospects?" *Africa Report,* 15, 3 (March 1970), 10-15.

Chazan, Naomi. *An Anatomy of Ghanaian Politics: Managing Political Recession, 1969-1982*. Boulder, Colo.: Westview Press, 1983. 350 p.

Danso-Boafo, Alex Kwaku. "The Political Biography of Dr. Kofi Abrefa Busia." Ph.D. Dissertation, Howard University, 1981. 343 p.

Davidson, Basil. *Black Star: A View of the Life and Times of Kwame Nkrumah*. London: Allen Lane, 1973. 225 p.

Dei-Anang, Michael. *The Administration of Ghana's Foreign Relations, 1957-1965: A Personal Memoir*. London: Athlone Press, University of London; Atlantic Highlands, N.J.: Humanities Press, 1975. 96 p. Dei-Anang was Principal Secretary at the Ministry of Foreign Affairs, 1959-1961, and head of the African Affairs Secretariat, 1961-1966.

Donkoh, C. E. *Nkrumah and Busia of Ghana*. Accra: New Times Corp., 1972. 147 p.

Dowse, Robert Edward. *Modernization in Ghana and the U.S.S.R.: A Comparative Study*. London: Routledge, 1969. 107 p.

Drake, St. Clair, and Leslie Alexander Lacy. "Government versus the Unions; the Sekondi-Takoradi Strike, 1961." In *Politics in Africa: Seven Cases*, ed. Gwendolen M. Carter. Harcourt Casebook in Political Science. New York: Harcourt, Brace, and World, 1966, 67-117.

Du Bois, Shirley Graham. *What Happened in Ghana? The Inside Story*. New York: Freedomways Associates, 1966. 223 p. Mrs. Du Bois was the wife of W. E. B. Du Bois.

Dzirasa, Rev. Stephen. *Political Thought of Dr. Kwame Nkrumah*. Accra: Guinea Press, 1962. 133 p. Dzirasa was a close associate of President Nkrumah.

Edoh, Anthony Adem. "Decentralization and Local Government Reforms in Ghana." Ph.D. Dissertation, University of Wisconsin, 1981. 412 p.

Erskine, Emmanuel A. *Mission with UNIFIL: An African Soldier's Reflections.* London: Hurst and Company, 1989. 215 p.

Fitch, Robert Beck, and Mary Oppenheimer. *Ghana: End of an Illusion.* New York: Monthly Review Press, 1966. 130 p. Also published as a special edition of the *Monthly Review*, vol. 2, 1966.

Frimpong, J. H. S. "The Ghana Parliament, 1957-1966: A Critical Analysis." Ph.D. Dissertation, University of Exeter, 1970. 426 p.

Goldschmidt, Jenny. "Ghana between the Second and the Third Republican Eras: Recent Constitutional Developments and Their Relation to Traditional Laws and Institutions." *African Law Studies*, 18 (1980), 43-62.

Goldsworthy, David. "Ghana's Second Republic: A Post-Mortem." *African Affairs* (London), 72, 286 (Jan. 1973), 8-25.

Gray, Paul S. *Unions and Leaders in Ghana.* Buffalo, N.Y.: Conch Magazine, 1981. 238 p.

Greenstreet, D. K. "Public Corporations in Ghana during the Nkrumah Period, 1951-66." *African Review* (Accra), 3, 1 (1973), 21-31.

Grundy, Kenneth W. "The Negative Image of Africa's Military." *Review of Politics* (Notre Dame), 30, 4 (Oct. 1968), 428-439.

___. "The Political Ideology of Kwame Nkrumah." In *African Political Thought: Lumumba, Nkrumah, and Toure*, ed. by W.Z.E. Skurnik. Denver: University of Denver, 1968.

Hansen, Emmanuel, and Paul Collins. "The Army, the State, and the Rawlings Revolution in Ghana." *African Affairs* (London), 79, 314 (Jan. 1980), 3-24.

Harris, D. J. "The Recent Political Upheavals in Ghana." *World Today*, 36 (June 1980), 225-232.

Hart, David. *The Volta River Project: A Case Study in Politics and Technology.* Edinburgh: Edinburgh University Press, 1980. 132 p.

Hart, Keith. "The Politics of Unemployment in Ghana." *African Affairs*, 75, 301 (Oct. 1976), 488-497.

Harvey, William Burnett. *Law and Social Change in Ghana.* Princeton, N.J.: Princeton University Press, 1966. 453 p. Harvey was Dean of the Law Faculty at the University of Ghana, 1962-1964. In 1964 Nkrumah had him deported for subversive activities.

Hevi, Emmanuel John. *An African Student in China.* London: Pall Mall Press, 1963. 220 p. Hevi was once Secretary-General of the African Students' Union of Ghana.

Hodgkin, Thomas. *African Political Parties.* Harmondsworth: Penguin, 1962. 217 p. Hodgkin was Director of the African Studies Program at Legon.

Hoeane, Patricia Masilo. "Economic Aid as an Instrument of Soviet Foreign Policy: The Case of Ghana, 1957-1966." Ph.D. Dissertation, Western Michigan University, 1981. 157 p.

Hyde, Emmanuel A. "The Role of Ghana in the Congo Crisis: A Study of a Small State's Involvement in a Post-Colonial System." Ph.D Dissertation, University of Pennsylvania, 1970-71. 498 p.

McKwartin, Dan B. "The Politics of Political Instability: State, Society, and Public Policy in Post-Independence Ghana, 1957-

1987." Ph.D. Dissertation, University of Illinois at Chicago, 1991. 231 p.

Mikell, Gwendolyn. *Cocoa and Chaos in Ghana.* New York: Paragon House, 1989. 284 p.

Milne, June, ed. *Kwame Nkrumah: The Conakry Years, His Life and Letters.* London: ZED Books Ltd., 1990. 432 p.

Ninsin, K. A., and F. K. Drah. *The Search for Democracy in Ghana: A Case Study of Political Instability in Africa.* Accra: Asempa Publishers, 1987. 176 p.

Nkrumah, Kwame. *Africa Must Unite.* New York: Praeger, 1963; London: Heinemann, 1965; New York: International Publishers, 1970. 229 p.

___. *Challenge of the Congo.* London: Nelson, 1967; New York: International Publishers, 1967. 304 p.

___. *Consciencism: Philosophy and Ideology for Decolonization and Development with Particular Reference to the African Revolution.* London: Heinemann, 1964; New York: Monthly Review Press, 1970. 122 p.

___. *Dark Days in Ghana.* London: Lawrence and Wishart, 1968; New York: International Publishers, 1969. 219 p.

___. *Ghana: The Autobiography of Kwame Nkrumah.* New York: Thomas Nelson and Sons, 1957. 302 p.

___. *I Speak of Freedom: A Statement of African Ideology.* London: Heinemann, 1961; New York: Praeger, 1961. 291 p.

___. *Neo-Colonialism: The Last Stage of Imperialism.* London: Nelson, 1965; Heinemann, 1968; New York: International Publishers, 1965. 280 p.

___. *Revolutionary Path.* New York: International Publishers, 1973. 532 p.

Nsarkoh, J. K. *Local Government in Ghana.* Accra: Ghana Universities Press, 1965. 309 p.

Ocran, Albert Kwesi. *A Myth Is Broken: An Account of the Ghana Coup d'Etat of 24 February 1966.* London: Longmans, 1968. 104 p.

___. *Politics of the Sword: A Personal Memoir on Military Involvement in Ghana and of Problems of Military Government.* London: Rex Collings, 1977. 167 p.

Ofusu-Appiah, L. H. *The Life of Lieut. Gen. E. K. Kotoka.* Accra: Waterville Publishing House, 1972. 156 p.

Ohene, Elizabeth. "Is Military Rule Really the Answer?" *West Africa* (London), 3382 (31 May 1982), 1451-1454.

Okeke, Barbara E. *4 June: A Revolution Betrayed.* Enugu, Nigeria: Ikenga Publishers, 1982. 185 p.

Oquaye, Mike. *Politics in Ghana, 1972-79.* Accra: Tornado Publications, 1980. 286 p.

Owusu, Maxwell. "Customs and Coups: A Juridical Interpretation of Civil Order and Disorder in Ghana." *Journal of Modern African Studies,* 24, 1 (1986), 69-99.

___. "The Search for Solvency: Background to the Fall of Ghana's Second Republic, 1969-1972." *Africa Today* (Denver, Colo.), 19, 1 (Winter 1972), 52-60.

___. *Uses and Abuses of Political Power: A Case Study of Continuity and Change in the Politics of Ghana.* Chicago: University of Chicago Press, 1970. 364 p. Paperback rpt. 1991.

Owusu-Ansah, David. "The Provisional National Defence Council of Ghana: A Move Toward Consolidation." *International Third World Studies Journal and Review*, 1, 1 (1989), 213-218.

Owusu-Ansah, Kwabena Asare. "Local Government under Political Integration: The Ghanaian Experience." Ph.D. Dissertation, University of Southern California, 1971. 536 p.

Pellow, Deborah, "Muslims Segmentation: Cohesion and Divisiveness in Accra." *Journal of Modern African Studies*, 23, 3 (1985), 419-444.

Phillips, E. A. "Ethnicity in Ghanaian Politics." *South African Journal of African Affairs*, 9, 1 (1979), 14-21.

Phillips, John. *Kwame Nkrumah and the Future of Africa*. London: Faber and Faber; New York: Frederick A. Praeger, 1960. 272 p. John Phillips was a member of the pre-independence civil service and was Executive Secretary of Nkrumah's State Enterprises.

Pickney, Robert. *Ghana under Military Rule, 1966-1969*. Studies in African History. London: Methuen, 1972. 182 p.

Pieterse, Jan. "Rawlings and the 1979 Revolt in Ghana." *Race and Class*, 23 (Spring 1982), 251-274.

Powell, Erica. *Kwame Nkrumah of the New Africa*. London: Thomas Nelson, 1961. 68 p. Erica Powell was the longtime private secretary and speechwriter of Kwame Nkrumah.

___. *Private Secretary, Gold Coast*. London: C. Hurst, 1984. 228 p.

Price, Robert M. "Military Officers and Political Leadership: The Ghanaian Case." *Comparative Politics*, 3 (Apr. 1971), 361-379.

___. *Society and Bureaucracy in Contemporary Ghana*. Berkeley, Calif.: University of California Press, 1975. 275 p.

___. "A Theoretical Approach to Military Rule in New States: Reference Group Theory and the Ghanaian Case." *World Politics*, 23, 3 (April 1971), 399-430.

Quaison-Sackey, Alex. *Africa Unbound: Reflections of an African Statesman.* New York: Frederick A. Praeger; London: Andre Deutsch, 1963. 174 p. Quaison-Sackey served both as President of the UN General Assembly and as Foreign Minister under Kwame Nkrumah.

Radix, A. "Foreign Participation in State Enterprises: The Case of Abbott Laboratories (Ghana) Ltd." *Legon Observer*, 2, 23 (Nov. 1967), 2-7.

Rathbone, Richard. "Businessmen in Politics: Party Struggle in Ghana." *The Journal of Development Studies*, 9, 3 (Apr. 1973), 391-402.

___. "Politics and Factionalism in Ghana." *Current History*, 60, 355 (Mar. 1971), 164-167, 175.

Rooney, David. *Kwame Nkrumah, The Political Kingdom in the Third World.* London: I. B. Touris and Company Ltd., 1988; New York: St. Martin's Press, 1989. 292 p.

Rothchild, Donald. "Military Regime Performance: An Appraisal of the Ghana Experience, 1972-1978." *Comparative Politics*, 12, 4 (July 1980), 459-79.

___, and E. Gyimah-Boadi. "Ghana's Return to Civilian Rule." *Africa Today*, 28, 1 (1981), 3-16.

Rubin, Leslie, and Paul Murray. *The Constitution and Government of Ghana.* Law in Africa series, 1. 1st ed., 1961. London: Sweet and Maxwell, 1964. 324 p.

St. Clair, Drake, and Leslie Alexander. "Government versus the Unions: The Sekondi-Takoradi Strike of 1961." In *Politics in*

Africa: Seven Cases, ed. Gwendolen Margaret Carter. New York: Harcourt, Brace and World, 1966, 66-118.

Sampson, Magnus J. *Makers of Modern Ghana*. Accra: Anowuo Educational Publications, 1969. 190 p.

Sekyi, H. V. H. "The Year of Revolution in Ghana." *African Affairs* (London), 72, 287 (April 1973) 197-201. Henry Van Hien Sekyi was Ghana's High Commissioner to the United Kingdom.

Shillington, Kevin. *Rawlings and His Moments; Ghana and the Rawlings Factor*. New York: St. Martin's Press, 1992. 184 p.

Smith, M. Brewster. *Peace Corps Teachers in Ghana; Final Report of Peace Corps Project in Ghana*. Berkeley, Calif.: Institute of Human Development, University of California, 1964. 195 p.

Thompson, Willard Scott. *Ghana's Foreign Policy, 1957-1966: Diplomacy, Ideology, and the New State*. Princeton, N.J.: Princeton University Press, 1969. 462 p.

Tiger, Lionel Samuel. "Bureaucracy in Ghana: The Civil Service." Ph.D. Dissertation, University of London, 1965.

Twumasi, Yaw. "Media of Mass Communication and the Third Republican Constitution of Ghana." *African Affairs* (London), 80, 318 (Jan. 1981), 13-28.

___. "The Newspaper Press and Political Leadership in Developing Nations: The Case of Ghana, 1964-1978." *Gazette* (Netherlands), 26, 1 (1980), 1-16.

Wallerstein, Immanuel M. *The Road to Independence: Ghana and the Ivory Coast*. London: Mouton, 1964. 200 p.

Warner, Douglas. *Ghana and the New Africa*. London: Muller, 1960. 181 p.

Welch, Claude E., Jr. "Ghana: The Politics of Military Withdrawal." *Current History*, 54 (Feb. 1968), 95-114.

___. "Return to Civilian Rule in Ghana." *Current History*, 56, 333 (May 1969), 286-291.

Woode, Samuel N. *Making the District Assembly Work*. Tema: Ghana Publishing Company, 1989. 48 p.

Woronoff, Jon. "Nkrumah--the Prophet Risen." *Worldview*, 16, 3 (1973), 32-36.

___. "Le Parti de la Convention du Peuple du Ghana." *Revue Française d'Études Politiques Africaines*, 86 (1973), 34-54.

___. *West African Wager: Houphouet versus Nkrumah*. Metuchen, N.J., and London: Scarecrow Press, 1972. 357 p.

Young, Crawford. *Ideology and Development in Africa*. New Haven, Conn.: Yale University Press, 1982. 320 p.

J. REGIONAL STUDIES

Addo-Fening, Robert, A. B. Holmes, et al. *Akyem Abuakwa and the Politics of the Inter-War Period in Ghana*. Basel Africa Bibliography, 12. Basel, Switzerland: Communications from the Basel Africa Bibliography, 1975. 166 p.

___. "Asante Refugees in Akyem Abuakwa 1875-1912." *Transactions of the Historical Society of Ghana* (Legon). 14, 1 (June 1973), 39-64.

___. "The Background to the Deportation of King Asafo Agyi and the Foundation of New Dwaben." *Transactions of the Historical Society of Ghana*, 14, 2 (Dec. 1973), 213-228.

Adjaye, Joseph K. "Asantehene Agyeman Prempe I, Asante History and the Historian." *History in Africa*, 17 (1990), 1-29.

___. *Diplomacy and Diplomats in Nineteenth Century Asante.* Lanham, Md.: University Press of America, 1984. 310 p.

Agbosu, L. K. "Land Administration in Northern Ghana." *Review of Ghana Law*, 12 (1980), 104-133.

Agyeman-Duah, J. "A Traditional History to the Reign of Nana Sofo Kantanka. With a Note on the Traditional History of Mampong by Ivor Wilks." *Transactions of the Historical Society of Ghana*, 4, 2 (1960), 21-29.

Agyemang Badu, Osagyefo O. "The Akan System of Government and Its Contributions to the Modern Government of Ghana." Graduate Thesis, Oxford University (UK), 1987. 324 p.

Aidoo, Agnes Akosua. "Asante Queen Mothers in Government and Politics in the Nineteenth Century." *Journal of the Historical Society of Nigeria* (Ibadan), 9 (Dec. 1977), 1-14.

___. "The Asante Succession Crisis of 1883-8." *Transactions of the Historical Society of Ghana*, 13, 2 (Dec. 1972), 163-180.

Akyeampong, Henry Kwasi. *The Akim Abuakwa Crisis.* With a foreword by J. B. Danquah. Accra: The Author, 1958. 63 p.

Alhasan, Malam. *A Short History of the Dagomba Tribe.* Trans. from a Hausa manuscript in the Library of the School of Oriental Studies by J. Withers Gill. Accra: Government Printer, n.d.

Allman, Jean Marie, "The National Liberation Movement and the Asante Struggle for Self-Determination, 1954-1957." Ph.D. Dissertation, Northwestern University, 1987.

Amenumey, D. E. K. *The Ewe in Pre-Colonial Times.* Accra: Sedco Publishing, 1986. 122 p.

___. "The Extension of British Rule to Anlo (Southeast Ghana) 1850-1890." *Journal of African History* (London), 9, 1 (1968), 99-117.

___. "The Pre-1947 Background to the Ewe Unification Question." *Transactions of the Historical Society of Ghana*, 10 (1969), 65-85.

___. "Some Aspects of Ewe Machinery of Government with Special Reference to the Anlo Political System." *Ghana Journal of Sociology* (Legon), 4, 2 (Oct. 1968), 100-108.

Anafu, Moses. "The Impact of Colonial Rule on Tallessi Political Institutions, 1898-1967." *Transactions of the Historical Society of Ghana*, 14, 1 (June 1973), 17-37.

Anti, A. A. *Akwamu, Denkyira, Akuapem, and Ashanti in the Lives of Osei Tutu and Okumo Anokye.* Accra: Ghana Publishing Corp., 1971. 100 p.

___. *The Ancient Asante King.* Accra: Volta Bridge Publishing Co., 1974. 80 p.

Arhin, Kwame. *Asante and the Northeast.* Legon: Institute of African Studies, 1970. 215 p.

___. "The Development of Market Centres at Atebubu and Kintampo Since 1874." Ph.D. Dissertation, University of London, 1969. 272 p.

___. *A Profile of Brong Kyempim.* Legon: Institute of African Studies, 1979. 180 p.

___. "Strangers and Hosts: A Study of Atebubu." *Transactions of the Historical Society of Ghana*, 12 (1971), 63-82.

___. "The Structure of Greater Ashanti (1700-1824)." *Journal of African History*, 8, 1 (1967), 65-85.

Armitage, Cecil Hamilton. "Notes on the Northern Territories of the Gold Coast." *United Empire*, 4 (Aug. 1913), 634-639.

___. *The Tribal Markings and Marks of Adornment of the Natives of the Northern Territories of the Gold Coast Colony*. London: Royal Anthropological Institute, 1924. 23 p.

Austin, Gareth. "The Emergence of Capitalist Relations in South Asante Cocoa-farming, c. 1916-1933." *Journal of African History*, 28 (1987), 259-279.

Beaton, Alfred Charles. *The Ashantees: Their Country, History, Wars, Government, Customs, Climate, Religion, and Present Position*. London: James Blackwell, 1877. 183 p.

Bening, Raymond B. "Foundations of the Modern Native States of Northern Ghana." *Universitas* (Legon), 5 (Nov. 1975), 116-138.

___. "The Location of Administrative Capitals in Ashanti, Ghana, 1896-1911." *International Journal of African Historical Studies* (Boston), 12, 2 (1979), 210-234.

___. "The Regional Boundaries of Ghana, 1874-1972," *Research Review* (Legon), 9, 1 (1973), 20-57.

Birmingham, David. "A Note on the Kingdom of Fetu." *Ghana Notes and Queries* (Legon), 9 (1966), 30-33.

Boahen, Albert Adu. "The Origin of the Akan." *Ghana Notes and Queries*, 9 (1966), 3-10.

___. "When Did Osei Tutu Die?" *Transactions of the Historical Society of Ghana*, 16, 1 (June 1975), 87-92.

Bourret, Florence Mabel. *The Gold Coast: A Survey of the Gold Coast and British Togoland, 1919-1946*. Stanford, Calif.: Stanford University Press, 1949. 231 p.

Braimah, J. A. *The Ashanti and the Gonja at War.* Accra: Ghana Publishing Corp., 1970. 63 p.

___, and J. R. Goody. *Salaga: The Struggle for Power.* London: Longmans, Green and Co., 1967. 222 p.

Britwum, K. A. "Kwadwo Adinkra of Gyaaman: A Study of the Relations between the Brong Kingdom of Gyaaman and Asante from c. 1800-1818." *Transactions of the Historical Society of Ghana*, 15, 2 (Dec. 1974), 229-239.

Brokensha, David W., ed. *Akwapim Handbook.* Accra: State Publishing Corp., 1972. 310 p.

___. "The Resilient Chieftaincy at Larteh, Ghana." In *West African Chiefs: Their Changing Status under Colonial Rule and Independence*, ed. Michael Crowder and Obaro Ikime. New York: Africana Publishing Corp.; Ile Ife, Nigeria: University of Ife Press, 1970, 393-406.

___. "Social Change in Larteh." Ph.D. Dissertation, Oxford University, 1962. Published by Clarendon Press, Oxford, 1966. 294 p.

Brown, David. "Anglo-German Rivalry and Krepi Politics, 1886-1894." *Transactions of the Historical Society of Ghana*, 15, 2 (Dec. 1974), 201-216.

___. "Borderline Politics in Ghana: The National Liberation Movement of Western Togoland." *The Journal of Modern African Studies* (Cambridge), 18, 4 (Dec. 1980), 575-610.

___. "Who Are the Tribalists? Social Pluralism and Political Idealogy in Ghana." *African Affairs* (London), 81, 322 (Jan. 1982), 37-69.

Brown, Susan Drucker. *Ritual Aspects of the Mamprusi Kingship.* African Social Research Documents, 8. Leiden: Afrika-

Studiecentrum; Cambridge: African Studies Centre, 1975. 172 p.

Busia, Kofi Abrefa. "The Ashanti." In *African Worlds*, ed. Daryll Forde. London: Oxford University Press, 1954, 190-209.

Butler, William Francis. *Akim-Foo: The History of a Failure.* London: Sampson, Low, Marston, Low, Searle, 1875. 300 p.

Cardinall, Allen Wosley. *Tales Told in Togoland to Which Is Added the Mythical and Traditional History of Dagomba by E. F. Tamakloe.* London: Oxford University Press, 1931; Westport, Conn.: Negro Universities Press (Greenwood), 1970. 290 p.

Case, Glenna Lea. "Wasipe under the Ngbanya: Polity, Economy, and Society in Northern Ghana." 2 vols. Ph.D. Dissertation, Northwestern University, 1979. 865 p.

Chambas, Mohamed Ibn. "The Politics of Agricultural and Rural Development in the Upper Region of Ghana: Implications of Technocratic Ideology and Non-Participatory Development." Ph.D. Dissertation, Cornell University, 1980. 241 p.

Daaku, Kwame Yeboa. "A History of Sefwi: A Survey of Oral Evidence." *Research Review* (Legon: Institute of African Studies), 7, 3 (1971), 32-47.

___. *Oral Traditions of Assin-Twifo, Adanse and Denkyira.* 3 vols. Legon: Institute of African Studies, University of Ghana, 1969-1970.

___. *Osei Tutu of Asante.* African Historical Biographies. London: Heinemann, 1976. 48 p.

Danquah, Joseph Boakye. *The Akim Abuakwa Handbook.* London: Forster Groom, 1928. 127 p.

___. *Gold Coast: Akan Laws and Customs and the Akim Abuakwa Constitution.* London: G. Routledge, 1928. 272 p.

Davis, David C. "Continuity and Change in Mampurugu: A Study of Tradition as Ideology." Ph.D. Dissertation, Northwestern University, 1984. 564 p.

Dougah, J. C. *Wa and Its People.* Legon: Institute of African Studies, 1966. 117 p.

Duncan-Johnstone, A. C., and H. A. Blair. *Enquiry into the Constitution and Organization of the Dagbon Kingdom.* Accra: Government Printer, 1932. 68 p. Duncan-Johnstone and Blair were both British officials in the Northern Territories.

Dunn, John, and A. F. Robertson. *Dependence and Opportunity: Political Change in Ahafo.* London and New York: Cambridge University Press, 1973. 400 p.

Fage, John Donnelly. "Reflections on the Early History of the Mossi-Dagomba Group of States." In *The Historian in Tropical Africa*, ed. Jan Vansina, Raymond Mauny, and L. V. Thomas. London: Oxford University Press, 1964, 177-192.

Ferguson, Phyllis. "Islamization in Dagbon: A Study of the Alfanema of Yendi." Ph.D. Dissertation, Cambridge University, 1973.

Field, Margaret Joyce. *Akim-Kotoku: An Oman of the Gold Coast.* London: Crown Agents for the Colonies, 1948. 211 p.

___. *Social Organization of the Ga People.* London: Crown Agents for the Colonies, 1940. 231 p.

Flight, Colin. "The Chronology of the Kings and Queenmothers of Bono-Manso: A Reevaluation of the Evidence." *Journal of African History*, 11, 2 (1970), 259-268.

Froelich, Jean Claude. *La Tribu Konkomba du Nord Togo.* Mémoires de l'Institut Français d'Afrique Noire, 37. Dakar: IFAN, 1954. 253 p.

Fuller, Sir Francis. *A Vanished Dynasty: Ashanti.* London: J. Murray, 1921; London: Frank Cass, 168. 241 p. Fuller was Chief Commissioner in Asante, 1902-1920.

Fynn, John Kofi. *Asante and Its Neighbors, 1700-1807.* Legon History Series. London: Longman, 1971. 175 p.

___. *Oral Traditions of the Fante States.* 7 vols. Legon: Institute of African Studies, University of Ghana, 1974-1976.

___. "The Reign and Times of Kusi Obedum, 1750-64." *Transactions of the Historical Society of Ghana,* 8 (1965), 24-32.

___. "The Rise of Ashanti." *Ghana Notes and Queries* (Legon), 9 (1966), 24-30.

Goody, Jack (John Rankine). *Death, Property and Ancestors: A Study of the Mortuary Customs of the La Dagaa of West Africa.* Stanford, Calif.: Stanford University Press, 1962. 452 p.

___. "The Ethnography of the Northern Territories of the Gold Coast West of the White Volta." London: Colonial Office, 1954. 59 p. Typescript.

___. "The Mande and the Akan Hinterland." In *The Historian in Tropical Africa,* ed. Jan Vansina, Raymond Mauny, and L.V. Thomas. London: Oxford University Press, 1964, 192-218.

___. "The Over-Kingdom of Gonja." In *West African Kingdoms in the Nineteenth Century,* ed. Daryll Forde and P. M. Kaberry. London: Oxford University Press, 1967, 179-205.

Gordon, James. "Some Oral Traditions of Denkyira." *Transactions of the Gold Coast and Togoland Historical Society* (Achimota), 1, 3 (1953), 27-33.

Greene, Sandra Elaine. "The Anlo-Ewe: Their Economy, Society and External Relations in the Eighteenth Century." Ph.D. Dissertation, Northwestern University, 1981. 483 p.

Haight, Bruce Marvin. "Bole and Gonja. Contributions to the History of Northern Ghana." Ph.D. Dissertation, Northwestern University, 1981. 1307 p.

Hamilton, Robert Earl. "Asante, 1895-1900: Prelude to War." Ph.D. Dissertation, Northwestern University, 1978. 401 p.

Haskett, Norman Dean. "Kete-Krakye and the Middle Volta Basin, 1700-1914: Cockpit of African and European Rivalry." Ph.D. Dissertation, University of California, Los Angeles, 1981. 777 p.

Henige, David P. "Abrem Stool: A Contribution to the History and Historiography of Southern Ghana." *The International Journal of African Historical Studies*, 6, 1 (1973), 1-18.

___. "Akan Stool Succession under Colonial Rule: Continuity or Change?" *Journal of African History*, 16, 2 (1975), 285-301.

___. "John Kabes of Komenda: An Early African Entrepreneur and State Builder." *Journal of African History*, 18, 1 (1977), 1-19.

___. "The Problem of Feedback in Oral Tradition: Some Examples from the Fante Coastlands." *Journal of African History*, 14, 2 (1973), 223-235.

___. "Seniority and Succession in the Krobo Stools." *International Journal of African Historical Studies*, 7, 2 (1974), 203-226.

Hilton, T. E. "Notes on the History of Kusasi." *Transactions of the Historical Society of Ghana*, 6 (1962), 79-86.

___. "Le Peuplement de Frafra, District du Nord Ghana." *Bulletin de l'Institut Français d'Afrique Noire*, 30, ser. B, 3 (July 1968), 868-883.

Holden, J. J. "The Zabarima Conquest of North-West Ghana, Part 1." *Transactions of the Historical Society of Ghana*, 8 (1965), 60-86.

Iddi, M. D. "The Ya Na of the Dagombas." Legon: Institute of African Studies, University of Ghana. Yendi Project, Report 12.

Iliasu, A. A. "The Origins of the Mossi-Dagomba States." *Research Review* (Institute of African Studies, Legon), 7, 2 (1971), 95-113.

Irwin, Graham W. "Ashanti East of the Volta." *Transactions of the Historical Society of Ghana*, 8 (1965), 33-59.

___. "The Population of Asante, 1817-1921: A Reconsideration." *Asantesem*, 8 (1978), 22-28.

___. "Precolonial African Diplomacy: The Example of Asante." *International Journal of African Historical Studies*, 8, 1 (1975), 81-96.

Jones, D. H. "Jakpa and the Foundations of Gonja." *Transactions of the Historical Society of Ghana*, 6, (1962), 1-29.

Kea, Ray A. "Akwamu-Anlo Relations c. 1750-1813." *Transactions of the Historical Society of Ghana*, 10 (1969), 29-63.

___. *Settlements, Trade, and Politics in the Seventeenth-Century Gold Coast*. Baltimore and London: Johns Hopkins University Press, 1982. 475 p.

Klein, A. Norman. "The Two Asantes: Competing Interpretations of 'Slavery' in Akan-Asante Culture and Society." In *The Ideology of Slavery in Africa*, ed. Paul E. Lovejoy. Sage Series on African Modernization and Development, 6. Beverly Hills and London: Sage Publications, 1981, 149-167.

Kropp Dakubu, Mary Ester. "Linguistic Pre-History and Historical Reconstruction: The Ga-Adangme Migrations." *Transactions of the Historical Society of Ghana*, 13, 1 (June 1972), 87-111.

Kumah, John Kweku. "The Rise and Fall of the Kingdom of Denkyira." *Ghana Notes and Queries* (Legon), 9 (Nov. 1966), 33-35.

Kwamena-Poh, M. A. *Government and Politics in the Akuapem State, 1730-1850*. Evanston, Ill.: Northwestern University Press, 1973. 177 p.

Kyerematen, A. A. Y. *Interstate Boundary Litigation in Ashanti*. African Social Research Documents, 4. Leiden: Afrika-Studiecentrum; Cambridge: African Studies Centre, 1972. 139 p.

___. "The Royal Stools of Ashanti." *Africa* (London), 39 (Jan. 1969), 1-10.

Labouret, Henri. *Nouvelles Notes sur les Tribus du Rameau Lobi: Leurs Migrations, Leur Evolution, Leurs Parlers, et Ceux de Leurs Voisins*. Mémoires de l'Institut Français d'Afrique Noire, 54. Dakar: IFAN, 1958. 296 p.

___. *Les Tribus du Rameau Lobi*. Paris: Institut d'Ethnologie, 1931. 512 p.

Ladouceur, Paul André. *Chiefs and Politicians: The Politics of Regionalism in Northern Ghana*. London: Longmans, 1979. 320 p.

___. "The Yendi Chieftaincy Dispute and Ghanaian Politics." *Canadian Journal of African Studies* (Montreal), 6 (1972), 97-115.

Levtzion, Nehemia. *Muslims and Chiefs in West Africa: A Study of Islam in the Middle Volta Basin in the Pre-Colonial Period*. Oxford: Clarendon Press, 1968. 228 p.

___. "Salaga--a Trading Town in Ghana." *Asian and African Studies* (Jerusalem), 2 (1966), 207-244.

Lewin, Thomas J. *Asante before the British: The Prempean Years, 1875-1900.* Lawrence, Kans.: Regents Press of Kansas, 1978. 312 p.

Lloyd, Alan. *The Drums of Kumasi: The Story of the Ashanti Wars.* London: Longmans, 1964. 209 p.

Maier, Donna Jane Ellen [Donna Maier Weaver]. *Priests and Power: The Case of the Dente Shrine in Nineteenth-Century Ghana.* Bloomington, Ind.: Indiana University Press, 1983. 258 p.

Mamattah, Charles M. K. *The Anlo-Ewes and Their Immediate Neighbors.* Vol. I of *The Ewes of West Africa.* Accra: Advent Press, Volta Research Publications, 1976. 763 p.

McCaskie, Thomas. "Komfo Anokye of Asante: Meaning, History and Philosophy in the African Society." *Journal of African History*, 26 (1986), 315-339.

Meyerowitz, Eva Lewin-Richter. *At the Court of an African King.* London: Faber and Faber, 1962. 244 p.

___. "Communication: The Chronology of Bono-Manso." *Journal of African History*, 13, 2 (1972), 348-352.

___. *The Early History of the Akan States of Ghana.* London: Red Candle Press, 1974. 228 p.

___. *The Sacred State of the Akan.* London: Faber and Faber, 1951. 222 p.

Northcott, Henry P. *Report on the Northern Territories of the Gold Coast.* London: HMSO (Harrison and Sons), 1899. 174 p. Northcott was the first British Commissioner of the Northern Territories.

Obeng, Ernest E. *Ancient Ashanti Chieftaincy.* Tema: Ghana Publishing Corp., 1988. 69 p.

Odonkor, Thomas Harrison. *The Rise of the Krobos.* Tema: Ghana Publishing Corp., 1971. 60 p. Odonkor was the Chief of Kpong, Manya Krobo.

Odotei, I. "The Ga and Their Neighbors." Ph.D. Dissertation, University of Ghana, 1972.

Owusu-Ansah, David. *Islamic Talismanic Tradition in Nineteenth-Century Asante.* Lewiston, N.Y.: Edwin Mellen Press, 1991. 253 p.

___. "Islamization Reconsidered: An Examination of Asante Responses to Muslim Influence in the Nineteenth Century." *Asian and African Studies,* 21, 2 (1987), 145-163.

Painter, Colin. "The Guang and West African Historical Reconstruction." *Ghana Notes and Queries* (Legon), 9 (1966), 58-65.

Paternot, Marcel. *Lumière sur la Volta, Chez les Dagari.* Paris: Association des Missionaires d'Afrique, 1953. 254 p.

Priestly, Margaret, and Ivor Wilks. "The Ashanti Kings in the Eighteenth Century: A Revised Chronology." *Journal of African History,* 1, 1 (1960), 83-96.

Rattray, Robert Sutherland. *Ashanti.* Oxford: Clarendon Press, 1923, 1955, 1969. 348 p.

___. *Ashanti Law and Constitution.* London: Clarendon Press, 1929, 1956, 420 p.; New York: Negro Universities Press, 1969.

___. *Tribes of the Ashanti Hinterland.* 2 vols. Oxford: Clarendon Press, 1932, 1969. 604 p.

Saaka, Yakubu. *Local Government and Political Change in Northern Ghana.* Washington, D.C.: University Press of America, 1978. 172 p.

Sanders, James Robert. "The Expansion of the Fante and the Emergence of Asante in the Eighteenth Century." *Journal of African History,* 20, 3 (1979), 349-364.

___. "The Political Development of the Fante in the Eighteenth and Nineteenth Centuries: A Study of a West African Merchant Society." 2 vols. Ph.D. Dissertation, Northwestern University, 1980.

Sanderson, R. W. "The History of Nzima Up to 1874." *Gold Coast Review* (Accra), 1 (1925), 95 ff.

Sarbah, John Mensah. *Fanti Customary Laws: A Brief Introduction to the Principals of the Native Laws and Customs of the Fanti and Akan Districts of the Gold Coast, with a Report of Some Cases Thereon Decided in the Law Courts.* 2nd ed. London: W. Clowes, 1904. 317 p. (First edition was in 1897.)

Schildkrout, Enid, ed. *The Golden Stool: Studies of the Asante Center and Periphery.* New York: American Museum of Natural History, 1987. 331 p. Collection of excellent chapters from leading scholars of Asante. Chapters were originally presented as papers at a 1984 conference held by the Museum during the visit of the Asantehene Otumfuo Opoku Ware II to America.

Sprigge, R. G. S. "Eweland's Adangbe: An Enquiry into an Oral Tradition." *Transactions of the Historical Society of Ghana,* 10 (1969), 87-128.

___. "A Note on the Ethno-Historical Background to the Ewe-speaking Villages of the Achimota-Legon Area." *Ghana Notes and Queries,* 11 (1970), 13-16.

Staniland, Martin. *The Lions of Dagbon: Political Change in Northern Ghana.* New York and London: Cambridge University Press, 1975. 241 p.

___. "The Manipulation of Tradition: Politics in Northern Ghana." *Journal of Development Studies*, 9, 3 (Apr. 1973), 373-390.

Strevens, P. D. "Konkomba or Dagomba?" *Transactions of the Gold Coast and Togoland Historical Society* (Achimota), 1, 5 (1955), 211-216.

Tait, David. *The Konkomba of Northern Ghana.* London: Oxford University Press, 1961. 255 p. This book made use of notes by Jack Goody.

___. "The Political System of the Konkomba." Ph.D. Dissertation, University of London, 1952. 266 p.

Tamakloe, Emmanuel Forster. *A Brief History of the Dagbamba People.* Accra: Government Printer, 1931. 76 p. The narrative also appears in A. W. Cardinall, *Tales Told in Togoland*, chapter 11. Tamakloe was an interpreter in Kete Krakye, 1897-1907, and served as a Census Clerk in the Northern Territories in 1910.

Tordoff, William. *Ashanti under the Prempehs, 1888-1935.* London and New York: Oxford University Press, 1965. 443 p.

Tufuo, J. W., and C. E. Donkor. *Ashantis of Ghana: People with a Soul.* Accra: Anowuo, 1969. 127 p.

Verdon, Michael. "Re-defining Pre-colonial Ewe Polities: The Case of Abutia." *Africa* (London), 50, 3 (1980), 280-292.

Wallis, J. R. "The Kwahus--Their Connection with the Afram Plain." *Transactions of the Gold Coast and Togoland Historical Society* (Achimota), 1, 3 (1953), 10-26.

Weaver, Donna J. E. [Maier]. "The Dente Oracle, the Bron Confederation, and Asante: Religion and the Politics of Secession." *Journal of African History*, 22, 2 (1981), 229-244.

Welman, Charles Wellesley. *The Native States of the Gold Coast: I Peki.* London: W. Clowes, 1925. 46 p.

___. *The Native States of the Gold Coast: II Ahanta.* London: W. Clowes, 1930. 88 p. The two parts were reprinted in 1969 as one volume by Dawson of London. Welman was once Secretary for Native Affairs on the Gold Coast.

Wilks, Ivor G. "Akwamu, 1650-1750: A Study of the Rise and Fall of a West African Empire." Master's Thesis, University of Wales, 1959. 203 p.

___. *Asante in the Nineteenth Century: The Structure and Evolution of a Political Order.* Cambridge: Cambridge University Press, 1975. Rpt (Paperback) with an extended "Preamble," 1989. 800 p.

___. "Aspects of Bureaucratization in Ashanti in the Nineteenth Century." *Journal of African History*, 7, 2 (1966), 215-232.

___. "The Growth of the Akwapim State: A Study in the Control of Evidence." In *The Historian in Tropical Africa*, ed. J. R. Vansina et al. London: Oxford University Press, 1964. 390-411.

___. *The Northern Factor in Ashanti History.* Legon: Institute of African Studies, University of Ghana, 1961. 46 p.

___. "The Northern Factor in Ashanti History: Begho and the Mande." *Journal of African History*, 2, 1 (1961), 25-34.

___. "A Note on the Chronology and Origins of the Gonja Kings." *Ghana Notes and Queries*, 8 (1966), 26-28.

___. "A Note on the Early Spread of Islam in Dagomba." *Transactions of the Historical Society of Ghana*, 8 (1965), 87-98.

___. "The Rise of the Akwamu Empire, 1650-1710." *Transactions of the Historical Society of Ghana*, 3, 2 (1957), 99-136.

___. *Wa and the Wala: Islam and Polity in Northwestern Ghana.* Cambridge and New York: Cambridge University Press, 1989. 256 p.

___, N. Levtzion, and B. Haight, *Chronicles from Gonja: A Tradition of West African Muslim Historiography.* Cambridge: Cambridge University Press, 1986. 258 p.

Wilson, Louis, L. *The Krobo People of Ghana to 1892: A Political and Social History.* Athens, Ohio: Ohio University Center for International Studies, 1992. 253 p.

Withers-Gill, J. *The Moshi Tribe: A Short History.* Accra: Government Printer, 1924. 24 p.

Yarak, Larry W. "The Chronology of the Asante Kings: A Further Revision." *Asantesem*, 8 (1978), 39-40.

K. TRAVEL

Anderson, Rosa C. *River, Face Homeward: An Afro-American in Ghana.* New York: Exposition Press, 1966. 120 p.

Barros, Joao de. "Extracts from the 'Decadas da India' of Joao de Barros," in *Voyages of Cadamosto and Other Documents on Western Africa in the Second Half of the Fifteenth Century*, trans. and ed. G. R. Crone, Hakluyt Society, 2nd series, 80. London: Cambridge University Press, 1937, 114-123. Barros was at Elmina from 1522 to 1532.

Beecham, John. *Ashantee and the Gold Coast: Being a Sketch of the History, Social State, and Superstitions of the Inhabitants of Those Countries.* London: J. Mason, 1841; rpt. London: Dawson, 1968; rpt. New York: Johnson Reprint Corp., 1970. 376 p. A secondhand collection of facts by a Wesleyan missionary.

Belcher, Wendy Laura. *Honey from the Lion: An African Journey.* New York: E. P. Dutton, 1988. 188 p.

Binger, Louis. *Du Niger au Golfe de Guinnée par le Pays de Kong et le Mossi, 1887-1889.* 2nd vol. Paris: Hachette, 1892. 416 p.

Biot, M. *Journal des Savants.* Paris: Editions Klincksieck, (1819), 514-529. Contains commentary on Bowdich's accounts from Kumase.

Bosman, William. *A New and Accurate Description of the Coast of Guinea, Divided into the Gold, the Slave, and the Ivory Coasts.* Utrecht: Anthony Schouten, 1704; London: J. Knapton, 1705 and later editions; London: Frank Cass, 1967. 577 p. Bosman, in Dutch service, was on the Gold Coast for 14 years. This is one of the best-known of the early accounts.

Bowdich, Thomas Edward. *An Essay on the Superstitions, Customs and Arts, Common to the Ancient Egyptians, Abyssinians and Ashantee.* Paris: Print by J. Smith, 1821.

___. *Mission from Cape Coast Castle to Ashantee.* London: J. Murray, 1819; London: Frank Cass 1966. 595 p. Bowdich was a representative of the African Company of Merchants. He visited Kumase, the capital of Asante, in 1817 to negotiate trade relations.

Boyle, Frederick. *Through Fanteeland to Coomasie.* London: Chapman and Hall, 1874. 411 p.

Burton, Richard Francis, and V. L. Cameron. *To the Gold Coast for Gold.* 2 vols. London: Chatto and Windus, 1883.

Cardinall, Allan Wolsey. *In Ashanti and Beyond.* London: Seeley, 1927. 288 p.

Carnes, Joshua A. *Journal of a Voyage from Boston to the West Coast of Africa.* Boston: J. P. Jewitt; Cleveland: J. Proctor and Worthington, 1852. 479 p.

Crouch, Archer Philip. *On a Surf-bound Coast: or, Cable-laying in the Tropics.* London: S. Low, Marston, Searle, and Rivington, 1887. 338 p. An interesting account by an English engineer who helped lay the cable along the west coast of Africa.

Cruickshank, Brodie. *Eighteen Years on the Gold Coast of Africa: Including the Account of the Native Tribes and Their Intercourse with Europeans.* 2 vols. London: Hurst and Blackett, 1853; London: Frank Cass, 1966. Cruickshank served as Lt. Governor and acted as Governor.

Curtin, Philip D., et al., eds. *Africa Remembered: Narratives of West Africans from the Era of the Slave Trade.* Madison, Wis.: University of Wisconsin Press, 1967. 363 p.

Dupuis, Joseph. *Journal of a Residence in Ashantee.* London: H. Colburn, 1824; London: Frank Cass, 1966. 502 p. Dupuis was the first Crown representative to visit Asante in 1820.

Eskelund, Karl. *Black Man's Country: A Journey through Ghana.* London: Alvin Redman, 1958. 164 p.

Fage, John Donnelly. "A Commentary on Duarte Packeco Periera's Account of the Lower Guinea Coastlands in His Esmeraldo de Situ Orbis and on Some Other Early Accounts." *History in Africa*, 7 (1980), 47-80.

François, Curt von. "Bericht des Hauptmann von François uber seine Reise im Hinterland des Deutschen Shutzgebiets Togo." *Mitteilungen für Forschungsreisenden und Gelehrten aus den deutschen Schutzgebieten*, 1 (1888), 143-171.

___. "Bericht von Hauptmann von François uber seine zweite Reise nach Salaga." *Mitteilungen für Forschungsreisenden und Gelehrten aus den Deutschen Schutzgebieten*, 2 (1889), 33-37.

Freeman, Richard Austen. *Travels and Life in Ashanti and Jaman.* London: A. Constable, 1898; New York: Frederich A. Stokes, 1898; London: Frank Cass, 1967. 559 p. Richard Freeman was a medical officer who accompanied a political mission to Asante in 1888-1889.

Freeman, Thomas Birch. *Journal of Various Visits to the Kingdoms of Ashanti, Aku and Dahomi in Western Africa.* London: J. Mason, 1844; London: Frank Cass, 1968. 298 p. Thomas Freeman was born in England to an African mother. He became a Methodist missionary to the Gold Coast in 1838. Other correspondence of Freeman can be found at the Methodist Mission Archives, London.

Gordon, Charles Alexander. *Life on the Gold Coast.* London: Balliere, Tindall, and Cox, 1874. 84 p. Sir Charles Gordon was a surgeon on the Gold Coast, 1847-1848.

___. *Recollections.* London: S. Sonnenschein, 1898. 320 p.

Gouldsbury, V. Skipton. "Report of His Journey into the Interior of the Gold Coast. Accra, 27 March 1876." CO. 96.119, no. 5162/S, enclosed in a letter to Lord Carnarvon, 30 April 1876, in Public Record Office. Gouldsbury was a surgeon in the British army medical corps. This letter is an early report on the territory from Krepi to Salaga. The photostat in the Public Records Office is 28 pages long.

Gros, Jules. *Voyages, aventures et captivité de J. Bonnat chez les Achantis.* Paris: Librairie Plon, 1884. 278 p.; Westport, Conn.: Negro Universities Press, 1976, 1970.

Harris, Elizabeth. *Ghana: A Travel Guide. Supplementary Notes on Togo.* Flushing, N.Y.: Aburi Press, 1976. 203 p.

Hutton, William. *A Voyage to Africa*. London: Longman, Hurst, Rees, Orme, and Brown, 1821. 488 p. William Hutton was a member of Dupuis's mission to Asante in 1820.

Huxley, Elspeth Joscelin. *Four Guineas*. London: Chatto and Windus, 1954. 308 p. Subtitled *A Journey through West Africa*, the part on Ghana is on pages 76 to 161.

Huydercoper, W. *Huydercoper's Diary, Journal from Elmina to Kumase, 28th April 1816 - May 1817*. Translated in 1962 by G. Irwin. Legon, Institute of African Studies. Original journal in General State Archives, The Hague, KvG 349. Huydercoper was a representative of the Dutch, who traveled to Kumase to discuss trade relations with Asante.

Ingrams, William Harold. *Seven across the Sahara from Ash to Accra*. London: Murray, 1950. 231 p. Ingrams was Chief Commissioner of the Northern Territories, 1947-1948.

Jones, Adam. "Four Years in Asante: One Source or Several?" *History in Africa*, 18 (1991), 173-203.

Klose, Heinrich. *Journey to Northern Ghana, 1894*. Inge Killick, trans. Legon: Institute of African Studies, University of Ghana, 1964.

___. *Togo unter deutscher Flagge*. Berlin: D. Reimer, 1899.

Makepeace, Margaret. "English Traders on the Gold Coast, 1657-1668: An Analysis of the East India Company Archives." *History in Africa*, 16 (1989), 237-284.

Marie Louise, Princess. *Letters from the Gold Coast*. London: Methuen, 1926. 240 p. Letters from a granddaughter of Queen Victoria written after a 1925 visit.

Pacheco Pereira, Duarte. *Esmeraldo de Situ Orbi* (Guide to Navigation). G. H. T. Kimble, trans. The Hakluyt Society. 2nd Series, No. 74, rpt. of 1937 ed. Nendeln, Liechtenstein:

Kraus Reprint, 1967. 193 p. This book was written about 1508 and was the earliest description of the Gold Coast. Pacheco Pereira was associated with Elmina from 1482, and was Governor from 1519 to 1522.

Ramseyer, F. A., and J. Kühne. *Four Years in Ashantee.* New York: R. Carter and Brothers, 1875. 320 p.

Robertson, G. A. *Notes on Africa.* London: Sherwood, Neely, and Jones, 1819. 460 p.

Rømer, L. F. *Tliforladelig Efterretning om Negotien Paa Kysten Guinea.* Copenhagen: Bey Friederich Christian Pelt, 1769. 304 p.

Rouch, Jane. *Ghana.* Lausanne: Editions Rencontre, 1964. 205 p.

Smith, William. *A New Voyage to Guinea.* London: J. Nourse, 1744. 276 p. With a companion volume of drawings--*Thirty Different Drafts of Guinea.* Smith made a survey for the Royal African Company in 1727 along the Gold Coast.

Thompson, Thomas. *An Account of Two Missionary Voyages.* London: Benj. Dod, 1758. 87 p. Thompson was a missionary for the SPG who went to the Gold Coast in 1752 and stayed there for four years.

___. *Memoirs of an English Missionary to the Coast of Guinea.* London: Shepperson and Reynolds, 1788. 31 p.

van Dantzig, A. "William Bosman's New and Accurate Description of the Gold Coast of the Guinea: How Accurate Is It?" *History in Africa,* 1 (1974), 100-108.

Wilks, Ivor. "Travellers in the Gold Coast Hinterland: Salih Bilali of Massina, Abu Bakr, and Wargee." In *Africa Remembered: Narratives by West Africans from the Era of the Slave Trade,* ed. Philip D. Curtin. Madison, Wis.: University of Wisconsin Press, 1967, 143-189.

L. GEOGRAPHY

Achanfuo-Yeboah, David J. "Internal Migration, Population Redistribution and Urbanization in Ghana." Ph.D. Dissertation, University of Alberta (Canada), 1990.

Adams, David Thickens. *Ghana Geography.* London: University of London Press, 1960. 192 p.

Adeetuk, Thomas A. "Land Tenure and Food Production in Northern Ghana: 1900-1985." Ph.D. Dissertation, University of Wisconsin--Madison, 1991. 215 p.

Agbolosoo, Emmanuel Kwami. "Mineral Processing in a Less Developed Country: Bauxite Processing in Ghana." Ph.D. Dissertation, University of Arizona, 1991. 235 p.

Asare, Benjamin D. "Urbanization and Agricultural Development: The Cocoa Economy in Ghana." Ph.D. Dissertation, Temple University, 1987. 386 p.

Boateng, E. A. *A Geography of Ghana.* 2nd ed. Cambridge: Cambridge University Press, 1966. 212 p.

Church, Ronald James Harrison. *West Africa: A Study of the Environment and of Man's Use of It.* 8th ed. New York: Wiley, 1981. 560 p.; London: Longmans, Green, 1981.

Dickson, Kwamina B. *A Historical Geography of Ghana.* Cambridge: Cambridge University Press, 1971. 379 p.

Dobson, George. "The River Volta, Gold Coast, West Africa." *Journal of the Manchester Geographical Society,* 8 (1892), 18-25.

Forde, Enid Rosamund. *The Populations of Ghana: A Study of the Spatial Relationship of Its Socio-Cultural and Economic Characteristics.* Studies in Geography, 15. Evanston, Ill.:

Department of Geography, Northwestern University, 1968 154 p.

Gaisie, S. K. *Dynamics of Population Growth in Ghana.* Legon: Ghana Universities Press, 1969. 118 p.

Ghana. Information Services. *Ghana at a Glance.* 4th ed. Accra: State Publishing Corp., 1967. 90 p.

Gill, H. E. *A Ground-Water Reconnaissance of the Republic of Ghana, with a Description of Geohydrologic Provinces.* Geological Survey Water Supply Paper 1757-K. Washington, D.C.: U.S. Government Printing Office, 1969. 38 p.

Gould, Peter R. *The Development of the Transportation Pattern in Ghana.* Studies in Geography, 5. Evanston, Ill.: Department of Geography, Northwestern University, 1960. 163 p.

Grove, David, and Laszlo Huszar. *The Towns of Ghana: The Role of Service Centres in Regional Planning.* London: Oxford University Press, 1965. 128 p.

Hilling, David. *Development of the Ghanaian Post System.* London: University of London Press, 1969, 350 p.

Hilton, Thomas E. *The Distribution and Density of Population in Ghana.* Legon: Ghana Universities Press, 1968. 60 p.

Kasanga, R. K., and M. R. Avis. *Internal Migration and Urbanization in Developing Countries: Findings from a Study of Ghana.* Reading: University of Reading, 1988. 108 p.

Lauer, Joseph J. *American and Canadian Dissertations and Master's Theses on Africa, 1974-1987.* GA.: Crossroad Press, Emory University, 1989. 377 p.

Nyamekye, Ambrose Lawrence. "Effect of Placement on the Utilization of Phosphorous by Maize (Zea Mays) in Northern

Ghana." Ph.D. Dissertation, University of Reading (UK), 1990. 205 p.

Ofori-Sarpong, E. *Impact of Drought in Ghana and Upper Volta, 1970-1977.* Legon: University of Ghana, 1980. 23 p.

Osei, William Yaw. "Woodfuel Use in Ghana: Its Nature and Impact at the Village Level." Ph.D. Dissertation, University of Western Ontario (Canada), 1989.

Tindall, Harold Donovan. *Fruit and Vegetables in West Africa.* Rpt. of 1965 ed. London: HMSO, 1971. 259 p.

Tsey, Christian E. "Gold Coast Railways: The Making of a Colonial Economy, 1879-1929." Ph.D. Dissertation, University of Glasgow (UK), 1986. 387 p.

Udo, Reuben K. *A Comprehensive Geography of West Africa.* New York: Holmes and Meier, Africana Publishing Co., 1978. 303 p.

U.S. Department of the Interior, Board on Geographic Names. Ghana: *Official Standard Names Approved by the United States Board on Geographic Names.* Washington, D.C.: U.S. Government Printing Office, 1967. 282 p.

Varley, William J., and H. P. White. *The Geography of Ghana.* London: Longmans, 1958. 313 p.

M. ARTS

Agyeman, Fred. *Amu the African: A Study in Vision and Courage.* Accra: Asempa Publishers, 1989. 208 p.

Antubam, Kofi. *Ghana's Heritage of Culture.* Leipzig: Koehler and Ameland, 1963. 242 p.

Asihene, Emmanuel V. *Understanding the Traditional Art of Ghana*. Cranbury, N.J.: Fairleigh Dickinson University Press, 1978. 95 p.

Assimeng, Max J., ed. *Traditional Life, Culture, and Literature in Ghana*. Buffalo, N.Y.: Conch Magazine, March 1976. 200 p.

Avorgbedor, Daniel K. "Modes of Musical Continuity among the Anlo Ewe of Accra: A Study in Urban Ethnomusicology." Ph.D. Dissertation, Indiana University, 1986. 362 p.

Bebey, Francis. *Musique de l'Afrique*. Paris: Horizons de France, 1969. 208 p.

Bennet-Clark, Margaret C. "Ghana." *Encyclopedia of World Art*, vol. 6. New York, Toronto, and London: McGraw-Hill, 1962, 298-299.

Bravmann, Rene A. *Islam and Tribal Art in West Africa*. London: Cambridge University African Studies Centre, 1974. 190 p. New ed., 1980.

___. *West African Sculpture*. Seattle: University of Washington Press for the Henry Art Gallery, 1970. 80 p.

Carter, William G. "Asante Music in Old and New Juaben: A Comparative Study." Ph.D. Dissertation, University of California at Los Angeles, 1984. 612 p.

Chernoff, John Miller. *African Rhythm and African Sensibility Aesthetics and Social Action in African Musical Idioms*. Chicago: University of Chicago Press, 1979. 304 p.

Cole, Herbert M., and Doran H. Ross. *The Arts of Ghana* (Exhibition Guide). Los Angeles: Museum of Cultural History, University of California, 1977. 230 p.

Collins, John. *Musicmakers of West Africa*. Washington, D.C.: Three Continents Press, 1985. 177 p.

Coplan, David. "Go to My Town, Cape Coast! The Social History of Ghanaian Highlife." In *Eight Urban Musical Cultures: Tradition and Change*, ed. Bruno Nettl. Urbana, Ill.: University of Illinois Press, 1978. 96-114.

DeVare, Evelyn G. "Music Education in Teacher Training Colleges in Ghana." Graduate Dissertation, University of Ghana (Legon), 1980. 484 p.

Ehrlich, Martha Judith. "A Catalogue of Ashanti Art Taken from Kumasi in the Anglo-Ashanti War of 1874." Ph.D. Dissertation, Indiana University, 1981. 789 p.

Garrard, Timothy. *Akan Weights and the Gold Trade.* New York and London: Longman, 1980. 393 p.

___. "Brass-Casting among the Frafra of Northern Ghana." Ph.D. Dissertation, University of California at Los Angeles, 1986. 1082 p.

Helwani, Faisal. *Roots of Highlife.* Film, 1988 production.

Kohler, William. *The Art of Goldweights: Words, Form, Meaning.* Philadelphia: University of Pennsylvania Museum and Anko Foundation, 1977. 68 p.

Kyermaten, A. A. Y. *Panoply of Ghana: Ornamental Art in Ghanaian Tradition and Culture.* New York: Praeger, 1964. 120 p.

Lamb, Venice, and Alastair Lamb. *The Lamb Collection of West African Narrow Strip Weaving.* Washington, D.C.: Textile Museum, 1975. 48 p.

Littrell, Mary Ann. "Ghanaian Wax Print Textiles." Ph.D. Dissertation, Purdue University, 1977. 195 p.

Mato, Daniel. "Clothed in Symbols: The Art of Adinkra among the Akan of Ghana." Ph.D. Dissertation, University of Indiana, 1987. 494 p.

McLeod, Malcolm D. *The Asante*. London: Published for the Trustees of the British Museum by British Museum Publications, 1981. 192 p.

Nketia, John Hanson Kwabena. *African Music in Ghana*. Evanston, Ill.: Northwestern University Press, 1963. 148 p.

___. *Drumming in Akan Communities of Ghana*. London: Nelson, for the University of Ghana, 1963. 212 p.

___. *Folk Songs of Ghana*. London: Oxford University Press for the University of Ghana, 1963. 205 p.

___. *Funeral Dirges of the Akan People*. New York: Negro Universities Press (Greenwood), 1969. 296 p.

___. "Historical Evidence in Ga Religious Music." In *The Historian in Tropical Africa*, ed. Jan Vansina, Raymond Mauny, and L. V. Thomas. London: Oxford University Press, 1964. 265-283.

___. "The Musical Traditions of the Akan." *Tarikh*, 7, 2 (1982), 47-59.

___. *The Music of Africa*. New York: W. W. Norton, 1974. 278 p.

Owusu, Brempong. "Akan Highlife in Ghana: Songs of Cultural Transition." Ph.D. Dissertation, Indiana University, 1986. 747 p.

Patton, Sharon Frances. "The Asante Stool." 2 vols. Ph.D. Dissertation, Northwestern University, 1980. 599 p.

Plass, Margaret W. *African Miniatures: The Goldweights of the Ashanti*. London and New York: Praeger, 1967. 26 p.

Prussin, Labelle. *Architecture in Northern Ghana: A Study of Forms and Functions.* Berkeley, Calif.: University of California Press, 1969. 120 p.

Ratton, Charles. *Fetish Gold.* Philadelphia: University of Pennsylvania Museum, 1975. 68 p.

Rattray, Robert Sutherland, et al. *Religion and Art in Ashanti.* Rpt. of the 1927 ed. New York and London: Oxford University Press, 1959. 432 p.

"Return to Mahe." Film from the National Film and TV Institute (Ghana) on the exile of Asantehene Prempe I.

Ross, D. H., and Timothy M. Garrard, eds. *Akan Transformations: Problems in Ghanaian Art History.* Los Angeles: Museum of Cultural History, 1983. 111 p.

Saighoe, Francis A. "The Music Behavior of Dagaba Immigrants in Tarkwa, Ghana: A Study of Situational Change." Ph.D. Dissertation, Columbia University, 1988. 304 p.

Sarpong, Peter. *The Sacred Stools of the Akan.* Tema: Ghana Publishing Corp., 1971. 83 p.

Schmidt, Nancy. *Sub-Saharan African Films and Filmmakers: An Annotated Bibliography.* London and New York: H. Zell, 1988. 401 p.

Smith, Fred Thomas. "Gurensi Architectural Decoration in Northeastern Ghana." Ph.D. Dissertation, Indiana University, 1979, 365 p.

Stapleton, Chris, and Chris May. *African All Stars: The Popular Music of the Continent.* London: Quartet, 1987. 373 p.

Swithenbank, Michael. *Ashanti Fetish Houses.* Accra: Ghana Universities Press, 1969. 68 p.

Underwood, Leon. *Bronzes of West Africa.* 2nd. ed. London: Tiranti, 1968. 32 p.

___. *Figures in Wood of West Africa.* 3rd. ed. London: Tiranti, 1964, 48 p.

N. LITERATURE AND PRESS

Abbs, Akosua. *Ashanti Boy.* London: Collins, 1959. 256 p.

Abruquah, Joseph Wilfred. *The Catechist.* London: Allen and Unwin, 1965. 202 p.

___. *The Torrent.* London: Longmans, Green, 1968. 280 p.

Addo, Peter Eric Adotey, comp. *Ghana Folk Tales: Ananse Stories from Africa.* Jericho, N.Y.: Exposition Press, 1968. 51 p.

Adzo, Zagbade-Thomas. *Emefa and Other Songs.* Python Publishers, 1990 (children's literature).

Agovi, Kofi Ermale. *Novels of Social Change.* Tema: Ghana Publishing Corporation, 1988. 290 p.

Aidoo, Christina Ama Ata. *Anowa.* London: Longmans, 1970. 66 p.

___. *The Dilemma of a Ghost.* Accra: Longmans, 1965. 50 p.

___. *No Sweetness Here.* London: Longmans, 1969; New York: Doubleday, 1970. 166 p.

Anokwa, Kwadwo. "Editorial Patterns of Ghanaian Daily Newspapers: A Study of Press Performance under Civilian and Military Regimes in Ghana." Ph.D. Dissertation, University of Arizona, 1991. 143 p.

Anyidoho, Kofi. *Earthchild with Brain Surgery (Poems)*. Accra: Woeli Publishers, 1985. 122 p.

___. *Elegy for the Revolution with a Harvest of Our Dreams (Poems)*. London: Heinemann, 1984; Accra: Woeli, 1985. 90 p.

___. *Interdisciplinary Dimensions of African Literature*. Washington, D.C.: Three Continents Press, 1985. 223 p.

___. *The Pan-African Ideal in Literatures of the Black World*. Accra: Ghana Universities Press, 1989. 49 p.

___, Masaemuru Zimunya, and Peter Porter. eds. *The Fate of Vultures: New Poetry from Africa*. London: Heinemann, 1989. 111 p.

Armah, Ayi Kwei. *The Beautiful Ones Are Not Yet Born*. Boston: Houghton Mifflin, 1968; London: Heinemann, 1969; New York: Macmillan, 1969. 215 p. Last print, 1981.

___. *Fragments*. Boston: Houghton Mifflin, 1970; New York: Collier-Macmillan, 1971; London: Heinemann, 1974. 287 p.

___. *The Healers*. London: Heinemann, 1979. 309 p.

___. *Two Thousand Seasons*. London: Heinemann, 1979; Chicago: Third World, 1980. Last print, 1984, 206 p.

___. *Why Are We So Blest?* New York: Doubleday, 1971; London: Heinemann, 1974; 2nd. ed. 1981. 288 p.

Asare, Bediako. *Rebel*. London: Heinemann, 1969; Nairobi, Kenya: Heinemann, 1972. 136 p.

___. *The Stubborn*. Kampala: East African Literature Bureau, 1976. 161 p.

Awoonor, Kofi [George Awoonor-Williams]. *The Breast of the Earth*. New York: Doubleday, 1975. 387 p.

____. *Guardians of the Sacred Word: Ewe Poetry.* New York: Nok, 1974. 104 p.

____. *A House by the Sea.* New York: Greenfield Review Press, 1978. 78 p.

. *Night of My Blood.* Garden City, N. Y.: Doubleday, 1971. 96 p.

____. *This Earth, My Brother.* New York: Doubleday; London: Heinemann, 1972. 183 p.

____. *Until the Morning After: Selected Poems, 1963-1985.* New York: Greenfield Review Press, and Accra: Woeli Publishing, 1987. 216 p.

____, and Geormbeeyi Adali-Mortty. *Messages: Poems from Ghana.* London: Heinemann, 1971. 190 p.

Bame, K. N. *Come to Laugh: A Study of African Traditional Theater in Ghana.* Accra: Baafour Educational Enterprises, 1982. 102 p.

Brown, Stewart, ed. *Writers from Africa.* London: Book Trust, 1989. 56 p.

Casely-Hayford, Joseph Ephraim. *Ethiopia Unbound.* London: C. M. Phillips, 1911; Frank Cass, 1969; New York: Humanities Press, 1969. 215 p.

Chick, John D. "The Ashanti Times: A Footnote to Ghanaian Press History." *African Affairs.* (London), 76, 302 (Jan. 1977), 80-94.

Danquah, Joseph Boakye. *Liberty: A Page from the Life of J. B.* Accra: J. K. Akyeampong, 1960. 35 p.

____. *The Third Woman.* London: United Society for Christian Literature, 1943. 151 p.

De Graft, Joe. *The Secret of Opokuwa.* Accra: Anowuo, 1967. 72 p.

___. *Through a Film Darkly.* London: Oxford University Press, 1970. 70 p.

Dei-Anang, Michael Francis. *Africa Speaks: A Collection of Original Verse.* 2nd ed. Accra: Guinea Press, 1960. 104 p.

___. *Cocoa Comes to Mampong.* Cape Coast: Methodist Book Depot, 1949. 47 p. Nendeln: Kraus Reprint, 1970.

___. *Ghana Glory: Poems on Ghana and Ghanaian Life.* London: Nelson, 1965. 69 p. Foreword by Kwame Nkrumah.

___. *Ghana Semi-Tones.* Accra: Presbyterian Book Depot, 1962. 28 p.

___. *Okomfo Anokye's Golden Stool: A Play in Three Acts.* Ilfracombe, Devon.: Stockwell, 1960; Accra: Waterville, 1963. 60 p.

Djoleto, Amu S. *Money Galore.* London: Heinemann, 1975. 182 p.

___. *The Strange Man.* London: Longman, 1967; New York: Humanities Press, 1968. 277 p.

Duodu, Cameron. *The Gab Boys.* London: Andre Deutsch, 1967; Fontana-Collins, 1969. 201 p.

Ellis, Alfred Burdon. *West African Stories.* London: Chapman and Hall, 1890. 278 p.

Fiawoo, F. Kwasi. *The Fifth Landing Stage.* Trans. from Ewe. London: United Society for Christian Literature, 1943. 87 p.

Fraser, Robert. *The Novels of Ayi Kwei Armah.* London: Heinemann, 1980. 113 p.

Hihetah, Robert Kofi. *Painful Road to Kadjebi*. Accra: Ananwuo, 1966. 194 p.

Jahn, Janheinz, et al. *Who's Who in African Literature: Biographies, Works, Commentaries*. Tubingen: Horst Erdmann Verlag, 1972. 411 p.

Johnevi, Eta. *Roses for Sondia*. Accra: Johnevi Publications, 1972. 208 p.

Jones-Quartey, Kwatei A. B. *History, Politics, and Early Press in Ghana*. Accra: Afram Publications, 1975. 130 p.

___. *A Summary History of the Ghana Press, 1822-1960*. Accra: Ghana Information Service, 1974. 68 p.

Kayper-Mensah, Albert. *The Dark Wanderer (Poems)*. Tubingen: Horst Erdmann Verlag, 1970. 133 p.

___, and Horst Wolff, eds. *Ghanaian Writing: Ghana as Seen by Her Own Writers as Well as German Authors*. Tubingen: Horst Erdmann Verlag, 1972. 240 p.

Knipp, Thomas R. "Myth, History and the Poetry of Kofi Awoonor." *African Literature Today* (New York), 11 (1980), 39-61.

Konandu, Samuel Asare. *Come Back Dora!* Rev. ed. Accra: Anowuo, 1968. 212 p. Later published as *Ordained by the Oracle*. London: Heinemann, 1969. 188 p.

___. *Devils in Waiting*. Accra: Anowuo Educational Publishers, 1989. 236 p.

___. *Don't Leave Me Mercy*. Accra: Anowuo, 1966. 118 p.

___. *The Lawyer Who Bungled His Life*. Accra: Waterville, 1965. 81 p.

___. *Night Watchers of Korlebu*. Accra: Anowuo, 1968. 99 p.

___. *Shadow of Wealth*. Accra: Anowuo, 1966. 173 p. Reprinted, 1990. 167 p.

___. *The Wizard of Asaman*. Accra: Waterville, 1964. 129 p. Rpt. Accra: Anowuo Press, 1988. 129 p.

___. *A Woman in Her Prime*. London: Heinemann, 1967. 108 p.

Kponkpongori, C. S., et al. *Gonja Proverbs*, ed. O. Rytz. Legon: Institute of African Studies, University of Ghana, 1966. 64 p.

Kwakwa, B. S. *Ghanaian Writing Today, 1*. Accra-Tema: Ghana Publishing Corp., 1974. 193 p.

Kwarteng, D. K. *My Sword Is My Life*. Accra: Ghana Publishing Corp., 1972. 158 p.

Laing, Kojo. *Godhorse*. Oxford: Heinemann, 1989. 56 p.

___. *Search Sweet Country*. London: Heinemann, 1986. 256 p.

___. *Woman of the Aeroplanes*. London: Heinemann, 1988. 196 p.

Mensah, Grace Osei. *Eight Delightful Folktales*. Accra: Waterville, 1965. 57 p.

Obeng, R. E. *Eighteenpence*. Ilfracombe, Devon.: Stockwell, 1943. 167 p.; Birkenhead: Wilmer, 1950. 167 p.; Accra: Ghana Publishing Corp., 1971. 145 p.

Okai, Atukwei. *The Anthills of the Sea*. Accra: Ghana Publishing Corp., 1989 (children's book).

Priebe, Richard K., ed. *Ghanaian Literatures*. New York: Greenwood Press, 1988. 300 p.

Quaye, Cofie. *Murder in Kumasi*. Accra: Moxon, 1970. 104 p.

___. *Sammy Slams the Gang*. Accra: Moxon, 1970. 62 p.

Rattray, Robert Sutherland. *Akan-Ashanti Folk-Tales.* Oxford: Clarendon Press, 1930. 275 p.

___. *Ashanti Proverbs.* Oxford: Clarendon Press, 1916. 190 p.; New edition, 1961.

___. *The Leopard Priestess.* New York: Appleton-Century, 1934. 224 p.

Sekyi, Kobina. *The Blinkards.* London: Heinemann, 1974. 160 p.

Selormey, Francis. *The Narrow Path.* London: Heinemann, 1966. 184 p.

Sutherland, Efua Theodore. *Edufa.* London: Longmans, 1967. 72 p.

___. *Foriwa.* Accra: State Publishing Corp., 1967. 60 p.

___. *Vulture! Vulture!* Accra: State Publishing Corp., 1968. 32 p.

___. *The Story of Bob Johnson, Ghana's Ace Comedian.* Accra: Anowuo, 1970. 25 p.

___. *The Marriage of Anansewa.* London: African Classics, 1987. 157 p.

Wright, Derek. *Ayi Kwei Armah, Africa: The Source of His Fiction.* London: Hans Zell, 1989. 334 p.

Yankah, Kwesi. *Woes of a Kwatriot: Reflections on the Ghanaian Situation.* Accra: Woeli Publishing, 1990. 127 p.

Yeboah-Afari, Ajoa. *A Decade of Thoughts of a Native Daughter: Collections of Her Column Articles.* Vol. I. The Author, 1988.

Zell, Hans, Helene Silver, et al. *A Reader's Guide to African Literature.* New York: Africana Publishing Corp., 1971. 218 p.

O. LANGUAGE

Abbot, Mary. *Collected Field Reports on the Phonology of Basari.* Legon: University of Ghana Institute of African Studies, 1966. 59 p.

Ablorh-Odijidja, J. R. *Ga for Beginners.* Accra: Waterville, 1968. 207 p.

Adjamah, Eli Koffi. *The Articulatory Settings of English and Ewe and Their Implications for Teaching English Phonology.* Ph.D. Dissertation, University of Kansas, 1987. 241 p.

Akrofi, C. A., and G. Borchey. *English-Twi-Ga Dictionary.* Accra: Waterville, 1968. 83 p.

Amankwaah, J. W. Y., et al. *Gonja-English Dictionary and Spelling Book,* ed. O. Ritz. Legon: University of Ghana, 1971. 273 p.

Balmer, William T., and F. C. Grant. *A Grammar of the Fante-Akan Language.* London: Atlantic Press, 1929. 223 p.

Bartels, Francis L. *Fante Word List with Rules of Spelling.* Cape Coast: Methodist Book Depot, 1944. 84 p.

Bendor-Samuel, J. T. "The Grusi Sub-Group of the Gur Languages." *Journal of West African Languages,* 2, 1 (1965), 47-55.

Berry, Jack. *English, Twi, Asante, Fante Dictionary.* London: Macmillan, 1960. 146 p.

___. *The Place-Names of Ghana.* Accra: University of Ghana, 1958. 190 p.

___. *The Pronunciation of Ewe.* Cambridge: Heffer, 1951. 28 p.

___, and Agnes Akosua Aidoo. *An Introduction to Akan.* Evanston, Ill.: Northwestern University Press, 1975. 336 p.

___, Joseph H. Greenberg et al., eds. *Linguistics in Subsaharan Africa.* The Hague, Paris, New York: Mouton, 1971. 972 p.

___, and Nii Amon Kotei. *An Introductory Course in Ga.* Washington, D. C.: U.S. Office of Education, Institute of International Studies, 1969. 148 p.

Blair, H. A. *Dagomba Dictionary and Grammar.* Accra: Government Printer, 1941. 151 p.

Brew, S. H. *Practical Fanti Course.* Cape Coast: Wesleyan Book Depot, 1917. 132 p.

Christaller, Johann G. *Dictionary of the Asante and Fante Language Called Tshi (Twi).* Basel: Evangelical Society, 1933. 607 p.

___. *A Grammar of the Asante and Fante Language Called Tshi (Twi) Based on the Akuapem Dialect with Reference to the Other Dialects.* Farnborough, Hampshire: Gregg International Publishers, 1964. 203 p.

Crouch, Marjorie. *Collected Field Reports on the Phonology of Vagala.* Legon: University of Ghana Institute of African Studies, 1966. 44 p.

Dolphyne, Florence Abena. "Akan Language Patterns and Development." *Tarikh*, 7, 2 (1982), 35-45.

Froger, Fernand. *Etude sur la langue du Mossi.* Paris: Leroux, 1910. 250 p.

___. *Manuel pratique de langue More.* Paris: Fournier, 1923. 326 p.

Gbedemah, Fui Fianyo Kosi. *Alternative Language Policies for Education in Ghana.* New York: Vantage Press, 1975. 204 p.

Ghana. Bureau of Ghana Languages. *Language Guide (Akuapem-Twi)*. 3rd ed. Accra: Bureau of Ghana Languages, 1973. 47 p.

____. *Language Guide (Asante-Twi)*. 3rd ed. Accra: Bureau of Ghana Languages, 1978; rpt. 50 p.

____. *Language Guide (Dagbani)*. 2nd ed. Accra: Bureau of Ghana Languages, 1968. 48 p.

____. *Language Guide (Ewe)*. 3rd ed. Accra: Bureau of Ghana Languages, 1977. 53 p.

____. *Language Guide (Fante)*. 3rd ed. Accra: Bureau of Ghana Languages, 1977; rpt. 52 p.

____. *Language Guide (Ga)*. 3rd ed. Accra: Bureau of Ghana Languages, 1976. 50 p.

____. *Language Guide (Nzema)*. 3rd ed. Accra: Bureau of Ghana Languages, 1977. 60 p.

Hall, H. F. *Dictionary of Practical Notes: Mossi-English Languages*. Ouahigouya: Assembly of God, n.d. 78 p.

Krass, A. C. *A Dictionary of the Chokosi Language: English-Chokosi*. Legon: University of Ghana, Institute of African Studies, 1973. 133 p.

Kropp-Dakubu, M. E. *Adangme Vocabularies*. Accra: Institute of African Studies, University of Ghana, 1970.

____. *Ga, Adangme, and Ewe with English Gloss*. Legon: University of Ghana, 1966. 79 p.

____. *Ga-English Dictionary*. Legon: University of Ghana, 1973. 248 p.

Lamothe, Charles. *Esquisse de système grammatical Lobi.* Paris and Ouagadougou: CNRS and CVRS, 1966. 168 p.

Migeod, Frederick William Hugh. *The Languages of West Africa.* 2 vols. Freeport, N.Y.: Books for Libraries Press, 1972; London: K. Paul, Trench, Trubner, 1911-1913. 350 p.

Painter, Colin. *Gonja: A Phonological and Grammatical Study.* Bloomington, Ind.: Indiana University Press, 1969. 523 p.

Prost, André. *Contribution à l'étude des langues voltaïques.* Dakar: IFAN, 1964. 461 p.

Rapp, Eugen L. *An Introduction of Twi.* Basel: Evangelical Society, 1948. 119 p.

Rattray, Robert Sutherland. *An Elementary Mole Grammar with a Vocabulary of over 1000 Words for the Use of Officials in the Northern Territories of the Gold Coast.* Oxford: Clarendon Press, 1918. 85 p.

Redder, J. E., N. Owusu, et al. *Twi Basic Course.* Washington, D.C.: U.S. Foreign Service Institute, 1963. 224 p.

Ring, James Andrew. "Planning for Literacy: A Sociolinguistic Survey of Multilingualism in Ghana." Ph.D. Dissertation, Georgetown University, 1987. 240 p.

Schachter, Paul, and Victoria Fromkin. *A Phonology of Akan: Akuapem, Asante, & Fante.* Working Papers in Phonetics, No. 9. Los Angeles: University of California, 1968. 268 p.

Schaeffer, Robert. *Collected Field Reports on the Phonology of Fra Fra.* Legon: University of Ghana Institute of African Studies, 1975. 43 p.

Steele, Mary, and Gretchen Weed. *Collected Field Reports on the Phonology of Konkomba.* Legon: University of Ghana Institute of African Studies, 1966. 77 p.

Warburton, Irene P., Prosper Kpotufe, and Roland Glover. *Ewe Basic Course.* Rev. ed. Bloomington, Ind.: African Studies Program, Indiana University, 1968. 271 p.

Warren, Dennis. *Bibliography and Vocabulary of the Akan (Twi-Fante) Language of Ghana.* African Series, 6, Research Center for Language and Semiotic Studies. Atlantic Highlands, N.J.: Humanities Press; Bloomington, Ind.: Indiana University Research Center for Language and Semiotic Studies, 1976.

Welman, Charles Wellesley. *A Preliminary Study of the Nzima Language.* London: Crown Agents, 1926. 113 p.

Welmers, William Everett. *A Descriptive Grammar of Fanti.* Baltimore: Linguistic Society of America, 1946. 78 p.

Westermann, Diedrich Hermann. *The Languages of West Africa.* London: Oxford University Press, 1952. 215 p.

___. *A Study of the Ewe Language,* trans. A. L. Bickford-Smith. London: Oxford University Press, 1930. 258 p.

Wilkie, M. G. *Ga Grammar, Notes and Exercises.* London: Oxford University Press, 1930. 239 p.

Yankah, Kwesi. *The Proverb in the Context of Akan Rhetoric: A Theory of Proverb Praxis.* Bern, New York: P. Lang, 1989. 313 p.

P. CULTURE AND SOCIAL LIFE

Abraham, William E. *The Mind of Africa.* Chicago: University of Chicago Press 1962; rpt. 1969. 206 p.

Achanfuo-Yeboah, David J. *Contraceptive Use in Africa.* University of Alberta, Department of Sociology Research Paper, 1988, #54. 10 p.

Acquah, Ione. *Accra Survey: A Social Survey of the Capital of Ghana, Formerly Called the Gold Coast, 1953-1956.* London: University of London, 1958. 176 p.

Akwabi-Ameyaw, Kofi. "Ashanti Social Organization: Some Ethnographic Clarifications." *Ethnology,* 21 (Oct. 1982), 325-334.

Alicoe, Thomas. *The Evolution of Gold Coast Chiefship.* Sheffield: Telegraph and Star, 1953. 102 p.

Ankama, S. K. "The Police and Maintenance of Law and Order in Ghana." Ph.D. Dissertation, University of London, 1967. 576 p.

___. *Police History: Some Aspects in England and Ghana.* Ilford, Essex: Silkan Books, 1983. 62 p.

Asante, S. K. B. *Property Law and Social Goals in Ghana, 1844-1966.* Accra: Ghana Universities Press, 1975; London: Rex Collings, 1977. 303 p.

Assimeng, Max. *Religion and Social Change in West Africa.* Accra: Ghana Universities Press, 1989. 327 p.

___. *Social Structure of Ghana.* Accra-Tema: Ghana Publishing Corp., 1981. 201 p.

Azu, Diana Gladys. *The Ga Family and Social Change.* African Social Research Documents, 5. Leiden: Afrika-Studies Centrum; Cambridge: African Studies Centre, 1974. 139 p.

Barkan, Joel D. *An African Dilemma; University Students, Development and Politics in Ghana, Tanzania and Uganda.* Oxford: Oxford University Press, 1976. 280 p.

Bebefo, Kofi Darkwa. *The Determinants of Family Size Preferences and Traditional Child-Spacing Practices in West Africa.* Ann Arbor, Mich.: University of Michigan, 1990. 296 p.

Birmingham, Walter, I. Neustadt, and E. N. Omamboe, eds. *A Study of Contemporary Ghana.* Vol. 1, *The Economy of Ghana*; Vol. 2, *The Social Structure of Ghana.* Evanston, Ill.: Northwestern University Press, 1966; London: Allen and Unwin for the Ghana Academy of Sciences, 1966.

Boamah-Wiafe, Daniel. "The Pattern and Correlates of Urbanbound Migration in Ghana." Ph.D. Dissertation, University of Wisconsin-Madison, 1978. 173 p.

Bukh, Jette. *The Village Woman in Ghana.* Uppsala: Scandinavian Institute of African Studies, 1979. 118 p. About life in the Ewe village of Tsito, a town near Ho.

Busia, Kofi Abrefa. *The Position of the Chief in the Modern Political System of Ashanti: A Study of the Influence of Contemporary Social Changes on Ashanti Political Institutions.* London: Oxford University Press for the International African Institute, 1951. 233 p. Rpt. London: Frank Cass, 1968.

___. *Report on a Social Survey of Sekondi-Takoradi.* London: Crown Agents, 1950. 164 p.

Caldwell, J. C. *African Rural-Urban Migration: The Movement of Ghana's Towns.* London: C. Hurst, 1977. 260 p.

___. *Population Growth and Family Change in Africa: The New Urban Elite in Ghana.* London: C. Hurst, 1977. 224 p.

Cardinall, Allan Wolsey. *The Natives of the Northern Territories of the Gold Coast: Their Customs, Religion and Folklore.* London: George Routledge and Sons, 1920; New York: Negro Universities Press (Greenwood), 1969. 158 p.

Chambers, Robert, ed. *The Volta Resettlement Experience.* New York and London: Praeger and Pall Mall, 1970. 286 p.

Christensen, James Boyd. *Double Descent Among the Fanti.* Behavior Science Monographs. New Haven, Conn.: Human Relations Area Files, 1954. 145 p.

___. "The Role of Proverbs in Fante Culture." *Africa* (London), 28 (July 1958), 232-43.

Cleveland, David Arthur. "The Population Dynamics of Subsistence Agriculture in the West African Savanna: A Village in Northeast Ghana." Ph.D. Dissertation, University of Arizona, 1980. 382 p.

Crowder, Michael, and Obaro Ikime. *West African Chiefs: Their Changing Status under Colonial Rule and Independence.* New York: Africana Publishing Corp.; Ile Ife, Nigeria: University of Ife Press, 1970. 453 p.

Datta, Ansu K., and R. Porter. "The Asafo System in Historical Perspective." *Journal of African History,* 12, 2 (1971), 279-297.

Elias, Taslim Olawale. *The Nature of African Customary Law.* Manchester: Manchester University Press, 1956. 318 p.

Ellis, Alfred Burdon. *The Ewe-speaking Peoples of the Slave Coast of West Africa; Their Religion, Manners, Customs, Laws, Languages.* London: Chapman and Hall, 1890. 331 p.

___. *The Land of Fetish.* London: Chapman and Hall, 1883. 316 p.

___. *The Tshi-speaking Peoples of the Gold Coast of West Africa; Their Religion, Manners, Customs, Laws, Languages.* London: Chapman and Hall, 1887. 343 p.

___. *West African Sketches.* London: S. Tinsley, 1881. 326 p. Alfred Burdon Ellis, 1852-1894 went out to the Gold Coast in 1874 and spent a number of years there as soldier and government official.

Field, Margaret Joyce. *Search for Security: An Ethno-psychiatric Study of Rural Ghana.* Evanston, Ill.: Northwestern University Press, 1960; London: Faber and Faber, 1960. 478 p.

___. *Social Organization of the Ga People.* London: The Crown Agents for the Colonies, 1940. 231 p.

Fikry, Mona. "Wa: A Case Study of Social Values and Social Tensions as Reflected in the Oral Traditions of the Wala of Northern Ghana." 2 vols. Ph.D. Dissertation, Indiana University, 1969. 1,063 p.

Fortes, Meyer. *The Dynamics of Clanship among the Tallensi: Being the First Part of an Analysis of the Social Structure of a Trans-Volta Tribe.* London: Oxford University Press, 1945. 270 p.

___. "Kinship and Marriage among the Ashanti." In *African Systems of Kinships and Marriage,* ed. A. R. Radcliff-Brown and Daryll Forde. London: Oxford University Press for the International African Institute, 1950. 252-284.

___. "Primitive Kinship." *Scientific American* (New York), 200, 6 (June 1959), 146-158. Patrilineal and matrilineal society compared.

___. *The Web of Kinship among the Tallensi.* London: Oxford University Press, 1949. 358 p. The second part of *Dynamics of Clanship among the Tallensi.*

Foster, Philip. *Education and Social Change in Ghana.* Chicago: University of Chicago Press, 1965. 322 p.

Gocking, Roger Stephen. "The Historic Akoto: A Social History of Cape Coast Ghana, 1843-1948." Ph.D. Dissertation, Stanford University, 1981. 391 p.

Goody, Jack [John Rankine]. *The Social Organization of the Lo Willi.* London: HMSO, 1956. 119 p.; 2nd ed. London: Oxford University Press for the International African Institute, 1967.

Howard, Rhoda. "Formation and Stratification of the Peasantry in Colonial Ghana." *Journal of Peasant Studies* (London), 8 (Oct. 1980), 61-80.

Jahoda, Gustav. *White Man: A Study of the Attitudes of Africans to Europeans in Ghana before Independence.* London: Oxford University Press, 1961. 144 p.

Kasanga, R. K., and M. R. Avis. *Internal Migration and Urbanization in Developing Countries: Findings from a Study of Ghana.* Reading: University of Reading, 1988.

Kelly, Gail Margaret. "The Ghanaian Intelligentsia." Ph.D. Dissertation, University of Chicago, 1959. 152 p.

Kilson, Marion D. *African Urban Kinsmen: The Ga of Central Accra.* London: C. Hurst, 1975; New York: St. Martin's, 1975. 122 p.

___. "Variations in Ga Culture in Central Accra." *Ghana Journal of Sociology.* 3 (Feb. 1967), 33-54.

Klein, Anatole Norman. "Inequality in Asante: A Study of the Forms and Meanings of Slavery and Social Servitude in Pre-Early Colonial Akan-Asante Society and Culture." 2 vols. Ph.D. Dissertation, Ann Arbor, Mich.: University of Michigan, 1980. 494 p.

___. "The Two Asantes: Competing Interpretations of 'Slavery' in Akan Asante Culture and Society." Chapt. 6 in *The Ideology of Slavery in Africa,* ed. Paul E. Lovejoy. Sage Series on African Modernization and Development. Beverly Hills, Calif.: Sage Publications, 1981. 312 p.

Lubeck, Paul. *Patterns of Assimilation of Hausa Families in Dagomba.* Evanston, Ill.: Northwestern University Press, 1968. 55 p.

Lystad, Robert A. *The Ashanti: A Proud People.* New Brunswick, N.J.: Rutgers University Press, 1958; Rpt. New York: Greenwood, 1968. 212 p.

Manoukian, Madeline. *Akan and Ga-Adangme Peoples of the Gold Coast.* Ethnographic Survey of Africa: Western Africa, pt. 5. London: International African Institute, 1952. 104 p.

Marshall, Margaret Ann. "A Preliminary Investigation of the Cultural and Service Factors Contributing to Maternal Mortality in the Central Accra Region, Ghana, as Perceived by Private Sector Midwives: Implications for Education Policy." Ph.D. Dissertation, George Washington University, 1989. 231 p.

Mate Kole, Nene Azu. "The Historical Background of Krobo Customs." *Transactions of the Gold Coast and Togoland Historical Society* (Achimota), 1, 4 (1955), 133-140.

McCall, Daniel Francis. "The Effect on Family Structure of Changing Economic Activities of Women in a Gold Coast Town." Ph.D. Dissertation, Columbia University, 1956. 125 p.

McCarthy, Mary O'Neil. "Social Change as a Prelude to Colonialism: The Fante States, 1807-1874." Ph.D. Dissertation, University of Minnesota, 1980. 298 p.

Meyerowitz, Eva Lewin-Richter. *The Akan of Ghana: Their Ancient Beliefs.* London: Faber and Faber, 1958. 164 p.

___. *Akan Traditions of Origin.* London: Faber and Faber, 1952. 149 p.

___. *At the Court of an African King.* London: Faber and Faber, 1962. 244 p.

____. *The Divine Kinship in Ghana and Ancient Egypt.* London: Faber and Faber, 1960. 260 p.

Morrison, Minion K. C. *Ethnicity and Political Integration: The Case of Ashanti, Ghana.* Foreign and Comparative Studies/African Series 38. Syracuse: Syracuse University, 1982. 208 p.

Murdock, George Peter. *Africa: Its Peoples and Their Culture History.* New York: McGraw-Hill, 1959. 456 p.

Nukunya, G. K. *Kinship and Marriage Among the Anlo-Ewe.* London: Athlone Press, 1969; New York: Humanities Press, 1969. 217 p. (London School of Economics Monograghs on Social Anthropology, 37.)

Opoku, A. A. "Festivals Change to Match Today's World." *Africa Report,* 17, 4 (April 1972), 23-26.

Oppong, Christine. *Domestic Rights and Duties in Southern Ghana.* Legon: Institute of African Studies, 1974. 382 p.

____. *Growing up in Dagbon.* Tema: Gha/na Publishing Corp., 1973. 79 p.

____. *Marriage among a Matrilineal Elite: A Family Study of Ghanaian Senior Civil Servants.* London and New York: Cambridge University Press, 1974. 186 p.

____, and Katharine Abu. *Seven Roles of Women: Impact of Education, Migration and Employment on Ghanaian Mothers.* Geneva: International Labour Office, 1983. 127 p.

Osei, Osafo Kwabena. *African Heritage of the Akan, Republic of Ghana.* Los Angeles: By the Author, 1979. 173 p.

Pellow, Deborah. *Women in Accra: Options for Autonomy.* Algonac, Mich.: Reference Publications, 1977. 272 p.

Robertson, A. F. "Anthropology and Government in Ghana." *African Affairs* (London), 74, 294 (Jan. 1975), 51-59.

Robertson, Claire C. *Sharing the Same Bowl: A Socioeconomic History of Women and Class in Accra, Ghana.* Bloomington, Ind.: Indiana University Press, 1984. 299 p.

Sandbrook, Richard, and Jack Arn. *The Labouring Poor and Urban Class Formation: The Case of Greater Accra.* Occasional Monograph Series 12. Montreal: Centre for Developing Area Studies, McGill University, 1977. 86 p.

Sarbah, John Mensah. *Fanti Customary Laws.* London: W. Clowes, 1897. 295 p.

___. *Fanti National Constitution and Fanti Law Report.* London: W. Clowes, 1906. 273 p.; London: Frank Cass, 1968.

Schildkrout, Enid. "Government and Chiefs in Kumasi Zongo." In *West African Chiefs: Their Changing Status under Colonial Rule and Independence,* ed. Michael Crowder and Obaro Ikime. New York: Africana Publishing Corp.; Ile Ife, Nigeria: University of Ife Press, 1970. 370-392.

___. *People of the Zongo. The Transformation of Ethnic Identities in Ghana.* Cambridge and New York: Cambridge University Press, 1978. 303 p.

Schmidt, Nancy J. *Social Impact of AIDS in Africa: A Working Bibliography.* Bloomington, Ind.: University of Indiana, 1987. 21 p.

Schott, John R., ed. *An Experiment in Integrated Rural Development: The Mampong Valley Social Laboratory in Ghana.* New York: International Institute of Rural Reconstruction, 1978. 252 p.

Scott, David. *Epidemic Disease in Ghana, 1901-1960.* London: Oxford University Press, 1965. 226 p.

Stenross, Barbara. "Customary Law, Colonialism, and the Courts: Land Law and Capitalist Class Formation in the Gold Coast Colony." Ph.D. Dissertation, Indiana University, 1981. 177 p.

Tranakides, G. "Observations on the History of Some Gold Coast Peoples." *Transactions of the Gold Coast and Togoland Historical Society*, 1, 2 (1953), 33-44.

Von Laue, Theodore H. "Anthropology and Power: R. S. Rattray among the Ashanti." *African Affairs* (London), 75 (Jan. 1976), 33-54.

Williams, Joy E. Stewart. "The Educated and Professional Elite in the Gold Coast and Sierra Leone, 1885-1914." Ph.D. Dissertation, University of California, Los Angeles, 1980. 168 p.

Wilson, Louis Edward. "The Evolution of Krobo Society: A History from c. 1400 to 1892." Ph.D. Dissertation, University of California, Los Angeles, 1980. 345 p.

Q. ECONOMICS

Abasa-Nyarko, Charles. "The Economic Performance of Civilian and Military Regimes, Ghana, 1957-1985." Ph.D. Dissertation, University of South Carolina, 1988. 183 p.

Agyeman-Badu, Yaw. *Essays in the Political Economy of Ghana.* Lawrenceville, Va.: Brunswick, 1987. 66 p.

Amoah, Frank Emmanuel Kwame. "The Growth and Decline of Seaports in Ghana, 1800-1962." Ph.D. Dissertation, University of California, Los Angeles, 1969. 248 p.

Andrae, Gunilla. *Industry in Ghana; Production and Spatial Structure.* Stockholm: University of Stockholm, Scandinavian Institute of African Studies, 1981. 181 p.

Antwi, Anthony Kwasi. *Public Expenditures: The Impact on Distribution of Income, the Ghana Case.* Washington, D.C.: University Press of America, 1978. 224 p.

Anyane, Seth. *Ghana Agriculture: Its Economic Development from Early Times to the Middle of the Twentieth Century.* London: Oxford University Press, 1963. 228 p.

Appiah, A. K. "The Development of the Monetary and Financial System of Ghana, 1950-64." Ph.D. Dissertation, University of Leeds, 1967. 374 p.

Arhin, Kwame. *The Expansion of Cocoa Production in Ghana: The Working Conditions of Migrant Cocoa Farmers in the Central and Western Regions.* Legon: Institute of African Studies, University of Ghana, 1985. 137 p.

___. *West African Traders in Ghana in the Nineteenth and Twentieth Centuries.* Legon History Series. London and New York: Longman, 1979. 224 p.

Asante, S. K. B. *The Political Economy of Regionalism in Africa: A Decade of the Economic Community of West African States (ECOWAS).* New York: Praeger, 1986. 267 p.

Beckman, Bjorn. *Organising the Farmers; Cocoa Politics and National Development in Ghana.* Uppsala. Sweden: Scandinavian Institute of African Studies, 1976. 299 p.

Beteman, Merrill J. "Cocoa in the Ghanaian Economy." Ph.D. Dissertation, Massachusetts Institute of Technology, 1965. 230 p.

Bevin, H. J., comp. *Economic History of the Gold Coast, 1874-1914: Select Documents.* Legon: Department of History, University of Ghana, 1960. 189 p.

___. "The Gold Coast Economy about 1880." *Transactions of the Gold Coast and Togoland Historical Society,* 2 (1956), 73-86.

___. "M. J. Bonnat, Trader and Mining Promoter." *Economic Bulletin* (Legon), 4, 7 (July 1960), 1-12.

Birmingham, Walter, I. Neustadt, and E. N. Omaboe, eds. *A Study of Contemporary Ghana.* Vol. 1, *The Economy of Ghana.* Evanston, Ill.: Northwestern University Press, 1966; London: Allen and Unwin for the Ghana Academy of Sciences, 1966. 472 p.

Byl, Adhemar. "Ghana's Struggle for Economic Independence." *Current History* (Philadelphia), 43, 256 (Dec. 1962), 359-365.

Carlsson, Jerdir. *The Limits to Structural Change: A Comparative Study of Foreign Direct Investments in Liberia and Ghana, 1950-1971.* Gothenburg: University of Gothenburg, Institute of African Studies, 1981. 299 p.

Clark, Gracia Courtright. "The Position of Asante Women Traders in Kumase Central Market, Ghana." Ph.D. Dissertation, Cambridge University (UK), 1986. 322 p.

Crisp, Jeff. *The Story of an African Working Class: Ghanaian Miners' Struggles 1870-1980.* London: Zed Press, 1984. 256 p.

___. "Union Atrophy and Worker Revolt: Labour Protest at Tarkwa Goldfields, Ghana, 1968-1969." *Canadian Journal of African Studies* (Guelph, Ontario), 13, 1-2 (1979), 265-293.

Daaku, Kwame Yeboa. "Aspects of Precolonial Akan Economy." *The International Journal of African Historical Studies* (Boston), 5, 2 (1972), 235-247.

___. *Trade and Politics on the Gold Coast, 1600-1720; A Study of the African Reaction to European Trade.* Oxford: Clarendon Press, 1970. 219 p.

Duffuor, Kwabena. "The Impact of the Post-1971 Exchange Rate System on the Economies of the Developing Countries with

Specific Reference to Ghana." Ph.D. Dissertation, Syracuse University, 1979. 263 p.

Dumett, Raymond E. "British Official Attitudes in Relation to Economic Development in the Gold Coast, 1874-1905." Ph.D. Dissertation, University of London, 1966. 395 p.

___. "John Sarbah, the Elder, and African Mercantile Entrepreneurship in the Gold Coast in the Late Nineteenth Century." *Journal of African History* (London), 14, 4 (1973), 653-679.

___. "The Rubber Trade of the Gold Coast and Asante in the Nineteenth Century: African Innovation and Market Responsiveness." *Journal of African History*, 12, 1 (1971), 79-101.

Dunn, John. "But How Will They Eat?" *Transactions of the Historical Society of Ghana*, 13, 1 (June 1972), 113-124.

Ewusi, Kodwo. *Economic Development Planning in Ghana*. New York: Exposition Press, 1973. 85 p.

Fage, John Donnelly. "Some Remarks on Beads and Trade in Lower Guinea in the Sixteenth and Seventeenth Centuries." *Journal of African History*, 3, 2 (1962), 343-347.

Feinberg, Harvey M., and Marion Johnson. "The West African Ivory Trade During the Eighteenth Century." *The International Journal of African Historical Studies*, 15, 3 (1982), 435-453.

Fry, Richard. *Bankers in West Africa: The Story of the Bank of British West Africa Limited*. London: Hutchinson Benham, 1976. 270 p.

Fynn, John Kofi. "Trade and Politics in Akan Land." *Tarikh* (Ibadan), 7, 2 (1982), 23-34.

Garlick, Peter Cyril. *African Traders and Economic Development in Ghana.* London: Oxford University Press, 1971. 172 p.

___. "The Development of Kwahu Business Enterprise in Ghana Since 1874--An Essay in Recent Oral Tradition." *Journal of African History,* 8, 3 (1967), 463-480.

Genoud, Roger. *Nationalism and Economic Development in Ghana.* New York: Praeger; Montreal: McGill; London: Pall Mall, 1969. 245 p.

Goody, Jack, John Rabkine, and T. M. Mustapha. "The Caravan Trade from Kano to Salaga." *Journal of the Historical Society of Nigeria* (Ibadan), 3, 4 (June 1967), 611-616.

Gray, Paul S. *Unions and Leaders in Ghana: A Model of Labor and Development.* New Brunswick, N.J.: Rutgers University, 1981. 356 p.

Grier, Beverly Carolease. *Pawns, Porters and Petty Traders: Women in the Transition to Export Agriculture in Ghana.* Boston: African Studies Center, Boston University, 1989. 24 p.

Handloff, Robert Earl. "The Dyula of Gyaman: A Study of Politics and Trade in the Nineteenth Century." 2 vols. Ph.D. Dissertation, Northwestern University, 1982. 692 p.

Hansen, E., and Kwame Ninsin, eds. *The State, Development and Politics in Ghana.* London: Codesria Book Series, 1989. 280 p.

Hendrixson, Karen Leslie. "Seeking the Economic Kingdom: The Impact of State Majority Ownership of the Ghana Bauxite Company on Company Performance." Graduate Thesis, Fletcher School of Law and Diplomacy (Tufts University), 1989. 309 p.

Hill, Polly. *The Gold Coast Cocoa Farmer: A Preliminary Survey.* London: Oxford University Press, 1956. 139 p.

___. *The Occupation of Migrants in Ghana.* Ann Arbor, Mich.: University of Michigan, 1970. 76 p.

___. *Studies in Rural Capitalism in West Africa.* Cambridge: Cambridge University Press. 1970. 173 p.

Hopkins, A. G. "Economic Aspects of Political Movements in Nigeria and in the Gold Coast, 1918-39." *Journal of African History*, 7, 1 (1966), 133-152.

___. *An Economic History of West Africa.* New York: Columbia University Press, 1973. 337 p.

Huq, M. M. *The Economy of Ghana: The First Twenty-five Years since Independence.* New York: St Martin's, 1989. 355 p.

Hutchful, Eboe. *The IMF and Ghana: The Confidential Records.* London: Institute for African Alternatives and Zed Books, 1987. 298 p.

Jefferies, Richard. "Rawlings and the Political Economy of Underdevelopment in Ghana." *African Affairs*, 81, 324 (July 1982), 307-317.

Johnson, Marion. "The Ounce in Eighteenth-Century West African Trade." *Journal of African History*, 7, 2 (1966), 197-214.

Kay, Geoffrey B., ed. *The Political Economy of Colonialism in Ghana: A Collection of Documents and Statistics, 1900-1960.* Cambridge: Cambridge University Press, 1972. 431 p.

Kennedy, Paul. "The Role and Position of Petty Producers in a West African City (Accra)." *The Journal of Modern African Studies* (Cambridge), 19, 4 (1981), 565-594.

Killick, Tony. *Development Economics in Action: A Study of Economic Policies in Ghana.* London: Heinemann, 1978. 392 p.

Konings, Piet. *The Political Potential of Ghanaian Miners: A Case-Study of the Ashanti Goldfields Corporation Workers at Obuasi.* Leiden, Netherlands: African Studies Centre, 1981. 116 p.

Kuruk, Paul. "Renegotiating Transnational Investment Agreements in the Natural Resource Industries in Aid of National Development: A Case Study of Bauxite and Hydropower Supply Arrangements between the Government of Ghana and the Volta Aluminum Company Limited." Ph.D. Dissertation, Stanford University, 1990. 462 p.

LaTorre, Joseph Raymond. "Wealth Surpasses Everything: An Economic History of Asante, 1750-1874." Ph.D. Dissertation, University of California, 1978. 518 p.

Leith, J. Clark. *Ghana.* National Bureau of Economic Research, Foreign Trade Regimes and Economic Development, 2. New York: Columbia University Press, 1974. 216 p.

Levy, Mildred Blitt. "Interregional Labor Migration in Ghana." Ph.D. Dissertation, Northwestern University, 1966. 144 p.

Lewis, William Arthur. *Report on Industrialization and the Gold Coast.* Accra: Government Printer, 1953. 23 p.

McCall, Daniel F. "The Koforidua Market." In *Markets in Africa,* ed. Paul Bohannan and George Dalton. Evanston, Ill.: Northwestern University Press, 1968. 667-697.

Meillassoux, Claude, ed. *The Development of Indigenous Trade and Markets in West Africa.* Tenth International African Seminar, Fourah Bay College. London: Oxford University Press, 1971. 444 p.

Milburn, Josephine F. *British Business and Ghanaian Independence.* London: C. Hurst; Hanover, N.H.: University Press of New England, 1977. 156 p.

Miracle, Marvin P., and Ann W. Seidman. *Agricultural Cooperatives and Quasi-Cooperatives in Ghana, 1951-1965.* Madison, Wis.: University of Wisconsin, 1968. 73 p.

___, and Ann W. Seidman. *State Farms in Ghana.* Madison, Wis.: University of Wisconsin, 1968. 54 p.

Ocansey, John Emanuel. *African Trading: Or the Trials of William Narh Ocansey of Addah, West Coast of Africa, River Volta.* Liverpool: B. J. Looney, ca. 1881. 92 p.

Okoso-Amaa, Kewku. *Rice Marketing in Ghana.* Thesis, Uppsala, Sweden: Scandinavian Institute of African Studies, 1975. 102 p.

Panford, Martin Kwamina. "The Influence of the International Labor Organization (ILO) on African Workers' Union and Collective Bargaining Rights: The Case of Ghana." Ph.D. Dissertation, Northeastern University, 1990. 300 p.

Patterson, David K. "The Veterinary Department and the Animal Industry in the Gold Coast, 1909-1955." *The International Journal of African Historical Studies*, 13, 3 (1980), 457-491.

Pedler, Frederick J. *The Lion and the Unicorn in Africa: A History of the Origins of the United Africa Company, 1787-1931.* London: Heinemann, 1974. 343 p.

Peil, Margaret. *The Ghanaian Factory Worker: Industrial Man in Africa.* Cambridge: Cambridge University Press, 1972. 254 p.

Posansky, Merrick. "Ghana and the Origins of West African Trade." *Africa Quarterly* (New Delhi), 11 (1971), 100-125.

Reynolds, Edward. *Trade and Economic Change on the Gold Coast, 1807-1874.* Legon History Series. London: Longman, 1974. 207 p.

Rodney, Walter. "Gold and Slaves on the Gold Coast." *Transactions of the Historical Society of Ghana*, 10 (1969), 13-28.

Rosenblum, Paul. "Gold Mining in Ghana: 1874-1900." Ph.D. Dissertation, Columbia University, 1972. 315 p.

Sanders, James. "Palm Oil Production on the Gold Coast in the Aftermath of the Slave Trade. Case Study of the Fante." *International Journal of African Studies*, 15, 1 (1982), 49-63.

Schwimmer, Brian. "Organization of Migrant Farmer Communities in Southern Ghana." *Canadian Journal of African Studies* (Guelph, Ontario), 14, 2 (1980), 221-238.

Shea, M. S. M. "The Development and Role of Trade Unions in a Developing Economy: The Case of Ghana." Ph.D. Dissertation, University of Edinburgh, 1968. 372 p.

Southall, Roger J. "Cadbury on the Gold Coast; 1907-1938: The Dilemma of the Model Firm in a Colonial Economy." Ph.D. Dissertation, University of Birmingham, 1975. 540 p.

___. "Polarisation and Dependence in the Gold Coast Cocoa Trade, 1890-1938." *Transactions of the Historical Society of Ghana*, 16, 1 (June 1975), 93-115.

Struthers, J. "Inflation in Ghana (1966-78): A Perspective on the Monetarist v. Stucturalist Debate." *Development and Change* (London), (April 1981), 177-213.

Sutton, I. B. "The Volta River Salt Trade: The Survival of an Indigenous industry." *Journal of African History*, 20, 1 (1981), 43-61.

Swanzy, Henry. "A Trading Family in the Nineteenth Century Gold Coast." *Transactions of the Gold Coast and Togoland Historical Society*, 2, 2 (1956), 87-120.

Tutu, Kwadwo Adjei. "The Impact of Coope tives on the Development of Ghanaian Agriculture: The Need for Self-Management as an Alternative System." Ph.D. Dissertation, Cornell University, 1988. 258 p.

Uzoigwe, G. N. "The Slave Trade and African States." *Transactions of the Historical Society of Ghana*, 14, 2 (Dec. 1973), 169-185.

Vercruijsse, Emile. *Transitional Modes of Production: A Case Study from West Africa (Ghana)*. Westport, Conn.: Lawrence Hill, 1982. 224 p. An account of canoe-fishing in Ghana.

Wehner, Harrison Gill, Jr. "The Cocoa Marketing Board and Economic Development in Ghana: A Case Study." Ph.D. Dissertation, University of Michigan, 1963. 264 p.

Wilks, Ivor. "A Medieval Trade Route from the Niger to the Gulf of Guinea." *Journal of African History*, 3, 2 (1962), 337-341.

Wills, John Brian, ed. *Agriculture and Land Use in Ghana*. London: Oxford University Press for the Ghana Ministry of Food and Agriculture, 1962. 503 p.

R. RELIGION AND PHILOSOPHY

Adu-Andoh, Samuel. "The Sacred in Ghana's Struggle for Justice and Communual Identity: The Legacy of Kwame Nkrumah." Ph.D. Dissertation, Princeton Theological Seminary, 1986. 274 p.

Affriefah, Kofi. "The Impact of Christianity on Akyem Society, 1852-1887." *Transactions of the Historical Society of Ghana*, 16, 1 (June 1975), 67-86.

Akrong, Abraham Ako. "An Akan Christian View of Salvation: From the Perspective of John Calvin's Soteriology." Ph.D. Dissertation, Lutheran School of Theology, 1991. 287 p.

Appiah-Kubi, Kofi. *Man Cures, God Heals: Religion and Medical Practice among the Akans of Ghana.* Totowa, N.J.: Allanheld, Osmun, and Co., 1981. 173 p.

Arhin, Kwame. "The Missionary Role on the Gold Coast and in Ashanti: Reverend F. A. Ramseyer and the British Take-over of Ashanti, 1869-1894." *Research Review* (Legon), 4, 2 (1968), 1-12.

Awasu, Wilson. "Religion, Christianity and the Powers in Ewe Society." Graduate Dissertation, Fuller Theological Seminary, 1988. 349 p.

Baeta, C. G. K. *Prophetism in Ghana: A Study of Some 'Spiritual' Churches.* London: SCM Press, 1962. 169 p.

___. *The Relationships of Christians with Men of Other Faiths.* Accra: Ghana Universities Press, 1971. 27 p.

___. *Theology as Liberation: Four Contemporary Third World Programmes.* Accra: Academy of Arts and Sciences, 1983. 43 p. Paper was originally presented in 1981 as part of the J. B. Danquah Memorial Lecture Series.

Bartels, Francis L. "Jacobus Eliza Johannes Capitein, 1719-47." *Transactionss of the Historical Society of Ghana,* 4, 1 (1959), 3-13.

___. "Phillip Quaque, 1741-1816." *Transactions of the Gold Coast and Togoland Historical Society,* : (1955), 153-77.

___. *The Roots of Ghana Methodism.* London: Cambridge Unive ity Press and Ghana Methodist Book Depot, 1965. 368 p.

Breidenbach, Paul S. "Maame Harris Grace Tani and Papa Kwesi John Nackabath: Independent Church Leaders in the Gold Coast, 1914-1958." *International Journal of African Historical Studies,* 12, 4 (1979), 581-614.

Busia, Kofi Abrefa. "Ancestor Worship, Libation, Stools, Festivals." In *Christianity and African Culture.* Accra: Christian Council, 1955, 17-23.

Chartey-Togoe, David Bright. "The Church's Understanding of Death and the Dead with Reference to Traditional Effutu Belief and Practices." Ph.D. Dissertation, St. Andrews University (UK), 1985. 328 p.

Danquah, Joseph Boakye. *The Akan Doctrine of God.* London: Lutterworth, 1944. 206 p.

___. *Ancestors, Heroes and God.* Kibi, Gold Coast: G. Boakie, 1938. 46 p.

Debrunner, Hans W. *A Church between Colonial Powers: A Study of the Church in Togo.* Trans. into English by Dorothea M. Barton. London: Lutterworth Press, 1965. 368 p.

___. *A History of Christianity in Ghana.* Accra: Waterville Publishing House, 1967. 375 p.

___. *Witchcraft in Ghana: A Study on the Belief in Destructive Witches and Its Effect on the Akan Tribe.* Accra: Presbyterian Book Depot, 2nd. ed., 1961. 213 p. Reprinted in 1978.

Field, Margaret Joyce. *Religion and Medicine of the Ga People.* London: Oxford University Press, 1937; Accra: Presbyterian Book Depot, 1961; Reprint of 1961 edition, New York: AMS, 1979. 214 p.

___. *Search for Security: An Ethno-Psychiatric Study of Rural Ghana.* Evanston, Ill.: Northwestern University Press; London: Faber and Faber, 1960. 478 p.

Fisher, Humphrey J. *Ahmadiyyah. A Study in Contemporary Islam on the West African Coast.* London: Oxford University Press for the Nigerian Institute of Social and Economic Research, 1963. 224 p.

Gaba, C. R. *Scriptures of an African People: Ritual Utterances of the Anlo.* New York: NOK Publishers, 1973. 154 p.

Gakpe-Ntsri, Theodore. "Aspects of Inculturation of the Eucharistic Sacrifice in the Traditional Worship of the Akan of Ghana: A Theology of the Eucharist in the Context of an Indigenous African Traditional Religion." Graduate Dissertation, Duquesne University, 1989. 367 p.

Grau, Eugene Emil. "The Evangelical Presbyterian Church (Ghana and Togo) 1914-1946." Ph.D. Dissertation, Hartford Seminary. 261 p.

Gyekye, Kwame. *An Essay on African Philosophical Thought: The Akan Conceptual Scheme.* Cambridge: Cambridge University Press, 1987. 246 p.

Haliburton, Gordon MacKay. *The Prophet Harris: A Study of an African Prophet and His Mass-Movement in the Ivory Coast and the Gold Coast 1913-1915.* London: Longman Group, 1971; abridged version, London and New York: Oxford University Press, 1973.

Jenkins, Paul. "The Anglican Church in Ghana, 1905-1924." *Transactions of the Historical Society of Ghana,* Part I, 15, 1 (June 1974), 23-39; Part II, 15, 2 (Dec. 1974), 177-200.

Kalu, O. U. *The History of Christianity in West Africa.* London and New York: Longman, 1980. 352 p.

Kilson, Marion. *Kpele lala; Ga Religious Songs and Symbols.* Cambridge, Mass.: Harvard University Press, 1971. 313 p.

Levtzion, Nehemia. *Muslims and Chiefs in West Africa: A Study of Islam in the Middle Volta Basin in the Pre-Colonial Period.* Oxford: Clarendon Press, 1968. 228p.

___, and H. Fisher, eds. *Rural and Urban Islam in West Africa.* Boulder, Colo.: Lynne Rienner, 1987. 176 p.

Lewis, I. M., ed. *Islam in Tropical Africa.* London: Oxford University Press for the Fifth International African Seminar, 1966. 470 p.

Mobley, Harris Witsel. *Ghanaian's Image of the Missionary: An Analysis of the Published Critiques of Christian Missionaries by Ghanaians, 1897-1965.* Leiden: Brill, 1970. 181 p.

Nyomi, Setriakor Kobla. "A Pastoral Theological Perspective on Ministry to Persons Dealing with Loss due to Natural Disaster in Ghana." Graduate Dissertation, Princeton Theological Seminary, 1991. 377 p.

Obeng, J. P. "Asante Catholicism: Ritual Communities of the Catholic Faith among the Akan of Ghana." Ph.D. Dissertation, University of Massachusetts, 1991. 213 p.

Opoku, Kofi Asare. *West African Traditional Religion.* Singapore: F.E.P. International Private, Ltd., 1981.

Owusu-Ansah, David. *Islamic Talismanic Tradition in Nineteenth-Century Asante.* Lewiston: Edwin Mellen Press, 1991. 253 p.

Parrinder, Edward Geoffrey. *West African Religion: A Study of the Beliefs and Practices of Akan, Ewe, Yoruba, Ibo, and Kindred Peoples.* London: Epworth Press, 1961. 203 p.

Pfann, Helene M. *A Short History of the Catholic Church in Ghana.* Cape Coast: Catholic Mission Press, 1965. 172 p.

Pobee, J. S. *Kwame Nkrumah and the Church in Africa, 1949-1966.* Accra: Asempa Publishers, 1988. 222 p.

___. *Towards an African Theology.* Nashville: Abingdon, 1979. 174 p.

___, ed. *Religion in Pluralistic Society: Essays in Honor of Professor Baeta.* Leiden: E. J. Brill, 1976. 236 p.

Rattray, Robert Sutherland. *Religion and Art in Ashanti.* Oxford: Clarendon Press, 1927. 414 p.; later editions, 1954, 1959, 1969, 1980.

Smith, Noel. *The Presbyterian Church of Ghana, 1835-1960.* London: Oxford University Press, 1966. 304 p.

Swithenbank, Michael. *Ashanti Fetish Houses.* Legon: Ghana University Press, 1969. 68 p.

Ward, Barbara E. "Some Observations on Religious Cults in Ashanti." *Africa* (London), 26, 1 (1956), 47-61.

Wilks, Ivor. "The Position of Muslims in Metropolitan Ashanti in the Nineteenth Century." In *Islam in Tropical Africa,* ed. I. M. Lewis. London: Oxford University Press for the International African Institute, 1966; 2nd. edition, 1980.

Williamson, S. G. *Akan Religion and the Christian Faith,* ed. Kwesi A. Dickson. Accra: Ghana Universities Press, 1965. 186 p.

___. *The Gold Coast: What of the Church?* London: Edinburgh House, 1953. 24 p.

Wiltgen, Ralph M. *Gold Coast Mission History, 1471-1880.* Techny, Ill.: Divine World, 1956. 181 p.

Yates, Walter Ladell. "The History of the African Methodist Episcopal Zion Church in West Africa, Liberia, Gold Coast (Ghana), and Nigeria, 1900-1939." Ph.D. Dissertation, Hartford Seminary, 1967. 398 p.

S. EDUCATION

Acquaye, Alfred A. "Ghanaian Education: Its Relevance for Ghana in Transition." Ph.D. Dissertation, University of San Francisco, 1990. 331 p.

Afrim, Albert Espinozar. "Aggrey in Retrospect: Some Aspects of J. E. K. Aggrey's Teaching and His Educational Theories and Their Relevance to Contemporary Ghana." Ph.D. Dissertation, Columbia University Teachers' College, 1986. 330 p.

Agbodeka, Francis. *Achimota in the National Setting*. Accra: Afram Publishers, 1977. 208 p.

Agyeman, Kofi D. *Ideological Education and Nationalism in Ghana under Nkrumah and Busia*. Accra: Ghana Universities Press, 1988. 81 p.

Annan, Akweley. "The Socio-economic Determinants of Mulnutrition among Pre-school Children in Ghana." Ph.D. Dissertation, Cornell University, 1985. 444 p.

Bugulo, Bening. *A History of Education in Northern Ghana, 1*; '-*1976*. Accra: Ghana Universities Press, 1990. 248 p.

Busia, Kofi Abrefa. *The Challenge of Africa*. New York: Praeger, 1962. 156 p.; London: Pall Mall, 1962.

___. *Purposeful Education for Africa*. The Hague: Mouton, 1969. 107 p.

Curle, Adam. *Educational Problems of Developing Societies: With Case Studies of Ghana, Pakistan, and Nigeria*. Expanded and Updated ed. Praeger Special Studies in International Economics and Development. New York: Praeger, 1973. 200 p.

Foster, P. J. *Education and Social Change in Ghana*. London: Routledge and Kegan Paul, 1963. 322 p.

Fraser, Alexander G. *Papers of Alexander Garden Fraser*. Oxford: Rhodes House Library, n.d. Oxford University Colonial Project Series, MSS. Brit. Emp. No. S. 283.

Graham, Charles Kwesi. *History of Education in Ghana from the Earliest Times to the Declaration of Independence.* London: Frank Cass, 1971. 232 p.

Grindal, Bruce. *Growing up in Two Worlds: Education and Transition among the Sisala of Northern Ghana.* Case Studies in Education and Culture, ed. George and Louise Spindler. New York: Holt, Rinehart, and Winston, 1972. 114 p.

Gyabaah, Samuel. "An Exploratory Study of Local Human Resource Utilization for Community-based Nonformal Adult Education in Ghana." Ph.D. Dissertation, University of Iowa, 1989. 185 p.

Hayward, Fred M. "Ghana Experiments with Civic Education: Center for Civic Education Aims to Inculcate Democratic Values." *Africa Report* (Washington), 16, 5 (May 1971), 24-27.

Hilliard, F. H. *A Short History of Education in British West Africa.* London: Nelson, 1957. 186 p.

Macartney, William M. *Dr. Aggrey, Ambassador for Africa.* London: SCM Press, 1949. 106 p.

McElligott, Therese E. "Education in the Gold Coast Colony, 1920-1949." Ph.D. Dissertation, Stanford University, 1950. 233 p.

McWilliams, Henry O. A. *Development of Education in Ghana.* London: Longmans, Green, 1959. 114 p.

Ofosu-Appiah, L. H. *The Life of Dr. J. E. K. Aggrey.* Accra: Waterville Publishing House, 1975. 103 p.

Setse, Theo. K. *Foundations of Nation-Building: The Case of Achimota School.* Accra: Presbyterian Press, 1974. 60 p.

Smith, Edwin W. *Aggrey of Africa: A Study in Black and White*. London: Student Christian Movement, 1929. 202 p; Freeport, N.Y.: Books for Libraries Press, 1971. 292 p.

Tenkorang, Samuel. "The Founding of Mfantsipim 1905-1908." *Transactions of the Historical Society of Ghana*, 15, 2 (Dec. 1974), 165-175.

Thomas, Roger G. "Education in Northern Ghana, 1906-1940: A Study in Colonial Paradox." *International Journal of African Historical Studies*, 7, 3 (1975), 427-467.

Ward, William E. F. *Fraser of Trinity and Achimota*. Legon: Ghana Universities Press, 1965. 328 p.

Williams, Charles Kingsley. *Achimota: The Early Years 1929-1948*. London: Longmans, 1963. 158 p.

APPENDIX A: BRITISH ADMINISTRATORS OF THE GOLD COAST

GOVERNOR

George C. Strahan	1874-1876
Stanford Freeling	1876-1879
Herbert T. Ussher	1879-1880
Samuel Rowe	1881-1884
William A. G. Young	1884-1885
William Brandford Griffith	1885-1895
William Edward Maxwell	1895-1897
Frederic M. Hodgson	1897-1900
Matthew Nathan	1900-1904
John P. Rodger	1904-1910
James J. Thorburn	1910-1912
Hugh Clifford	1912-1919
Frederick Gordon Guggisberg	1919-1927
Alexander R. Slater	1927-1932

Thomas S. W. Thomas	1932-1934
Arnold W. Hodson	1934-1941
Alan C. M. Burns	1941-1948
Gerald H. Creasy	1948-1949
Charles N. Arden-Clarke	1949-1957

GOVERNOR-GENERAL

Charles N. Arden-Clarke	1957
William Francis Hare, Earl of Listowel	1957-1960

This list is adapted from David P. Henige, *Colonial Governors from the Fifteenth Century to the Present* (Madison, Wis.: University of Wisconsin Press, 1970), p. 120-121.

APPENDIX B: GHANAIAN LEADERS FROM 1951

KWAME NKRUMAH: Leader of Government Business, 1951-1952; Prime Minister, 1952-1960; President, 1960-1966.

JOSEPH A. ANKRAH: Chairman, National Liberation Council, 1966-1969.

AKWASI A. AFRIFA: Chairman, National Liberation Council, 1969; Head, Presidential Commission, 1969-1970.

KOFI A. BUSIA: Prime Minister (Second Republic), 1969-1972.

EDWARD AKUFO-ADDO: President (Second Republic), 1970-1972.

IGNATIUS K. ACHEAMPONG: Chairman, National Redemption Council, 1972-1975; Chairman, Supreme Military Council, 1975-1978.

FREDERICK W. K. AKUFFO: Chairman, Supreme Military Council, 1978-1979.

JERRY JOHN RAWLINGS: Chairman, Armed Forces Revolutionary Council, 1979.

HILLA LIMANN: President (Third Republic), 1979-1981.

JERRY JOHN RAWLINGS: Chairman, Provisional National Defense Council, 1982-1992.

JERRY JOHN RAWLINGS: President (Fourth Republic), January 1993.

ABOUT THE AUTHORS

DAVID OWUSU-ANSAH is Associate Professor of African History at James Madison University, Harrisonburg, Virginia. He holds a B.A. (Hons.) Ed. from the University of Cape Coast, Ghana. His M.A. in Islamic Studies is from McGill University, Montreal, Canada, and his Ph.D. is in African Studies from Northwestern University, Evanston, Illinois. He is the author of a number of scholarly articles on Asante history. His *Islamic Talismanic Tradition in Nineteenth Century Asante* was published in 1991 by Edwin Mellen Press, New York. His chapters on the "History of Ghana" and "Ghana: The Society and Its Environment" are included in *Ghana: A Country Study*, a forthcoming publication by the Library of Congress, Washington, DC.

DANIEL MILES McFARLAND, former Professor of African Studies at James Madison University, Harrisonburg, Virginia, authored the first editions of the *Historical Dictionary of Upper Volta* (Burkina Faso) and the *Historical Dictionary of Ghana* (Scarecrow Press, 1978 and 1985, respectively). Dr. McFarland holds a B.A. from the University of North Carolina and an M.A. and a Ph.D. from the University of Pennsylvania. He also studied at the Institute of African Studies, University of Ghana, Legon. Dr. McFarland retired from active teaching in 1988.